Decision Support Systems

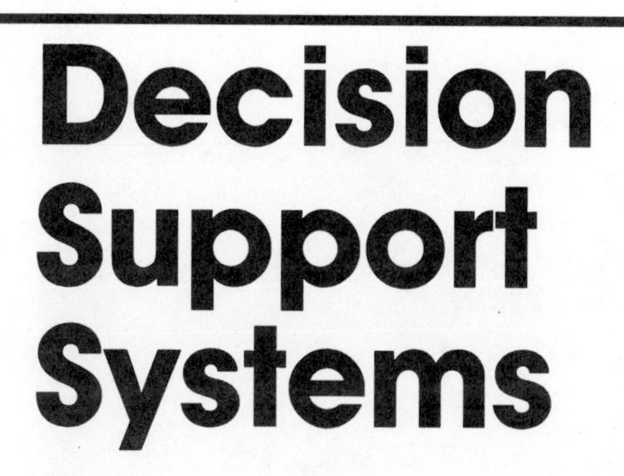

Decision Support Systems

Principles and Practice

Hossein Bidgoli
California State University, Bakersfield

West Publishing Company

St. Paul ▪ New York ▪ Los Angeles ▪ San Francisco

Copy Editor: Linda Thompson
Text Design: Melinda Grosser
Cover Design: *IMAGESMYTHE, INC.*
Cover Image: Garry Gay—The Image Bank
Composition: Carlisle Communications, Ltd.

50 W. Kellogg Boulevard
P.O. Box 64526
St. Paul, MN 55164-1003

Printed in the United States of America

96 95 94 93 92 91 90 89 8 7 6 5 4 3 2 1 0

Library of Congress Cataloging-in-Publication Data

Bidgoli, Hossein.
Decision support systems.

Includes bibliographies and index.
1. Decision support systems. I. Title.
T58.62.B53 1989 658.4'03 88-27816
ISBN 0-314-46560-X

To my parents Ashraf and Mohammad
for their continued support throughout my life

About the Author

Dr. Hossein Bidgoli is Professor and Coordinator of Management Information Systems at California State University, Bakersfield. He holds a Ph.D. degree in systems science from Portland State University with a specialization in design and implementation of MIS. His master's degree is in MIS from Colorado State University. Dr. Bidgoli's background includes experience as a systems analyst, EDP consultant, and financial analyst. He was director of the Microcomputer Center at Portland State University and has done computer-related consulting for numerous organizations including Tektronix, Inc., in Oregon.

Dr. Bidgoli has authored four texts and numerous professional papers and articles presented and published throughout the United States on the topics of computers and MIS. Dr. Bidgoli has also designed and implemented over twenty executive seminars on all aspects of information systems and decision support systems.

Contents in Brief

part four New Trends in DSS Environment

part five The Future Outlook

part six DSS Products and Applications

Contents

part one: Getting Started

part two: Architecture of DSS

part four: New Trends in DSS Environment

11 Distributed Processing and DSS 215

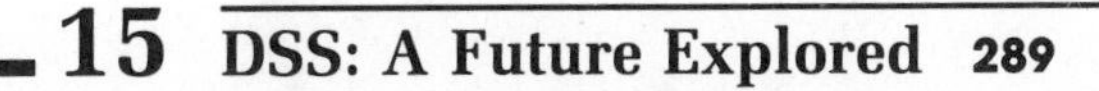

part five: The Future

part six: DSS Products and Applications

Preface

Cost reduction and significant improvement in all areas of computer technology have made computers a viable alternative in the decision-making process. During the past decade, microcomputer technology has grown extensively. Today an executive can connect to a wealth of information through a desktop computer. Specific improvement in networking, data base design, input/output devices, menu driven systems, and so on have made the computer a true decision companion. Computers are becoming easier to use, more affordable, and more powerful.

To be able to design and utilize a decision support system (DSS) two important concepts must be understood. First, the philosophical aspects of DSS must be explained. The second concept is the understanding of the architecture of a DSS and the integration of the philosophical issues in the architecture.

This text attempts to incorporate the philosophical foundations as well as the practical issues regarding a DSS design, implementation, and utilization. The text covers the existing technology of DSS and then explores the near future by introducing artificial intelligence, expert systems, and the integration of these technologies with DSS.

The text is divided into six sections, which include fifteen chapters and four appendices.

Part I starts with a general discussion of the past, present, and future of decision support systems. The unique characteristics of DSS compared with EDP and MIS are amplified. A general discussion of the decision-making process and computer technology as a decision aid is provided. Materials presented in this part should provide the reader with the necessary background for an understanding of the rest of the book.

Part II presents an architecture for DSS. The three main components of DSS, data base, model base, and dialog management are explained in detail. This part provides the reader with the necessary background for the conceptual design of a DSS and also highlights the requirements for establishing a DSS.

In Part III, systems analysis and design in the DSS environment are discussed. Guidelines for establishing a successful DSS are given and tools and techniques for design and implementation of a DSS are discussed. Several functional DSS are explained. This part concludes with an integrated framework for DSS products selection and implementation. Part III puts the discussion in Part II in perspective.

In Part IV some recent issues related to DSS design and utilization are discussed. Topics such as microbased DSS, teleconferencing, group DSS, executive information systems, executive support systems, artificial intelligence, and expert systems are examined. Research data show these issues and technologies are gaining in popularity. A thorough treatment of these topics should arm DSS users for the challenges of tomorrow.

Part V, by investigating the past, presents an outlook about the future. Important aspects of DSS, including hardware, software, and human elements, are explained.

Part VI provides a listing of the popular DSS generators on the market. DSS capabilities in several areas are highlighted and several successful DSS in action are examined. The last appendix provides a comprehensive and updated bibliography on all aspects of DSS definition, components, design, and utilization.

Each chapter begins with a brief introduction. This introduction provides initial information and lists materials covered in that particular chapter. Each chapter ends with a summary. The summary provides the reader with the essence of the particular chapter, leaving the reader with an understanding of the materials discussed.

Each chapter concludes with 15 to 25 review questions. These questions reinforce the material covered. At the end of each chapter, there are 5 to 8 projects that can be used as class assignments or for further investigation of a particular topic. Also, each chapter includes a list of the key terms and a comprehensive reference list.

Few books, if any, provide a comprehensive coverage of microbased DSS, group DSS, executive information systems, artificial intelligence, expert systems, and most importantly, the relationship of these technologies to DSS. This book devotes five entire chapters to these topics. These topics undoubtedly will play very important roles in future DSS design and utilization, and we expect the text will prepare the reader for tomorrow's challenge in the DSS field.

There is a vast array of DSS products on the market. Several of these products can enhance and facilitate DSS design and utilization. Appendix A provides a comprehensive coverage of 27 DSS products for both micro- and mainframe computers. To facilitate the selection task for DSS practitioners, Chapter 9 provides a series of guidelines and a comprehensive model for selection and implementation of these products.

To inform the reader about the versatility of the DSS field, we have devoted Appendices B and C to the applications of DSS in diverse disciplines. Some of the more successful DSSs on the market, such as GADS and BRANDAID, are discussed, putting the DSS field into perspective. Also, these materials guide the reader to investigate a particular discipline in which he or she may have special interest. Appendix D provides a comprehensive and up-to-date bibliography on all aspects of DSS design and use. This should help the readers in further investigation on specific aspects of DSS.

Several versions of these materials have been tested as a series of notes by groups of graduate and undergraduate students and executives in profit and nonprofit organizations. Classroom testing has provided us with excellent feedback on the suitability of the material to a variety of levels of understanding.

Acknowledgements

Several colleagues reviewed different versions of this manuscript and made constructive suggestions. Without their assistance the text could not have been in its present shape. Their help and comments are greatly appreciated.

Marvin D. Troutt, Southern Illinois University

James K. Carter, University of Wisconsin, Stevens Point

Sue A. Block, University of California, Santa Barbara

Jerry D. Sawyer, Kennesaw College

Cherian S. Thachenkary, Georgia State University

Cary T. Hughes, University of North Texas

Rammohan R. Kasuganti, Youngstown State University

Sohail S. Chaudhry, University of Wisconsin, La Crosse

Timothy Shea, University of Lowell

Lloyd J. Buckwell, Jr., Indiana University, Northwest

Robert A. Rademacher, Colorado State University

Al B. Schwartzkopf, University of Oklahoma

Rose M. Laird, Northern Virginia Community College

Many different groups assisted me in completing this project. I am grateful to students in my undergraduate and graduate classes who have provided feedback. Also, executives who attend my executive seminars on DSS provided me with insights regarding the practicality of the materials. They helped me fine-tune the manuscript during its various stages.

Two of my students, Judy Buchanan and Catherine Begg, deserve special thanks for providing feedback regarding the classroom acceptance of the material. I also thank Andrew Prestage for his assistance in putting together the Instructor's Manual. My colleagues and friends, Dr. Michael Flanagan and Reza Azaumsa, provided me with several useful references for Chapter 2. Their help is very much appreciated. David Koeth designed all the graphs and charts in the first phase of the text development. His help and thoroughness is appreciated. Gloria Dumpler read the first draft and provided editorial suggestions. Johanna Alexander assisted me in locating numerous reference materials. Their contributions are appreciated. Sylvia O'Brien and Jacki Lawson, deserve special recognition for their patience and thoroughness for typing and retyping drafts of this manuscript. Denise Simon, Tamborah Moore, Thomas Modl and Theresa O'Dell from West Educational Publishing Company were supportive and constructive in their suggestions concerning this project. I appreciate their help.

Last, but not least, I want to thank my family for their support and encouragement throughout this project and many other projects in my professional life.

part one

Getting Started

1 Decision Support Systems at a Glance

1-1 Introduction

This chapter reviews decision support systems (DSS), elaborating on the unique characteristics of DSS as compared with electronic data processing (EDP) and management information systems (MIS). A brief history of DSS and a discussion of its present status follows, touching on implementation and the cost and benefit of these systems. To show the versatility and power of DSS, a summary of a survey covering DSS applications in several disciplines is presented, which clearly illustrates the real power of these systems, and finishes with a look into the future. The design and implementation of DSS have been improved by products readily available on the market. A sample of these packages (products) is provided for future reference. The material in this chapter is discussed in detail in later chapters.

1-2 Background for DSS

For the past 40 years electronic data processing has been applied to structured tasks such as record keeping, simple clerical operations, and inventory control. Payroll, for example, was one of the first applications to be automated. The emphasis in these systems has been on data collection and data processing [14].

Since their inception in the mid-1960s, MISs have been used to process information. The objective of these systems has been the production of timely, accurate, and useful information for middle management on a scheduled basis. An MIS, though it supplies more information, lacks flexibility and is not suitable for ad hoc applications. However, the majority of MISs are becoming more flexible and more suitable for ad hoc applications. This is due to the sophistication in hardware/software technologies and users' requirements.

Although much has been written over the past few years about DSSs, there is no common or acceptable definition for these systems. Most experts define a DSS as a series of integrated computer software and as any computer-based information system that helps decision makers with semistructured and unstructured tasks [49].

DSSs have been applied to many different disciplines, including manufacturing, marketing, human resource management, accounting, small business, and the like. The power of these systems has been demonstrated in the business world, leading many to conclude that DSS is the way of the future. The decreasing cost and the increasing sophistication of both hardware and software have made these systems available not only to large organizations but to small businesses as well. Recent studies illustrate the overall effectiveness of these systems for decision-making purposes [51]. In this chapter we attempt to present a comprehensive review of this rapidly growing discipline.

1-3 What is a DSS?

Because the field is in flux, an exact definition of DSS is elusive. However, Keen and Scott-Morton offer this comprehensive description [45]:

> A DSS is a coherent system of computer-based technology (hardware, software, and supporting documentation) used by managers as an aid to their decision-making in semistructured decision tasks.

For our purpose we define DSS as:

> A computer-based information system consisting of hardware/software and the human element designed to assist any decision-maker at any level. However, the emphasis is on semistructured and unstructured tasks.

This simple definition underscores several requirements for a DSS:

- DSS requires hardware
- DSS requires software
- DSS requires human elements (designers and users)
- DSS is designed to support decision making
- DSS should help decision-makers at all levels
- DSS emphasizes semistructured and unstructured tasks

DSSs differ from traditional electronic data processing and MISs in many ways. For example, Keen and Scott-Morton address the distinction between EDP/MIS and DSS. They describe DSS as the use of computers to

- Assist the manager in his or her decision making process for semistructured tasks.

- Support rather than replace managerial judgment.
- Improve the effectiveness of decision making rather than its efficiency.

They describe the characteristics of MIS somewhat differently:

- Efficiency through cost reduction is the key point.
- The emphasis is on structured tasks.
- Data storage, access, and report generation are the major processing tasks.

In comparing EDP, MIS, and DSS, we can set up a normative approach regarding design and utilization of DSS. Table 1-1 identifies some of the key factors that differentiate DSS from the other systems [11]. (We explain this table in detail in Chapter 3.) However, DSS is not a disjoint technology—it shares a number of common technologies. We can also say DSS is a natural progression or expansion of EDP/MIS systems.

1-4 The History of DSS

We can trace the history of DSS to the origin of all electronic data-processing systems. Since the mid-1940s, the data-processing field has entered a new era. Increases in the speed and accuracy of electronic data processing systems, massive cost savings, and improvement in the quality of decision making in many organizational settings have added a new dimension to data storage and retrieval systems.

Information technology (and computer applications in general) has developed and improved in parallel with computer technology as computers have moved from first-generation (vacuum tube), to second-generation (transistor), to third-generation (integrated circuit), to fourth-generation (miniaturization and massive utilization of microcomputers), and, finally, to fifth-generation computers (smart computers and artificial intelligence machines—computers that can mimic human thought behavior).

However, this era has not been without problems. We have experienced many failures in the design and utilization of computer-based information systems. The majority of these failures have been directly associated with

- Lack of familiarity of users with these systems
- Complexity involved in the operation of these systems
- Inadequate training for the users
- Intensive cost associated with design and implementation of these systems
- Most importantly, lack of user involvement in design and implementation of these systems

Overall, we have seen more successes than failures, and the state of technology supports the utilization of these systems on a broader scale. Table 1-2 presents highlights of the important events of the past that have had a direct relationship to the development of DSS in today's form.

Table 1-1 ▪ Unique Characteristics of DSS

Key Factor	EDP/MIS	DSS
Central focus	To automate routine and repetitive tasks (EDP) and to some degree MIS	To aid decision making and decision implementation
Mode of usage	Mostly passive and scheduled reports	Active use—each instance of system use is initiated by user(s) and designer(s)
Types of activities	Mostly line	Line, staff, and management
Orientation	Efficiency	Overall effectiveness of the system and organization
Time horizon	Mostly on past	Focus on present and (primarily) future
Design emphasis	Periodic report and standard format	Flexibility and ad hoc utilization
Key words	Replacement and automation	Interaction and support for decision maker
System evaluation	Based on hard benefit	Primarily based on behavioristic criteria, e.g., user satisfaction, decision-making improvement, etc.
Computational focus	Mostly basic	Basic and complex
Output orientation	Mostly for control	Mostly for planning and control
Problems addressed	Quantitative	Qualitative,* quantitative, unstructured, and semistructured
Output format options	Limited	Numerous (e.g., hard copy, soft copy, graphic, exception reporting, tabular, etc.)
Tailoring to personality and status of the user	Rare	Frequent
Mode of system/user interaction	Mostly scheduled reports	Numerous options, e.g., scheduled reports, intermediary, terminal, command mode, menu driven, etc.
Design principles	Users minimally involved (but this is changing)	Users initiate, design, and control the implementation of the system
Design tools	Traditional life-cycle approach	Prototyping, iterative, and adoptive design

Key Factor	EDP/MIS	DSS
Flexibility of the operation	Not flexible	Quite flexible—responds quickly to the changing environment
Organizational target group	Mostly operational and tactical	All levels (operational, tactical, and strategic)
Data used	Mostly internal	Both internal and external
Implementation	Mostly from tools (e.g., FORTRAN, COBOL, etc.)	Both from DSS tools and DSS generators—primarily by DSS generators (e.g., IFPS, FOCUS, etc.)
Interactiveness	Not usually regarded	Highly regarded
Types of analysis	More data analysis	Both modeling and data analysis

*By increasing the integration between expert systems (discussed in Chapter 13) and DSS, qualitative analysis is becoming more common in DSS environment.

1-5 DSS in More Recent Times

DSSs, as a concept of how computers could be used in the decision-making process, were initially developed from a synthesis of ideas originating from two major engineering institutions. The theoretical studies of organizational decision making were completed at the Carnegie Institute of Technology during the late 1950s and early 1960s; the technical work on different aspects of computer systems was carried out at the Massachusetts Institute of Technology in the early 1960s. For more information consult Gorry and Scott-Morton [33], Alter [1], and Keen and Scott-Morton [45].

More recently, Steven L. Alter surveyed 56 systems with DSS characteristics. According to their generic operations, he divided them into a seven-category taxonomy:

1. File drawer systems
2. Data analysis systems
3. Analysis information systems
4. Accounting models
5. Representational models
6. Optimization models
7. Suggestion models

He further divided them into two groups: data-oriented systems (the first three) and model-oriented systems (the last four).

A file drawer system is basically the automated version of a simple file cabinet. The major difference between these systems and file cabinet–type systems is improved accuracy and speed.

Table 1-2 ▪ How Did It All Happen: From Abacus to . . .

Approximate Date of the Event	People Involved	Product/Idea Introduction
2600 B.C.	Egyptians/Chinese	Abacus
A.D.1614	John Napier	Logarithms
1621	William Oughtred	Slide rule
1623	Wilhelm Schichard	First mechanical calculator
1642	Blaise Pascal	First automatic mechanical calculator
1666	Samuel Morland	First multiplying machine
1673	Gottfried Leibniz	First general-purpose calculating machine
1777	Charles Mahon	First logic machine
1804	Joseph Marie Jacquard	First punched card machine
1820	Charles Thomas de Glmau	First commercially successful calculating machine
1822	Charles Babbage	Difference engine
1833	Ada Augusta	First idea of programming
1854	George S. Boole	Publishing of Boolean algebra
1869	William Jerons	Invention of a logic machine
1874	W. T. Odhner	First pinwheel adding machine
1879	William Thomson	The analog tide predictor
1885	Door Eugene Telt	First successful key-driven calculator
1886	Dr. Herman Holerith	First electromechanical punched-card system
1890	William S. Burroughs	First adding and listing machine
1893	Otto Steiger	First scientific calculator
1920	Leonardo Torres y Queredo	First automatic calculating machine
1931	Dr. Vannevar Bush	First analog computer for differential equations
1933	Wallace J. Echert	First mechanical program
1936	Alan M. Turig	First general model of logic machines
1937	Claude Shannon	First application of Boolean algebra to switching functions
1938	George R. Stibitz	First electromechanical calculator
1939	Dr. John V. Atanasoff	First electronic digital computer
1941	Konaud Zuse and Helmut Schreger	First general-purpose program-controlled computer
1946		Electronic numerical integrator and computer (ENIAC)
1947	J. Bardeen, W. H. Brattain, and W. Shockley	First transistor
1949	Maurice Wilkes	First full-scale stored program computer

Approximate Date of the Event	People Involved	Product/Idea Introduction
1951	J. Presper Eckert and John W. Mauchly	First computer dedicated to data processing applications
1957		First high-level programming language (FORTRAN)
1958	John McCarthy	First artificial intelligence programming language (LISP)
1959	Texas Instruments and Fairchild Semiconductor	First integrated circuit
1960	Theodore H. Maiman	First laser
1961		First virtual memory
1961		GPSS (general-purpose systems simulator)
1963		First minicomputer
1970	Corning Glass Works, Inc.	First commercially produced fiber optic cable
1971	Intel Corp.	First microprocessor
1971		First expert system product (DENDRAL)
1974	Micro Instrumentation and Telemetry Systems (MITS)	First commercial microcomputer
1977	Datapoint Corporation	First local area network (ARCNET)
1978	Peter G. W. Keen and Michael S. Scott-Morton	First comprehensive DSS Text
1979	Robert Frankston, Dan Brincklin, and Dan Fylstra	VisiCalc introduced
1982	Lotus Development Corp.	Lotus 1-2-3 introduced
1983		First experimental version of an optical transistor
1983		There are 13 million computers in the world
1986	Intel/Compaq Computer Corp.	The first 80386 microprocessor PC
1989	Bolt, Beranek and Newman, Inc.	Expected completion of Monarch Computer (computes 8 million floating point calculations per second). The parallel processing computer is to be used by U.S. Department of Defense.
1990		More advancement in parallel processing
2000		The electronic industry is expected to be a $900-billion-per-year industry

Sources: Robert H. Blissmer, *Computer Annual* (New York: John Wiley & Sons, Inc., 1975), 375–429. *Computerworld* (November 3, 1986): 13–18.

Data analysis systems, such as on-line budgeting systems, perform simple data analysis. The present results of operations can be compared with the past or with a target budget, and variation can be reported.

Analysis information systems, such as regional analysis and sales force analysis, utilize a series of decision-oriented data bases and small models in order to provide management information [1]. These systems can analyze the present situation by using internal data. They can also generate a forecast for the next period based on the past performance.

Accounting models use definitional relationships and formulas in order to calculate the consequences of a particular action [1]. Any "what-if" analysis type of model can be classified within this group. Sources and uses of funds are one example; break-even analysis is another.

Representational models include simulation models that do not use definitional relationships available in accounting models, such as Monte Carlo simulation models. The outcome of this type of system is usually the estimation of consequences of a particular action over the entire system. For example, using Monte Carlo simulation one can see the effects of varying the number of operators assigned to a service station.

Optimization models, the most commonly used models, are designed either to maximize the profit or to minimize the cost. Any type of allocation model, including linear programming techniques, can be classified within this group. This technique is discussed in Chapter 5.

Suggestion models are more structured than optimization models [1]. The output of a suggestion model is the answer to a problem. A good example is a manufacturing control system. Based on a series of constraints and the existing situation, the system will calculate the production mix. This type of system can utilize any kind of model or formula in order to come up with the solution.

The major distinction between data-oriented systems and model-oriented systems is that the first group uses pure data analysis and the second group uses modeling analysis. To illustrate the difference, consider Tely-Tak, a manufacturer of electronic devices. Tely-Tak has collected the sales data for the past 18 months from the corporate data base. In a data-oriented analysis we can organize these data based upon sales regions (e.g., which region is the best, which region is the worst) or we can organize it based on the performance of different products (e.g., which product generated the highest total sales, which product generated the lowest total sales). Now, suppose we create a regression model using the past 18 months' sales in order to generate a sales forecast for the next period. In this case we can say we have performed a modeling analysis. The objective is to provide managerial support for decision making. Throughout this book we provide other examples of these types of analyses.

The findings from this 56-system study show that applications are being developed and used to support rather than to replace a decision maker in making, justifying, and implementing decisions. In other words, people in a growing number of organizations are using DSS to improve their managerial effectiveness.

1-6 Implementation of DSS

Implementation is usually associated with change. Change may be physical or organizational and may involve one or several individuals or departments. It may be moderate or widespread. In any event, this stage determines the ultimate success and/or acceptance of a new system.

As we discuss in Chapter 8, a user or designer can minimize the negative issues related to implementation through a series of appropriate tools. For example, in recent years using a prototype as a design tool has provided DSS users with a better understanding of the operation of the system. As a result, users have been more involved, and the systems have been better received by the users. Implementing DSS is an involved, complex venture because the information requirements and decision styles of each user are unique. In the recent past management scientists and MIS personnel have failed in their efforts to implement computerized systems in business organizations because they did not support the needs, attitudes, and abilities of the users. It is imperative, that the overall implementation of DSS be an interactive and iterative process. We talk about this in detail in Chapters 7 and 8, when we discuss the process of building a DSS. From the very beginning, the designer, the user, and the system must be integrated to achieve a unified developmental effort. Ideally the designer, who understands management decision processes, and the user should work together to resolve the following issues:

1. *The particular task or decision to be supported.* This should be defined as narrowly as possible. The major players also must be identified.
2. *The objectives of the system.* Care must be taken to define the objectives from the user's perspective, *not* the data processing expert's. Users must know what the system is going to achieve.
3. *The decision-maker's current decision process.* DSS must complement and extend this process through the use of proper analytical models and methods. Care must be taken not to change drastically the present processes and procedures to which the decision maker is accustomed. Any change that takes place must be gradual.

To be successful, the interface, which handles the user-system interface (dialog management is discussed in Chapter 6), should be flexible, easy to use, reliable, reasonably self-explanatory, and responsive. These traits may be achieved by the use of commands and other flexible interfaces developed as a part of the user-system interface. Commands can be either general or specific. General commands are those common to most DSSs, such as REPORT, GRAPH, DISPLAY, PLOT, and SELECT. These commands support the manager's existing verbs. Specific commands relate to implementation issues, the three issues just discussed, to be resolved by the decision-maker and designer. They tend to extend the decision maker's decision-making abilities, replacing the intuitive or judgmental abilities of the manager. An example of a specific command is SMOOTH, a command designed to provide the decision-maker with a forecasting technique based on exponential smoothing that replaces intuitive "guesstimates."

When implementation is complete, the final product is a tailored decision-support aid. The success of implementation hinges on user participation and responsibility, instead of mere user compliance, in order to help the user feel he or she has been a part of the entire effort; this individual then continues to support "our" system.

1-7 Costs and Benefits of DSS

The costs and benefits of a DSS are difficult to assess, since DSS is aimed at effectiveness rather than efficiency and because it is said to facilitate, but not directly cause, improvements. How does one assign monetary values to facilitating interpersonal communication, to expediting and improving problem-solving activities, or to receiving information in 15 minutes as opposed to 2 hours?

Peter G. Keen [46] conducted an interesting study of a number of organizations regarding their DSS use. He concluded that the decision to build a DSS appears to be based on value rather than cost. He outlined the benefits of a DSS:

1. Increase in the number of alternatives examined
2. Better understanding of the business
3. Fast response to unexpected situations
4. Ability to carry out ad hoc analysis
5. New insights and learning
6. Improved communication
7. Improved control
8. Cost savings
9. Better decisions
10. More effective teamwork
11. Time savings
12. Making better use of data resources

As this study indicates, most of the benefits generated by a DSS are intangible and are difficult to assess.

The so-called intangible benefits generated by a DSS can be quantified. However, this quantification may be subjective, and different individuals may come up with different figures. For example, the opportunity cost of wasting 2 hours of a manager's time can be measured and transferred into monetary values—the 2 hours spent by a manager looking for information that could have been readily available by using a DSS. A decision-maker could have spent this time more productively making decisions. A less frustrated manager is also generally more productive.

The fact that DSS increases communication and interaction between clients and organizations, between organizations and employees, and among employees is also a benefit worth mentioning. (For more discussion on this issue, see Steven Alter, Chapter 3 [1]). DSS facilitates the way in which decision-makers view themselves, their jobs, and the way they spend time. In fact, improving communication and expediting learning are among the objectives of a DSS.

A DSS is said to have achieved its goals if employees have found it useful in doing their jobs. Some DSSs have resulted in definite clerical savings, whereas others have caused significant improvements in the decision-making process.

Overall, it seems that most DSSs can be developed from the existing resources in an organization. One may assume that the cost of developing a DSS compared to the benefits generated by these systems is minimal.

1-8 DSS at Present

Steven L. Alter's study of DSS users and their 56 systems (discussed earlier) and his taxonomy of these systems offer more recent data and assertions that DSSs are not homogeneous. Some DSSs may contain *descriptive* models such as the budgeting model, in which relationships among variables can be either probabilistic or deterministic. Other DSSs contain optimization models such as linear programming, allocation, inventory, and networking models.

Finally, a DSS such as geodata analysis and display system (GADS) contains no models at all. Instead it relies on language, software, and sometimes instructions to construct models appropriate for specific situations. Appendices A and B contain a comprehensive coverage of DSS generators (products) and popular DSSs in action. These two appendices provide a summary of the real power of DSS in today's business organizations. Appendix C highlights DSS applications in several disciplines.

Before we leave this discussion we should remind you that a DSS can be developed by using either DSS tools or DSS generators. DSS tools are hardware or software technologies available to DSS designers. For example, the COBOL language could be used as a DSS tool. DSS generators include hardware and software facilities as a package for developing a DSS, for example, IFPS (interactive financial planning system). We talk about these technologies further in Chapter 3.

1-9 DSS in Different Disciplines

During recent years, DSS has appeared in a variety of disciplines. Table 1-3 summarizes some of the most recent applications, which can be categorized under the following major functions:

1. *What-if analysis.* Many analyses can be performed using the what-if approach. The effect of a change in one variable on the entire system can be easily illustrated. If, for example, labor costs increase by 4%, what is going to happen to the final cost of a unit? Or if the advertising budget increases by 2%, what is the impact on total sales?
2. *Goal-seeking.* Goal-seeking is the reverse of what-if analysis. As an example, you may ask for how much you should sell a particular unit in

Table 1-3 ▪ Most Recent Applications of DSS

Area of Application	References	Specific Application
Manufacturing	[37], [12], [10], [56], [55], [42], [22]	Shop floor planning Job scheduling Different modeling
Marketing	[50], [19], [47], [9], [41], [30], [39]	Market analysis Product analysis Experimental design Modeling and simulation Sales forecast Analysis of different marketing scenarios
Accounting and budgeting	[8], [43]	Testing various financial scenarios by using what-if analysis Budgeting and long-range planning Lease/buy decisions
Purchasing	[7]	Price/cost analysis Inventory/production planning Material management Statistical purchasing analysis
Finance and investment	[21], [15], [25], [6], [5], [32], [48]	Predictive profiles Different spreadsheet applications Better planning Simulation capability
Sales	[53], [20], [16], [40]	Sales force allocation Sales forecast Price analysis Measurement of the effectiveness of marketing activities such as advertising and promotion Sales force effectiveness evaluation
Banking	[34], [39], [35], [23], [44]	Defining market segments What-if analysis over different investment scenarios Cost analysis
Office automation	[57], [4]	Integration of traditional office operation, e.g., word processing, electronic mail, message distribution Improve timeliness of information

Area of Application	References	Specific Application
Insurance	[54], [3]	Different modeling analyses Graphics analysis Access to external and internal data
Facility planning	[2], [29], [36]	Analysis of geographical location Project analysis Plant analysis
Law firms	[27]	Modeling the expected outcome of litigation to schedule or match lawyer's skills and legal tasks Planning litigation strategy

order to generate $200,000 profit or how much you should advertise in order to generate $50,000,000 total sales.

3. *Sensitivity analysis.* Using sensitivity analysis will enable you to perform analyses applying different variables. For example, what is the maximum price that you should pay for raw material and still make a profit, or how much overtime can you pay and still be cost-effective.
4. *Exception reporting analysis:* This application monitors the performance of variables that are outside a predefined range. It keys in on the region that generated the highest total sales or the production center that spent more than the predefined budget.

These are only some of the capabilities of a typical DSS. There are many more analyses and capabilities available, such as graphic analyses, forecasting, simulation, statistical analyses, modeling analyses, and so on. For further information, see Appendix C, which highlights DSS applications in diverse disciplines.

1-10 DSS Products: What is Available?

The available DSS software can be classified into two main categories: modeling products and data-management products. Although there is some overlap between these products, each group is still identified by one capability or the other. These products can also be classified as either mainframe-based or microbased. Recently some vendors have been offering microbased versions of mainframe-based DSS products. The microversions are less powerful than their mainframe counterparts. Table 1-4 provides a summary of some of the most powerful DSS products on the market. In Appendix A we provide a detailed description of some of the popular DSS products on the market.

Table 1–4 ▪ Decision Support Systems Products

Mainframe-Based Modeling	Mainframe-Based Data Management
IFPS by Execucom	RAMIS II by Mathematical Products Group
EIS by Boeing Computer	FOCUS by Information Builders, Inc.
SYSTEM W by ComShare	TOTAL by CINCOM
EXPRESS by MDS	IMAGE by Hewlett-Packard
FCS-EPS by EPS	ADABAS by Software Ag
SIMPLAN by Simplan Systems	IMS, DMS by IBM
AUTOFAB by Capex	IDMS by Cullinet Software, Inc.
CUFFS by Informatics	SQL/DDS by IBM
REVEAL by Infotym, a division of McDonnell Douglas	INGRES by Relational Technology
SAS by SAS Institute, Inc.	
Microbased Modeling	**Microbased Data Management**
Lotus 1-2-3 and Symphony by Lotus Development Corporation	R-BASE 5000 and System V by Microrim Corporation
FRAMEWORK by Ashton-Tate	dBASE III and III Plus by Ashton-Tate
MULTIPLAN by Microsoft	MICRORIM by Microrim Corporation
CONTEXT MBA by Context Management	CLOUT by Microrim Corporation
PLANNERCALC by ComShare	Oracle by Oracle Corporation
OVATION by Ovation Technologies	10-Base by Fox Research, Inc.
20/20 by Access Technology	Knowledge Man by Micro Data Base Systems
SAS/PC by SAS Institute, Inc.	FOCUS/PC by Information Builder, Inc.
SMART by Innovative Software	
SuperCalc by Sorcim Corporation	

1-11 A Look in the Past

To understand the future better, a review of the past would be helpful. The three main components of a DSS, the user, the software, and the hardware, have gone through major improvements.

Highly trained computer personnel are not the only users of computer technology in an organization. Computer education and computer awareness are found at all levels of the management team. Computers have become easier to use and more widespread, and so a majority of business organizations either provide computer training inside the organization or send their employees to college classes, seminars, or vendor training sessions. Also, the availability of graphic interfaces such as the mouse, the touch screen, and menu-driven systems has made it easier to train employees with minimum computer backgrounds.

Software technology has improved significantly. When the first computers were introduced in the early 1940s, the only language understood by these computers was machine language, which consists of a series of 0s and 1s. Because it is difficult to program a computer using machine language, the only users of these early computers were highly trained data-processing personnel. The second generation of computer language, called assembly language, consisted of a series of short codes or mnemonics. In general, assembly language was easier to use than machine language, but it still required rigorous training to become proficient. The third generation of computer languages, called high-level languages, or higher-level languages, are more like English and are more user-oriented. For example, a user can get a general idea of what is happening in a program written in the COBOL language by just reading through the program. High-level languages are easier to learn and to use than the first two; however, they are still very specific in nature, and do not have very flexible structures. The fourth level of computer languages, or 4GL's, are more forgiving than the first three, and are by far easier to learn and to use. Many fewer lines are needed to perform a task using these languages compared to their earlier counterparts. To use these languages requires some basic computer training and a familiarity with the keyboard. The fifth generation of computer languages, natural language processing (NLP), promises a great deal of flexibility and power. If these languages ever become a reality, computers will become a lot easier to use, friendlier, and more flexible.

Computer hardware has also gone through major improvements. The first generation of computers were operated by vacuum tubes and were bulky and unreliable. The second generation, the transistor era, brought power, speed, and reliability to the computer industry. Second-generation computers were much smaller and a lot more powerful than their ancestors. The third generation of computer technology is associated with chip technology. With the integrated circuit as the building block of the third-generation computer, computer technology improved in all dimensions. In the early 1970s the fourth generation of computer technology was introduced to the market. The fourth generation was basically a miniaturization era: Computers became smaller and more powerful than before. The widespread use of microcomputers and desktop computing are the main features of this generation.

The fifth generation features the AI (artificial intelligence) computers, the computers that are more "intelligent" than traditional computers.

1-12 Outlook for DSS

After addressing the question What is DSS? the next question is, What is the future of DSS?

By identifying what it is, we have suggested that DSS is a new part of the MIS concept that will in no way replace MIS. It is called DSS because its purpose is to support decision-makers in making and implementing decisions. DSS is characterized by its active use in all aspects of management activities. It is used at all organizational levels to facilitate communication, interaction, and learning among a myriad of users, not necessarily all of whom are managers. Successful implementation is assured when there is interaction between users and designers. The emphasis in DSS is on increased individual and organizational effectiveness. The philosophy of DSS is to improve or expedite the processes by which people make decisions. Because DSS is both flexible and evolutionary, its effectiveness should steadily increase as it is applied.

To address the question of DSS in the future, we choose to look at the short-range rather than the long-range situation. Only recently has DSS begun to take hold in the business world. For some time, research (as well as technology) has been ahead of the practical application of DSS. Users have only recently accepted the concept of DSS and begun using their creativity and the resources of their organizations to make DSS applications a reality. People who use DSS are continuing to learn what can be done and how to use the systems more effectively.

We feel that DSS will continue to grow; however, decision-makers must *first* accept the idea that computers can be used to support rather than replace human decision-makers. *Second*, interpersonal and technical relationships between decision-makers and designers must be improved. DSS will become more prevalent in the future if these two conditions are met and if the users continue to take an active part in the development of DSS. The ability of DSS to meet the decision makers' needs with ever-increasing effectiveness will ensure its continued existence. In the ultimate sense, we regard DSS as the most significant, current frontier in the organizational application of computers.

We cannot end this discussion without remarking on the almost unlimited possibilities of the future. AI and its supporting technologies will undoubtedly play an important part in the future of DSS because AI is concerned with humanlike reasoning. The potential integration of AI products and DSS could be exciting. Some applications of AI, called expert systems, have already proved to be very promising. AI, expert systems, and their relationship to DSS are discussed in detail in Chapters 12–14. For now, keep in mind that AI technologies try to mimic human thought behavior.

The future of DSS will be influenced by three factors:

1. *Computer hardware*. Computers are becoming more powerful, faster, less expensive, and more manageable. Microcomputers will continue to play an important role in information storage, retrieval, and analysis. Telecommunications and networking will be improved. A mainframe micro (high-powered desktop computer) will become a reality.
2. *Computer software*. We will see more and more integration among the software packages. Integrated software such as FRAMEWORK, SMART, Lotus 1-2-3, and Symphony will become more common. User-friendly and menu-driven software will become a reality. Artificial intelligence and expert systems will become more common and more business-oriented. Also, we should see more integration among AI, ES, and DSS.
3. *Users of computers*. The users and managers of the future will be computer sophisticates and will have higher expectations. Computer support will be more acceptable and less threatening. All of us, not just hard-core computer scientists, will use computers. Chapter 15 explores the future of DSS in detail.

1-13 Summary

Decision support systems have been around for several years, yet there is no common definition for these systems. The power of DSS has been demonstrated in many applications, but skeptics still believe DSS is a new name for traditional MIS and EDP. But through comparative analysis the unique characteristics of DSS have been demonstrated. The historic progression from EDP to MIS to DSS showed the natural progression that is continuing today. The future seems very promising as further development in artificial intelligence and expert systems enhances the power and utilization of DSS.

What does all this mean to DSS? The trend for hardware, software, and even users indicates an increasing utilization of DSS. DSS should become much easier to use, while at the same time becoming more powerful and user-friendly. It is hard to imagine a significant corporate enterprise in the near future *without* DSS.

Review Questions

1. What is EDP?

2. What is MIS?

3. What is DSS?

4. Mention unique characteristics of each technology.

5. Is DSS really something new? Discuss.

6. Give one example of Alter's taxonomy of DSS.

7. What is the major difference between data-oriented and model-oriented DSS?

8. Is implementation of DSS different from EDP and MIS? If yes, how?

9. What are some of the costs and benefits of a typical DSS?

10. Mention different fields that have benefited from DSS.

11. What is the difference between what-if analysis and goal seeking in the DSS environment?

12. What is sensitivity analysis?

13. Give an example of each of these three types of analysis.

14. Give some examples of mainframe-modeling DSS software and micromodeling DSS software.

15. Give some examples of mainframe DBMS DSS software and micro DBMS DSS software.

16. Give some indications of the future trend for DSS.

17. What is AI, and in what ways may it affect DSS?

Projects

1. Identify one example of EDP, MIS, and DSS in a typical college or university. What are the basis of your classification? What are the differences in these three applications as far as the users are concerned?

2. What are some DSS applications in a typical bank? What can a DSS do for a loan officer? What can a DSS do for a stock analyst?

3. Give an example of how inventory-control systems such as those used at grocery stores have evolved from the typical EDP to an MIS system. Explain how this could be taken one step further and evolve into a DSS system.

4. Research three DSS modeling products and three DSS data base products for microcomputers. How are these different? How are they similar? Why do we have so many of these products?

Key Terms

Decision support systems
Electronic data processing
Management information systems
Efficiency
Effectiveness
Quantitative analysis
Qualitative analysis
Design tools
Internal data
External data
Life-cycle approach
File drawer systems
Data analysis systems
Optimization models
Accounting models
Analysis information systems
Representational models
Suggestion models
Implementation of a DSS
Costs and benefits of a DSS
What-if analysis
Goal-seeking analysis
Sensitivity analysis
Exception reporting analysis
Vacuum tube
Transistor
Integrated circuits
Miniaturization
Data-oriented systems
Model-oriented systems
Artificial intelligence
Expert systems
Resistance to change
User-system interface
User-friendly
Menu-driven system

References

[1] Alter, Steven L. 1980. *Decision Support Systems Current Practice and Continuing Challenges*. Reading, Mass.: Addison-Wesley Publishing Company.

[2] Anonymous. 1982. Decision Support Helps Dominion Choose Store Sites. *Canadian Datasystems* (Canada) (October): 85.

[3] Anonymous. 1983. End-User Computing Facility Aids Insurer. *Computerworld* (May 30): 47, 52.

[4] Anonymous. 1982. Why Decisions Come Quicker at Airco. *Sales & Marketing Management* (December 6): 56–57.

[5] Anonymous. 1983. Batch to On-Line Transition Eased by IFPS. *Computerworld* (June 27): Special Report 57, 60.

[6] Anonymous. 1983. Systems in Action. *Office Administration & Automation* (August): 85–86.

[7] Anonymous. 1984. User Friendly Software Now Available for Purchasing, *Purchasing World* (October): 70–71.

[8] Anonymous. 1984. Distiller Used DSS System to Change Budgeting Procedure. *Computing Canada* (Canada) (December 27): 10–11, Software Report.

[9] Anonymous. 1985. Kodak's MIDSS Zooms In On DSS Role. *Computerworld* (January 21): 42, 52.

[10] Anonymous. 1984. Thanks to DSS, Manufacturer Builds Powerful Analysis Tool. *Data Management* (July): 36–37.

[11] Attaran, Mohsen, and Hossein Bidgoli. 1986. Building an Effective Manufacturing DSS. *Business* (October/December): 9–16.

[12] Bellack, Paul M. 1984. Dofasco's Microcomputer Decision Support System. *Planning Review* (July): 21–23, 44.

[13] Bennett, John L. 1983. *Building Decision Support Systems*. Reading, Mass.: Addison-Wesley Publishing Company.

[14] Bidgoli, Hossein, and James Vigen. 1986. *Introduction to Management Information Systems: A User Perspective*. Dubuque, Ia.: Kendall/Hunt Publishing Company, pp. 1–19.

[15] Bryan, Shawn W. 1984. Complex Financial Modeler Surpasses Mainframe Rivals. *Business Computer Systems* (June): 162–65.

[16] Buchin, Stanley, and Timothy A. Davidson. 1983. Computer-Aided Sales Forecasting: How the Skeptics Can Learn to Love It. *Business Marketing* (August): 74–81.

[17] Chan, K. Harry. 1984. Decision Support System for Human Resource Management. *Journal of Systems Management* (April): 17–25.

[18] Chandler, John, et al. 1983. Decision Support Systems Are for Small Businesses. *Management Accounting* (April): 34–39.

[19] Coleman, David. 1984. Decision Support Systems. *Data Processing* (UK) (October): 35–36.

[20] Cravens, David W., and Raymond W. LaForge. 1983. Salesforce Deployment Analysis. *Industrial Marketing Management* (July): 179–92.

[21] Crawford, Diane. 1984. Software Support for the Intuitive Thinker. *Wall Street Computer Review* (November): 53–58.

[22] Crescenzi, Adam D., and Gary K. Gulden. 1983. Decision Support for Manufacturing Management. *Information & Management* (Netherlands) (April): 91–95.

[23] Davis, Donald L. 1983. Computing the Advantages of Detailed Datasystems. *Personnel Journal* 62, no. 11 (November): 888–892.

[24] Davis, Samuel G. et al. 1983. Expressend: A Check Clearing Decision Support System for Endpoint Selection. *Journal of Bank Research* (Fall): 203–211.

[25] Donnelly, Robert M. 1983. Keep Up With Decision Support Systems. *Financial Executive (August):* 44–46.

[26] Dressler, Michael et al. 1983. Why Marketing Managers Love DSS. *Business Marketing* (April): 77–81.

[27] Emerson, Jeff D. 1983. Litigation Management Support Systems. *Legal Economics* 9, no. 5 (September-October): 49–52.

[28] Enrico, Jack F. 1984. More Facts in Less Time. *Cost Engineering* (December): 22–29.

[29] Filley, Richard D. 1984. A Survey of Software for Facilities Planning & Design. *Industrial Engineering* (May): 71–79.

[30] Frank, Jonathan, and Jacques Schnabel. 1983. Timing of Borrowing Decisions—A Decision Support System. *Journal of Systems Management* (April): 6–9.

[31] French, Graham. 1984. Better Support for Top Decision-Makers. *Chief Executive* (UK) (November): 47, 49.

[32] Gerrity, T. P., Jr. 1971. Design of Man-Machine Systems: An Application to Portfolio Management. *Sloan Management Review* 14, no. 2 (Winter): 59–75.

[33] Gorry G. A., and Michael S. Scott-Morton. 1971. A Framework for MIS. *Sloan Management Review* 13, no. 1 (Fall): 55–70.

[34] Goldberg, Joan B. 1984. RB3 Boosts Personal Selling, Enhances Bank's 'Pro' Image. *Bank Systems & Equipment* (April): 72–73.

[35] Green, Christopher. 1984. Emergence of Rapid Response. *Mortgage Banking* (April): 41–48.

[36] Hales, H. Lee. 1984. Computerized Facilities Planning and Design: Sorting Out the Options Available Now. *Industrial Engineering* (May): 60–70.

[37] Hehnen, M. T. et al. 1984. An Integrated Decision Support and Manufacturing Control System. *Interfaces* (September/October): 44–52.

[38] Hirouchi, Tetsuo, and Takeshi Kosaka. 1984. An Effective Database Formation for Decision Support Systems. *Information & Management* (Netherlands) (August): 183–195.

[39] Horn, Sheri. 1984. Bank of OK Uses DSS to Determine Profitable Products. *Bank Systems & Equipment* (April): 70–71.

[40] Hughes, G. David. 1983. Computerized Sales Management. *Harvard Business Review* (March/April): 102–112.

[41] Israni, Sharat S., and Jerry L. Sanders. 1984. A Manufacturing Decision Support System for Flamecutting. *Computers & Industrial Engineering:* 207–214.

[42] Jaffe, Merle. 1983. Decision Support Systems for Manufacturing. *Infosystems* (July): 112–114.

[43] Johnson, Bart. 1984. Why Your Company Needs Three Accounting Systems. *Management Accounting* (September): 39–46.

[44] Justice, Karen. 1982. Electronic Decisions for Bankers. *Interface: Banking Industry* (Winter): 6.

[45] Keen, Peter G., and Michael S. Scott-Morton. 1978. *Decision Support Systems: An Organizational Perspective*. Reading, Mass.: Addison-Wesley Publishing Co.

[46] Keen, Peter G. 1981. Value Analysis: Justifying Decision Support System. *MIS Quarterly* 5, no. 1 (March): 1–15.

[47] Lampert, Anne. 1985. Expert Systems Get Down to Business. *Computer Decisions* (January 15): 138–144.

[48] Moskowitz, Robert. 1983. Decision Support System/Analysis (DSS/A). *Interface Age* (April): 62–68.

[49] Rector, Robert L. 1983. Decision Support Systems—Strategic Planning Tool. *Managerial Planning* (May/June): 36–40.

[50] Reimann, Bernard C. 1985. The "New Wave" of Decision Support Software: Is It For You? *Woman CPA* (January): 20–26.

[51] Sharda, Ramesh, Steve H. Barr, and James C. McDonnell. 1988. "Decision Support System Effectiveness: A Review and an Empirical Test. *Management Science* 34, no. 2 (February): 139–59.

[52] Sprague, Jr., Ralph, and Eric D. Carlson. 1982. *Building Effective Decision Support Systems*. Englewood Cliffs, N. J.: Prentice-Hall, Inc.

[53] Taylor, Thayer C. 1984. Honeywell's Computer Makes Managers Out of Salespeople. *Sales & Marketing Management* (May 14): 59–61.

[54] Viste, Gerald D. 1984. Making Decisions Are a Snap, Because of DSS, at Wausau Insurance. *Data Management* (June): 22–24.

[55] Viviers, Francois. 1983. A Decision Support System for Job Shop Scheduling. *European Journal of Operational Research* (Netherlands) (September): 95–103.

[56] Waliszewski, David. 1983. The Decision Maker's Guide to MRP/Vendor Roundup: A Who's Who in Manufacturing Software. *Interface: Manufacturing & Engineering* (Fall): 12–21, 36–39.

[57] Walkinshaw, Ian. 1984. Development and Use of a Flexible DSS. *Data Processing* (UK) (October): 37–40.

2 Decision Making and Computer Technology

2-1 Introduction

This chapter provides a general overview of the decision-making process. Generally, theoretical decision-making techniques fall into five different schools of thought: the rational actor view, the satisficing view, the organizational view, the political view, and the individual differences view. This chapter examines aspects of efficiency and effectiveness in the decision-making process and discusses types of decisions and stages of decision making in an organization. Since the rational actor view is the most frequently employed method of decision making due to its structure it has the potential to gain significantly from DSS. Therefore, a more in-depth discussion of this method is provided. Different tools, techniques and models used in this view are highlighted. Finally, this chapter concludes with a discussion of decision making in a real-life situation by focusing on external and internal constraints facing a decision-maker. These constraints must always be considered in designing a DSS.

2-2 Computers as Decision-Making Aids

During the past 40 years, we have witnessed numerous applications of computers in different disciplines. Throughout this period more applications have been introduced and earlier applications improved in order to cover a broader perspective.

In an organizational setting, we have witnessed three categories of computer applications. These include electronic data processing (EDP), management information systems (MIS), and decision support systems (DSS). As discussed in Chapter 1, EDP and MIS have been used primarily for automating simple record-keeping procedures and for activities in which a well-defined operating procedure exists within the organization.

DSSs, on the other hand, have centered on decision making and decision implementation in all levels of the organization. These systems utilize computer hardware and software to assist the decision-maker. Given the rapid advancement in the computer field, these systems offer broad potential for helping decision-makers in their decision-making tasks.

In the last few years the areas of artificial intelligence (AI) and expert systems (ES) have attracted much attention. AI and ES technologies are concerned with intelligent computers, which try to mimic human thought behavior.

We talk about these issues in detail in later chapters. In this chapter, we examine the decision-making process and highlight those areas in this process that may benefit from computer technology in general and from DSS in particular.

2-3 The Decision-Making Process

Throughout the literature, decision making has been classified in terms of five main schools of thought [1, 10]. Graham T. Allison provides an excellent discussion in his book *Essence of Decision* [1], explaining the decision-making process in the Cuban Missile Crisis. Although much has been written on various aspects of decision making, including organizational, individual, and group [13], [14], we believe Allison's classical approach is more suitable to the specific environment of DSS. Understanding Allison's model can help the designer gain insight into organizational decision making and the role of DSS in this process. But first let us briefly explain the different schools of thought.

The Rational Actor Decision-Maker's View

The rational actor school of thought advocates that decisions are made by an individual, rational decision-maker who is always consistent, considers economic factors, and is cognizant of relevant cost/benefit ratios. This school of thought assumes that a decision-maker has all the required tools and information for making and implementing a decision and also assumes an ideal situation that rarely exists in the dynamic business world.

The rational actor school follows the classic approach to decision making by progressing through the following steps:

- Defining the problem
- Generating the alternatives
- Evaluating the alternatives
- Implementing the best alternative
- Performing a follow-up evaluation to see how the solution is working

A classic example using this approach is a transportation problem. The problem is well defined: Product A is to be shipped from city X to city Y. Alternatives include sending it by plane, bus, train, and private transportation. The criteria for evaluation of these alternatives are based on either the cost of shipping or the pertinent time constraint. Naturally, the alternative chosen will be either the cheapest or the fastest; it depends upon the objectives of the organization. The follow-up phase may suggest a corrective action for the future if the organization is faced with such decisions again.

Another example is a business's selection of a medium or combination of media for advertising purposes. Several options may be available to the business, but only one combination of media may maximize the number of potential customers reached by the organization. After the desired alternative is implemented, the follow-up phase may suggest a different action based on the results of the survey related to the effectiveness of the previous advertising campaign.

The "Satisficing" View

The ideal situation necessary for the rational actor does not always exist. If the requirements for the rational view *are* present, this school is the best, since it seeks the optimal solution, a solution that yields the highest payoff in monetary or non-monetary terms.

The *satisficing* view seeks a "good enough" alternative and uses feedback to improve the next solution if possible. This school advocates that an organization should survive with the present solution and should try to obtain a more satisfactory solution in the future.

To understand this method of problem solving, consider this example. An organization is trying to decide where to start in implementing a hiring procedure. There is probably no best way to implement a recruitment policy, so for the time being, the organization may choose to follow a procedure that includes the following steps:

- Advertise the position rigorously.
- Conduct comprehensive interviews.
- Check résumé's and references of the candidates.
- Screen the applicants for the top five candidates.
- Conduct second interviews.
- Hire the top candidate.

This may be considered an adequate solution for the time being; however, this process may be improved in the future. In the next round, the organization may include different methods of advertising, choose different media for advertising, or ask the candidates to answer a questionnaire before their interviews. An organization may continuously learn from the present situation and improve its status in the future.

The Organizational View

The organizational school of thought tries to generate and implement decisions as the outputs of standard operating procedures (SOPs) imposed by organizational units within the organization. A typical business organization may include marketing, finance, personnel, and manufacturing departments as its organizational units. For this approach, understanding organizational roles, relationships, and channels of communication is very important.

Consider this example. A business organization is trying to decide where to put a new plant in one of the 50 states. The organization, as a system, may gather input from four major players in the organization: the vice presidents of marketing, manufacturing, finance, and personnel. Each of these vice presidents has a unique set of concerns. For example, the vice president of finance may recommend a location that has the cheapest capital outlay. Or he or she may consider only an investment that yields at least a 15% rate of return. This may be the SOP of the finance department.

Other players in the organization may be concerned about other factors. For example, the marketing vice president may recommend a location that provides the best potential market or the location that has the best access to present and future customers. The personnel vice president may suggest the plant be located where the cost of labor is the cheapest. The manufacturing vice president may be concerned with the location of the plant relative to raw material suppliers, transportation, and environmental factors. As you can see, in a situation like this, organizational roles, channels of communication, different relationships, and the power status of different players are extremely important.

The organization as a unit may choose a solution that is good enough for all the players and is consistent with the SOPs of the organization as a whole.

The Political View

The political school of thought emphasizes the bargaining process involved in the decision-making process. There are several players involved in this process, and each one may influence the outcome of the decision-making process differently. The power and influence of each player determine the outcome of any given decision. Usually this type of decision making ends with a compromise among the players.

The major difference between this school and the organizational view is the lack of control imposed by the organization as a unit on the final outcome. In the political decision-making process, there is no organizational entity to have the final word on the decision.

One good example of this school is the Organization for Petroleum Exporting Countries (OPEC). There are 13 different players implementing decisions in the organization, and each one has a different interest and background, representing a country with different economic and political structures. Players have various levels of power and influence. The negotiation process usually ends with a compromise. Sometimes it may take days or even months before a compromise is reached. And sometimes the players are unable to come to a compromise.

The organizational view and the political view should be very helpful for understanding group DSS (GDSS) and processes involved in making decisions in this type of setting. In GDSS there are usually several decision-makers involved in the decision process. Understanding the "bargaining" process that exists in any group decision-making process is important. The organizational and the political view highlight the issues involved in such settings. We discuss GDSS in Chapter 11.

The Individual Differences View

The individual differences school of thought puts a heavy emphasis on the individual decision-maker's personality, background, style, and so forth. The designer of an effective DSS must take these idiosyncrasies into account. For instance, the output format of the information provided by any computer-based information system can be tabular or graphic, in summary form or detailed. Do all decision-makers like graphs? Do all decision-makers like summary reports? Naturally, these issues must be considered and investigated individually with regard to each decision-maker's personal style and organizational status.

2-4 Efficiency and Effectiveness in the Decision-Making Process

Efficiency in decision making is concerned mainly with cost factors [10]: the cheapest way to implement a task, to manufacture a product, to travel to a place. On the other hand, effectiveness is concerned with the appropriateness of a decision. You may implement a task in the cheapest possible way; however, the task as a whole may accomplish no known goal. To see this more clearly, consider this example. Assume you can manufacture an electronic calculator for a total cost of $5. You may have made a big effort to minimize the cost/benefit ratio and may think nobody else in the world could manufacture such a calculator at this cost. In this case, you can say you have been efficient. However, there may not be anybody who is willing to pay even $2 for this calculator. If this is the situation, you have been efficient but not effective.

In decision-making processes, a decision-maker must be both efficient and effective. A DSS, if it is designed properly, should enable a decision-maker to accomplish these goals. As you will see in Chapter 3, effectiveness may be achieved by being efficient in some cases. Overall, however, a decision-maker cannot be effective without being efficient. That is, you cannot implement a good decision with too much cost, thus sacrificing efficiency for effectiveness.

Efficiency in organizational decision making may involve the utilization of the internal resources in the best possible way. Effectiveness is usually concerned with the factors outside the organization. A DSS utilizes both internal and external data in order to achieve both goals. These issues are addressed throughout this book.

2-5 Types of Decisions in an Organization

Decisions in an organization can be classified into three groups [4]:

- Structured decisions
- Semistructured decisions
- Unstructured decisions

Structured decisions, or programmable tasks, do not need a decision-maker for implementation, because a well-defined standard operating procedure exists for the execution of these types of decisions. Record-keeping operations, payrolls, and simple inventory problems are examples of this type of task, in which computer technology can be of significant help.

Semistructured decisions are those that are not quite as well-defined by standard operating procedures as are structured decisions. However, these decisions include structured aspects that greatly benefit from information retrieval, analytical models, and information-system technology in general. Sales forecasting, budget preparation, and capital acquisition analysis are some decisions within this group.

Unstructured decisions are unique in nature, are mostly nonrecurring, and have no standard operating procedure that pertains to their implementation. In these circumstances, the decision-maker's intuition plays the most significant role and computer technology offers the least support. There are numerous instances of these types of decisions, including research and development, hiring and firing, and introduction of a new product. Future development in artificial intelligence may be of great assistance to organizations confronted with qualitative types of decisions. The possible integration of DSS and artificial intelligence is discussed in Chapter 14.

Figure 2-1 illustrates organizational levels and types of decisions [3]. This figure highlights the potential of information technology in general and DSS specifically in all levels of an organization.

2-6 Stages of the Decision-Making Process

Herbert Simon defines the three stages in the decision-making process [15] as intelligence, design, and choice. A fourth stage, implementation, may be added to these three stages. Figure 2-2 illustrates these four stages.

Intelligence

In the intelligence phase, the environment of an organization is studied for conditions requiring decisions. Data are collected from a variety of sources (internal and external) and are processed. From this information, the problem-solver may discover ways of approaching his or her problem.

As an example, an organization may experience a decrease in total sales over a 6-month period. In order to pinpoint the source of the problem, the

Figure 2-1 Organizational Levels and Types of Decisions

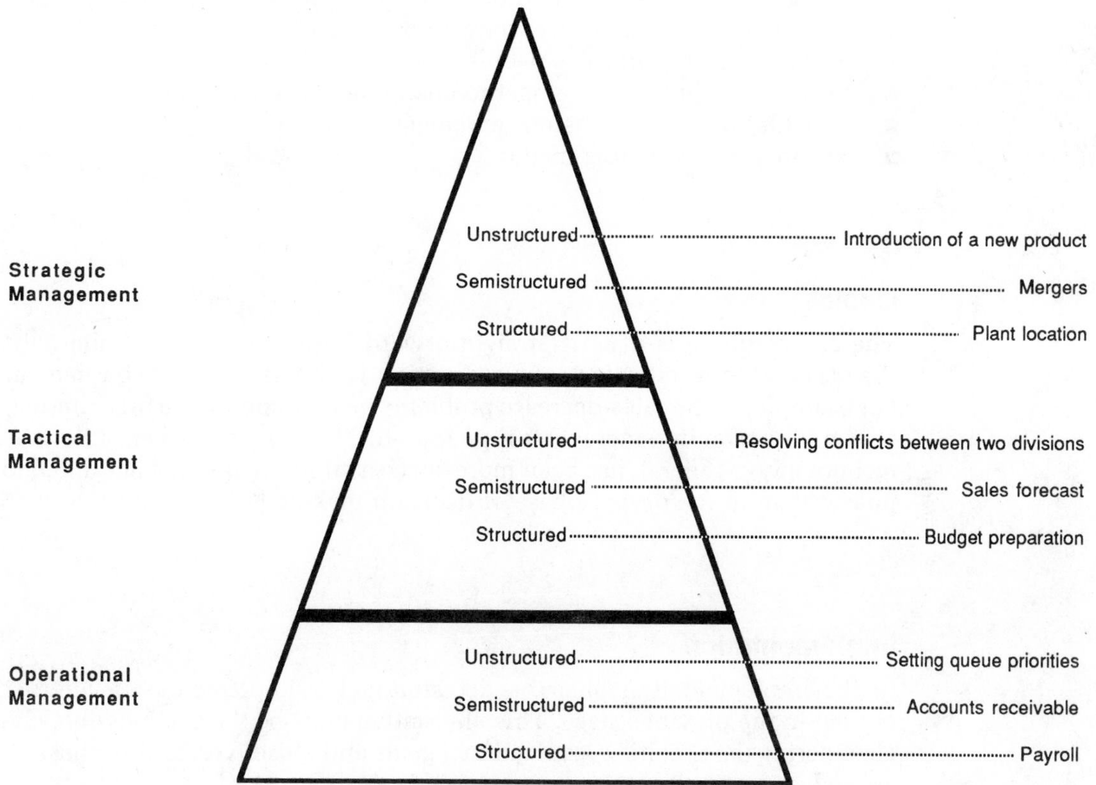

organization can collect data from customers, the marketplace, and the competition, to name a few sources. Once the data are processed, analysis of the information might suggest possible remedies.

Design

In the design stage, the objective is to generate alternatives, evaluate different alternatives creating courses of action, and evaluate the feasibility and accessibility of each solution.

Figure 2-2 Four Stages in the Decision-Making Process

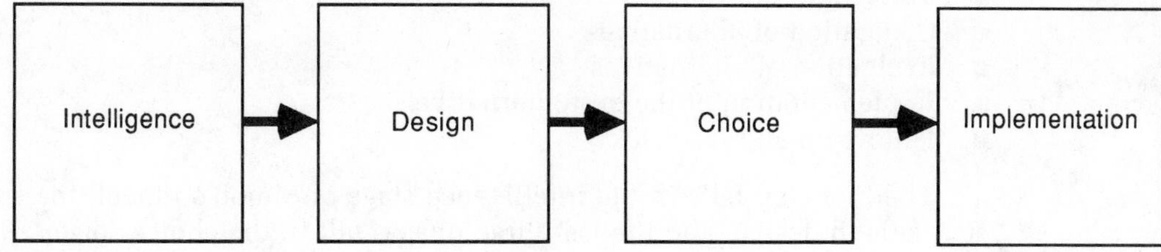

In the sales-decrease problem, we may generate a number of alternatives:

- Assign more sales people to the target market
- Retrain and motivate the current sales people
- Reroute the current sales people
- Revamp the product to adjust to changing consumer tastes
- Consider a new advertising campaign
- Reallocate the existing media

Choice

The choice phase is usually straightforward. From the practical alternatives, the best and most effective course of action is chosen and then implemented. For example, in the sales-decrease problem, we may choose the first alternative, which is assigning more sales people to the target market. Information technology, in general, has been more successful in the intelligence and choice phases than in the design phase of decision making [17].

Implementation

In the implementation phase, a decision-maker implements the alternative chosen in the previous stage. This alternative must be the best possible choice considering the specific organizational goals and objectives. In this phase ideas are transferred into action.

2-7 The Rational Actor: A Second Look

Among the five views of decision making, the rational decision-making process stands to gain the most from computer technology in general and DSS specifically. The major reason for such a direct gain is the existence of the rigorous structure and standard operating procedures in this approach to decision making that are lacking in the other views of decision making. As discussed earlier, in this school of thought, the following five steps are usually followed:

- Problem definition
- Generation of alternatives
- Evaluation of alternatives
- Implementation of the best alternative
- Follow-up and feedback

The first step falls in the intelligence stage of Simon's model, the second step falls in design, and the last three phases fall in the choice stage.

Computer technology can be of some assistance in these steps. Automated data bases, for example, can help a decision-maker to collect and analyze data in order to pinpoint a problem. When more integration between AI technologies and DSSs is possible, we may be able to ask "why" and "how" questions of a computer-based information system in order to define a particular problem more clearly. We discuss AI-related technologies in Chapters 12 through 14. For now, remember AI computers refer to those computers that can perform with some degree of intelligence by mimicking and possibly reproducing the human expert's thought behavior.

In the generation of alternatives, computers have not been of much help to human decision-makers. This may be changed in the future, when we witness more integration between DSS and AI technologies.

In the evaluation of alternatives, computer technology has been of great help. Such factors as the outcome of each alternative, its cost/benefit, and its net gain, can be calculated; then a decision-maker can choose the best alternative.

In terms of implementation, computers have always been a part of the operation, since implementation of particular solutions is usually faster and more effective when computers are involved. In the follow-up and feedback stages, computers can help a decision-maker to analyze data faster and come to a conclusion sooner if the system is doing what it is supposed to do.

Problem Definition

Problem definition, or the intelligence stage, is probably the most important part of the decision-making process. At this time, a decision-maker must define the problem, not the symptoms of the problem, as precisely as possible. This information-gathering exercise can be a costly and time-consuming endeavor. Using a rational view of decision making, the goal of a decision-maker is either to maximize the profit or minimize the cost. A classic example is an inventory problem faced by any business organization, where the objective is to minimize the total cost of the inventory (ordering cost, capital cost, opportunity cost, and so on). In a transportation problem, the objective is to minimize the cost of transportation.

Generation of the Alternatives

Alternative generation, or as Simon calls it, the design stage, can be very easy or very complex, depending on the problem. In this phase a variety of tools may be employed to assist a decision-maker. Two commonly used tools are brainstorming and Delphi techniques.

During a brainstorming [9] session, a group of individuals gets together and tries to generate as many alternatives as possible. Initially, some of these alternatives may seem infeasible and even ridiculous. However, in a later stage, each alternative can be given individual attention in order to investigate its practicality.

In the Delphi [11] process, a decision is reached by collecting and reviewing the opinions of a group of experts in a particular discipline. In succeeding meetings the opinions are supported or criticized by an expert group. After several meetings the group usually comes to a conclusion regarding a particular problem.

Alternatives generated to solve an advertising problem may focus on the choice of a medium:

- Television
- Radio
- Newspaper
- Brochure
- Promotional activities
- Combination of media

Evaluation of the Alternatives

The alternative with the highest payoff is the desired alternative. However, the best choice may not be easily recognized. Generally speaking, a decision-maker makes a decision under either certainty or uncertainty. In decision making under certainty, a decision-maker has access to all the needed information for making and implementing a decision, which is not the case in decision making under uncertainty. A decision-maker is faced with a series of alternatives and states of nature. Sometimes there is a probability factor associated with each state of nature, or there may be no probability information available to the decision-maker.

To illustrate this situation, consider the following example. North Text, a major multinational northwestern textile company, is considering the implementation of a new computer system. This is the result of a detailed study aimed at improving the market share and competitiveness of this company in the international arena.

A consulting team has provided a detailed analysis, which recommends three alternatives to North Text. These recommendations include:

- Maintenance of the current manual system with added computer support
- Implementation of a new EDP/MIS system
- Implementation of an EDP/MIS with DSS support

Generally speaking, each system has some advantages and disadvantages and each has different associated costs and benefits. However, the level of success will be measured by North Text employees' enthusiasm for working with the new system. Factors in this judgment of success may include employee reaction, usability, acceptance, and so forth.

There are three scenarios identified by the consulting team:

- High success
- Moderate success
- Low success

Table 2-1 ▪ Payoff Table for North Text (Figures are in thousands)

	State of Nature		
Alternatives	High Success S_1	Moderate Success S_2	Low Success S_3
a_1 Manual system with added computer support	50	55	26
a_2 EDP/MIS system	60	46	30
a_3 EDP/MIS with DSS support	70	40	21

In decision theory, these scenarios are referred to as states of nature. Each alternative and state of nature may generate a payoff, or net gain, to North Text. An estimate of potential gains is summarized in Table 2-1, the payoff table. The alternative that should be chosen by North Text in order to maximize its gain depends upon the degree of success offered by the decision-making environment.

Decision Making Under Certainty. In decision making under certainty, only one column in the payoff table must be considered. For example, if North Text knows it will have a high success regardless of which system is implemented, the payoff table will be as represented in Table 2-2.

In this case, North Text will implement a_3, since that alternative offers the highest payoff, meaning North Text will implement an EDP/MIS with DSS support.

Decision Making Under Uncertainty with No Probability. In decision making under uncertainty, a decision-maker either knows some probability associated with each state of nature or has no knowledge regarding the probability of occurrence of each state of nature. Consider first the existence of no probability regarding the state of nature. If this is the case, one of the following three techniques may be considered:

- Maximin
- Maximax
- Minimax

Table 2-2 ▪ Payoff Under High Success

Alternatives	Potential Payoff
a_1	50
a_2	60
a_3	70

Table 2-3 ▪ Minimum Payoff

Alternative	Potential Payoff
a_1	26
a_2	30
a_3	21

Table 2-4 ▪ Maximum Payoff

Alternative	Potential Payoff
a_1	55
a_2	60
a_3	70

Maximin. The maximin is a pessimistic, or conservative, approach for implementing a decision. The goal is to maximize the minimum potential gain.

First the decision-maker lists the minimum payoff of each alternative regardless of the state of nature (Table 2-3) and then chooses the alternative that yields the maximum payoff.

Under these conditions, alternative a_2 is chosen, since it maximizes the minimum payoff.

Maximax. The maximax technique considers the problem from an optimistic view point. A decision-maker first lists the maximum payoff of each alternative regardless of the state of nature and then chooses the alternative with the highest payoff from the list. Table 2-4 illustrates this process.

In this case, alternative a_3 will be chosen.

Minimax. In the minimax technique, the opportunity cost, or the cost of the next best alternative, must be determined. In Table 2-1, if the state of nature is

Table 2-5 ▪ Opportunity Loss Table

	State of Nature		
Alternative	S_1	S_2	S_3
a_1	20	0	4
a_2	10	9	0
a_3	0	15	9

Table 2-6 ▪ Highest Opportunity Loss

Alternatives	Potential Payoff
a_1	20
a_2	10
a_3	15

S_1, the best alternative for a decision-maker to choose is a_3. The opportunity loss for a_1 is 20 (70 − 50), meaning a decision-maker could have made \$20 more by implementing the alternative a_3. For a_2 the opportunity cost is 10 (70 − 60), meaning a decision-maker could have made \$10 more by implementing the a_2 alternative.

If the state of nature is S_2, the best alternative for a decision-maker is a_1. If the state of nature is S_3, the best alternative is a_2. Based on these calculations, we can generate Table 2-5, called the opportunity loss table.

Table 2-6, which shows the highest opportunity loss under each alternative, is derived from the preceding information.

Based on the minimax technique, the decision-maker chooses the alternative that generates the minimum opportunity loss. As Table 2-6 shows, this alternative is a_2, meaning North Text should implement an EDP/MIS system.

Decision Making Under Uncertainty With Probability. North Text has collected some statistics from its own experience in the past and from the experience of its competitors in the industry. The payoff shown in Table 2-7 has been generated.

Generally speaking, those problems where probabilities are known (or can be estimated) with the various states of nature are called problems under risk. In such cases, two options are available to the decision-maker, either use the expected value of the payoff table or use the expected value from the opportunity loss table.

To calculate the expected value, the probability factor must be multiplied by the payoff for each alternative for each state of nature. The alternative with the highest expected value is selected. The calculation is as follows:

Table 2-7 ▪ Payoff Table with Probabilities

	State of Nature		
Alternative	S_1	S_2	S_3
a_1	50	55	26
a_2	60	46	30
a_3	70	40	21
Probability	.45	.40	.15

$$\text{Expected value of } a_1 = (50)(.45) + (55)(.40) + (26)(.15) = 48.40$$
$$\text{Expected value of } a_2 = (60)(.45) + (46)(.40) + (30)(.15) = 49.90$$
$$\text{Expected value of } a_3 = (70)(.45) + (40)(.40) + (21)(.15) = 50.65$$

In this case, a_3, the EDP/MIS with DSS support, is implemented.

In order for the expected opportunity loss technique to yield a decision, Table 2-8 is used to calculate the expected opportunity loss for each alternative.

$$\text{Expected opportunity loss of } a_1 = (20)(.45) + (\ 0)(.40) + (4)(.15) = 9.60$$
$$\text{Expected opportunity loss of } a_2 = (10)(.45) + (\ 9)(.40) + (0)(.15) = 8.10$$
$$\text{Expected opportunity loss of } a_3 = (\ 0)(.45) + (15)(.40) + (9)(.15) = 7.35$$

As this calculation shows, the alternative with minimum expected opportunity loss, a_3, must be chosen, meaning the decision-maker must implement the EDP/MIS with DSS support.

Implementation of the Best Alternative

During the implementation phase, a decision-maker will implement the best alternative, the alternative that either maximizes the profit or minimizes the cost. For example, in the advertising problem, a decision-maker may choose the medium or combination of media that reaches the largest number of potential customers.

Follow-Up

Though frequently ignored, the follow-up step is important for several reasons. First, the decision-maker needs to find out whether an appropriate selection has been made. Second, the decision-maker needs to know if his or her decision is successfully achieving its intended goal and, if not, whether further changes are required. Finally, a thorough review may provide the decision-maker with corrective action for future decision-making tasks.

2-8 Tools and Techniques Used by the Rational Actor

Major factors governing the rational decision-maker are economic principles and cost/benefit considerations. Mathematical and statistical models can be of

Table 2-8 ▪ Opportunity Loss with Probability

	State of Nature		
Alternative	S_1	S_2	S_3
a_1	20	0	4
a_2	10	9	0
a_3	0	15	9
Probability	.45	.40	.15

Table 2-9 ▪ Optimization Models

Linear Optimization Models

Allocation models
Assignment models
Transportation models
Network models

Inventory Optimization Models

Economic Order Quantity
Economic Manufacturing Quantity

Portfolio Optimization Models

Present value
Future value
Internal rate of return

Dynamic Programming Optimization Models

Nonlinear Optimization Models

great help to the decision-maker. Each model is examined in detail in Chapter 5. Tables 2-9 and 2-10 summarize these models, some of which we have not discussed. For comprehensive discussions of these methods, see [2, 9, 11].

2-9 Decision Making in Action

We conclude this chapter with a general review of the decision-making process. Decisions encountered by a decision-maker may be structured, semistructured, or unstructured, and the nature of the support provided by a DSS is directly related to the structure involved in the problem under investigation—the higher the structure, the more support a DSS can provide. After defining a particular problem, the next step is to analyze the problem in the context of constraints surrounding the problem. In any case, there are two sets of constraints surrounding a particular problem: internal and external. A decision-maker has some control over internal constraints, which are those sets of constraints imposed internally. Under certain conditions some of these constraints, which are shown in Table 2-11, may be removed or modified in order to fit a particular situation. The more rigorous types of constraints imposed on a decision-making process are external constraints, which are externally imposed on the organization. Unfortunately, these constraints are usually fixed, and a decision-maker cannot change or modify them. The organization must modify its operations in order to comply with these constraints, which may be a very difficult task. Table 2-12 provides a listing of some of the important external constraints.

Table 2-10 ▪ Nonoptimization Models

Forecasting Models
- Statistical (quantitative)
  - Exponential smoothing
  - Moving average
  - Mean
  - Simple linear regression
  - Multiple linear regression
  - Nonlinear regression
- Technological (qualitative)
  - Delphi
  - Forecasting by analogy
  - Technology transfer

Decision Tree Models

Simulation Models

Table 2-11 ▪ Internal Constraints

Resource limitations (labor, raw materials, etc.)
Physical limitations (plant layout)
Organizational policies (power struggle)
Employee welfare
Geographical layout (region, location, etc.)
Staffing policies
Corporate arrangements (contracts, procurement, etc.)
Image issues (concern for the public, product backing, etc.)
Human issues (motivation, morale, . . .)
Economic factors (economics of scale, investment structure, etc.)

Table 2–12 ▪ External Constraints

Suppliers
Customers
Unions
Public images
Labor pools
Legal issues
Environmental constraints
Cultural issues
Financial communities
Tax structures
Market conditions
Government regulations
Economic conditions
Distribution networks
Political changes
Technological breakthroughs

Figure 2-3 Decision Making in Action

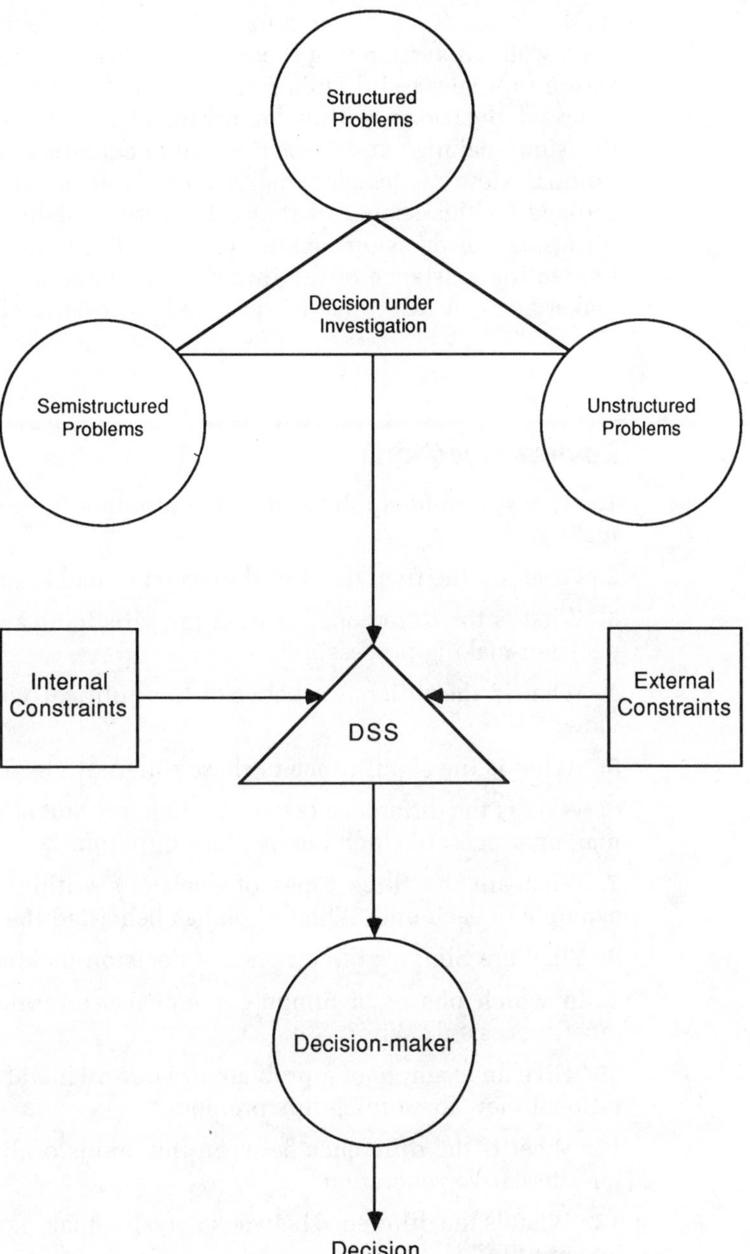

The solution proposed by a decision-maker to be addressed by a DSS must be in agreement with both types of constraints; in return, a DSS should provide a decision-maker with a solution that fits a given context. Figure 2-3 displays these relationships graphically. Throughout the text we discuss different ways in which this simple architecture can be supported.

2-10 Summary

In this chapter, different approaches to the decision-making process were discussed. Understanding these approaches is necessary for design and utilization of a successful DSS. Phases in the decision-making process, different types of decisions within an organization, efficiency and effectiveness in decision making, and decision implementation were also discussed. The rational view of decision making—as well as several tools and techniques utilized by this school of thought—were explained. The chapter included a discussion of decision making in a real-life situation. This discussion highlighted the existence of the internal and external constraints that a decision-maker faces. A DSS must be designed considering both of these constraints.

Review Questions

1. What are some applications of computers in organizational decision making?

2. What are the five views of the decision-making process?

3. What is the difference between the satisficing and optimizing views of the decision-making process?

4. What is the difference between the political view and the organizational view?

5. What is the significance of these different views in the DSS environment?

6. What is the difference between efficiency and effectiveness in the decision-making process? Which one is more important?

7. What are the three types of decisions within an organization? Give an example of each one. Which type has benefited the most from computers?

8. What are Simon's three stages of decision-making?

9. In which phases of Simon's model has information technology been the most successful? Why?

10. Give an example of a problem of your own and explain the five steps of a rational view for solving this problem.

11. What is the difference between the brainstorming and Delphi techniques for alternative generation?

12. What is the difference between decision making under certainty and under uncertainty?

13. Explain maximin, maximax, and minimax techniques as they are used for alternative evaluation.

14. Which technique is used by an optimistic decision-maker? Which technique is used by a pessimist?

15. Which technique is used if the probability factor of the state of nature is given to a decision-maker?

16.What are some other tools mentioned in this chapter that may be useful for the rational decision-making process?

17. Give an example of an optimization technique.

18. Give an example of a nonoptimization technique.

19. Discuss internal and external constraints imposed on a private organization. How are these constraints different in a public organization? What can a decision-maker do regarding the external constraints?

Projects

1. Which school of thought in decision making may be the most suitable to describe the introduction of a new medicine. Why? Which school is more suitable for putting a new plant in a foreign country?

2. Tek-Electronic, the manufacturer of disk-drive systems, is faced with four alternatives and three states of nature with some probability as follows:

	State of Nature		
Alternative	S_1	S_2	S_3
a_1	10	9	15
a_2	15	20	17
a_3	18	11	21
a_4	12	19	13
Probability	.30	.37	.33

a. Which alternative will be chosen using maximin?
b. Which alternative will be chosen using maximax?
c. Which alternative will be chosen using minimax?
d. Which alternative will be chosen using expected value?

3. Tek-Electronics is trying to design a full-featured inventory-control system that can potentially be used in all three levels of management. What are some of the behavioral issues here? How might they resolve these issues?

4. Tek-Electronics' board of directors has decided to put a new plant in the northwestern part of the country. Identify all the important external constraints imposed on Tek-Electronics. What type of support may be provided by a computer-based information system regarding the external constraints?

5. Apply the four phases of decision making (intelligence, design, choice, and implementation) to Tek-Electronics' new project. What is the design phase in this particular situation? Is putting in a new plant a structured, semistructured, or unstructured decision? Discuss.

Key Terms

Electronic data processing
Management information systems
Decision support systems
The rational actor view of decision making
The satisficing view of decision making
The organizational view of decision making
The political view of decision making
The individual differences view of decision making
Efficiency
Effectiveness
Structured decisions
Semistructured decisions
Unstructured decisions
Intelligence
Design
Choice
Brainstorming
Delphi technique
Decision making under certainty
Decision making under uncertainty
Maximin
Maximax
Minimax
Payoff table
Opportunity loss table
Optimization models
Nonoptimization models
Internal constraints
External constraints

References

[1] Allison, Graham T. 1971. *Essence of Decision: Explaining the Cuban Missile Crisis.* Boston: Little, Brown and Company.

[2] Anderson, D. K., D. J. Sweney, and T. A. Williams. 1988. *An Introduction to Management Science*, 5th ed., St. Paul, Minn.: West Publishing Company.

[3] Anthony, R. N. 1965. Planning and Control Systems: A Framework for Analysis. Harvard University Graduate School of Business Administration, Studies in Management Control, Cambridge, Mass.

[4] Gorry, G. A., and Michael S. Scott-Morton. 1971. A Framework for MIS. *Sloan Management Review* 13, no. 1: (Fall): 55–70.

[5] Goslar, M. D., G. I. Green, and T. H. Hughes. 1986. Decision Support Systems: An Empirical Assessment for Decision Making. *Decision Science* 17.

[6] Harrison, E. Frank. 1981. *The Managerial Decision Making Process.* Boston: Houghton Mifflin Company.

[7] Heiller, F. S., and G. J. Lieberman. 1974. *Operations Research*, 2d ed. San Francisco: Holden-Day, Inc.

[8] Inbar, M. 1979. *Routine Decision Making Process.* Beverly Hills: Sage Publications.

[9] Jones, Harry, and Brian C. Twiss 1978. *Forcasting Technology for Planning Decisions.* New York: Business Publications, Inc. pp. 98–106.

[10] Keen, Peter G. W., and Michael S. Scott-Morton 1978. *Decision Support Systems: An Organizational Perspective.* Reading, Mass.: Addison-Wesley Publishing Company, pp. 61–77.

[11] Martino, Joseph P. 1978. *Technological Forecasting for Decision Making.* New York: Elsevier Science Publishing Company, Inc., pp. 18–64.

[12] McKenney, James L., and Peter G. W. Keen. 1974. How Manager's Minds Work. *Hardwood Business Review* (May-June): 79–90.

[13] McMillan, C. J. 1980. Qualitative Models of Organizational Decision Making. *Journal of Management Studies* 5: 22–39.

[14] Nutt, P. C. 1984. Types of Organizational Decision Processes. *Administrative Science Quarterly* 29: 414–50.

[15] Simon, Herbert A. 1960. *The New Science of Management Decision*. New York: Harper & Row Publishers, Inc.

[16] Snyders, J. 1984. Decision Making Made Easier. *Infosystems* (August): 52–54.

[17] Sprague, Jr., Ralph H., and Eric D. Carlson. 1982. *Building Effective Decision Support Systems*. Englewood Cliffs, N.J.: Prentice-Hall, Inc., pp. 26–27.

[18] Taylor, R. 1984. *Behavioral Decision Making*. Glenview, Ill: Scott, Foresman & Company.

3 Important Issues in Design, Implementation, and Utilization of a DSS

3-1 Introduction

In this chapter the unique characteristics of a DSS that were introduced in Chapter 1 are explained, highlighting the potential of DSS systems for effective decision making at all levels of the organization. The three technologies of DSS are examined, including specific DSS, DSS generators, and DSS tools. A specific DSS is built by using either a DSS generator or a DSS tool. This chapter also provides several views regarding different players in the entire cycle of DSS design, implementation, and use. The equal importance of the technical designer and the managerial designer in this process is emphasized. This chapter concludes with a brief discussion about the components of a DSS and the advantages of an effective DSS. Material discussed in this chapter should provide the DSS user with a better appreciation and understanding of DSS operations, which are somewhat different from EDP and MIS.

3-2 Unique Characteristics of DSS

As highlighted in Table 1-1, DSSs present a series of unique characteristics that make the design and utilization of these systems somewhat different from the earlier applications (EDP and MIS). Understanding these features in some detail will help the designer and user of these systems to develop a more successful DSS.

Central Focus

EDPs and some MISs have been utilized to automate routine, programmable, and repetitive functions. Once these tasks are automated, little or no human intervention is required for the execution of such tasks. The central focus of EDPs is data; that of MISs is information.

Conversely, DSS tries to aid decision making and decision implementation for nonroutine and nonrepetitive tasks. This system always works in conjunction with a decision-maker. The central focus of a DSS is decision making and decision implementation.

Mode of Usage

EDPs and MISs are utilized primarily in a passive mode, which means these systems are usually based on a series of well-defined standard operating procedures. They generate a series of scheduled reports on a regular basis.

DSSs are utilized primarily in an active mode. This means each instance of the system's use is initiated by the designer/user of the system.

Type of Activities

EDPs and MISs are usually used by clerical personnel and supervisory staff. DSSs are designed for line managers and key decision-makers. Wherever in the organization a decision is being made, a DSS has potential for implementation.

Orientation

As discussed in Chapter 2, there are two issues of paramount importance in any decision: efficiency and effectiveness. Whereas EDPs and MISs are concerned mostly with the efficiency of a decision, DSSs are concerned with both the efficiency and the effectiveness of a decision. In other words, DSSs are concerned not only with financial savings; other aspects of implementation such as improved communication, learning, and ease of decision making are also highly regarded.

Time Horizon

EDPs and MISs are concerned primarily with the past. Sometimes these systems, such as a balance sheet and an income statement, are referred to as the "blaming information systems." When the fiscal year is over, a report is generated that highlights what was done wrong last year. A decision-maker cannot do anything about the past but must learn from it!

DSSs focus on the present and, to a large degree, the future. These systems usually tell the decision-maker what is happening now and what may happen in the future. These systems naturally use past data as well as projected data in conjunction with analytical models to project and predict the present and future status of an organization.

Design Emphasis

EDPs and MISs are designed to generate periodic reports with minimum flexibility. Again, a good example is an accounting information system, which generates periodic financial reports.

Conversely, DSSs place heavy emphasis on flexibility and ad hoc utilization. The ability to manipulate information is essential if a DSS is going to be utilized effectively for semistructured and unstructured, nonrecurring, one-of-a-kind decisions.

Key Words

Throughout the computer literature, EDPs and MISs are associated with a series of key words such as replacement, automation, and computerization [2, 4]. This factor is probably the most important cause of resistance to change. Employees are concerned about losing their jobs and being replaced by computers. Some recordkeeping, simple inventory, and clerical systems are designed to replace humans.

The key words associated with DSSs are usually interaction, support, learning, and coexistence [2, 4]. No DSS is intended to replace a decision-maker. These systems are designed to improve the quality of decision making and implementation by assisting decision-makers and improving their effectiveness.

System Evaluation

To evaluate an EDP/MIS system, usually a cost/benefit analysis is performed and then the system is evaluated based on these potential economic gains and losses.

DSS places equal emphasis on noneconomic gains (such as user satisfaction), decision-making improvement, and the overall performance of the decision-maker after the implementation of a DSS. In other words, a DSS may not generate any tangible economic gain, yet it still may be considered a successful venture by its user and designer.

Computation Focus

EDPs and MISs usually perform basic and simple analyses. These analyses address a well-defined problem where the parameters and variables under investigation are clearly delineated. DSSs, on the other hand, utilize a variety of models for numerous computational tasks. These models and computations cover a broad range of analyses from the very basic to the very complex. As an example, a DSS can be used for simple price analysis using a break-even model. At the same time, a comprehensive econometric model can be used by a DSS in order to predict a more realistic price for gasoline in the year 2000.

Output Orientation

As mentioned earlier, the output of EDP/MIS systems is usually used for operational control. Like accounting systems, the output of the system tells the user whether he or she has operated within an acceptable range. The output of DSS can also be used for control, but for the most part it is used for planning. The system's output will tell the user, based on the past performance, what he or she should do in the next round of operations. The extensive employment of forecasting, statistical, and simulation models is a good indication of the orientation of the output of these systems.

Problems Addressed

EDP and MIS systems have been utilized for quantitative analysis. Although DSSs have been used for the same purpose, the integration of expert systems (ES) and artificial intelligence (AI) products should assist DSSs in performing qualitative as well as quantitative analysis in the near future. We have already witnessed some limited applications of these types of analyses by using rule data models and knowledge-based systems in the data base component of DSSs. This feature of DSS represents a clear departure of such a system from the domain of traditional EDP/MIS systems. These features are examined in detail in Chapters 12 through 14.

Output Format Options

The format of the output generated by EDPs and MISs has been limited primarily to scheduled reports.

In the DSS environment the format for the output provided is quite varied. Because these systems are designed to help a variety of decision-makers with assorted decision-making styles, different output format is both essential and needed for such operations. These outputs may be in graphic, exception reporting, tabular, detail, or summary format, for example.

Tailoring to the Personality and Status of the User

With EDPs and MISs the user may not be heavily involved in the design and implementation phases of the systems, since these systems are usually designed by data-processing personnel. In the process of building these systems, the personalities, status, and information needs of different decision-makers are largely ignored. However, this is changing.

Such is not the case in the DSS environment. The user is heavily involved in all phases of analysis, design, and implementation of the system. In many cases the design of the system is initiated by the user. This means that a DSS is usually tailored to the status and styles of individual decision-makers. This custom fit may be the key factor for the relative success of these systems in recent years.

Mode of User/System Interface

Once again, with EDPs and MISs the scheduled report, or "subscription" mode [2], is the dominant type of user/system interface. Obviously the flexibility is minimal when this type of user/system interface is employed. On the other hand, with DSS (as you will see in Chapter 6) the user can interact with the system in a variety of modes. These include question/answer, command language, menu, and input/output. Since the majority of the users of a DSS are not computer-trained personnel, the user/system interface is highly regarded in the DSS environment. The interface should be straightforward and easy to use.

Design Tools

With EDPs and MISs, as is discussed in Chapters 7 and 8, a traditional life-cycle approach is the dominant design tool. The designers of these systems follow the classic approach of problem definition, systems analysis, systems design, systems implementation, and post-implementation audit.

DSSs, with intensive user involvement, combine all the phases in the life-cycle approach into one phase and, by using a prototype, perform an iterative design. The design process in a DSS environment is never final. The system is continuously improved to incorporate the varying needs of the decision-maker. Other tools used in DSS design, such as adoptive design and middle-out approach, which are not commonly used in traditional EDPs and MISs, are discussed in Chapter 7 in detail. The main objective of these new tools is to make the user the focal point; design systems are thus tailor-made to the specific needs of a decision-maker.

Flexibility of the Operation

EDPs and MISs are not usually flexible. Flexibility may include input/output formats, types of reporting, user/system interface, and so on. With EDPs and MISs, the input/output of the system is defined in advance, and changes usually cannot be made without a major redesign of the system. DSSs, on the other hand, are quite flexible and are very responsive to changing environments. As you will see in Chapter 6, flexibility is built into the architecture of any DSS by the provision of several types of user/system interfaces that fit a diverse group of users with different styles and statuses as well as different computer backgrounds.

Organizational Target Group

EDPs and MISs are concerned chiefly with the operational level in an organization. At times they are also concerned with the tactical level. In contrast, DSSs are designed to assist decision-makers in all levels of an organization, including operational, tactical, and (especially) strategic management. Use of internal/external data and diverse modeling techniques provides DSS with a good opportunity for success at all levels of management, particularly at the strategic level. This is another departure of these systems from traditional EDP/MIS systems.

Data Used

EDPs and MISs usually use internal data, including transaction data and data collected internally from other departments within the organization. DSSs utilize both internal and external data. These data may be collected from a variety of sources. Utilization of both internal and external data and analytical models is another departure of these systems from traditional EDP/MIS systems.

Implementation

Generally, EDPs and MISs are designed using tools available in the computer field. For example, COBOL, a high-powered, high-level language, is an example of a tool used to develop a computer-based information system. In such a case, the development time is long and the system may go through several revisions before it is finalized.

On the other hand, DSSs are developed by using both DSS tools and recently available highly sophisticated DSS generators. These generators include a nonprocedural language that is easier than high-level languages such as FORTRAN and COBOL and are more forgiving and provide more flexibility. The user can enter the codes in any order; there is no rigorous programming involved. After a few hours of training, a user can write simple programs using these languages. In this process the development time is usually short. A workable system (an operational prototype) is designed and is improved in the next round of the operation. We provide a comprehensive coverage of popular DSS generators in Appendix A.

Interactiveness

EDPs and MISs are used primarily in batch mode (but this is changing). In batch mode, data and information are sent to the computer periodically. DSSs, on the other hand, are highly interactive. Interactiveness may expedite decision making by providing on-line and what-if facilities for DSS users.

Types of Analyses

As mentioned in Chapter 1, there are two types of analyses that can be performed by any computer-based information system. EDPs and MISs usually perform data analysis and, to some degree, may perform limited modeling analysis.

DSSs perform data analysis as well as modeling analysis, which is made possible by incorporating a data base and a model base as integral parts of the DSS architecture.

3-3 Three Technologies of DSS

In a DSS environment there are three areas of technology that must be understood by both DSS users and designers. These include specific DSS (SDSS), DSS generators (DSSG), and DSS tools (DSST) [12]. Following is a brief explanation of each technology.

Specific DSS

A specific DSS is a combination of hardware and software that is used to assist a decision-maker with a specific task. This capability may be utilized for any task in any level of the organization. These systems have been successfully used for many years, supporting decision-makers in a variety of settings. BRANDAID, a marketing mix model [7] developed by John Little, and AAIMS (An Analytical Information Management System) [6], which performs forecasting, planning, and financial analysis for American Airlines, are examples of such systems. In Appendix B, we provide a comprehensive listing of several successful, specific DSSs currently being used. In a typical business organization, systems may be designed for use in different functional areas. For example, an SDSS for a manufacturing department assists in manufacturing decisions. This system may provide timely information on various aspects of a manufacturing environment such as production and distribution decisions. An SDSS may provide on-line sales forecasts for a marketing department. An SDSS for a finance department may assist the portfolio analyst with information to minimize the risk of investment by monitoring and providing timely information on stocks, bonds, and financial activities.

DSS Generators

DSS generators use a combination of hardware and software as a package to develop a specific DSS. These generators provide most of the capabilities needed by an SDSS. A typical DSS generator has a data base management system (DBMS), graphics, built-in functions, modeling analysis, statistical analysis, optimization, and simulation models. It is capable of macroprogramming, which is more powerful than high-level languages such as FORTRAN and COBOL.

DSS generators continue to grow in popularity. Interactive Financial Planning System (IFPS) by Execucom Systems of Austin, Texas, and EXPRESS by TYMSHARE are two examples of these generators. By using IFPS, many different specific DSS in the areas of finance, accounting and marketing can be developed.

Appendix A provides a comprehensive coverage of popular DSS generators for both micro- and mainframe computers.

DSS Tools

DSS tools are computer hardware or software used to develop either a specific DSS or a DSS generator. For example, either a graphics package or COBOL may serve as a DSS tool. In general, development of an SDSS from a DSS generator is faster and it may be more economical than the development of these systems from DSS tools. This area of technology has improved continuously. For example, computer languages have gone through several generators, from machine language to assembly, high-level languages, to fourth-generation languages. Finally, developers are working on natural language-processing systems. Another example of such improvement is the enhancement of operating systems for the microcomputers. Very soon these operating systems should simulate the same level of sophistication first found in larger computers. Hardware technology has improved hand-in-hand with software technology. For example, graphic terminals, laser printers, and sophisticated modems all are examples of DSS tools. Figure 3-1 illustrates these three technologies of DSS and their relationships.

3-4 Different Players in the DSS Environment

To design, implement, and utilize a DSS, several different groups of individuals must be involved; these are called "roles in system usage" by Steven Alter. [2, pp. 110–12] He recognizes five different roles:

1. A *user* is a person who communicates directly with the DSS in either an on-line or off-line mode.
2. A *decision-maker* is a person who makes decisions by using the output of the DSS.
3. An *intermediary* is a person who interprets the output of a DSS for the decision-maker.
4. A *maintainer* is a person who maintains the technical aspects of the DSS. This may include the entire input/output cycle.

Figure 3-1 Three Technologies of DSS

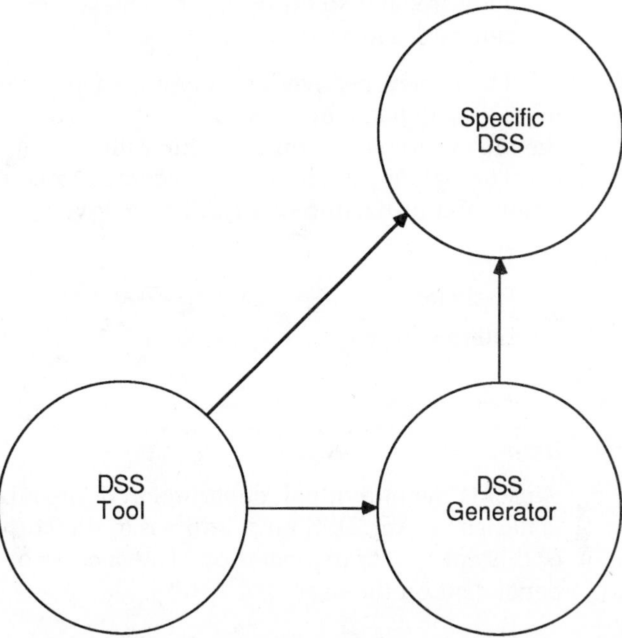

5. A *feeder* is a person who provides data to the system. This individual may or may not use the DSS for his or her direct operation. However, this individual may gain indirect benefit from the operation of the system. As an example, consider the accounting department as a feeder when data are given to a marketing DSS to perform regional sales analysis. As a matter of fact, accounting departments, in conjunction with accounting information systems, serve as the base for any other information systems developed and utilized in any organization. These systems gather and analyze all the important internal data critical to other functional information systems in the organization.

Ralph Sprague [Sprague and Watson, p. 15] also identifies five roles in the DSS environment but defines them differently than Alter. They are as follows:

1. The *manager* or *user* is the principal user of the system. This person uses a DSS for decision-making purposes in order to improve his or her effectiveness and the efficiency and effectiveness of the organization.
2. The *intermediary* is a person who helps the user in order to make the system as effective as possible. This individual may interpret the output of DSS or explain the user needs to the designer of the DSS.
3. The DSS *builder* "configures" the specific DSS, which may be built either from a DSS generator or from DSS tools.
4. The *technical supporter* develops additional technical capabilities that may not be included in a generator or in the tools used to build the specific DSS (e.g., an external linkage program for multivariate analysis).

5. The *toolsmith* is a person who develops new technology, hardware/software, and so on in order to make the operation of an SDSS or DSS generator more effective.

There may be overlaps among these roles. The degree to which roles overlap is dependent upon the scope of the problem under investigation and the organizational setting in which the system is going to be implemented.

Throughout this book we recognize three roles for the design, implementation, and utilization of a DSS:

User
Designer
Intermediary

User

A user is the individual, department, or organizational unit for whom the DSS is designed. An SDSS must address and incorporate the specific requirements of this entity into its operation. The success or failure of the system is heavily dependent on the user.

Designer

The role of designer may include two different groups: managerial designer and technical designer.

A *managerial designer* is the individual (or individuals) who defines the management issues related to a DSS. This role is very similar to the role of an architect building a house: The architect provides the general design of a house. In simple terms, he or she highlights the important aspects of the house. In a DSS environment, this individual may be the MIS specialist in the organization, the decision-maker, or anyone else who can define the requirement of the DSS. For example, to develop an on-line forecasting DSS, some of the managerial issues may include:

- What data must be collected?
- From what source must the data be gathered?
- How recent must the collected data be?
- How must the data be indexed?
- How must the data be updated?

The *technical designer* usually is not concerned with the issues specified under the managerial designer's domain. Instead, his or her role is very similar to the role of a construction engineer charged with the task of building a house. The technical designer is concerned with the technical issues related to the DSS design and use. Some of the questions addressed by a technical designer are:

- How must the data be stored?
- What type of file structure must be implemented?

- What type of user access must be implemented?
- What type of response time is required?
- How must the security measures be installed?

This role may be occupied by the computer specialist or a consultant from outside the company. The technical designer may incorporate these facilities into an SDSS by using a DSS generator, DSS tools, or inventing new capabilities from scratch.

Intermediary

An intermediary is the liaison between the user and the DSS. This individual may play different roles. For example, during the design phase for the preceding forecasting DSS, the intermediary may explain the user's needs to the managerial designer or technical designer of the system. This same individual, at a later date, may explain the provided output to the user, or this individual may explain the output of the regression analysis provided by forecasting DSS mentioned earlier. He or she may tell the user about the assumptions underlying the model, limitations, strengths, and so on, as well as suggest new or different applications of the system. Figure 3-2 graphically illustrates these roles in a DSS environment.

3-5 Components of a DSS

As you will see in the next three chapters, a DSS includes three major components: data base, model base, and dialog management [12]. Chapters 4, 5, and 6 provide a comprehensive coverage of each of these components. For now, let us briefly explain them.

The *data base* component includes both internal and external data. Internal data are either transaction data or data collected internally from other subsystems in the organization. Associated with the data base is software called the DBMS. This software creates, modifies, and maintains the data base as required by the user. The data base component enables a DSS to perform any type of data analysis operation. For a detailed discussion of data bases and DBMSs, see Chapter 4.

The *model base* component includes a series of mathematical and statistical models, which—in conjunction with the data base—enable a DSS to perform any type of modeling analysis. For more information, see Chapter 5.

Finally, the *dialog management* component is the user/system interface. This component provides a user with different interface procedures that enable him or her to access the DSS and is, from the user's point of view, probably the most important part. It is imperative that this component be as flexible and as user-friendly as possible. Since the majority of DSS users are discretionary in their usage, user-friendliness is an even more important consideration in such a situation.

Figure 3-2 Roles in a DSS Environment

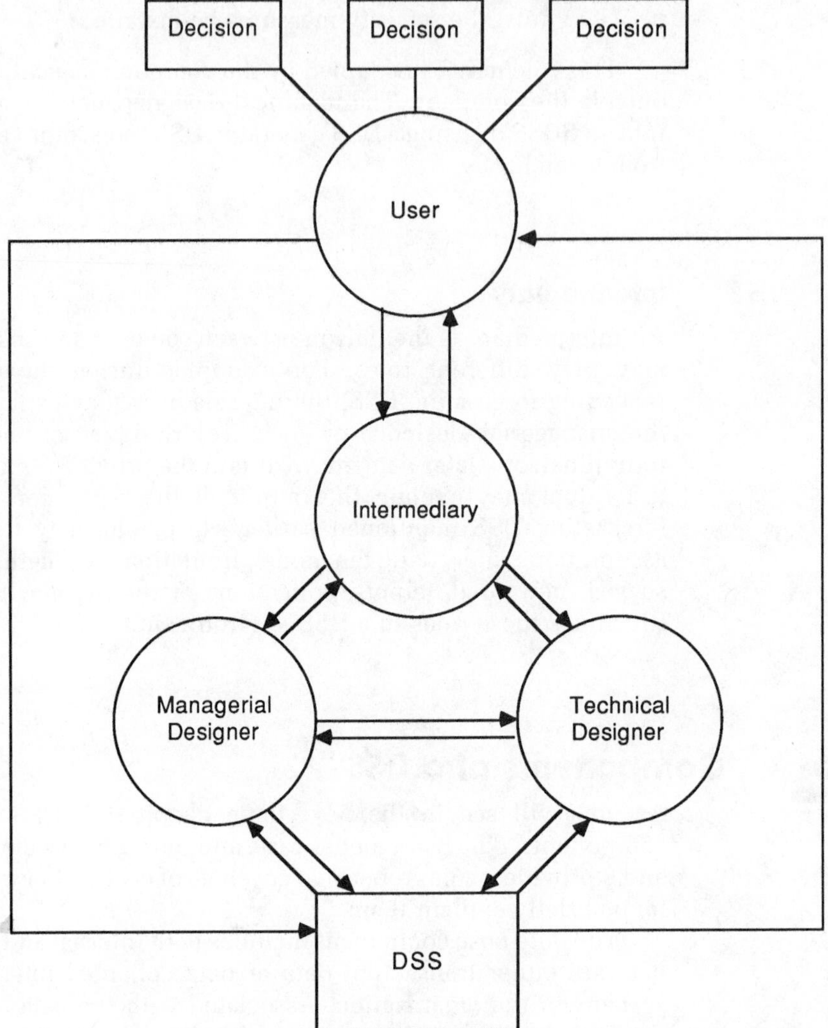

Figure 3-3 illustrates a graphic model for DSS within the organization. As this figure indicates, a DSS user, who may occupy a position in any one of the three management levels of the organization (operational, tactical, or strategic), may be faced with the need to make a decision. The decision process may include the three stages, intelligence, design, and choice. The user, through dialog, may query either the data base, model base, or both for decision help. As discussed in future chapters, this simple architecture incorporates most (if not all) of the necessary capabilities needed by a decision-maker for making a decision.

Figure 3-3 DSS in the Organization

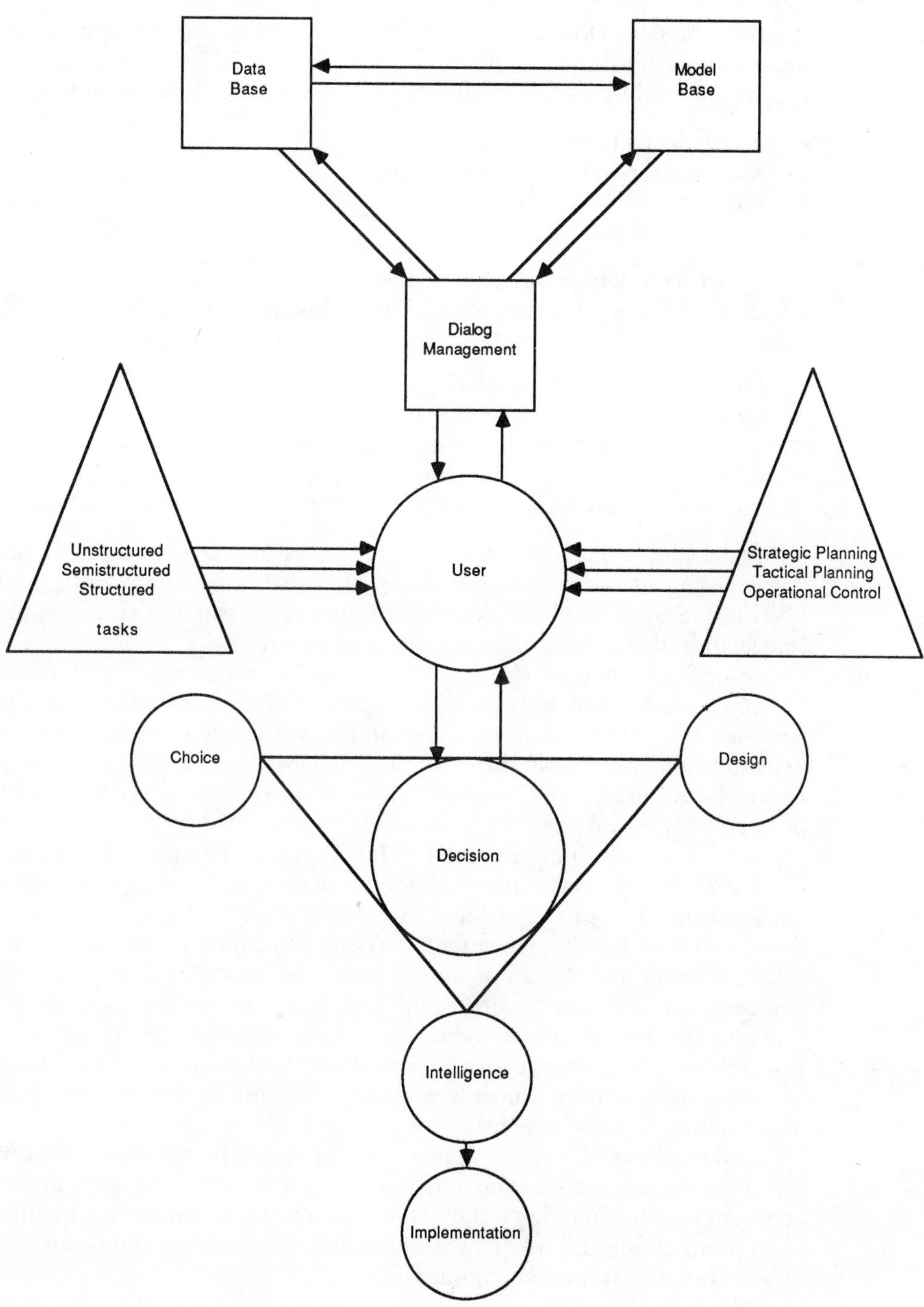

3-6 Advantages of a DSS

A comprehensive DSS that has followed and incorporated the objectives of an organization into its architecture should provide all the advantages and features offered by any computer-based information system, such as:

- Faster decision making
- More comprehensive information
- Improved communication
- Improved accuracy

As we mentioned earlier, the major objective of a DSS is to improve the effectiveness of a decision-maker. The following five factors highlight how a DSS may improve the effectiveness of a decision-maker [2]:

1. Improving personal efficiency
2. Expediting problem solving
3. Facilitating interpersonal communication
4. Promoting learning or training
5. Increasing organizational control

A decision-maker who has on-line access to a DSS capable of providing timely, integrated, accurate, and comprehensive information can spend his or her time making effective decisions rather than wasting time searching for information that should have been available initially.

A DSS can expedite problem solving by providing rapid turnaround, increased accuracy, detailed examination of different scenarios, and improved consistency. A DSS can assist a decision-maker in identifying a solution in an expedited manner. Capabilities such as what-if, goal seeking, and sensitivity analysis (discussed in Chapter 1) are all instrumental in accelerating the problem-solving process.

Interpersonal communication is facilitated and improved because everyone using the DSS has a new channel to access, a "language" common to all participants. DSS provides "tools for persuasion" [2] and a vocabulary and discipline that facilitate negotiations and coordination across the organizational boundaries. As an example, consider the situation of a high-tech company that did not have a cost-based DSS. Due to the absence of such a system, division managers were providing different prices for a finished product in the bidding process. The establishment of an on-line cost-based DSS significantly improved the interpersonal communication and the intergroup coordination of these executives.

DSS can have an impact on learning or training by telling the user why and how a particular decision must be made in a particular way. This may not be a common practice in today's DSS. However, as mentioned earlier, by integration of AI products and ES into DSS architecture, the learning and training features of a DSS can be improved significantly.

Again, by providing comprehensive information regarding the entire organizational boundaries, the overall control of the organization, including control over costs, inventory, and personnel, will be improved.

3-7 Summary

This chapter highlighted the unique characteristics of DSS and made a comparison of DSS to EDP/MIS. It discussed the power of DSSs and their potential for decision making and decision implementation at all levels of an organization. DSS characteristics should provide guidelines for the design and implementation of these systems. It also explained three different levels of DSS, including specific DSS (SDSS), DSS generators (DSSG), and DSS tools (DSST). This explanation should clarify the options available to a DSS user/designer for construction of DSS. The players involved in DSS design and implementation were examined as well. This chapter also introduced some advantages of a DSS. In the next three chapters, the architecture of DSS will be discussed.

Review Questions

1. List unique characteristics of DSS that are different from EDP/MIS.

2. If we introduce the three focal points data, information, and decision, which system (EDP, MIS, DSS) emphasizes which focal points? Explain.

3. What is meant by active use? What is passive use?

4. What are the criteria for evaluation of an EDP system?

5. What are the criteria for the evaluation of a DSS?

6. What is qualitative analysis?

7. What is quantitative analysis? Which analysis is best achieved by a DSS?

8. What are design tools in DSS environment?

9. What does flexibility mean in a DSS environment?

10. What type of data are used by DSS? Internal or external? Or does it depend on the task?

11. What is interactiveness in a DSS environment? Is interactiveness always needed?

12. What is the difference between modeling analysis and data analysis? Which type of analysis is performed by a typical DSS?

13. What is a specific DSS? What function does it serve?

14. What is a DSS generator? What function does it serve?

15. What is a DSS tool? What function does it serve?

16. What is the fastest way to build an operational DSS, using DSST or DSSG? Discuss.

17. Who are the major players in DSS design and implementation?

18. Who is the intermediary in a DSS environment?

19. What is the difference between the managerial designer and the technical designer? Who occupies these roles?

20. Why are both of these designers needed for a successful DSS design?

21. What are the three main components of a DSS?

22. List the advantages of a DSS in a typical business organization.

Projects

1. A student record-keeping system in your school may be considered an EDP-, MIS-, or a DSS-type system. Why and how can this system be classified within each group? Explain three features of such a system that may qualify the system within each group.

2. Consult a local bank and see if they are using a DSS. Investigate the process of building this DSS. Was it developed from DSST or DSSG? Who were the people involved in constructing this DSS? Identify and investigate the role of an intermediary in such a system. Who occupies such a role?

3. How may a DSS improve the effectiveness of the operation of a city hall? Consult your local city hall and see what type of system they are using.

4. Identify five DSS tools and five DSS generators and five specific DSSs. What are some of the unique features of each system? How is a DSS generator developed?

5. Investigate the office of a graduate school of a college or university with which you are familiar. How may a DSS improve the operation of this office? How is the office running now? How can it be improved by a DSS?

Key Terms

Routine tasks
Programmable tasks
Passive mode
Active mode
Efficiency of a decision
Effectiveness of a decision
Periodic reports
Ad hoc utilization
Replacement
Support
Economic gain
Economic loss
Control
Planning
Quantitative analysis
Expert systems
Artificial intelligence
Qualitative analysis
Output format
Internal data
External data
Specific DSS (SDSS)
DSS generator (DSSG)
DSS tool (DSST)

Intermediary
Maintainer
Feeder
DSS builder
Technical supporter
Toolsmith
Managerial designer
Technical designer
Data base
Model base
Dialog management
DSS architecture

References

[1] Alloway, Robert, and Robert E. Umbaugh. 1987. Decision Support Systems Mission Accomplished? *Computer Decisions* (April 6): 41–42.

[2] Alter, Steven. 1980. *Decision Support Systems: Current Practice and Continuing Challenges*. Reading, Mass.: Addison-Wesley Publishing Company.

[3] Anonymous. 1977. Getting the Requirements Right. *EDP Analyzer* (July): 1–13.

[4] Keen, Peter G. W., and Michael S. Scott-Morton. 1978. *Decision Support Systems, An Organizational Perspective*. Reading, Mass.: Addison-Wesley Publishing Company, pp. 1–15.

[5] Kopcych, Tony. 1986 Evolution of the MIS Function. *Infosystems* (April): 56–58.

[6] Klaas, Richard L. 1977. A DSS for Airline Management. *Data Base* (Winter): 3–8.

[7] Little, John D. C. 1972. BRANDAID: A Marketing-Mix Model, Part I: Structure. *Operations Research* (July/August): 628–55.

[8] Lucas, Henry C. 1987. The Evolution of an Information System: From Key-Man to Every Person. *Sloan Management Review* (Winter): 39–52.

[9] Maritote, Regina. 1986. Decision Support Systems Provide Powerful Armor for Corporate Survival. *Data Management* (October): 40–41.

[10] Ntuen, Celestine. 1986. The Seven 'R' Paradigms: What Managers Should Know About Decision Support Systems. *Industrial Management* (January/February): 19–21.

[11] Sol, Henk G. 1985 DSS: Buzzword or Challenge? *European Journal of Operational Research*: 1–8.

[12] Sprague, Ralph H., Jr. 1980. A Framework for the Development of Decision Support Systems. In *Decision Support Systems: Putting Theory Into Practice*. Ed. by Ralph H. Sprague, Jr. and Hugh J. Watson. 1986. Englewood Cliffs, N.J.: Prentice-Hall, pp. 7–32.

part two

Architecture of DSS

4 Data Base for DSS

4-1 Introduction

This chapter provides an overview of data bases and data base management systems (DBMS). Types of data used in the DSS environment are discussed and several views for data base design in a DSS environment are given. Data can be presented in different formats within a data base. These varying formats are referred to as data base models, and six commonly used models in the DSS environment are explained. Major functions of DBMS needed for effective DSS operations are explored. The chapter concludes by introducing new trends in the data base environment, including natural language processing, distributed data bases, and data base machines. Discussion in this chapter highlights the importance of data and a data base for successful design of a DSS.

4-2 What Is a Data Base?

A data base is simply a collection of relevant data stored in a central location. Data base and data base design are by no means new topics in the computer field. These topics have been discussed thoroughly by several authors [4, 7, 14]. In this chapter an overview of this important component of DSS is provided as well as guidelines and instructions for the design and implementation of a data base in the DSS environment.

Data bases are utilized even in manual systems. A file cabinet is a good example of a data base. Various information and data are stored using a series of manila folders. However, in this type of data base, speed and accuracy are not high. In this chapter we are interested exclusively in computerized data bases in order to satisfy the specific need of a DSS.

In computer terminology, a data base is defined as a series of integrated files. A file is a series of related records. A record is a series of related fields.

A data base is a critical component of any DSS. Regardless of whether a DSS is concerned primarily with modeling or data base management, it must have an adequate data base. An operational data base must be in place to support modeling analysis as well as data analysis performed by any DSS.

The data base is closely associated with DBMS software. A DBMS is a series of computer programs that create, store, maintain, and access a data base. The features offered depend on the type and level of sophistication of the DBMS.

The data base environment in comparison with a non–data base environment (flat files) [14, 16] offers a series of unique advantages:

- More information can be generated from the same amount of data.
- Ad hoc requests can easily be fulfilled.
- Data duplication is minimal.
- Programs and data are independent.
- Data management is enhanced and improved.
- More sophisticated programming is affordable and feasible.
- Data relationships can be presented and maintained easily.
- More sophisticated security measures can be implemented.
- Less space is needed for data maintenance.

Design and implementation of a data base is done by data base administrators (DBAs). The scope of the responsibility of DBAs depends on the complexity of the data base. Some organizations devote an entire office to data base design and maintenance. In smaller organizations one individual may carry the entire responsibility of data base design. Generally speaking, the following are some of the responsibilities of a DBA:

- Designing and implementing a data base
- Protecting a data base
- Establishing security measures
- Establishing the recovery procedures
- Documenting the data base
- Establishing data base performance evaluation
- Adding new data base functions
- Fine-tuning the existing data base functions

In a data base environment, both a DBA and data base administration are critical, and careful consideration is needed in order to establish an effective data base administration office and DBA.

Generating a data base increases cost and creates more complexity in an operation. However, the implementation of an effective DSS requires an on-line and comprehensive data base regardless of its cost and complexity.

4-3 Types of Data in the DSS Environment

To function as a support for operational management, management control, and strategic planning, a DSS must have access to two types of data: internal and external.

Internal data, as the name implies, are generated and collected internally. They can involve transaction data, which are usually supported by an accounting subsystem in an organization, or other types of data collected internally from other subsystems such as marketing, manufacturing, or personnel. An accounting information system serves as the basis for any other information system in the organization by collecting and maintaining all the internal data. This may include payrolls, accounts receivable, accounts payable, purchasing and receiving, fixed assets, and general ledgers.

A DSS, if it is designed to support strategic planning, must also have access to data that cannot be generated internally. These are external data and may come from various sources:

- Competition
- Cultural change indicators
- Labor markets
- Labor union activities
- Government activities
- Suppliers
- Economic conditions
- Population trends
- Customers
- Technological breakthroughs
- Political climates and changes in these climates
- Consumer behavior
- Distribution networks
- Tax structures
- Bank policies
- Money markets

These different sources play different roles in different DSSs. The specific objective of a DSS determines the sources of data to be considered in designing a data base for a DSS.

4-4 Data Base Design for DSS

In designing a data base for a DSS, two views are recognized: the managerial view and the technical view. The managerial view of a data base emphasizes issues concerning the user of a data base and the way in which he or she views a data base. From this perspective, the methods of collecting data and the types, sources, and nature of the data to be collected are important. This view also emphasizes issues such as the maintenance and storage of data within the data base, such as the following:

- Should data be aggregated (lump sum) or disaggregated (itemized)?
- How should data be indexed?
- How often should a data base be updated?
- What sources of data should be considered?
- What method of data collection should be used?

On the other hand, the technical view of a data base is concerned with the technical issues associated with data base design and maintenance. Some of the issues important in a technical view may be as follows:

- How must data files be designed (sequential, random, indexed sequential)?
- What type of access system must be implemented (on-line, batch, or both)?
- How can an effective security feature be implemented?
- How must backup and recovery procedures be implemented?

In data base design, file structures include sequential, random, and indexed sequential. In a sequential file, records are organized sequentially so that all records before a particular record either must be read or skipped in order to reach it. On the other hand, a random file or record can be accessed in any order regardless of its physical location. Indexed sequential files are similar to a card catalog in a library. This type of file can be processed either sequentially or randomly. To protect data and information, which are among the most valuable resources in an organization, an effective security system must be designed. Data files must be fully backed up and only authorized personnel must have access to the organization's data files.

For design and implementation of an effective data base, both views are important and each must be carefully investigated. In the following pages we discuss these issues further.

4-5 Data Base Design: a Functional View

A data base for a corporate-level DSS usually integrates and augments data from the four major functional areas of a business:

- Accounting
- Manufacturing
- Marketing
- Personnel

Figure 4-1 illustrates a typical corporate data base. Table 4-1 highlights detailed data items that should be maintained in these individual data bases.

4-6 Issues Related to the Data Component of a Data Base

Regardless of the sophistication of the data base and DBMS, a DSS may not be effective if the data contained in the data base are not properly gathered and stored. A series of "data problems" must be carefully analyzed before the data base component of a DSS is designed [1]:

1. Data are not correct. Incorrect data may be caused by entering inaccurate data (typing error) or using data that were wrong initially. This issue may be resolved by more rigorous collection and entry procedures. In the days of punch-card machines, a verifier machine was used to double-check the accuracy of the data. However, verification does not eliminate errors caused by collecting the wrong data. Standard procedures must be developed to ensure collection of the right data, the sources of data must be identified, and their validity must be verified.
2. Data are not timely. No matter how sophisticated a DSS is, if it does not generate timely and accurate information, its effectiveness will be jeopardized. Data entry procedures and data validation methods must be monitored in order to assure timeliness of data.
3. Data are not measured or indexed properly. This problem is less serious than those mentioned earlier. Designers and users of DSSs should be able to develop a system for rescaling and reindexing the data in order to meet the requirements of the DSS.
4. Too many data are needed. Sometimes the DSS may require a series of data values in order to produce a single variable such as when forecasting total sales based on the organization's performance for previous years. Or a model may include several variables for which the data base does not include values. If the user or designer of a DSS defines the objectives of the DSS, a comprehensive data base should be able to resolve the first problem by maintaining adequate data related to all important variables. The second problem may be resolved by using alternative models that require fewer variables—for example, choosing a multiple linear regression model that requires fewer variables than the original model.
5. Needed data simply do not exist in the data base. This may be caused by improper definition of the objectives of a DSS, or it may be caused by a simple oversight of the user or designer of the DSS. In any event, this data must be identified, gathered, and stored for future use.

Figure 4-1 A Typical Corporate Data Base

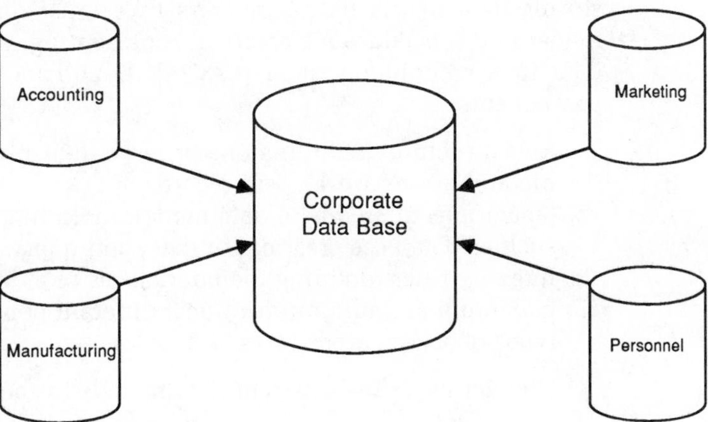

Table 4-1 ▪ Corporate Data Base: A Typical Example

Functional Area	Data to be Collected and Maintained
Accounting	Payroll
	Cost
	Taxes
	Income/loss statements
	Balance sheets
	Cash flow
	Sources of funds
	Uses of funds
Manufacturing	Warehousing
	Transportation
	Purchasing
	Inventory
	Production
	Technology
	Legal environment
Marketing	Economy
	Consumer behavior
	Competitors
	Sales
	Promotional activities
	Advertising
Personnel	Wages and salaries
	Contracts
	Skills inventory
	Personal history
	Training

4-7 Conceptual Design of a Data Base

We now consider how a data base is designed and the different formats for storing data in the data base. First, we must define a data model: A data model is a procedure for creating, representing, organizing, and maintaining data in a computer system [13, 24]. Usually a data model includes three components:

1. Data structure, including one or more data structures such as relations, hierarchies, networks, and records.
2. Operations offered by a data model, including a variety of operations such as data base creation, update, and query.
3. Integrity rules, defining the boundaries of a data base. These include maximum and minimum values, different constraints, and different types of access procedures.

Now let us define different data models in the DSS environment.

Table 4-2 ▪ An Example of a Flat File

Name	Major	Age	GPA
Mary	MIS	25	3.00
Sue	CS	21	3.60
Debra	MGT	26	3.50
Bob	MKT	22	3.40
George	MIS	28	3.70

4-8 The Flat File Model

A file management system, or a flat file model, is simply a file or a series of files with a series of records and fields. These files are called flat because there are no relationships among them. The flat file system does not allow sophisticated data base operations performed by other data models. Table 4-2 illustrates an example of a flat file system.

Basic data management operations such as file creation, deletion, updating, and simple data query can be performed using this model. However, as mentioned earlier, this type of data model is limited in its capacity to support complex DSS requirements.

4-9 Relational Model

A relational model uses a mathematical construct called a relation (table), which is simply a table of rows and columns of data. Rows are records (tuples) and columns are fields (attributes). Different relations can be linked together on the basis of a common field (key). To clarify this concept, look at the two relations in Tables 4-3 and 4-4.

As you can see, the common field in these two relations is the customer number. A relational DBMS can utilize these two relations and generate a report like the one in Table 4-5.

Table 4-3 ▪ A Customer Relation

Customer Number	Name	Address
2000	ABC	Broadway
3000	XYZ	Jefferson
9000	TRY	Madison

Table 4-4 ▪ An Invoice Relation

Invoice Number	Customer Number	Amount	Method of Payment
111	2000	$2000.00	Cash
222	3000	$4000.00	Credit
333	3000	$1500.00	Cash
444	9000	$6400.00	Cash
555	9000	$7000.00	Credit

The relational model is straightforward. Creation and maintenance of this type of data base is easy as are addition and deletion of records. Overall, relational models offer a great degree of flexibility. General operations handled by a relational model include:

- Creation of relation
- Updating (insertion, deletion, and modification)
- Selection of a relation or a subrelation
- Join operation
- Projection (selection of a subset of a field or a subset of a series of fields)
- General query operation

A major shortcoming of this model is in dealing with complex data operations. Establishing many relations, with the key included in each one, may use a lot of disk space, and modification may be time-consuming. This model may limit the complexity and insertion of new records. Advance planning may resolve some of these problems. However, specific problems associated with some relational data bases may include [26]:

- The enforcement of data integrity
- The lack of automatic maintenance of data redundancy
- Uncontrolled update anomalies

Table 4-5 ▪ Invoice and Customer Relations Are Joined by Using Customer Number

Invoice	Customer Number	Amount	Method of Payment	Name	Address
111	2000	$2000.00	Cash	ABC	Broadway
222	3000	$4000.00	Credit	XYZ	Jefferson
333	3000	$1500.00	Cash	XYZ	Jefferson
444	9000	$6400.00	Cash	TRY	Madison
555	9000	$7000.00	Credit	TRY	Madison

Overall, the relational model presents a series of unique advantages not easily found in the other data models [26]:

- Smaller applications can be developed easily.
- There are fewer application errors.
- Development time is shorter.
- Fewer resources are invested in different applications.
- Applications may have a longer life span due to insulation from changes in the data base structure.

A relatively new type of data model is gaining popularity. This data model, an extension of object programming, is called an object-oriented data model [19]. The model reduces the semantic gap between complex business applications and the data storage supporting these applications. It carries the relational model one step further, providing support for more complex data management applications and making it easier to model the complex real business world. This model represents an object in the real world with a corresponding object in the data base, which is a realistic way of modeling a real-life system. We shall see many DBMSs built based on this model in the near future.

4-10 Hierarchical Model

Like the relational model, a hierarchical data model is made up of records, called nodes, each of which can have several fields. The presentation is similar to a one-dimensional array. The relationships between the records are called branches. The node at the top of the hierarchy is called the root, and every node of the tree except the root node has a parent. The nodes with the same parents are called twins or siblings. For example, P1 and P2 in Figure 4-2 are twins.

In the relational model, as discussed earlier, the connections among the files are based on a common key field. In the hierarchical model the connections between files do not depend on the data contained within the files. The connections are defined initially when the data base is designed and are maintained for the entire life of the data base. For example, file X is linked to file Y regardless of their contents. The connection between records is hierarchical. These connections are sometimes called the structure, or schema, of the data base.

The hierarchical model is sometimes called an upside-down tree (a tree with its roots up). Figure 4-2 illustrates an example of a hierarchical model; it indicates that a supplier may supply three different families of products. In each family, there may be several different product categories. As an example, Supplier X may supply soap, shampoo, and toothpaste. Within each product category there may be many brands of the same product—for example, ten different shampoos or five different toothpastes. Such a relationship is called a one-to-many data structure, which means a parent can have many children; however, each child has only one parent. In the hierarchical model a search in the parent node can lead you to children nodes and vice versa. Any updating in a parent node should automatically update the children nodes.

Figure 4-2 An Example of the Hierarchical Model

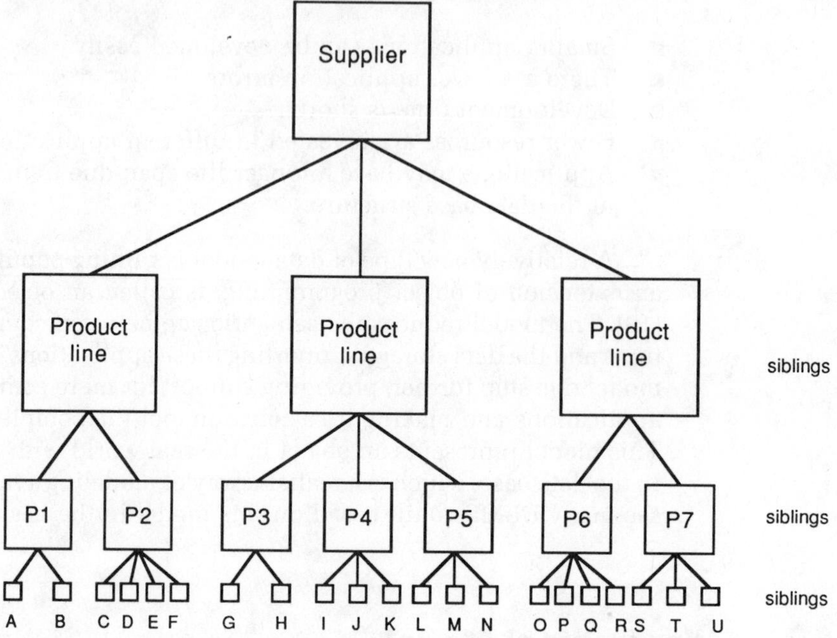

The operations associated with the hierarchical model include:

- File creation
- File updating (insertion, deletion, addition, modification)
- Query operation
- Retrieval of next descendent record
- Retrieval of parent record

When compared with the relational data model, the hierarchical model is less flexible primarily because the designer should know the reporting procedure of a particular system ahead of time.

4-11 The Network Model

The network model is very similar to the hierarchical model. However, the records and fields of a network model are organized differently. Figure 4-3 illustrates the customer/invoice relations in a network model.

As can be seen in this figure, in place of related key fields, there is a link between the invoice number, the customer number, and the method of payment. In this case the customer number no longer needs to remain in the invoice record. As Figure 4-3 illustrates, invoice numbers are linked to the header link in the same order in which they were entered (from Table 4-3).

The network model is not as flexible as the relational model. Also, the DSS reporting procedure must be defined ahead of time in order to see if the network model will be suitable for a particular DSS operation. Operations associated with a network model include:

- File creation
- File updating (insertion, deletion, addition, modification)
- Query operations

The network model can be considered to be an enhanced version of the hierarchical model. In this data structure the relationship can be one-to-many (simple network) as well as many-to-many (complex network). Figure 4-3 illustrates a one-to-many relationship. Each child (invoice) has two parents (method of payment and customer number). Figure 4-4 illustrates a many-to-many relationship. In a real estate organization, each agent is selling several properties. (For example, agent A-1 sells properties P-1, P-2, and P-6 at the same time property P-1 has been listed under agents A-1 and A-2.) At the same time, each property has been listed under several agents. In a many-to-many relationship, the parent-child relationship breaks down, since any record can be the parent and any record can be the child.

4-12 The Rule Model

Another data model used in the DSS environment is the rule model [24]. This model is mostly used in "knowledge-based," or expert, DSS systems. This model describes data by using a set of rules. These rules may be conditional or unconditional. We talk about expert systems in detail in Chapter 13. For now, remember that this type of data model not only provides data queries to the DSS users, it also provides some explanation capabilities. It tells the user about the facts in the data base and their meanings. Table 4-5 is an example of this type of data model in a university data base.

Figure 4-3 An Example of a Simple Network Model

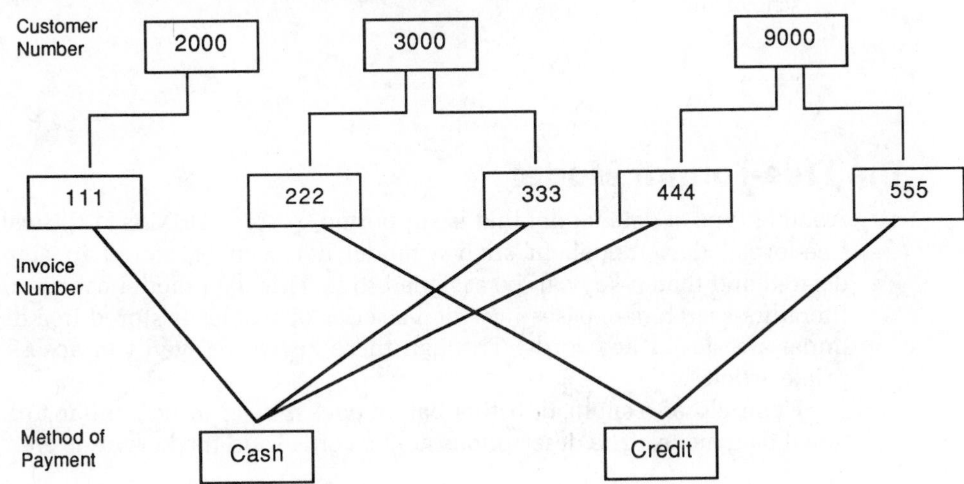

Figure 4-4 An Example of a Complex Network Model

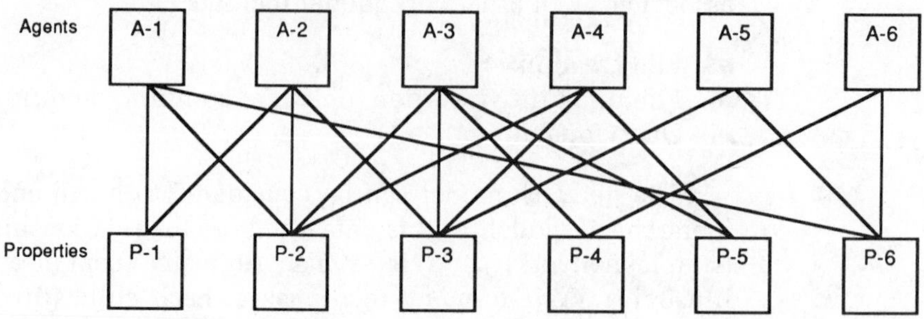

The rule model is very suitable for data bases that require complex relationships and include many related data items. Like the other data models, basic data base operations such as file creation, file update, modification, deletion, and insertion are possible. However, there are at least three unique operations associated with this model that are not usually available in the other data models [24]:

- Computation (some relational data modeles perform this feature)
- Deduction
- Explanation

An example of computation in our sample data base is:

Compute average age for honor students or compute GMAT/GPA ratios for MIS students

An example of deduction in our sample data base is:

A set of honor students chosen from the entire data base.

Finally, an example of explanation in our data base is:

Listing of all the rules that define why a student should be awarded a scholarship.

4-13 The Free-Format Model

Another type of data model that is supported by some DBMSs [12] is called the free-format data model. In such a model data can be stored in any format desired and then a key can be assigned to it. This data model can be useful in literature-search data bases in which a series of articles is stored in a data base under a series of keywords. Through these keywords, you can access appropriate articles.

Upon closer examination this data model is seen to be similar to the relational data model. The descriptions are "records" and the keywords are "fields."

4-14 What Data Model To Choose

All the data models are capable of performing basic data-management functions. Before choosing a DBMS, the designer of a DSS should consider the operations supported by a DBMS, *not* the way in which the data is presented in a particular data model. Table 4-7 summarizes the types of data models and DSSs that use each data model [24]. Appendix A provides a comprehensive coverage of popular DSS products on the market and various data models used by these products. Appendix B highlights several popular DSSs, including the ones in Table 4-7.

4-15 DSS and DBMS Functions

A DBMS, regardless of its data structure (data model), must be able to perform the following operations for effective use in a DSS environment.

1. *Basic data-management operations.* The basic operations include data base creation, modification, deletion, addition, insertion, and maintenance. These operations are supported even in a file manager system.

Table 4-6 ▪ An Example of the Rule Model

Rule 1	Graduate student rules Name = any name Age > 19 Language status = any GPA > 3.00 GMAT > 500 Major = any Deficiency Status > 10 courses
Rule 2	Classified student rules GPA > 3.20 GMAT > 550 Deficiency Status = 1 course
Rule 3	Honored Rules GPA > 3.50 Language status = bilingual
Rule 4	Scholarship rules Major = MIS or CS Language status = English or German GPA > 3.80

Table 4-7 ▪ Data Models and DSS in Use

Data Model	DSSs Using the Model
Record (flat file system)	SIMPLAN
Relational	REGIS
Hierarchical	AAIMS
Network	GPLAN
Rule	MYCIN

2. *Basic arithmetic operations.* These include simple arithmetic operations performed on different records and fields in a data base, including addition, subtraction, multiplication, and division. These basic operations may be quite useful for simple query operations.
3. *Projection operation.* This function may be a special case of a general query operation, which may generate a subset of the fields. For example, in a student data base that includes each student's name, GPA, age, sex, address, and nationality, a projection operation may generate a listing of name and GPA of all these students.
4. *Search* (Query). This function may include different searches on a data base for specific conditions. As an example, a triple-criteria search on the preceding student data base is

```
DISPLAY ALL STUDENTS FOR GPA >= 3 and MAJOR = "CS" AND AGE <=22
```

   Search operations can include as many criteria as the number of the fields existing in the data base. They may include an AND search (all criteria specified must be met), an OR search (only one of the specified criteria must be met; failure to meet others does not matter), and a NOT search (opposite criteria must be met).
5. *Sort.* This operation puts the data base in a specific order. Data can be sorted with one key or multiple keys in ascending or descending order.
6. *Summary.* The summary operation may be a special case of basic arithmetic operations. For example, you may generate a subtotal of all MIS students and all acounting students in the student data base.
7. *Union (merge) operation.* This operation enables a user to combine two files, tables, or relations, thereby generating a third file, table, or relation that includes all the information from the first two files, tables, or relations. In other words, the union operation does concatenation over the existing data. Figure 4-5 presents this operation on a student data base. File 3 is the union of Files 1 and 2.
8. *Join operation.* This operation combines two files, tables, or relations within one and the same data base on a common field in order to generate the third file, table, or relation. Figure 4-6 illustrates one example of this operation. In this example, the common key is the customer name.

Figure 4-5 An Example of Union Operation

File 1

Student	Major
Bob	MIS
Barry	CS
James	MIS
Sue	Accounting

File 2

Student	Major
Mary	Marketing
Sherry	MIS
Sandy	Math

File 3 (Union of Files 1 and 2)

Student	Major
Bob	MIS
Barry	CS
James	MIS
Sue	Accounting
Mary	Marketing
Sherry	MIS
Sandy	Math

9. *Intersection Operation* This operation generates the intersection of two relations in a third relation containing a common tuple(s) (common rows). The relations must be union compatible, which means that each relation must have the same number of identical attributes. Figure 4-7 illustrates this operation. The result of the intersection of relations 1 and 2 is relation 3, which contains only one tuple, the one belonging to the first two relations.

Figure 4-6 An Example of Join Operation

Relation 1

Customer	Purchase no.
Barry	112
James	118
Susan	129
Bob	135

Relation 2

Customer	Purchase amount
Barry	2000
James	5000
Susan	1000
Bob	1500

Relation 3 (Joining of Relations 1 and 2)

Customer	Purchase no.	Purchase amount
Barry	112	2000
James	118	5000
Susan	129	1000
Bob	135	1500

Figure 4-7 An Example of Intersection Operation

Relation 1

Student	Major	GPA
Bob	CS	3.60
Bobby	MIS	3.80
Tom	ACC	2.90

Relation 2

Student	Major	GPA
Tom	ACC	2.90
Jerry	CIS	3.70
Don	MGT	3.90

Relation 3 (Intersection of Relations 1 and 2)

Student	Major	GPA
Tom	ACC	2.90

4-16 New Trends in Data Base Design and Utilization

Several new trends, including natural language processing, distributed data base, and data base machines, have recently developed in data base design and utilization. The advancement in artificial intelligence and natural language processing will have a definite impact on the design and utilization of data bases [2]. AI technology should facilitate the construction of a data base. Natural language processing should provide an easier access for the DSS user by providing an interface that is more similar to the user's native language. We discuss natural language processing in detail in Chapter 12. Currently, these issues may be of limited practical importance; however, they may be quite significant in the near future, and this may have direct impact on the design and utilization of DSSs. A brief explanation of these new trends follows:

Distributed Data Base

So far in our discussion, we have assumed a central data base for all the users of a DSS. However, there a number of actors that indicate a data base that is distributed throughout an organization is better than acentralized operation [3, 6]

- *Economic constraints.* For remote users of a DSS (those users who are not located in the same place where the DSS is located), it may not be economically feasible to access the central data base all the time. It may be more economical to store some of the data at the remote site(s).
- *Lack of responsiveness.* Centralized data bases may not be responsive to the immediate needs of a DSS user.
- *Enhanced sophistication in microcomputers.* The increasing sophistication and decreasing cost of microcomputers has made distributed processing more feasible and the utilization of these computers a more viable option in a distributed environment.

- *Change in data processing organizational structure.* Since the mid-1970's there has been a trend toward distributed processing. This trend certainly includes data base design and implementation. When considering user needs, the responsiveness of this type of system is evidently higher than that of a centralized system.

These issues support a distributed DBMS. In distributed data base the data are not located at the same site as the user and/or the computer. Rauch-Hindin [20] identifies some specific advantages with a distributed DBMS:

- The design reflects an organization's structure.
- Local storage of data decreases response times and communication costs.
- Data distribution involving multiple sites minimizes the effects of a computer breakdown, restricting it to its point of occurrence.
- The size and number of users is not limited by one computer's size or processing power.
- Multiple, integrated small systems might cost less than one large computer.
- Most important of all, a distributed data base need not be constrained by the physical organization of data.

This type of data base may follow the data model discussed earlier; however, more than one user can access the same data base at the same or different times. DBAs must design specific features and access codes in order to allow only one user to update the data base at any time. Otherwise data discrepancies may occur.

Also, security issues are more important in a multiuser environment due to multiple access from both inside and outside of the organization. Security policies must be clearly defined and the authorized users must be identified. The scope of users' access and their times of access must also be clearly defined. Generally speaking, the designer of a data base and DSS must bear in mind that not all applications are suitable for distributed processing.

A distributed data base may be designed in several configurations. Figure 4-8 [6] illustrates one example of this type of data base.

Data Base Machines

Data base machines have also attracted some attention in recent years because they enhance efficiency. Data base machines simply serve as back-end processors [10, 18] to the main computer system. Since a second processor handles the whole operation related to the DBMS, the first processor (the main computer system) can be dedicated to the application programs. In other words, data base machines provide an environment for parallel processing. This technology has not been around long, so it is difficult to judge its effectiveness, but it seems to have merit in complex business environments. However, its real effectiveness is yet to be seen.

Figure 4-8 An Example of a Distributed Data Base

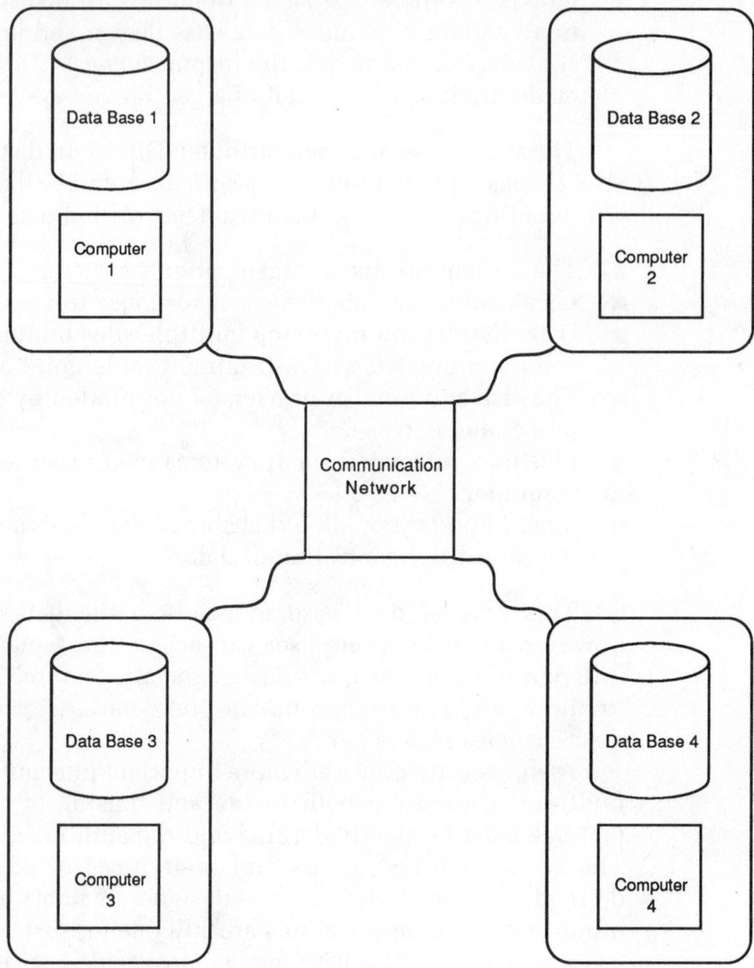

4-17 Summary

This chapter introduced and discussed the data base as one of the major components of a DSS. Several views related to data base design, different types of data, and problems associated with data were expanded upon. Types of data base models used in DSS design were also discussed. The latter part of this chapter concentrated on functions and operations supported by a DBMS. Understanding of these functions should help a DSS user/designer to choose a more suitable DBMS for DSS design. Finally, some of the new trends in data base environment were introduced. These new trends should play an important role in DSS design and utilization in the near future. Table 4-8 illustrates some examples of popular DBMSs and data models used by these systems [15].

Table 4-8 ▪ Examples of DBMS and Data Models Used

Name/Vendor	Data Model	Hardware Support
IDMS/R by Cullinet Software, Inc.	Network	IBM and compatible mainframes
Model 204 by Computer Corporation of America	Relational	IBM and compatible mainframes
IMB/VS-DB by IBM	Hierarchical	IBM
SQL/DS by IBM	Relational	IBM
DB2 by IBM	Relational	IBM
System 2000 by Intel Corp.	Hierarchical	IBM and compatible mainframes
IDM 500 by Britton-Lee, Inc.	A relational data base machine	Any computer
IDM System-PC by Britton-Lee Inc.	A relational data base machine	IBM-PC and compatibles
INGRES by Relational Technology, Inc.	Relational	DEC VAX under VMS or UNIX operating system
Oracle by Oracle Corp.	Relational	IMS, SQL, and DB2 compatible
Informix by Relational Database Systems, Inc.	Relational	IBM PC and compatibles
System V by Microrim, Inc.	Relational	MS-DOS and Eagle computers
dBASE III Plus by Ashton-Tate	Relational	IBM PC and compatibles

Review Questions

1. What is a data base?

2. What is the difference between a data base and a file cabinet?

3. What are some of the advantages of a data base compared with a flat file system?

4. What are the different types of data used in DSS design?

5. List some external sources for data used in a DSS environment.

6. What is a functional view of data base design?

7. Why is a data base so crucial to DSS design?

8. What types of analyses are supported by a data base? Modeling analysis or data analysis, or both?

9. Give some examples of data used in finance, manufacturing, marketing, and personnel.

10. What are "data problems" discussed in the chapter? How can these problems be resolved in a DSS environment?

11. What is a data model? What is supported by a data model?

12. Briefly discuss six types of data models discussed in this chapter: flat file, relational, hierarchical, network, rule, and free-format.

13. What are some of the limitations of each data model?

14. What are some of the advantages of the relational data model compared with the others?

15. What are some of the unique operations supported by the rule model not found in the other types?

16. List major operations supported by any DBMS.

17. What is an example of projection operation?

18. What is the difference between the union and join operations?

19. When should a user use each operation: join, merge, sort, and intersection?

20. What is a distributed data base?

21. What are some of the advantages of a distributed data base?

22. What are data base machines? What are some of the advantages of this type of processing?

23. What is natural language processing? What are some of its impacts on data base design and DSS utilization?

Projects

1. There are 20 students in our DSS class. For each student we keep track of eight fields: first name, last name, social security number, major, GPA, age, nationality and status (freshman, sophomore, and so on.) Organize this simple 20 × 8 file in six different data models discussed in this chapter. Which one is the easiest, and why?

2. Nine basic operations associated with any DBMSs were discussed. Using a DBMS with which you are familiar, perform these operations on the above data base. (*Hint*: You may have to generate a couple of other relations first, then perform these basic operations.)

3. Table 4-6 presents five major data models used in specific DSS in action. By referring to Appendix B of this book, investigate the functions performed by the data base component of these specific DSS.

4. dBASE III Plus is a well-known DBMS for microcomputers. Investigate the strengths and weaknesses of this DBMS for DSS utilization.

5. Table 4-7 presents popular DBMSs on the market. Research SQL/DS by IBM and IDM 500 by Britton-Lee, Inc. Both of these systems offer relational DBMSs. Compare and contrast these two. What are the unique features of a data base machine not found in a regular DBMS?

6. The object-oriented data model shows some promising signs. Starting with reference [19] research this. What is the present status?

Key Terms

Data base
File cabinet
Data base management system (DBMS)
Internal data
External data
Managerial view
Technical view
Functional view
Data problems
Conceptual design
Data model
Flat file
Relational model
Object-oriented data model
Hierarchical model
Network model
Rule model
Free-format model
Query operation
Projection operation
Search
Sort
Union operation
Join operation
Intersection operation
Artificial intelligence
Natural language processing
Distributed data base
Data base administrator
Data base machines

References

[1] Alter, Steven L. 1980. *Decision Support Systems Current Practice and Continuing Challenges*. Reading, Mass.: Addison-Wesley Publishing Company, Inc., pp. 127–132.

[2] Barbary, Clifton L. 1987. A Database Primer on Natural Language. *Journal of Systems Management* (April): 20–25.

[3] Bradley, James. 1987. *Introduction to Data Base Management in Business*. New York: Holt, Rinehart and Winston.

[4] Courthney, James F., Jr., and David B. Paradice. 1988. *Database Systems for Management*. St. Louis: Time Mirror/Mosby College Publishing.

[5] Cunningham, Lloyd. 1985. Developing a Database Management System for Decision Support. *Computer in Healthcare* (August): 34–36.

[6] Ceri, Stefano, and Giuseppe Pelagatti. 1984. *Distributed Database Principles and Systems*. New York: McGraw-Hill Book Company.

[7] Date, C. J. 1977. *An Introduction to Data Base Systems*, 2d ed.. Reading, Mass.: Addison-Wesley Publishing Company, Inc.

[8] Gil, Philip J. 1987. Distributed Databases, Still in Test Phase, Hold Great Promise. *PC Week* (May 5): 33–34.

[9] Hirouchi, Tetsuo, and Takeshi Kosaka. 1984. An Effective Database Formation for Decision Support Systems. *Information Management*: 183–95.

[10] Hsiao, D. K. 1983. *Advanced Data Base Machine Architecture*. Englewood Cliffs, N.J.: Prentice-Hall, Inc.

[11] Inmon, William. 1986. Building the Best Data Base. *Computerworld* (July 9),: 73–75.
[12] Krajewski, Rich. 1984. Database Types. *Byte* (October): 137–42.
[13] Kruglinski, David. 1987, The Network Model DBMS. *Applications Software Today* (Summer): 25–31.
[14] Kroenke, David M. 1983. *Database Processing*, 2d ed. Chicago: Science Research Associates, Inc.
[15] Manuel, Tom. 1984. The Growing Surge in Data-Base Systems. *Electronics* (May 17): 131–42.
[16] McFadden, Fred R. and Jefferey A. Huffer. 1985. *Data Base Management*. Menlo Park, Calif: The Benjamin/Cummings Publishing Company.
[17] Melymuka, Kathleen. Newest Database Technology Effect on PCs Debated. *PC Week* (October 28): 151–54.
[18] Myers, E. 1985. Database Machines Take Off. *Datamation* (May 15): 52–63.
[19] Peterson, Robert W. 1987. Object-Oriented Data Base Design. *AI Expert* (March): 26–31.
[20] Rauch-Hindin, Wendy. 1987. True Distributed DBMS's Presage Big Dividends. *Mini-Micro Systems* (May): 65–73.
[21] Schroeder, Matthew T. 1986. What's Wrong with DBMS. *Datamation* (December 15): 67–70.
[22] Sol, Henk G. 1985. Aggregating Data for Decision Support. *Decision Support Systems:* 111–21.
[23] Spencer, Cheryl. 1986. Building a Data Base. *Personal Computing* (November): 99–105.
[24] Sprague, Ralph H. Jr., and Eric D. Carlson. 1982. *Building Effective Decision Support Systems*. Englewood Cliffs, N.J.: Prentice-Hall, Inc., pp. 221–55.
[25] Sullivan, Kristina B. 1986. Distributed Database for PCs Could Help Systems Managers. *PC Week* (September 16): 131–32.
[26] Wood, David. 1985. Relational Systems Meet the Real World. *Data Management* (July): 10–15.

5 Model Base for DSS

5-1 Introduction

In this chapter the second DSS component, the model base, is addressed. For DSS to be able to support all phases of decision making (intelligence, design, and choice), a model base, a data base, and dialog management are needed. This chapter provides a background for and examples of models, modeling analysis, and types of models. Later in this chapter problems associated with traditional modeling techniques are highlighted. The majority of these problems can be solved when models are used in the DSS environment. At the end of the chapter modeling analysis for functional areas of business is presented. The chapter ends with guidelines for implementation of modeling techniques in a DSS environment. The capabilities of Lotus and IFPS as DSS modeling products, chosen because of their popularity both in the academic and business worlds, are introduced. Also, the important capabilities of SPSS and SAS, two of the strong modeling tools easily available for both academic and business use, are highlighted. Other modeling software is introduced as well.

5-2 What is a Model?

A model is a representation of a real-life situation. Because the study of a real-life situation is usually difficult, costly, and, in many cases, not practical, we instead build a model of the real-life situation and then conduct a study of the model.

A model is made up of a series of elements and relationships. In modeling terms, the elements are called variables and the relationships are the constraints imposed, either internally or externally.

There are many types of models. An organizational chart is a model representing a particular organization and the relationships existing among individuals in the organization. For DSS purposes we are interested primarily in mathematical and statistical models, which are presented using a series of variables and possibly a series of constraints.

A simple example of a model is a balance sheet:

$$\text{Total assets} = \text{fixed assets} + \text{current assets}, \quad \text{or} \quad TA = FA + CA$$

If two of the variables are defined, the third is automatically defined.

Another example of a model is a break-even analysis formula:

$$\text{Break-even point} = \text{Fixed cost} \div (\text{sales price} - \text{variable cost})$$

If the fixed cost is $500, the sales price is $15, and the variable cost is $10, then the break-even point is 100 units. At this point the company is neither losing money nor gaining any profit. Above this point the company is making profit, and below this point the company is losing money.

The models used in the DSS environment are more complicated and involve many more variables and constraints; however, the principle is the same.

5-3 Model-Building Process

To build a model for DSS the following steps are used:

1. *Defining the Problem.* Problem definition is the most important step. The problem under investigation must be defined as precisely as possible. A comprehensive problem definition makes the task of model building an easier one. The following are some examples of problems to be addressed by a DSS:

Example 1

An on-line sales forecast for a department store. This model provides decision-makers with a tool to avoid forecasting over or under. Either forecast error can be very costly.

Example 2

Effective advertising media for a service agency. This model assists decision-makers in spending the advertising budget effectively. A company can choose any medium or combination of media. But which combination is the best? Which combination will reach the highest number of potential customers?

Example 3

An on-line budget for city hall for the next 5 years. An on-line budgeting model may save time and frustration for the budgeting specialist in the organization. This model, if properly designed, can provide sophisticated features, such as what-if analysis, goal seeking, sensitivity analysis, and so on. This powerful tool can help an organization meet its financial goals in a comprehensive manner.

2. *Constructing the model.* After careful definition of the problem, the model is constructed. This means all variables, constraints, assumptions, and so forth are stated in mathematical terms. In a forecasting assignment, the most appropriate forecasting model—such as time series or regression—is selected. In a linear programming model, all the decision variables and constraints are formulated using mathematical terms.
3. *Solving the model.* The constructed model must be solved in order to determine the numerical value of each variable. This is usually done with a computer.
4. *Analyzing the solution.* At this point, the solution must be analyzed and conclusions drawn. The model may require some correction, but models in a DSS environment go through continuous updating procedures. It is a natural process because the information needs of decision-makers and the environmental factors are continuously changing.
5. *Testing and validating the model.* Discussion of model building and computerized models should not lead you to the conclusion that computerized models in DSS solve all the problems. Also, it is far from the truth that a decision-maker directly uses and relies on the modeling analyses. Computerized models can be misleading. Only expert statisticians and operations researchers are aware of all the assumptions underlying these models. The decision-maker must use his or her judgment and utilize the advice of intermediaries, in this case, usually experts from operation research (OR) departments. The "amateur" use of computerized models must be avoided, and the output of these models must be thoroughly interpreted before their actual use. A good example of amateur use of a model would be in multiple linear regression (MLR) analyses. In MLR, the value of R^2 usually indicates the strength of correlation between dependent and independent variables. But at the same time a large R^2 may have been generated by severe multicollinearity problems or a gross failure of the model's normality assumptions. For a detailed discussion of MLR and its assumptions, see [6, 7].

5-4 Modeling Analysis versus Data Analysis

Data base, model base, and dialog management are integral components of a DSS. If the DSS is designed to support all phases of decision making (intelligence, design, and choice), all three components are necessary. The data base component (as discussed in Chapter 4) supports the intelligence phase of decision making. The modeling component is required for the design and choice phases of decision making [17, pp. 25–27].

All information provided by a typical DSS is generated by data analysis, modeling analysis, or a combination of both. To clarify this idea consider the

Table 5-1 ▪ On-Line Automated Corporate Data Base

City (Figures in thousands)					
Salespersons	L.A.	Denver	Portland	St. Paul	Detroit
Sue	100	600	680	600	625
Jack	150	510	750	500	980
Bob	180	580	900	480	640
Robin	200	610	830	900	720
Mary	600	920	650	600	690
Becky	250	630	490	400	950
Silvia	350	640	500	600	250
John	750	510	610	720	700
Melani	550	650	450	950	900

following example: The data presented in Table 5-1 have been extracted from the corporate data base of On-Line Automated, a wholesaler of electronic devices.

By manipulating these data, valuable information such as the following can be generated:

Who has the highest total sales?

Who has the lowest total sales?

Which city has the highest total sales?

Which city has the lowest total sales?

Can anything be said about the future by examining these data? Can any statistical conclusion be drawn, either for the salespersons or the sales regions? Using such simple data analysis, the answer to these questions is no. Using modeling analysis, however, we can provide answers to these questions and more. Using a simple forecasting model we can generate a forecast for total sales for any city or salesperson. Statistical models can be used to compare the performance of cities or salespersons and to spot significant differences. Here the key point is that modeling is attempting to look into the future to analyze alternatives in the design and choice phases of decision making.

Modeling analysis makes use of data available in the data base and, by using mathematical and/or statistical models, generates some insight into what may happen in the future. As we will see, there are many models that have been successfully utilized in a DSS environment.

5-5 Limitations of Traditional Modeling Techniques

Traditional modeling techniques have been criticized because [17, 4]:

1. Their output has not been easily understood by the typical model user.

2. They have an inability to cope with discontinuities, especially in model input data.
3. They have an inability to evaluate model validity based on its output.
4. They are unable to guide the user through possible analyses beyond the output of the model.
5. They are unable to explain why the model acted the way it did.
6. All necessary input data have not always been available for models to analyze.
7. Models have not always included all necessary variables.
8. Interaction between the model and the user has been minimal.
9. Certain variables and/or relationships are not easily quantified or are not mathematically tractable.

In a DSS environment, the majority of these problems are either resolved or significantly reduced.

Output of a DSS can be in a variety of formats, such as graphic, tabular, detailed, and summary. These options are designed to suit different styles and needs of decision making. In a DSS environment there are two types of intermediaries trained to obtain and explain DSS output to the DSS user (this is discussed at length in Chapter 6). Of course, these intermediaries are used if they are needed.

DSS is designed to involve different models, which, by their nature, are supposed to utilize both continuous and discrete data input. Through the screening process, DSS utilizes the most relevant data for further analysis. Through feedback control, the validity of DSS models can be continuously evaluated. By using some of the output generated by a model as input to the model in the next round, models in the DSS environment are controlled and updated continuously. By using the most current data, either the parameters of the model can be modified, the structure of the model can be modified, or both. Parameters are the constant values or coefficients in the model, and structure indicates either the number and types of variables included in the model or replacing a model with another model in the same group.

When models are used in the DSS environment, diverse analyses can be made and more insight can be gained. This feature is possible with the help of either an intermediary or some of the built-in features, such as what-if, goal seeking, and the sensitivity analysis available in the DSS modeling component.

Models in the DSS environment use the most relevant, accurate, and recent data, which indicate why the model acts the way it does. As discussed in Chapter 4, the DBMS continuously modifies, updates, and integrates all data available in the data base component of the DSS, which maintains the most relevant data in the data base for a more accurate modeling analysis.

The data base component of DSS provides all necessary data needed by the modeling component of a DSS. (We discussed types and sources of data needed by a DSS in Chapter 4.) Both the quality and quantity of data needed by the modeling component are guaranteed by virtue of an extensive information pool.

Since all relevant data needed for modeling analysis are included in the data base and since the user/designer of DSS has complete control regarding the type and the quantity of data to be entered into the model, it is possible to decide which variables will be included in the model. For example, by including some of the most relevant data, stepwise multiple linear regression can tell the user which variable should be included or which should be excluded from the model. The user can include all variables and later eliminate those that prove insignificant.

Other examples include moving average or exponential smoothing models for forecasting. These models utilize the most relevant data available, assigning the heaviest weight to the most recent data. When new data become available, the older data are automatically dropped out. This generates the best possible forecast.

Finally, by including user-friendliness and intermediaries, there can be maximum interaction between the DSS and the user.

As discussed in Chapter 7, using flexible and progressive design methodologies will encourage the use of DSS, and, ideally, the majority of earlier problems will be resolved.

5-6 Modeling in a DSS Environment

To be able to support all three phases of decision making (intelligence, design, and choice), the following capabilities are needed:

The modeling component of the DSS should be able to *analyze* the data in the data base component using different types of analysis, such as arithmetic operations, statistical, trend analysis, and so on.

The modeling component of the DSS should be able to *generate alternatives* for solving a problem by using alternative data sets and/or alternative models in the same family.

The modeling component of the DSS should be able to *compare alternatives* and choose the best or make suggestions regarding each alternative, for example, by comparing the number of errors generated by each forecasting technique and then choosing the one that generated the smallest number. This feature can be built into the DSS modeling component.

The modeling component of the DSS should also perform *simulation*, *optimization*, and *forecasting*. These techniques can be included in the model base component of the DSS.

The most challenging task in model building and modeling analysis in a DSS environment is the inclusion of the most appropriate data and variables in the model, particularly relevant external data. Fig. 5-1 highlights the relevant factors in the environment of a DSS that might be included in modeling analysis. Naturally, these factors are not suitable for all DSSs. Depending on the situation, the relevant external factors must be carefully identified and then, if possible, be integrated into the model-base component of the DSS.

Finally, models in DSS should include what-if, goal seeking, and sensitivity analysis. As we will see later in this chapter, these features can be either

Figure 5-1 External Factors to be Considered by Model Base Component of a DSS

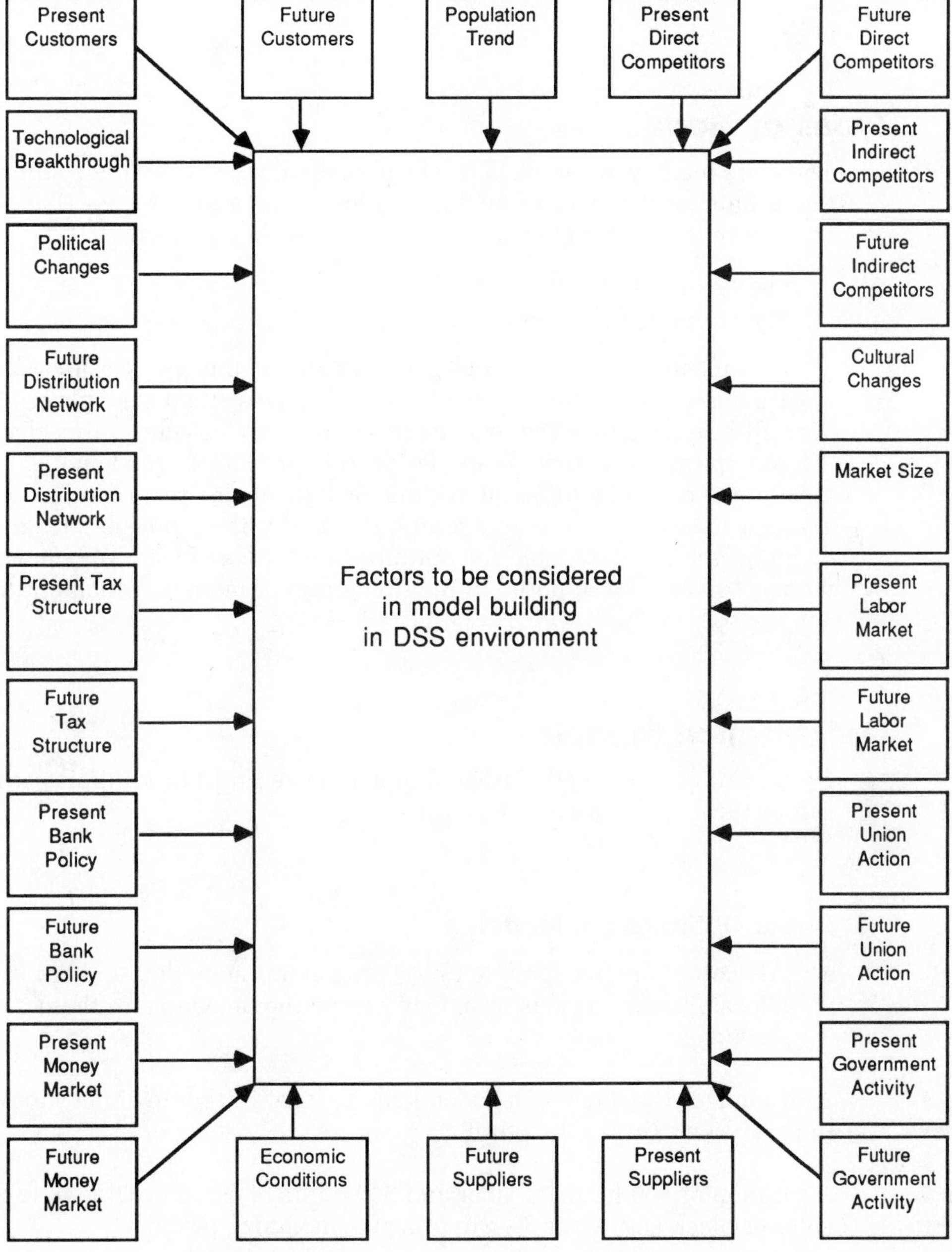

built into the modeling component of a DSS or provided by commercial DSS products available on the market.

As discussed in Chapter 3 and Appendix A, DSS generators include some impressive modeling capabilities, which can be adapted for a specific DSS. It is also expected that DSS generators will evolve toward more sophisticated and comprehensive inclusion of modeling techniques as their integral component. We talk more about these generators in Appendix A.

5-7 Types of Models

There are many ways models can be classified, such as by their functions, by the techniques they use, or by their mathematical structure. For DSS purposes we choose to classify models by the functions they perform:

Optimization models

Nonoptimization models

Optimization models are designed to generate the best possible solution to a particular problem. Linear programming is an excellent example of this type. We will provide a detailed explanation of this model later in this chapter.

Nonoptimization models are designed to provide a "good enough" answer to a problem using different techniques. However, this solution does not presume to be the best possible solution. Actually, the problems solved by these techniques are not suitable for optimization-type analysis. We can say these models "satisfy" as opposed to the first group of models, which optimize.

5-8 Optimization Models

Optimization models are designed to maximize profit or minimize cost. They can be further classified as follows.

Linear Optimization Models

- *Allocation models* include linear programming models and are used to allocate limited resources among competing demands for these resources.

Example 1 Allocation of 100 hours of labor and 200 units of leather to either shoes or bags in order to maximize the profit.

Example 2 Allocation of 400 hours of labor and 300 hours of assembly line time to either color or black-and-white TVs in order to maximize profit.

- *Assignment models* are special applications of linear programming models. They are used to assign activities to individuals, machines to operators, and so forth.

Example 1 Assignment of 5 machines to 5 operators to minimize the total cost or total time of operation.

Example 2 Assignment of 4 runners to 4 races in order to minimize total running time.

- *Transportation models* are also applications of linear programming models and are designed to establish the best possible link between sources (origin) and sinks (destination) in a transportation-type problem.

Example 1 There are 5 warehouses and 10 shopping centers. Which warehouse should ship to which shopping center in order to minimize shipping costs?

Example 2 There are 12 tankers and 6 oil rigs. Which tanker should be assigned to which oil rig in order to minimize traveling distance and total cost?

- *Network models* are used as PERT (program evaluation review technique) or CPM (critical path mèthod) in order to determine the critical path for the completion of a series of interrelated activities. Network models are also used to establish a telecommunication network system to minimize distance and wiring cost.

Example 1 Site preparation for a computer center. How must all activities be organized in order to minimize the total construction time? Which activity or activities can be delayed without delaying completion of the project?

Example 2 Establish a local area network (LAN) in a ten-story building that includes 36 offices on each floor. How should all these nodes (offices) be connected in order to minimize the wiring cost?

There are two other models used in this group: MOST (management operation system technique), used to improve some features of PERT, is used primarily in production-oriented organizations. LOB (line of balance), developed by the U.S. Navy as a graphic method for industrial programming, is useful in a production setting. PERT, MOST, and LOB can be combined to provide a more effective scheduling tool for decision-making purposes [10, 14].

Inventory Optimization Models

Inventory models are used to minimize the cost of inventory. These models assist the decision-maker in solving problems regarding the amount of products ordered and the timing of the order. Economic order quantity (EOQ) and economic manufacturing quantity (EMQ) are two good examples of this type.

Example A shoe company sells 480,000 pairs of shoes. When and how many pairs of shoes should be ordered to minimize the total inventory cost?

Portfolio Optimization Models

A combination of capital budgeting (such as present value, future value, and internal rate of return) and mathematical models is used to determine the best possible combination of securities in an investment setting problem.

Example

A newly established high-tech company decides to establish a sound portfolio policy that minimizes the risk to capital. What is the best combination of common stocks, preferred stocks, bonds, real estate, and so on?

Dynamic Programming Optimization Model

The dynamic programming optimization model is suitable for interrelated decisions, which can be either deterministic or probabilistic. In this type of model, each outcome is usually related, directly or indirectly, to the previous outcome. The model's emphasis is on the overall effectiveness of the entire system, a technique suitable for multistage problems that allows decomposition of one large problem into a series of subproblems, which are easier to solve. For example, a 12-month decision can be broken down into four separate decisions per quarter. The dynamic programming model may utilize different techniques, such as linear programming, network techniques, and inventory models. The specific technique depends on the nature of the problem.

Example

Replacement of machines in a manufacturing operation. When should machinery be replaced? Should a machine be replaced or repaired?

Nonlinear Optimization Models

In the nonlinear optimization model variables do not have a linear relationship, which—in mathematical terms—means the variables are of the second degree or higher. For instance, X, Y, and Z are linear but X^2, XY, and XYZ are nonlinear. Quadratic models exemplify this model.

Example

A linear model that includes all linear constraints but has objective function that is quadratic with regard to decision variables. To illustrate, the cost of an item decreases in a nonlinear fashion when the quantity sold increases. This means that subsequent units will generate profit at a different rate than previous units. (In a linear programming problem all units must generate the same amount of profit.)

5-9 An Example of an Optimization Model

To show the steps involved in model building and model formulation, we explore a simple problem faced by a local manufacturer of leather products.

1. *Problem definition.* A manufacturer of leather products is planning to allocate two limited resources—300 units of leather and 600 hours of labor—to two competing products, shoes and bags. The following data from past operations have been collected from the data base.

   Each pair of shoes requires 6 units of leather

Each pair of shoes requires 15 hours of labor

Each leather bag requires 3 units of leather

Each leather bag requires 5 hours of labor

Each pair of shoes generates $8 profit

Each leather bag generates $5 profit

All assumptions of a classic linear programming model are present:

All units of the same product will generate the profit specified.

All units of both products will use the amounts of resources just specified.

2. *Construction of the model.* At this point we would like to formulate the preceding problem as follows:

x_1 is the number of pairs of shoes
x_2 is the number of leather bags
z is the objective function to be maximized

$6x_1 + 3x_2 \leq 300$	Constraint 1
$15x_1 + 5x_2 \leq 600$	Constraint 2
$z = 8x_1 + 5x_2$	Objective function
$x_1, x_2 \geq 0$	Production cannot be negative

Constraint 1 indicates that there are at most 300 units of leather and constraint 2 indicates that there are at most 600 hours of labor that can be allocated to the two competing activities.

3. *Solving the model.* This problem, though simple, shows how modeling works. The problem can be solved either graphically, by using the simplex method, or by using one of the commercial software packages. In any event, the numerical values are:

$$x_1 = 20$$
$$x_2 = 60$$
$$z = \$460$$

This is the best possible solution. No other combination can generate a profit as high as $460.

4. *Analyzing the solution.* Now the decision-maker may want to perform some sensitivity analysis. If the profit generated by each pair of shoes is decreased by 15%, what will happen to the product mix? If manufacturing each leather bag requires four units of leather instead of three units, what will the product mix be?

Other important and interesting questions can be put to the model, and the DSS will answer them. Actually, in linear programming problems, these questions can be answered using a technique called shadow pricing [1].

5. *Model Testing and Validation.* As discussed earlier, model testing is an important phase in modeling analysis. In this phase, the decision-maker, with the help of an intermediary, must make sure the underlying assumptions of a particular model are well understood and must use his or her judgment in order to make sure the provided answers make

sense and are consistent with the overall goals and objectives of the organization. After careful analysis, the provided solution can be put into action.

5-10 Nonoptimization Models

Nonoptimization models provide a satisfactory rather than optimal solution to many problems. These models include forecasting models, regression models, trend analysis models, simulation models, and decision trees.

Forecasting Models

There are two types of forecasting models: statistical (quantitative) and technological (qualitative). In a DSS environment we are interested primarily in statistical forecasting models. There are a variety of forecasting models that can be used for short-, medium-, and long-range forecasting problems; for example, exponential smoothing, moving average, and mean are used for short- to medium-range forecasting. This group also includes trend analysis (linear and nonlinear models). In a trend-analysis model, time is always one of the variables. Based on data available in the data base, these models can generate a reliable forecast.

Regression Models

There are two types of regression models: simple linear regression and multiple linear regression. In a simple regression, the relationship between two variables is established and a forecast is generated.

Example

Based on the advertising budget, you are interested in predicting the company's total sales for the next period. You may want to first find out how strong such a relationship is and then generate a forecast. The linear regression model can be a valuable tool in a situation such as this.

In multiple linear regression, the performance of one variable, called the dependent variable, is predicted by a series of other independent variables.

Example

You want to predict the potential sales performance of a sales person based on education, years of experience, and sales territory. The sales performance in this case is a dependent variable, and the other three variables are independent.

Decision Tree

The decision-tree model is used when a decision-maker must deal with several alternatives, each having a different result. Usually there are probabilities associated with each alternative. A decision tree can help you graphically

Table 5-2 ▪ Payoff Table For Tri-Teck

	State of Nature		
Alternative	Hitting Water S_1	Hitting Low-quality Oil S_2	Hitting High-quality Oil S_3
a_1 Drilling	12	13	17
a_2 Drilling with condition	14	15	16
a_3 Leasing	11	12	18
a_4 Leasing with condition	16	11	14
Probability	.25	.40	.35

depict the entire tree and evaluate the expected value of each branch (or each alternative) of the tree. The alternative with the highest expected profit or the lowest expected cost will be selected.

Example

Tri-Teck, an oil company, is dealing with four alternatives in its newest oil field: drilling, drilling with condition, leasing, and leasing with condition. There are three states of nature related to each alternative: hitting water, hitting low-quality oil, and hitting high-quality oil. Also, there is a probability asssociated with each state of nature. The probabilities are based on historical data stored in a data base. The question is: Which alternative must be chosen in order to minimize the risk or maximize the profit? A decision-tree model can demonstrate the process and help the decision-maker calculate the expected value of each alternative (outcome multiplied by its probability is the expected value). Table 5-2 presents the payoff table for this oil company and Figure 5-2 illustrates the decision tree generated based on data in Table 5-2.

Expected values for the following five alternatives are as follows:

Expected value of alternative 1 = (12*.25) + (13*.40) + (17*.35) = 14.15
Expected value of alternative 2 = (14*.25) + (15*.40) + (16*.35) = 15.10
Expected value of alternative 3 = (11*.25) + (12*.40) + (18*.35) = 13.85
Expected value of alternative 4 = (16*.25) + (11*.40) + (14*.35) = 13.30

Alternative 2, drilling with condition, has the highest expected value; therefore, regardless of the status of the state of nature, this alternative must be chosen.

Simulation Models

Simulation models are used to evaluate alternative courses of action based on variables and constraints built into the model.

Figure 5-2 A Decision Tree for Tri-Teck

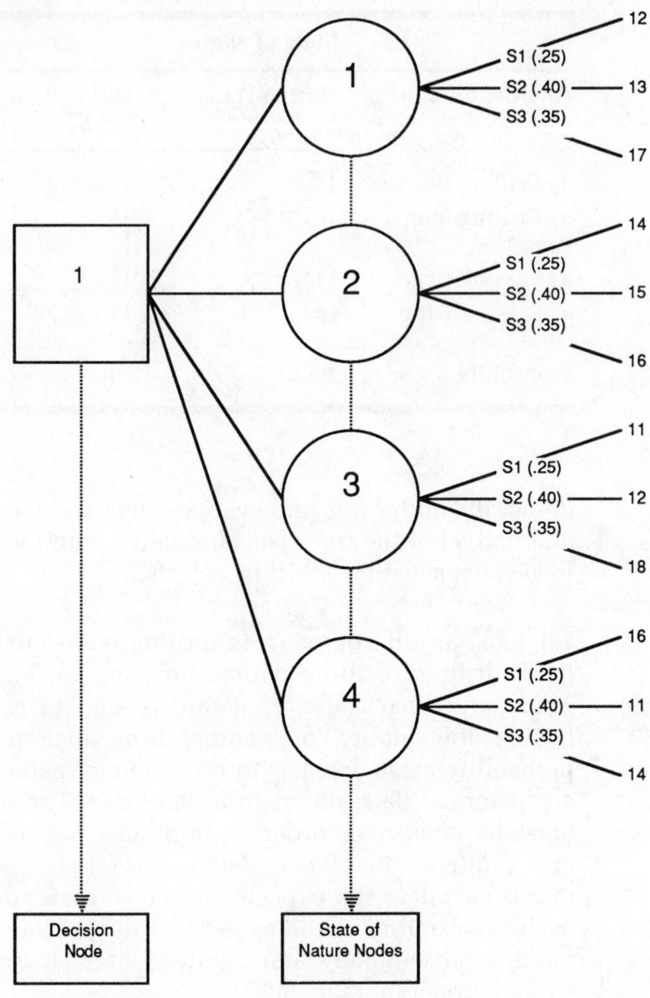

Example

A newly established service center is deciding on the number of operators to be assigned to run the service center. If there are too many operators, the company may lose a lot of money. At the same time, if too few operators are assigned, the company may lose customers because of long waiting lines. A simulation model can help in a situation like this. The pattern of customer arrival can be simulated by a computer program and, based on this pattern, the waiting time, the length of the queue, and the service time can be calculated.

5-11 An Example of a Nonoptimization Model

An example of a nonoptimization model uses data extracted from the corporate data base of Tasty Cool, a soft-drink distributor, presented in Table 5-3.

Table 5-3 ▪ Tasty Cool Data Base

Year	Advertising Expenses (in thousands)	Total Sales (in thousands)
1980	6,000	67,000
1981	7,000	81,000
1982	7,500	85,000
1983	9,200	87,000
1984	10,800	91,000
1985	11,600	105,000
1986	15,700	116,000
1987	16,900	125,000

The marketing vice president is planning to spend $18,000,000 for advertising and she would like answers to two questions:

- How strong is the relationship between advertising expense and total sales?
- If she spends $18,000,000 on advertising, how much would the estimated total sales be, assuming other factors are constant?

Using a simple linear regression should provide a reasonable answer to both questions. We used Lotus 1–2–3 and came up with the following equation: $Y = 45{,}028{,}790 + 4684.41X$ and $R^2 = .94$. This means that first of all, there is a very high correlation between advertising expenses and total sales. Secondly, if the company does not spend any money on advertising, the estimated total sales would be $45,028,790, and if the company spends $18 million, the estimated total sales would be 45,028,790 + 4684 × $18,000,000 = $84 billion. Remember, this is just an example to show how this technique works. In reality, this may not be the final conclusion because there may be other variables having direct impact on total sales. Also in this analysis, we have presumed that the assumptions of regression analysis are valid.

5-12 Types of Decisions and Organizational Levels

DSS is designed to support a decision-maker at any level of the organization. However, the emphasis is on middle and upper levels of the organization, on semiunstructured and unstructured tasks. Decision-makers in different levels of the organization have different information needs and personal and organizational styles, so DSS should consider these differences. Also, different models can be used in different levels. Figure 5-3 shows an organizational pyramid and the different types of decisions that can be found at each level.

Figure 5-3 also shows the potential of an effective DSS in all levels of an organization and reiterates the versatility of DSS as a decision-making aid.

Figure 5-3 Organizational Levels and Types of Decisions

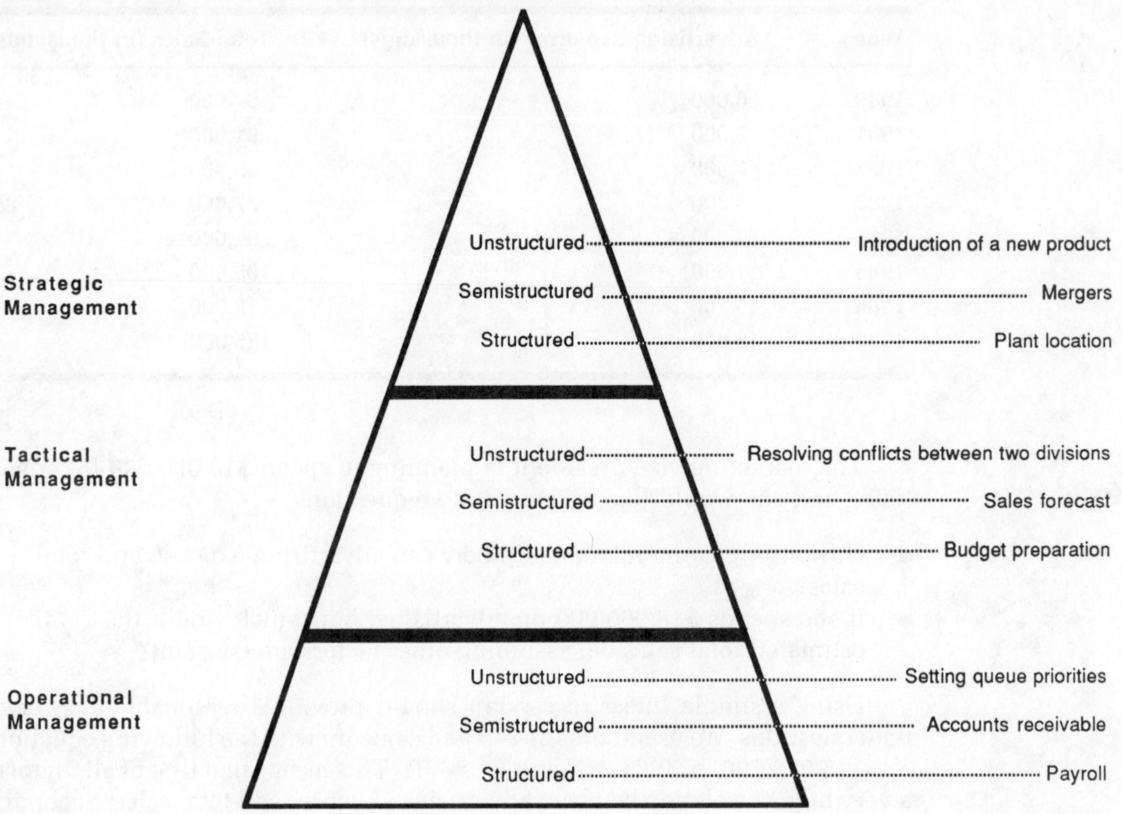

5-13 Business Functions and Modeling Techniques Used in DSS

A DSS can be designed to assist decision-makers in all functional areas of a business. Some areas may benefit more from DSS than others because of the structure available in the specific business function. However, a DSS, if properly designed, should be a valuable tool in all business functions. Table 5-4 highlights areas within each business function that may benefit directly from DSS and models used by a DSS. Appendix C provides more diverse applications of DSS in different disciplines.

5-14 Implementation of Modeling Techniques in DSS Environment

Modeling techniques can be implemented in several ways, with subroutine or prepackaged programs being two of the most common methods. A subroutine can either be developed in-house or purchased commercially. Two other methods for implementation of a modeling technique are models as statements and models as data [17].

Models as statements are simply a series of modeling statements grouped together. This group of statements, if used repeatedly, can serve as a subroutine. In models as data, the modeling statements are created like a data set and are manipulated by data-management functions. At this point, however, these methods are not widely accepted or utilized.

If the subroutine approach is selected, each model is written as one subroutine. Each subroutine can be retrieved with a CALL statement, and a RETURN statement marks the end of a subroutine where control will be transferred back to the main program. The model-base component of DSS has a close analogy to the data base component. This means that a general-purpose program equivalent to DBMS can retrieve the model-base component of a DSS. Fig. 5-4 shows this process graphically. The general-purpose program Model Base Management System (MBMS) has a built-in facility for access, manipulation, and updating of these subroutines.

SPSS (statistical package for social sciences) is a good example of a subroutine oriented package. A variety of statistical, forecasting, and optimization problems can be solved with it. If the user is interested in a particular analysis not included in the package, that analysis can be developed in-house. Table 5-5 highlights the important features of SPSS and SPSS/PC. Table 5-6 highlights the important features of SAS and SAS/PC.

There are a number of commercial packages on the market known as DSS products or DSS generators able to perform a variety of modeling analyses. We provide a thorough coverage of these products in Appendix A. Tables 5-7 and 5-8 provide basic capabilities of Lotus 1–2–3 and IFPS (Interactive Financial Planning System) as modeling DSS products.

Table 5-4 ▪ DSS in Different Business Functions

Business Functions	Particular Area	Model Used by DSS
Accounting	Cost Accounting	Inventory models
Corporate planning	Budgeting	Allocation models
Distribution	Effective distribution	Linear programming/ transportation
Engineering	Product design	Simulation, capital budgeting
Finance	Cash flow analysis	Simulation
Inventory/warehousing	Inventory problems	EOQ, EMQ
Investment	Investment structure	Portfolio models
Manufacturing	Waiting-line problems	Queuing
Marketing	Advertising problems	Simulation, allocation models
Purchasing	Vendor performance	Combined models
Personnel	Skill Evaluation/promotion	Statistical models
Sales	Sales forecast	Forecasting models

Figure 5-4 Model Implementation in DSS Environment

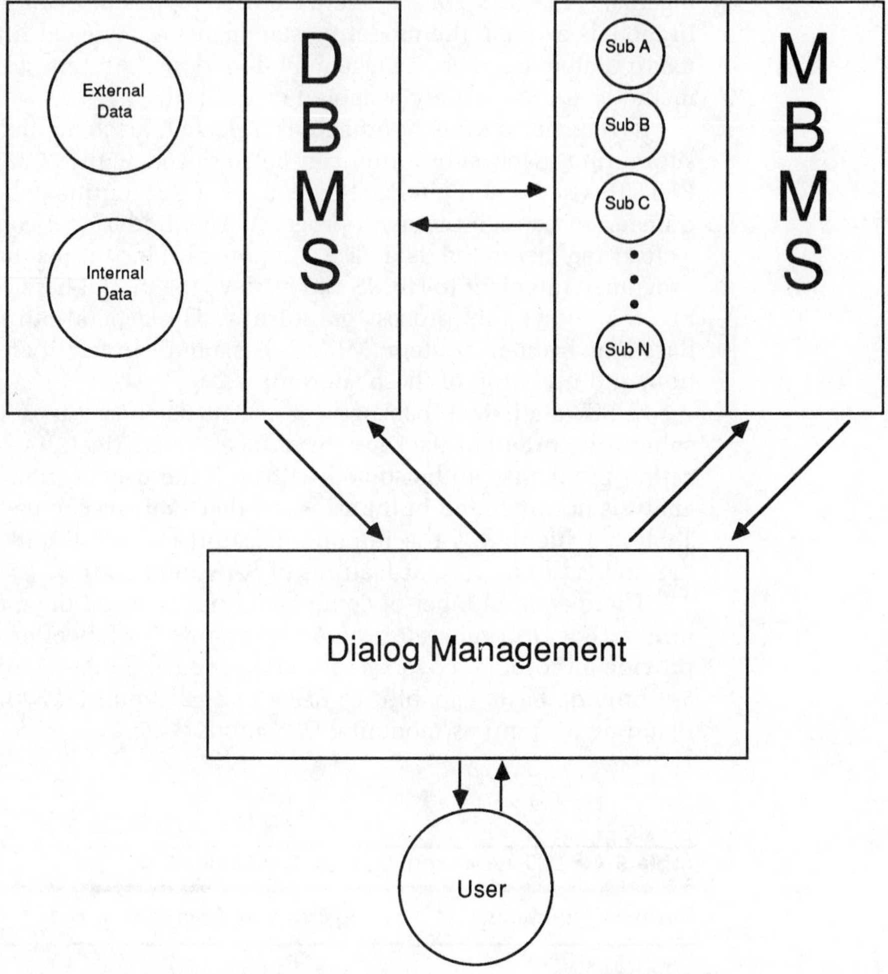

Table 5-5 ▪ SPSS and SPSS/PC + Family

Data entry and editing procedure
Direct interface between SPSS/PC with SPSS-X, Lotus, and dBase
File handling routines
Descriptive statistics including categorical, correlation, regression, and analysis of variance
Report writing and plotting functions
Advanced statistics, including factor, cluster, log linear, discriminant analyses, and multivariate analysis of variance
Time series analysis
Forecasting including curve fitting, smoothing, regression, and Box-Jenkins
Full-color "snapshot" graphics
Tabulation analysis
Direct interface with other graphics programs

Table 5-6 ▪ SAS and SAS/PC + Family

Information storage and retrieval
Full-screen editing
Data modification and interactive programming
Report writing
Diverse statistical analysis including regression, multivariate, discriminant, cluster analyses
Survival analysis
Scoring procedures
Tabulation analysis
Color graphics and plotting
Analysis of variance
Forecasting and time series analysis
Software interface with graphic and OR packages
Financial analysis and planning
Optimization models

Table 5-7 ▪ Lotus as a Modeling DSS Product

Feature	Examples
Arithmetic operations	+, −,*, /
Predefined functions	@EXP, @RAND, @SORT, @NPV, @MAX, @MIN,
Forecasting support	Simple and multiple regressions
Programming support	Extensive programming support by using Macro commands, such as BRANCH, FOR, IF
Graphic support	Line, bar, pie, stacked-bar, and XY
Data base support	Sort, different search
Direct DSS support	Table handling with 1 and 2 variables
Matrix operations	Manipulation of up to 90-by-90 matrix

Table 5-8 ▪ IFPS as a Modeling DSS Product

Feature	Examples
Arithmetic operations	+, −, *, /
Predefined functions	NPVS, IRR, BCRATIO
Forecasting support	Time series, exponential smoothing, simple and multiple regression
Programming support	Extensive nonprocedural programming support
Graphic support	Extensive graphic capabilities
Direct DSS support	Simulation, what-if, goal seeking
Matrix operations	Extensive matrix operations available

Table 5-9 ▪ Main Capabilities of a DSS Product

Data base capabilities
Spreadsheet capabilities
General modeling capabilities
Graphic capabilities
Statistical capabilities
Forecasting capabilities
Micro-mainframe linkage
What-if capabilities
Goal-seeking capabilities
Sensitivity analysis capabilities

The variety of packages available on the market makes the task of selection difficult. We provide a comprehensive and integrated model for DSS product selection and evaluation in Chapter 9. For now, Table 5-9 summarizes the minimum capabilities a package must possess in order to perform data analysis, modeling analysis, or both.

5-15 Interaction between Model Base and Data Base Components

There is a two-way relationship between the model base and data base components of a DSS. Figure 5-5 illustrates this relationship graphically.

Models receive their input data from the data base. This input generates integrity in the information generated by the DSS, since all models use the same data base. At the same time the models can input information generated by their analysis to the data base, making this new information available to all models for future analysis.

Being able to return data generated by analysis to the data base is one advantage of modeling analysis in a DSS environment over traditional modeling analysis. In traditional modeling analysis, each model has access only to its own data set, creating a possible inconsistency in the final result because separate and independent data sets may be created and updated differently. In a DSS environment, all data are stored, manipulated, and updated by a DBMS, nullifying the issue of consistency.

5-16 Interaction between Model Base and Dialog Management

The linkage between the dialog management and model base is also a two-way relationship. A user may request an analysis using a specific model, and the model base may query the data base for the necessary data. The necessary data are sent to the model, and the model base performs the analysis and then sends the result back to the user. Such a process can be iterative and continuous and continues until the user stops the process or exits that routine. Figure 5-6 illustrates this process [17].

Figure 5-5 Interaction Between Data Base and Model Base Components

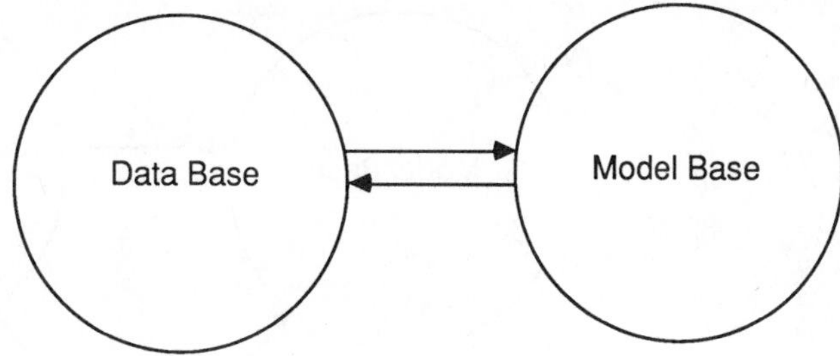

5-17 Summary

This chapter discussed the second component of a DSS, a model base. Like the other two components, it is essential for a successful DSS design. Types of modeling techniques used in DSS were introduced. Some of the problems associated with traditional modeling techniques and how these problems are resolved in a DSS enviroment were highlighted. Methods used for implementation of a model base in a DSS environment and basic capabilities of Lotus and IFPS as DSS modeling products were also discussed. General capabilities of SPSS and SAS were introduced.

Review Questions

1. What is a model?

2. Why is modeling needed in a DSS environment?

3. What are the ingredients of a model?

4. What are the steps for building a model?

5. What is the difference between modeling analysis and data analysis? Can both types of analysis generate the same information? If yes, how? If not, why?

6. How are the limitations of traditional modeling techniques resolved or partially resolved in a DSS environment?

7. What modeling capabilities are needed to build a DSS for the design and choice phases of decision making?

8. Give some examples of optimization models.

9. Give some examples of nonoptimization models.

10. Give some examples of forecasting models.

11. How can a DSS assist accounting functions of an organization? Marketing functions? Manufacturing? Personnel?

12. How do you implement a modeling technique in a DSS?

13. Aside from Lotus and IFPS, what are some other DSS products with Lotus and IFPS type capabilities?

14. To design a DSS for budgeting analysis, what modeling techniques are needed?

Figure 5-6 Relationships among the Three Components of a DSS

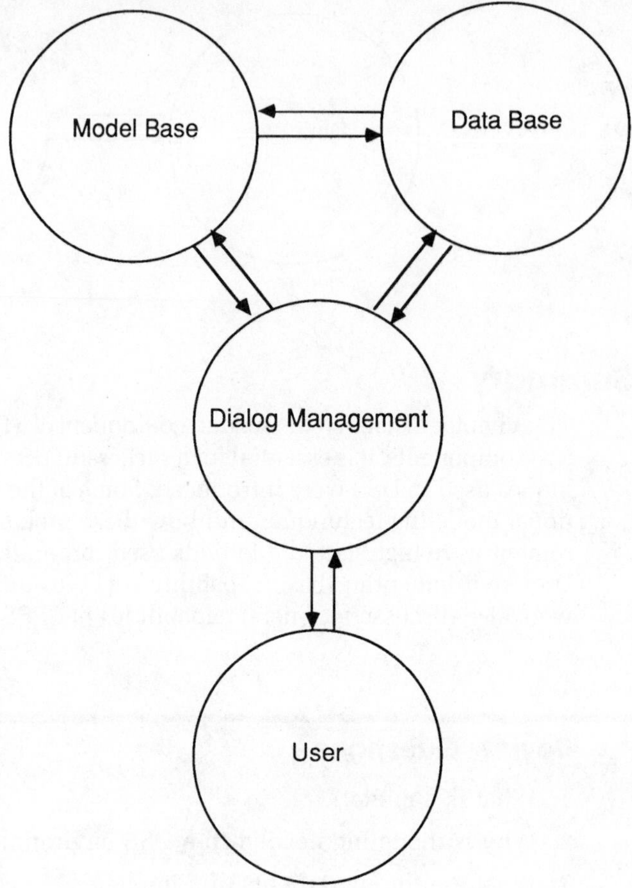

Projects

1. Research FRAMEWORK and IFPS/Personal as DSS modeling products. Which product is a stronger choice? Why?

2. Consult the computer center of your school or an organization with which you are familiar, and identify three modeling packages available. What are the general capabilities of these packages? What are their specific uses?

3. You have been asked to design a forecasting DSS to predict the enrollment of a 4-year college. Which model should be used and what data are needed? How are you going to implement this modeling task?

4. Which model(s) discussed in this chapter may be the most helpful for a community bank? Why? How may this model improve the effectiveness of the financial officers of the bank?

5. What is needed to design a DSS for the allocation of the advertising budget? Which model may be used here?

6. Research SAS as one of the popular modeling tools. What are some of the specific tasks that can be handled by this package? How is SAS/PC different from SAS/mainframe?

7. Compare and contrast SAS and SPSS. In your opinion, which one is a more powerful tool in a DSS environment?

8. Using Lotus 1–2–3, IFPS, or any other package with which you are familiar, design an on-line forecasting DSS. The model should ask the user for the past 10 years of data on total sales. Based on the data, the system should generate the forecast of total sales for the next period using simple regression. The model should also generate all the statistics needed for such a model. Use a DSS tool such as BASIC or FORTRAN and design the same system. Which method is easier?

9. Using any DSS tool or generator with which you are familiar, design a simple DSS for inventory decisions. Your system should be fully interactive and it should generate EOQ and EMQ based on diverse input data. For specific formulas for these models consult reference [1].

Key Terms

Model
Model base
Mathematical models
Statistical models
Model construction
Modeling analysis
Data analysis
Traditional modeling techniques
Optimization models
Nonoptimization models
Optimizing
Satisficing
Linear programming models
Assignment models
Transportation models
Network models
Local area network (LAN)
PERT (program evaluation review technique)
CPM (critical path method)
MOST (management operation system technique)
LOB (line of balance)
Inventory models
Portfolio models
Dynamic programming models
Nonlinear optimization models
Forecasting models
Regression models
Decision tree
Simulation models
EOQ (economic order quantity)
EMQ (economic manufacturing quantity)
Queuing problems
Subroutine
SPSS (Statistical Package for Social Sciences)
SAS
Lotus 1–2–3
IFPS (Interactive Financial Planning System)

References

[1] Anderson, D. K., D. J. Sweeny, and T. A. Williams. 1988. *An Introduction to Management Science*, 5th ed. St. Paul, Minn.: West Publishing Company.

[2] Bonczek, R. H., C. W. Holsapale, and A. B. Whinston. 1979. Computer Based Support of Organizational Decision-Making. *Decision Sciences* 10, no. 2 (April): 268–91.

[3] Bonczek, R. H., C. W. Holsapale, and A. B. Whinston. 1980. The Evolving Roles of Models in Decision Support Systems. *Decision Sciences* 11, no. 2 (April): 337–56.

[4] Brennan, T. J., and Jon Elam. 1986. Enhanced Capabilities for Model-Based Decision Support Systems. In *DSS Putting Theory into Practice* by R. H. Sprague, Jr. and H. J. Watson. Englewood Cliffs, N.J.: Prentice-Hall, Inc.,pp. 130–37.

[5] Eden, C., and D. Sims. 1981. Subjectivity in Problem Identification. *Interfaces* 11, no. 1 (February): 68–74.

[6] Edwards, Allen L. 1976. *An Introduction to Linear Regression and Correlation*, 2d ed. New York: W. H. Freeman and Company.

[7] Harnett, Donald L., and James L. Murphy. 1980. *Introductory Statistical Analysis*, 2d ed. Reading, Mass.: Addison-Wesley Publishing Company.

[8] Hayes, R. H., and R. L. Nolan. 1974. What Kind of Corporate Modeling Functions Best. *Harvard Business Review* (May-June): 102–12.

[9] Heiller, F. S., and G. J. Lieberman. 1974. *Operations Research*, 2d ed. San Francisco: Holden-Day, Inc.

[10] Iannone, A. L. 1971. *Management Program Planning With PERT, MOST and LOB*. Englewood Cliffs, N.J.: Prentice-Hall, Inc.

[11] Little, J. D. C. 1970. Models and Managers: The Concept of a Decision Calculus. *Management Science* (April): 466–85.

[12] McKenney, J. L., and P. G. W. Keen. 1974. How Managers' Minds Work. *Harvard Business Review* (May-June): 79–90.

[13]Mintzberg, H., D. Raisinghan, and A. Theoret. 1976. The Structure of "Unstructured" Decision Processes. *Administrative Science Quarterly* 21, no. 2 (June): 246–75.

[14] Mittra, Sitansu S. 1976. PERT, LOB and MOST: United for More Efficient Project Scheduling. *Supervisory Management (November): 30–35.*

[15] Rivett, P. 1980. *Model Building for Decision Analysis*. New York: John Wiley & Sons.

[16] Scott, J. H. 1978. The Management Science Opportunity: A Systems Development Management Viewpoint. *MIS Quarterly* 2, no. 4 (December): 59–61.

[17] Sprague, H. Ralph Jr., and Eric C. Carlson. 1982. *Building Effective Decision Support Systems*. Englewood Cliffs, N.J.: Prentice-Hall, Inc., pp. 256–78.

[18] Taseen, Jose, and Arshad A. Tomasini. 1986. Evaluation of Forecasting Methods for Decision Support. *International Journal of Forecasting* (Netherlands) 2, no. 2: 139–52.

[19] Stott, K. L., Jr., and B. W. Douglas. 1981. A Model-Based Decision Support System for Planning and Scheduling Ocean-Borne Transportation. *Interfaces* 11, no. 4 (August): 1–10.

6 Dialog Management for DSS

6-1 Introduction

This chapter discusses the third important component of DSS: dialog management. First, it treats the importance of dialog management for successful DSS design and utilization. Then it explains the major types of dialog used for DSS design as well as future dialog—natural language processing. It also covers hardware and software support for successful design and utilization of the dialog component of DSS, and highlights the important criteria for dialog selection in a DSS environment. It concludes with a discussion on graphics and the strengths and weaknesses of this technique used as dialog by DSS users.

6-2 What Is Dialog Management?

Dialog management can be defined as a combination of software, hardware, and people that enables the user to interact with a DSS. It can be defined in a broader sense as the entire user/system interface. Dialog management, or user/system interface, is generally the most important component of a DSS for a typical DSS user. To many users, the dialog component is the entire system.

Two views of the user/system interface must be examined more closely: user view and designer view. The user view is the way in which the system appears and functions for the user, whereas the designer view is concerned with the construction of the dialog system. Technical aspects play an important role for the designer of the dialog system. The user view is concerned with the simplicity and functionality of the interface, but the designer's view is concerned with the simplicity and soundness of the system from the technical standpoint. These issues are discussed in detail in this chapter.

6-3 Types of Dialogs

Any DSS can be used and operated by one of the following methods [1, 7]:

- Scheduled reports (periodic reports)
- Question and answer
- Menu
- Command language
- Input form/output form
- Input-in-context-of-output
- Combination
- Natural language interface

Dialog can be either direct or indirect. In direct dialog, the user operates the DSS. In indirect dialog, the user does not directly use and operate the system; instead, a third party (intermediary) operates the system and submits the result to the user. The intermediary can play many roles in the organization. Let us describe different types of dialog within each category.

6-4 Indirect Dialog

Indirect dialog can include generating scheduled reports, using a staff clerk as a "go-between," and relying on a staff analyst for advice and assistance.

Scheduled Reports

Scheduled reports such as monthly financial reports, have been the most commonly used type of user/system interface in computer-based information systems. Any of these systems, including DSS, can generate periodic reports. Based on differing organizational schemes, these reports can include diverse information presented in various formats. Advantages of the scheduled report interface include simplicity and versatility of application; generation of these reports requires no direct interaction with the DSS. However, report formats tend to be inflexible and, in many cases, not effective. The reports are generally produced on a regular basis and, regardless of changes in the existing situation, provide the same information over and over. The effectiveness of this type of interface may be improved by utilizing exception reporting, which means the system will generate reports only when there is a case that needs to be reported. Exception reporting gives the user the capacity to request a detailed report of transactions affecting only a particular area.

Staff Clerk

A DSS can be designed to be used and operated by an individual or group of individuals other than the end-users themselves. The operator—in this case the staff clerk—serves as the go-between for the DSS and the end-user. The end-user can request a report, and the staff clerk operates the system to generate the desired reports. For example, a staff member might generate a personnel status report for the vice president of personnel. The advantage of this type of interface is that the end-user does not need to have any knowledge of the system. However, such interface lacks the advantage of direct interaction between the system and the end-user. Staff clerk dialog may be more flexible than the scheduled report style because the user requests that he or she exercise some control over the system. The decision-maker asks for a report if the particular report is needed.

Staff Analyst

The staff analyst interface is very similar to the staff clerk interface; however, the analyst is capable not only of operating the system but also providing interpretive advice to the end-user [1]. With complex decisions that involve the input of several experts, this type of user/system interface may be quite powerful. Also, the staff analyst may assist decision-makers who are not familiar with the different analyses done by a DSS to avoid the amateur use of these analyses. This type of interface may become very common in the near future when desktop computers put massive data and modeling analyses at the fingertips of nonexperts. An example of this type of user/system interface is a financial analyst in an organization who generates financial reports for the vice president of finance and at the same time interprets the results and makes recommendations.

6-5 Direct Dialog

Since DSS is usually designed for interactive use and for ad hoc applications, indirect dialog is not a suitable type of user/system interface in a variety of cases. When direct dialog is used, it simply means that the user and the DSS interact directly and there is no third party involved in the process. A brief explanation of different types of direct dialog follows [7].

Question and Answer

In the question-and-answer user/system interface, the system asks a series of questions and the user answers them. The DSS questions may vary depending upon prior user answers. Based on this conversation, a report or a response will be generated.

Figure 6-1 Question and Answer Dialog

```
Welcome to Online Automated. Please answer all the questions.
When you are ready press the Enter key.
_____________________________________________________________

   * What is the employee name? John Brown
   * What is the employee's marital status (M, S, or D)? M
   * What is the employee's degree status (BS, MS, PhD)? BS
   * Does the employee speak German (Y, N)? Y
   * Has the employee been employed over 10 years (Y, N)? Y
   * Do you have another question to ask? (Y, N)? N
_____________________________________________________________

   John Brown qualifies for an overseas assignment. If you
need another inquiry, press the Enter key. Thank you.

>>>>>>>>>>>>>>>>>>>>>>>>>>>>>>>>>>>>>>>>>>>>>>>>>>>>>>>>>>>>>>>>
```

For example, a personnel DSS may ask for the following information:

- Name of the employee
- Marital status
- Degree status
- Languages spoken
- Length of employment

Based on the answers given by the user, the system may report the name of an employee who qualifies for an overseas assignment.

This type of dialog is easy to use; however, it may be slow and not suitable for experienced users (too elementary). Figure 6-1 illustrates an example of this type of dialog.

Menu

A menu interface is probably the most common method of direct dialog. In this type of dialog the system presents a series of choices, and the user selects one of these options. Based on the selection, a response may be generated or the user may be transferred to another menu or submenu. This type of interface may be faster than question-and-answer dialog; however, it may become tedious for an experienced user.

Lotus 1-2-3 is a good example of a menu system. The user can select an option by pointing to the option or by typing the first letter of the option. Once a selection is made, Lotus will put the user into another menu and/or ask for further input.

Figure 6-2 illustrates an example of menu dialog. The menu gives the user eight choices. The decision-maker can either move the cursor to one of these choices and press the enter key or he or she can type the choice number and press the enter key. In any case, the menu choice puts the user in the selected option. For example, if the user chooses option 1, which is the spreadsheet programs, he or she may be given another menu that lists all the spreadsheet programs included in the system, such as Lotus, SuperCalc, and VisiCalc. From this menu, the desired option is chosen, and the user is in the program of his or her choice. A menu dialog usually brings the user back to the main menu.

Command Language

A command language interface consists of a series of commands or short codes. Based on the user's request, which is communicated to the system using the codes, the system generates a response. For example, (1) the user may type NPV (net present value), in which case the system calculates the net present value of a given portfolio, and (2) the user may specify the parameters of a graph in a DRAW or PLOT command, and the system then generates the specified graph.

The command language interface is similar to programming or "macro" programming. Macro programming uses a series of short codes or simple commands which have special meaning to the user. For example LIST, DRAW,

Figure 6-2 Menu Dialog

```
Welcome to the Community Microcomputing Lab. Type the Number
of your choice or just move the cursor to the desired option
and then press the Enter key.

>>>>>>>>>>>>>>>>>>>>>>>>>>>>>>>>>>>>>>>>>>>>>>>>>>>>>>>>>>>>>>>>

--> 1) Spreadsheet programs

    2) Database programs

    3) Word processing programs

    4) Graphics Programs

    5) Statistical Analysis programs

    6) Listing of the entire directory

    7) Exiting to disk operating system

    8) Exiting the system
```

Figure 6-3 Command Language Dialog

```
? Solve                      (User types this)

? Plot                       (User types this)

Enter plot options           (IFPS asks the user)

? Plot Revenue, Income       (User types this)


(Now IFPS plots these two variables from a given model using
its default settings)
```

PLOT, etc. It is faster than the other two types of direct dialog, and it is more suitable for experienced users. Lotus 1-2-3 macros can be considered a command language for the package. Simple user/system interfaces can be designed using macros in Lotus. Figure 6-3, which illustrates the PLOT command in Interactive Financial Planning System (IFPS) [12], is an example of this type of dialog.

Input Form/Output Form

When there is a correspondence between the input and the output, the input/output type of interface can be very effective. In this interface the system provides an input form for which the user supplies data and/or commands. Based on these inputs, the system may generate either a response or another input form for further questioning.

For example, an employee checklist that requires five inputs from the user may appear on the screen. When the user supplies the necessary data, the system generates an output, which may be a listing of the selected employees based on specified criteria. The system may present another input form in order to ask more questions of the user. This type of interface is suitable for both experienced and inexperienced users, and the response time is relatively high. (In some ways this interface is similar to question/answer interface, but in the latter there is no correspondence between the input and the output.) Figure 6-4 illustrates an example of this type of dialog from query-by-example [7, p. 69].

Input-In-Context-Of-Output

Input-in-context-of-output is a special case of the input form/output form interface; however, the interface process is significantly different and deserves special attention. In this type of interface both the input and the output forms are combined, and the user always provides response in the context of the previous output from the system.

The system may present an output such as a table, which the user may fill in or from which the user may select items. This will modify the current output or generate a new output.

For example, a screen that displays a graph and a series of variables generating a financial forecast may be given to a user. The user may either add new variables or input new values for the existing variables. When the new values are inputted, the system may present a new screen with a different graph and different values. This type of interface works well for experienced users and for decisions that involve a series of variables and parameters to be determined by the user and can be very effective for model building and graph design, both of which require numerous user inputs.

Figure 6-4 Input Form/Output Form Dialog

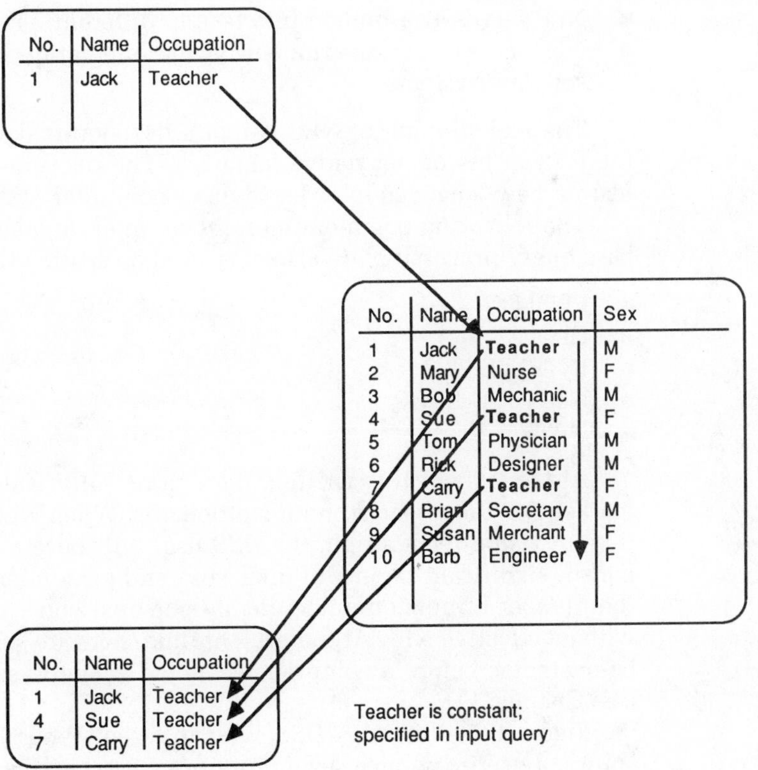

Combination

A DSS can present all the options we have just discussed and allow the user to select his or her preference. Conversely, one type of dialog may utilize more than one option. For example, in Lotus 1-2-3 the user selects a menu option, which in turn invokes a command.

6-6 Future Dialog: Natural Language Processing

For all these types of interfaces the user must have certain knowledge about his or her particular DSS, and the decision-maker must follow a restricted format. In the majority of dialog styles, the user must know how to operate a keyboard and specify certain features. But computer scientists have been working on a new type of interface called natural language processing (NLP) [11, 14], which permits increased flexibility for the user of a DSS. For example, a user may ask:

PLOT THE TOTAL SALES OF ALL THE NORTHWEST REGIONS
TELL ME THE TOP THREE SALESPERSONS IN THE STATE OF OREGON
TELL ME WHICH MONTH GENERATED THE HIGHEST TOTAL SALES

As Lawrence Harris [13] mentions, the use of NLP includes two important applications:

- NLP serves as a human interface to different data base systems.
- NLP serves as an instrument for the integration of a variety of traditional software systems.

The real strength of NLP is that a decision-maker can communicate with the DSS in his or her native language. The decision-maker does not need to learn a new language in order to use a computer system and/or a DSS.

The following common natural computer languages already used for data base query processing are also classified as artificial languages [2, 11]:

- PROLOG
- CLOUT
- INTELLECT
- NATURALLINK
- NATPACK

At the time of this writing, there is no fully workable NLP dialog on the market. But the research sounds promising. When NLP is combined with voice [9] and vision recognition, the DSS user will have a much easier time. There may be significant savings of time, cost, and personnel and a drastic increase in the number of noncomputer literate persons who would like to use the DSS with an effective NLP. At the present time there are several problems that must be overcome before a comprehensive and easy-to-use NLP becomes available (see Chapter 12).

Figure 6-5 illustrates DSS with different types of dialog. As this figure shows, a user may have several options for accessing a DSS.

Figure 6-5 DSS and Different Types of Dialog

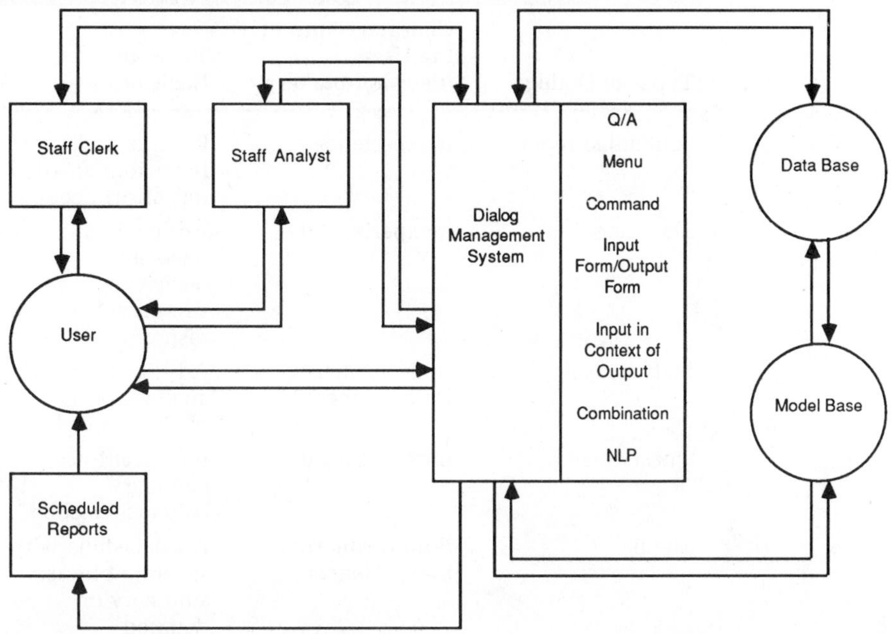

6-7 Types of Dialogs and Different Users

As discussed earlier, using different dialogs involves trade-offs. Also, selection by a DSS user of a dialog type is directly related to his or her status, computer knowledge, style, and preference in using computers in the organization. Each type of user/system interface has advantages and disadvantages and may be more suitable for one particular user and/or a particular decision than another. Table 6-1 [3, 6] summarizes the different types of dialog and the different users in an organization.

6-8 Hardware and Software Support for Dialog Management

To design an effective dialog system, two important components are needed. These include hardware and software components. The ultimate goal of a DSS designer is the optimum combination of these two components for the most effective design of a dialog system. The hardware support is straightforward and may include devices used in general input/output operations of any computer system [16, 18]. Table 6-2 provides a listing of these devices. Table 6-3 summarizes different types of hardware that have been commonly utilized in the DSS environment and the advantages/disadvantages of each. Let us briefly explain some of these commonly used devices.

Table 6-1 ▪ Different Users and Different Types of Dialog

Types of Dialog	Characteristics of the User (decision-maker)	Types of Decisions	Organizational Focus
Scheduled reports	Inexperienced	Routine and recurring; detailed responses needed	Operational management
Staff clerk	Inexperienced	Ad hoc and one-shot decisions; summary response needed	Middle and strategic levels
Staff analyst	Both (primarily inexperienced)	Ad hoc decisions; analysis of the response needed	Middle and primarily strategic level
Question/answer	Inexperienced	Infrequent use; summary response needed	All levels (primarily middle and operational)
Menu	Both (primarily inexperienced)	All decisions with several options; summary or detailed	Primarily middle and strategic levels
Command language	Experienced	All decisions; summary response needed	All levels (primarily middle and operational)
Input form/output form	Experienced	Routine decisions; summary response needed	Operational and middle
Input-in-context of-the-output	Experienced	Routine decisions; summary response needed	Operational and middle
Combination	Both	Routine and non-routine decisions	Operational and middle
Natural language processing	Both (primarily inexperienced)	All decisions (primarily when summary response needed)	All levels (primarily middle and strategic)

Keyboards are the first (after the punch card) and most widely used input device. Originally, keyboards were designed with a configuration very similar to a typewriter. In recent years, there have been several modifications. In order to make the user's task easier, the majority of keyboards now include control keys, arrow keys, function keys, and several special keys. Keyboards are capable of performing any type of computer input task. However, for some special tasks, the use of a scanner or a mouse is faster and more accurate.

Touch screens are a combination of several input devices. First of all, they are touch devices; second, they work with a menu; third, they can also be classified as vision devices. Some touch screens rely upon light detection in order to determine which item from the menu is chosen. Others accomplish the same task by activating a pressure-sensitive device. Touch screens may be easier to use than typical keyboards; however, in some cases they may not be highly accurate due to misreading the chosen instruction.

Light pens are similar to conventional pens and are connected to the terminal through a cable. They are particularly useful to engineers, drafters, and designers for graphic applications. When the pen is located at a particular location on the CRT, the information in this particular spot is sent to the system. The data can be characters, lines, or blocks. This device is easy to use, inexpensive, and accurate.

A *mouse* is a device used for rapid cursor movement. The mouse is moved around under the user's control until the cursor is located on the desired item; the user then pushes a button to enter a command or an instruction.

A *data tablet* device is a small pad and a pen classified within the vision input category. Any menus generated by the user are presented on the tablet and any selections are indicated via the pen. Its widest current application is in CAD and CAM, where the user draws on the tablet with the pen rather than using a CRT or light pen.

Bar code readers are optical scanners that use laser light to read bar codes. These devices are very fast and accurate and have many applications in inventory systems, data entry, and tracking systems.

Optical character readers (OCRs) work on the same principle as do optical scanners. However, since there are special characters, upper- and lowercase

Table 6-2 ▪ General Input/Output Devices for Dialog Management

Input Devices	Output Devices
Bar code	Camera
Camera	Dot matrix printer
Graphics tablet	Flat panel display
Keyboard	Ink jet printer
Light pen	Laser printer
Magnetic ink character reader	Letter-quality printer
Mouse	Thermal and electrostatic printer
Optical character reader	Plotter
Sensor	Video display terminal (VDT), cathode-ray tube (CRT)
Touch technology	Voice synthesizer
Digitizer	
Voice recognition unit	

Table 6-3 ▪ Hardware Support for Dialog Management

Type of Device	Advantages	Disadvantages
Keyboard	Versatile	Lack of familiarity with different keys by many users
Touch screen	Easy to use	May not always generate a desired report; also may be limited in use
Light pen	Lightweight, less space, easy to use, fast, accurate	May make the user tired; limited software support
Mouse	Occupies more space than light pen, easy to use	Limited software support
Data tablet	Very effective for CAD/CAM* applications	Limited use
Bar code reader	Speed and accuracy	Limited use
Optical character reader	Speed and accuracy	Limited use
Voice-recognition system	Ease of use	Not available yet; the present ones are very limited

*CAD (computer-aided design) and CAM (computer-aided manufacturing) are applications of computer-based information systems and DSS in a manufacturing environment.

characters, and special spacing, using OCRs is more difficult than using bar code readers. However, these systems have achieved remarkable success and have been improving steadily.

Voice-recognition systems, the newest types of dialog, have attracted much attention in recent years. The principle behind these systems is to enable the user to talk to the system and formulate queries. The integration of voice-recognition systems, NLP, and menu systems should be the ultimate in dialog for any DSS user. However, at the time of this writing, there is no workable, full-feature voice recognition system on the market. Many problems must be overcome before we can have an effective voice-recognition system [9, 17]. These issues are discussed in detail in Chapter 12.

The software support of dialog management can be provided by commercial packages or developed internally [5]. If an organization chooses to implement the dialog component in-house, a high-level language such as Pascal or FORTRAN is usually selected.

A more viable and comprehensive option would be to utilize the dialog component of a DSS product or DSS generator. Appendix A provides a comprehensive coverage of numerous DSS products on the market. The majority of DSS generators offer an easy-to-use and comprehensive dialog component.

6-9 Criteria for a User-Friendly Dialog

Most DSS users are not computer experts. They are experts in their own fields and see the DSS as a productivity and survival tool. Dialog should be easy to learn and use and should match the organizational and personal style of the user. In choosing a dialog system several factors must be carefully considered [15]:

1. *Simplicity.* Simplicity indicates user-friendliness, a familiar concept in the computer field. As mentioned earlier, different types of interfaces may be suitable for different users or applications. Dialog should be straightforward with a minimum amount of computer jargon.
2. *Consistency.* Different parts of the system should utilize the same command for a specified task, thus providing consistency. A good example is the Delete command in Lotus 1-2-3, which deletes a record in both a worksheet and a data base. However, there are many counter examples in the computer field. To delete a file in MS-DOS the command is DEL; BASIC uses KILL; Wordstar uses Y; other systems use Release and Purge.
3. *Familiarity with the user's world.* The system prompts should be designed to match a user's established thought patterns. For instance, a date is presented as year-month-day in the majority of systems. This is a logical format for programmers because it makes sorting very easy. However, DSS users are used to a month-day-year format.
4. *Informativeness.* Most systems give you only error messages when you do something wrong. Very few, if any, indicate the source of errors and suggest remedies. A good dialog system informs the user about how to get out of a problem and continue with the process.
5. *Flexibility.* Flexibility generally pertains to entering and exiting a system. A good dialog helps a user navigate through the system in any direction. The user should be able to exit from the system from any given location.

Other important issues regarding selection and implementation of an effective dialog system include [5]:

- Training time for DSS users (should be minimal)
- Elapsed time before a user can operate a DSS without help (should be minimal)
- Type and rate of errors (should be minimal with minor errors)
- Time to recover from errors (should be short)
- Warm-up time after time away from the DSS (should be short)
- Attitude toward wanting to use the DSS (should be very positive)

Factors related to user-friendly dialog should serve as a checklist for choosing a DSS generator with a dialog component that matches the preceding criteria.

The designer of a DSS dialog component should use modularity in design to assure the user satisfaction and minimize the consequences of change in user needs and system requirements. This means each function must be performed within one module and each module should be independent from the other modules. Naturally, if a system is designed in this fashion, new requirements can be easily added to the system. The system can be enhanced with minimum effort. We talk about tools and techniques regarding design and implementation of DSS in Chapter 7.

6-10 Graphics as a Prominent Dialog

Graphs and graphic capabilities can be accessed using either direct or indirect dialog. Due to decreasing cost and increasing sophistication of graphics software, this type of data format has gained popularity in recent years. In the DSS environment graphs are used [8, 10]:

- To improve communication
- To support presentation
- To organize complex networks (PERT/CPM)
- To enhance group decision making
- To monitor financial status
- To facilitate plant management
- To facilitate budget management
- To monitor trends in the market, in consumer behavior, and in population characteristics
- To analyze cost structure
- To evaluate employee performance

Different types of graphs have been successfully utilized for exhibiting data relationships, for presentations of frequently updated information, for quick decision making where precise accuracy is not essential, and for trend analysis.

A majority of DSS products on the market are now capable of providing a variety of graphs:

- Pie charts
- Scatter plots
- Line and bar graphs
- Stacked-bar graphs
- Maps and flow charts
- Three-dimensional displays

However, the user of DSS must be aware of some of the serious limitations of graphics [8].

As mentioned before, the accuracy a user may expect from a graph is limited. Graphs can facilitate decision making by indicating an area of likely possibilities and/or trends. If an exact calculation is required, however, a graph is seldom capable of producing answers that are sufficiently precise. Another common pitfall is the use of an inappropriate graph for an application. Not all data have the same or even similar attributes. The astute DSS user will select graphs that highlight the aspects of the data to which he or she wishes to draw attention.

6-11 Summary

This chapter explained the third component of a DSS, dialog management. Dialog management for the majority of DSS users is considered to be the entire system. DSS users usually are not concerned with how the system is working, how sophisticated the system is, or what the technical aspects of system design are. However, users are very much concerned with the simplicity of the system. The designers of DSS should consider all the options available as well as the trade-offs before implementation of a particular dialog system. This chapter reviewed the major types of dialog; the advantages and disadvantages of each; and hardware/software support and presented a series of guidelines for successful dialog selection and implementation. It also briefly highlighted the strengths and weaknesses of graphics as a dialog device and data format.

Review Questions

1. What is dialog management?
2. Why is dialog management so important to a DSS user?
3. What is a direct dialog?
4. What is an indirect dialog?
5. Explain the strengths and weaknesses of scheduled reports, staff clerk, and staff analyst as indirect dialog.
6. Explain the strengths and weaknesses of question/answer, menu, and command language as direct dialog.
7. When should you use input form/output form as a dialog device?
8. What are some of the uses of input-in-context-of-output dialog?
9. What are the unique advantages of NLP as a prominent dialog choice?
10. What are some obstacles associated with NLP use at the present time?
11. Are all dialog types suitable for strategic planning? If not, why?
12. Which dialog is the most suitable for operational management personnel? Tactical? Strategic?
13. State two types of hardware and two types of software to support a dialog system.
14. What are some of the limitations of the keyboard as an input device?
15. What are some of the uses of touch technology as a dialog system?
16. State several criteria for a user-friendly dialog.
17. What are some of the strengths and weaknesses of graphs as a dialog device?
18. Which decisions can benefit the greatest from graphics: operational management, tactical decisions, or strategic planning? Why?

Projects

1. Among the DSS generators presented in Appendix A, which generator has the best dialog and why? (*Hint:* Use the criteria given in this chapter for user-friendliness.) Why have graphics interfaces such as the mouse and menu systems attracted so much popularity? What are the unique advantages of these types of interfaces compared with the traditional ones?

2. Investigate the dialog management of a DSS with which you are familiar. Can this system be improved in any possible direction?

3. Research one of the NLPs presented in this chapter and analyze its strengths and weaknesses for use as a dialog management.

4. Discuss a dialog system from two perspectives: the managerial designer and the technical designer. What are some of the concerns of each group and why?

5. Research an organization of your choice that is using graphics. In what area have graphics been the most successful? In what area the least successful?

6. Using a DSS tool with which you are familiar, such as FORTRAN or PASCAL, design a menu which gives a user six options. These options may include six different financial analyses by a given system. Repeat the same task; however, this time use a DSS generator such as IFPS, FOCUS, dBASE, or Lotus. Which method is easier? Why?

7. The DSS in Corner Community Bank generates four types of graphs: line, bar, pie, and stacked-bar. What are the specific uses of each graph in the bank? For which analysis might these graphs not be useful? Investigate a DSS generator that provides these types of graphs.

Key Terms

Dialog management
User/system interface
User view
Designer view
Scheduled reports
Question and answer
Menu
Command language
Input form/output form
Input-in-context-of-output
Natural language processing
Direct dialog
Indirect dialog
Staff clerk
Staff analyst
Ad hoc applications
Voice recognition
Vision recognition
Keyboard
Mouse
Touch technology
Data tablet
Optical character reader
Bar code
Sensor
Camera as I/O device
Voice as I/O device
Dot matrix printer

Letter-quality printer
Ink jet printer
Thermal and electrostatic printer
Laser printer
Camera output
Plotter
Video display terminal

References

[1] Alter, Steven L. 1980. *Decision Support Systems Current Practices and Continuing Challenges*. Reading, Mass.: Addison-Wesley Publishing Company, pp. 109–142.
[2] Andriole, Stephen J. 1985. The Promise of Artificial Intelligence. *Journal of Systems Management* (July): 8–17.
[3] Attaran, Mohsen, and Hossein Bidgoli. 1986. Developing an Effective Manufacturing Decision Support System. *Business* (October-December): 9–16.
[4] Barbary, Clifton L. 1987. A Database Primer on Natural Language. *Journal of Systems Management* (April): 20–25.
[5] Bennett, John L. 1983. *Building Decision Support Systems*. Reading, Mass.: Addison-Wesley Publishing Company, pp. 41–65.
[6] Bidgoli, Hossein, and Robert R. Harmon. 1987. Marketing Decision Support Systems. *Business Insights* 3, no. 1 (Spring): 20–26.
[7] Carlson, Eric D. 1983. Developing The User Interface for Decision Support Systems. In *Building Decision Support Systems*, by John L. Bennett, Reading, Mass.: Addison-Wesley Publishing Company, pp. 65–88.
[8] DeSanctis, Gerardine. 1984. Computer Graphics as Decision Aids. *Decision Sciences* (Fall): 463–82.
[9] E. F. 1985. Voice Recognition on Intelligent Machines. *Personal Computing* (April): 66.
[10] Evans, Sherli. 1984. Business Graphics Software. *Office Administration and Automation* (May): 35–38.
[11] Fersko-Weiss, Henry. 1985. Natural Language: The Dialog Has Begun. *Personal Computing* 9, no. 11 (November): 93–96.
[12] Gray, Paul. 1983. *Student Guide to IFPS*. New York: McGraw-Hill Book Company.
[13] Harris, Lawrence. 1984. Teaching Computers English Proves Easier Than Training People. *Mini-Micro Systems* 17, no. 15 (December): 163–72.
[14] Johnson, Tim. 1986. NLP Takes Off. *Datamation* (January 15): 91–93.
[15] Lustman, Francois, Pierre Mercier, and Luc Grantton. 1985. A Dialog-Based Architecture for Interactive Information Systems. *Data Base* (Spring): 18–23.
[16] Markoff, John, and Phillip Robinson. 1985. LightTouches. *BYTE* (January): 416–17.
[17] Mordoff, Keith F. 1985. Computerized Voice System Speeds GE Engine Inspection. *Aviation Week and Space Technology* (May 6): 92–93.
[18] Osgood, Donald. 1985. The Koala Pad. *BYTE* (March): 283.
[19] Sprague, Ralph Jr., and Eric D. Carlson. 1982. *Building Effective Decision Support Systems*. Englewood Cliffs, N.J.: Prentice-Hall, Inc., pp. 197–220.
[20] Wofsey, Marvin M. 1984. User Identity Must Precede User Friendly Computer Systems. *Data Management* (December): 15–16.

part three

Putting Theory into Practice

7 Systems Analysis and Design in the DSS Environment

7-1 Introduction

This chapter reviews the principles of systems analysis and design. First it discusses the classic life-cycle approach, explaining its phases. Then it discusses the product life cycle as it relates to the development of a computer-based information system as well as to a DSS. By synthesizing these two approaches the chapter provides a "revised approach," which is more suitable for development of a DSS. It should provide a good background for building an effective DSS, which is discussed in the next chapter.

7-2 Classic Life-Cycle Approach

The classic life-cycle approach, which has been utilized for many years [41, 42, 43] in traditional EDP/MIS design and implementation, is a series of well-defined steps. Understanding this approach should help the user to understand better DSS design and implementation, which employs a special version of this approach. Figure 7-1 illustrates phases involved in the classic life-cycle approach.

Problem Definition

During the problem-definition stage, the user and the designer of the system try to define and understand the problem faced by the organization. This very important step must be undertaken with great care. It is possible to mistakenly identify the symptoms of the problem instead of the problem itself.

Figure 7-1 Phases Involved in Classic Life Cycle Approach

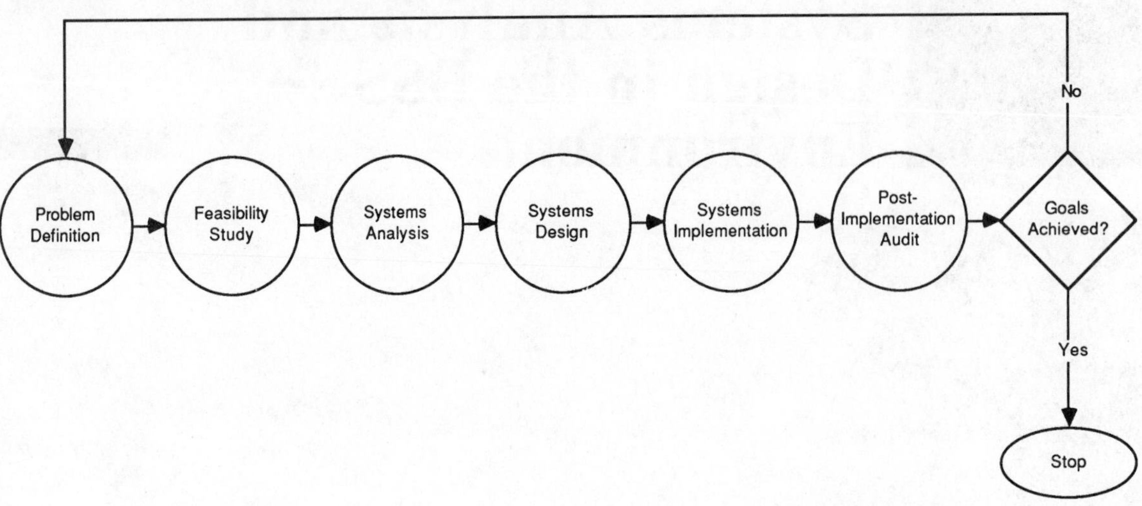

The problem may have been identified internally or brought to the attention of the organization by customers, employees, external agencies, and so forth. The following are some examples of problems in a typical business organization:

Problem 1. Improper allocation of resources
Problem 2. Inaccurate billing system
Problem 3. Inefficient inventory system
Problem 4. Inaccurate budgeting system
Problem 5. Complaints from customers regarding the timeliness of services

In a DSS environment the problem may not be as well defined as these problems are. For example, the problem may be the improvement of competitiveness in the market place or employment of a new technology in order to be able to analyze the environment of the organization in a more thorough manner. Problems in a DSS environment are usually novel, nonrecurring and unstructured.

Feasibility Study

During the feasibility stage of the life cycle, the system analyst or a team of system analysts tries to investigate the feasibility of a solution proposed to resolve the problem. The feasibility study may include the following different dimensions.

Economic feasibility is concerned with the cost or benefit of the system. For example, if the net gain of implementing an inventory system is $250,000 and the cost of implementation is $500,000, the system is not economically feasible. To conduct an economic feasibility study, the systems analyst team must identify all the costs and benefits of the proposed system, which may be either tangible or intangible. Tangible costs include cost of equipment, training, new employees, and so forth. Intangible costs include the social issues related to automation—for example, privacy, security, and employee turnover. Benefits usually include all the cost savings of the new system.

The real challenge for the systems analyst team is accurately assessing intangible costs and benefits. The system analyst should attach a realistic monetary value to intangible costs and then conduct an economic feasibility study.

To make the assessment of intangible benefits clearer, consider an example. Suppose one of the intangible benefits of a new system is improved customer service. One way to assign a monetary value to this benefit is to quantify the intangible benefit. Customer service means maintaining the present total sales and possibly increasing the total sales by a certain percentage in a business organization. If improved customer service means 10% growth, it means 10% of $15,000,000 for Company X, or a $1,500,000 increase in sales. If Company X has a 20% net margin, this means a $300,000 net profit just by increasing the customer service. The same type of analysis can be performed for the assessment of intangible costs.

Technical feasibility is concerned with the technical aspects of the new system. One way to investigate the technical feasibility is to study the state of technology. A proposed solution may not be technically feasible for implementation because the technology does not exist for the implementation of the new system. For example, a voice-activated monitoring system at this point is not technically feasible. However, given today's computer technology, this is not a major problem, and for many proposed solutions the technical support is available.

Lack of technical feasibility may also stem from an organizational deficiency. A specific system may not be feasible because the organization lacks the expertise, time, or personnel required to implement the new system. This has been referred to as a lack of organizational readiness.

Operational feasibility investigates the workability of the proposed system in the organization [43, p. 787]. This dimension may investigate the organization's response to the system, employee reaction, and general feelings toward the system. In traditional EDP/MIS, operational feasibility is not always a choice given to the user. The system may be implemented even if it is somewhat operationally unfeasible (feasibility is a continuum). DSS users, however, are discretionary in their usage, and so operational feasibility becomes an even more important issue than it is in EDP/MIS.

Social feasibility investigates the proposed system within the context of social issues. This dimension is generally concerned with social issues of automation. This may include employee replacement, privacy issues, turnover, employee dissatisfaction, and so forth. An organization may choose not to implement a new system because of the social problems that may be caused by the new system. As discussed in Chapter 8, some of the social issues can be overcome by a series of design measures performed by the systems analyst

Figure 7-2 Different Dimensions of Feasibility Study

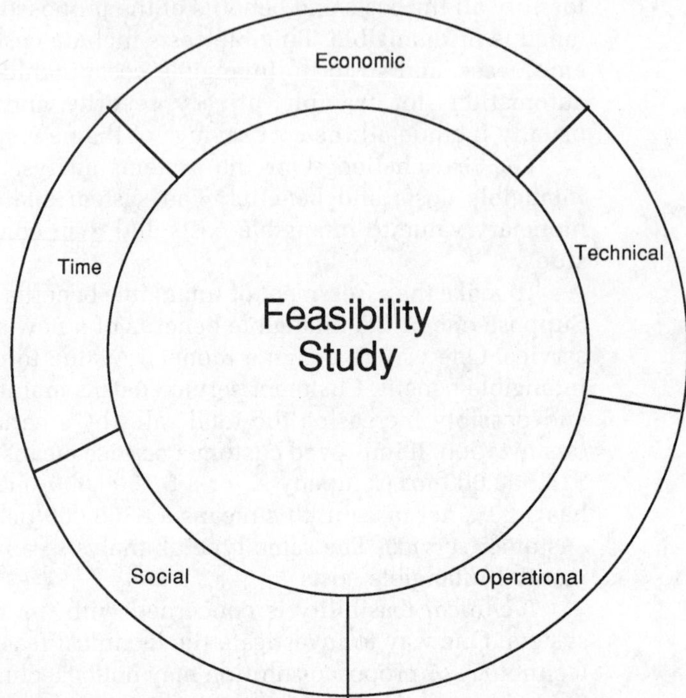

team. However, some of these issues are an inherent part of any automation, and there is no way for complete elimination of such problems.

Finally, a feasibility study may be concerned with the *time*, factor. Let us say a system is feasible economically, technically, operationally and socially; however, it will not be ready within the time frame needed by an organization. If this is the case, you may say the proposed system is not feasible from the time-factor viewpoint. Figure 7-2 illustrates the five dimensions of a feasibility study.

Systems Analysis

The third step in the life-cycle approach is systems analysis. In this phase, the system analyst or a team of analysts specifically defines the problem and come up with some possible alternatives for solving it. A variety of tools may be utilized during this phase:

- Interview
- Questionnaire
- Observation
- Work measurement
- Form investigation and control
- Flowchart
- Data flow diagram (DFD)

The output of this phase, as mentioned earlier, will be a clear problem definition, one or several alternatives, and some initial documentation relating to the operation of the new system.

Interview, questionnaire, and observation are used to understand the problem area better. Graphical tools such as flowcharts and data-flow diagrams (DFDs) are used for highlighting the problem area, gaining a clear understanding of the input/process/output cycle, and eliminating the bottlenecks encountered throughout the entire system operation. Flowcharts usually show the *logic* involved in the system and highlight the detail by using special symbols. DFDs, by using bubbles and arrows, show the *process* in the system and highlight the overall operations of the system. Again, these tools are very useful when the prespecifications can be done, but they may not be suitable if the problem under investigation is unstructured. Figure 7-3 illustrates a typical flowchart and Figure 7-4 depicts a DFD.

Systems Design

During the systems design phase the team of analysts tries to choose the alternative that is the most realistic and presents the highest payoff to the organization. At this point, the details of the proposed solution are outlined. The output produced by the team is a document very similar to a blueprint for implementation, which includes file and data base design, form and report design, documentation design, procedure design, hardware and software selection, and general system specifications.

Systems Implementation

During the implementation phase, the solution is transferred from paper to action. A variety of tasks take place while the implementation phase is underway:

- Acquisition of the new equipment
- Hiring new employees
- Training new employees
- Physical planning and layout design
- Coding
- Testing
- Security and recovery design
- Conversion planning and documentation

When a system is ready to be converted, there are several options available to the designer:

- Parallel conversion
- Phased-in, phased-out conversion
- Direct (crash) conversion
- Pilot conversion

Figure 7-3 An Example of a Flowchart

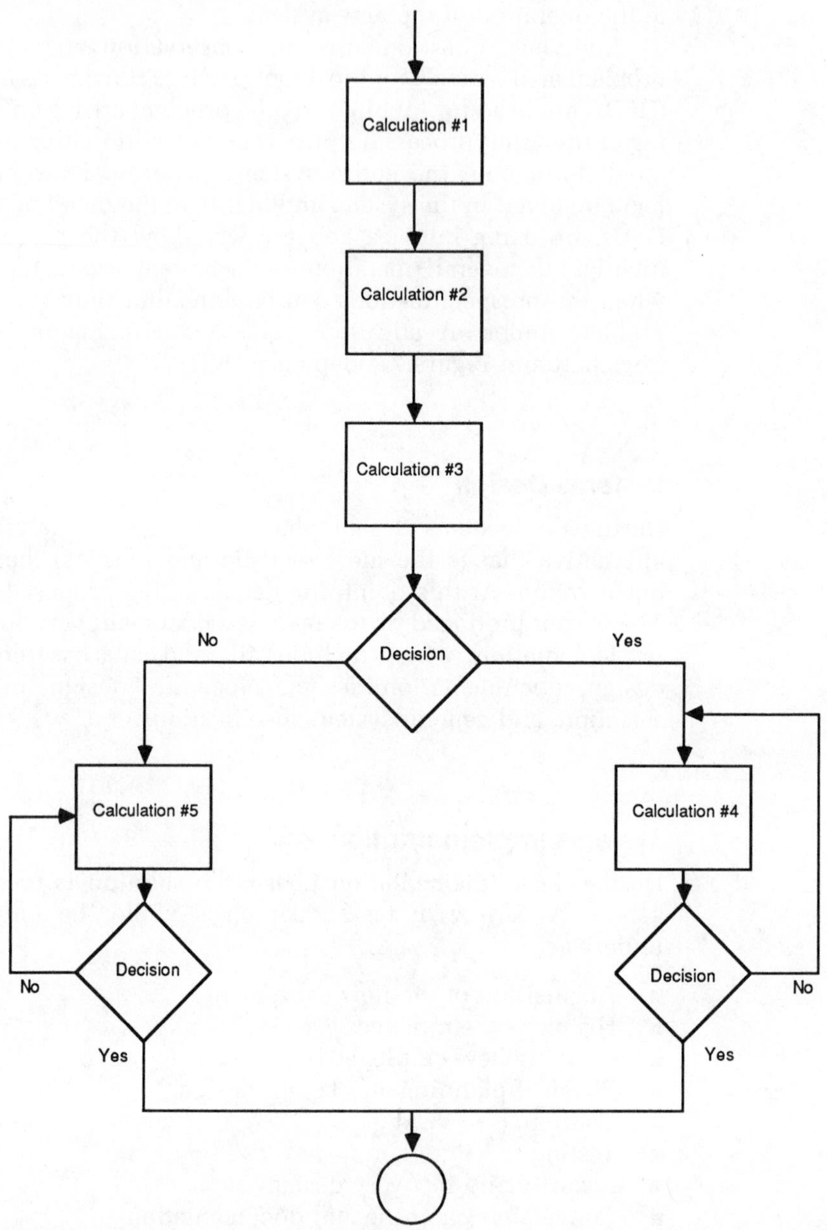

Using the *parallel* conversion approach, the old and the new systems will run simultaneously for a short time in order to ensure that the new system will operate properly. However, this approach is costly.

In the *phased-in, phased-out* approach, depending on the suitability of the system for such conversion, as each module of the new system is converted the corresponding part of the old system is retired. This process continues until the entire system is converted. In accounting and finance areas, this approach may be very effective, but it is not suitable for all applications.

Using the *direct (crash)* conversion approach, the old system is stopped and the new system is implemented. This approach is risky but the organization may save a lot of money by not running the old and new systems concurrently.

Finally, using a *pilot* conversion approach, the analyst develops the system with some selected data and enhances the system to work for any other possible data. This approach, depending on the system and whether test data are selected correctly, can be a relatively safe approach.

Postimplementation Audit

The last phase in the life-cycle approach, the postimplementation audit, attempts to verify the suitability of the system after the implementation. The

Figure 7-4 An Example of a DFD

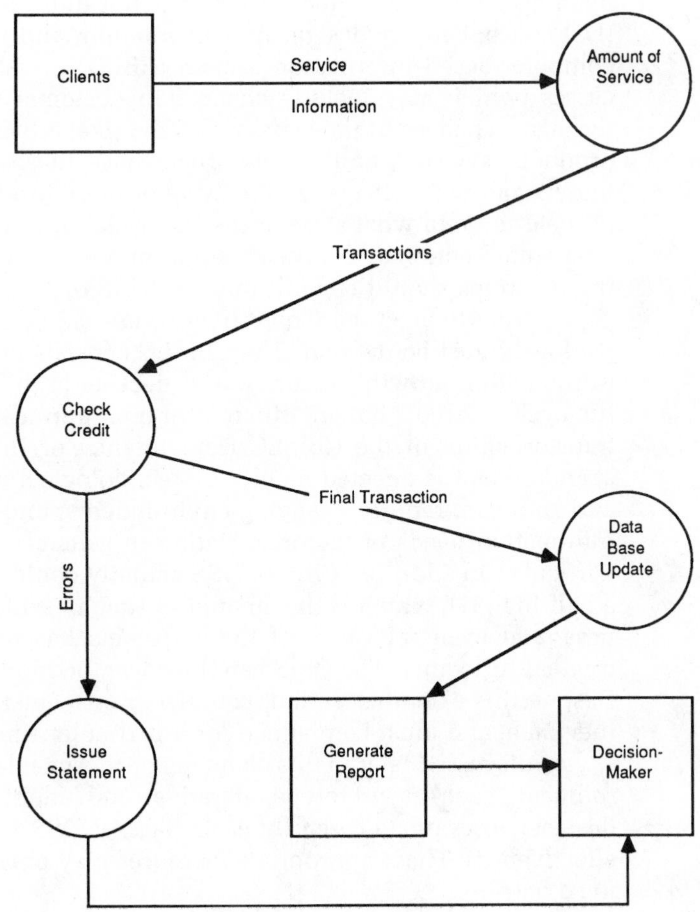

team of analysts tries to collect data and talk with the users, customers, and other people affected by the new system to make sure that the system is doing what it was designed to do.

7-3 Product Life Cycle

Design and implementation of computer-based information systems, particularly EDP/MIS and, to some degree, DSS, follow the product life cycle [7, 17], which means that these systems follow the four distinguished stages of the life cycle, including introduction, growth, maturity, and decline. Understanding of this life cycle is important and should help the designer of a DSS with a series of tools that can be used to design a more successful DSS.

Traditionally, a *life cycle* has been discussed in terms of product obsolescence due to factors such as change in consumer preference and technological change. Increasingly, the life-cycle concept is being more broadly defined, being applied to various professionals, including engineers and physicians [37], as well as to such unusual areas as organizational rules [23] and even plant openings and closings [34]. Thus, it is not unusual to consider the life cycle (LC) concept in the design, implementation, and continuous evaluation of a computer-based information system (CBIS) as well as a DSS. Entropic processes (which may include changes in customer taste, technological breakthroughs, changes in the market, and the like) adversely affect the life cycle of products, systems, and people. To manage these processes, we need to (1) understand what affects the life cycle of these products, systems, and people; (2) determine in what stage of the life cycle they currently are; and (3) decide what interventions, if any, are appropriate for that particular stage. These interventions should be built into the CBIS or DSS framework.

In order to meet these objectives or needs, the concept of a CBIS life cycle (CBISLC) must be defined. The CBISLC consists of the four specific stages of introduction, growth, maturity, and decline [17]. These are similar to other life-cycle concepts but are different in their application. More specifically, the transformation of the CBISLC from infancy or introduction to decline and abandonment is affected mainly by technological advancements in hardware and software, rapidly changing environments, and continuous change in the information needs of the organization in general and the decision-makers in particular. In addition, CBIS or DSS actually could be suggested to experience a half-life [37], which is the amount of time in which the efficiency, effectiveness, and even relevance of these systems has been reduced to half of its original full value. The CBIS can, however, be modified to extend its full life. Despite this extended period, complete replacement of the existing system is inevitable and must be planned for a particular time frame.

As discussed later in this chapter, appropriate design tools in the DSS environment, such as prototype, iterative, and adoptive design, help the DSS designer to evaluate carefully each stage of DSS life cycle and determine its effectiveness. These appropriate measures may prevent a DSS from experiencing a half-life.

The most important features of an information system life cycle (ISLC) are characteristics that are unique or indigenous to different stages of the cycle. By understanding these characteristics or determinants, the CBIS user/designer can identify not only the stage in which the CBIS is (macro) but where it is within that stage (micro). This will help the designer take whatever action is appropriate at that particular time for resolving possible problems. The following are stages of the ISLC and their characterizations.

Introduction. Characterized by a series of technical problems, unrealistic demand by users, lack of interest and familiarity, and so on [17]. There may even be adverse feelings or attitudes toward the introduction of this new technology due to individual, group, or organizational habit structures [29].

Growth. Characterized by an increase in awareness and interest, multiple use, new applications suggested and incorporated, and the like.

Maturity. Characterized by a high degree of efficiency and effectiveness, low cost/benefit ratio, widespread satisfaction with "our" systems, and so forth.

Decline. Characterized by lack of interest, slow response time to requests, and the inevitable bypassing of the CBIS by using "personal" micros and individually contrived or procured data bases, technological obsolescence, and so on. Though a CBIS designer would want to anticipate this stage, many do not understand the human or technical responses to the decline process.

Figure 7-5 illustrates the stages of information systems life cycle.

The classic phases involved in building a CBIS, as mentioned earlier, include problem definition, analysis, design, implementation, and postimplementation audit. A careful examination of variables involved in each phase should significantly improve the life cycle of the CBIS. The use of appropriate tools, techniques, and methodologies for each phase or step should bring about a more successful CBIS introduction. When these phases are applied to a DSS, they should include the following:

1. *The analysis phase* should include economic, technical, operational, time, and human concerns. The user(s) of the system must be identified, and style, status, and preferences of these users must be considered. Both quantitative and qualitative benefits must be evaluated in this phase. Also, a combination of top-down and bottom-up methodologies should be utilized.
2. *The design phase* should include more flexible methodologies such as iterative design, task force design, and/or modular design in order to reflect the information needs of the user. This phase should also consider potential technological advancements and changing user needs.
3. *The implementation phase* provides the first impression of the DSS to the users. Fortunately or unfortunately, user acceptance is based to a great extent on the user's first impressions and is akin to a job interview for the system. In order to smooth the implementation process and minimize human resistance, parallel conversion might be considered the

Figure 7-5 Stages of ISLC

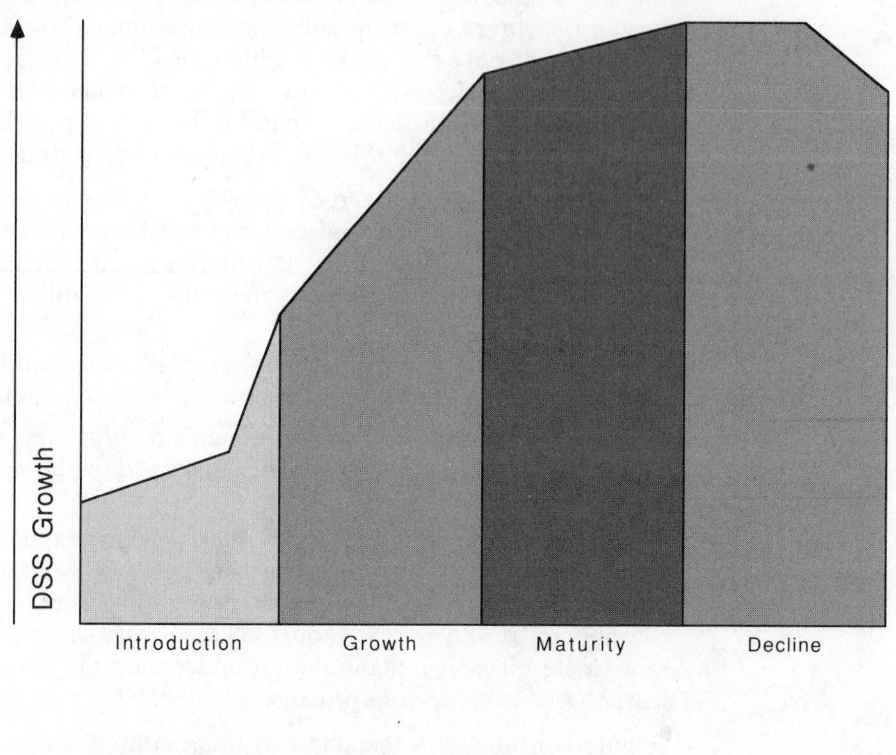

best method. Parallel conversion provides the users with such advantages as more on-the-job training than the other methods and a safety net in case of system failure. In the particular case of DSS, on-line prototyping may achieve the same goal as parallel conversion. On-line prototyping provides the user with an idea regarding the operation of the DSS and makes it possible to integrate the views of the user into the system during the final stages of completion.

4. *The postimplementation audit* should continuously monitor the system. Implementation of a CBIS is no different than any other organizational change that requires evaluation of operations as an absolute necessity. The behavior of the system *and* the users indicate the stage in the ISLC. The designer must make appropriate decisions in each situation.

7-4 Product Life Cycle and DSS Design Considerations

As discussed in Chapter 3, the conceptual model of a DSS includes three components: data base, model base, and dialog management. The major players involved in DSS design and implementation include the user, intermediary, and managerial and technical designers. Considering these issues, the life-cycle approach identifies several major elements in construction of a successful DSS.

User

The user and his or her information needs are among the most important elements and can expand or reduce the life expectancy of a DSS. These needs may have been generated either by company requirements or industry pressure. Also, a variety of attributes related to the user—such as style, acceptance, convenience, and status—are important for an expanded and productive DSS life. A DSS that is not responsive to these factors will have a shorter life expectancy or reduced quality of life.

Technology

Hardware and software technologies and their proper augmentation into the conceptual model for a DSS are also important factors for an expanded and effective DSS life. In many cases a DSS has failed to respond to the user needs because of improper employment of software and/or hardware technologies. Production of timely, integrated, and useful information, which is the prime objective of any DSS, could have a significant impact on the proper employment of these technologies. As mentioned in Chapter 3, DSS can be built by using either DSS tools or DSS generators. The proper selection of these technologies has direct impact on the effective life of a DSS.

Top Management

Heavy involvement of top management in all phases of analysis, design, and implementation can facilitate the introduction of a more viable DSS, speed up the introduction phase, and improve the cost/benefit ratio of the system during the growth and maturity phases. This involvement can also accelerate the planned abandonment of the DSS and consequently shorten the CBISLC.

Environment

There are many elements outside the boundary of the DSS that can have a very significant impact on the life expectancy of such a system. One such element is increasing business volume. Other factors can involve changes in present and future competition, customer preferences, government action, suppliers, union activity, labor market, tax structure, and economic conditions.

7-5 Monitoring Mechanisms for DSS Implementation

When considering the design and implementation of a DSS, it is essential to establish monitoring mechanisms that gather information and evaluate the status of these internal and external determinants of the DSS life cycle. If significant variance or change occurs in these determinants, the DSS designer may need to take action to minimize any adverse impact. This is analogous to political risk analysis as a monitoring mechanism for the investment decision process with respect to a project in a foreign country. The investment process (or life cycle) can be abandoned or redesigned if the value of the investment project has changed significantly. This variance has, in effect, changed the potential or useful life of the project.

An example of external determinants is a drastic breakthrough in hardware technology. Microcomputer capacity has increased significantly in the past few years; many companies that were using minicomputers are now able to use microcomputers for the same and even expanded service capability. Some individual or individuals must be responsible for providing continuous evaluation of the status of hardware and software technologies so that the abandonment of current technology can be anticipated prior to the actual decline phase of the DSS life cycle.

With these monitoring mechanisms in place, the DSS designer can both enhance the design and implementation of the DSS and manage its movement through its useful life cycle. These monitoring mechanisms should also tell the DSS designer where he or she is in the life cycle at any moment in time.

Some examples of monitoring mechanisms and how they might be used include the following:

1. If the user need is not satisfied, then the DSS designer should change the data-collection strategy in order to reflect the quality and quantity of collected data.
2. If the information provided does not match the user's personal and organizational style and status, then the DSS designer should vary the format of provided information.
3. If the user has problems with the acceptance of DSS, then the introduction phase should provide for on-going education or the DSS should hide the complexity (i.e., through use of a user-friendly system). In other phases, redesign and/or planned abandonment should be considered.
4. If the user is not comfortable in using the DSS, then the DSS designer should provide easy access to the system.
5. If the DSS is not responsive to volume increase; then the DSS designer should upgrade the data base, improve the data input/output channels, or use modular design.
6. If the user is bombarded by the information provided, then the DSS designer should use intelligent filtering.
7. If the views of top management and/or users have not been considered in any phases of DSS design and implementation, then the DSS designer should use task force design and/or interface design.
8. If hardware/software components of DSS are not responsive to various needs of the user and/or environment, then the DSS designer should employ more suitable hardware/software, upgrade these components, or plan abandonment.
9. If DSS does not provide information related to the changing environment, then the DSS designer should modify data collection strategy or redefine the data base.

Numerous other examples that are related to the conceptual model of the DSS can also be generated.

7-6 Design Methodologies in DSS Environment

As mentioned earlier, understanding of the life-cycle approach is necessary but not sufficient for designing a DSS. Life-cycle approach and traditional design methodologies are not appropriate in a DSS environment. The major reasons for this unsuitability are:

1. Lack of prespecification in DSS environment. The problem under investigation is not always well defined. The input/output process cannot be fully identified and the problem itself is usually ill-defined.
2. Changing needs of the user. The user needs in DSS environment are continuously changing; therefore, a system may have to undergo several changes until it satisfies the unique user needs. Such a system may be suitable for a short time but not over the long run. Due to the existence of these issues, traditional methodologies are not suitable in a DSS environment, and the designer of DSS must utilize other methodologies. The following sections explain some of these methodologies.

Prototyping

Prototyping as a methodology for DSS construction has gained popularity in recent years [24, 30, 40]. Since the construction of a complete system is time-consuming, difficult, and expensive, a prototype of the system is developed first. A prototype is usually a small-scale version of the system under investigation, which is significant enough to highlight the value of the DSS to the user. Prototyping makes it possible for the user to express his or her views regarding the final DSS and is also the fastest way to put the DSS into operation. There are two types of prototypes: throwaway and evolving prototypes [39, pp. 155–61]. The throwaway prototype is designed for the purpose of illustration and gaining feedback. If the user does not like the prototype, it is thrown away. If the user is happy with the prototype, it may either evolve to the final system or be used until a separate, full-featured DSS is constructed. The evolving prototype starts from a small-scale system and evolves into the final system as new features are added and existing features are upgraded.

Middle-out Methodology

To understand the middle-out methodology, we should first explain top-down and bottom-up methodologies. In top-down design a global view of a problem is identified first. Then the problem under investigation is divided into a series of subproblems, or modules. Each module is designed separately. At the end these different pieces are put together. This methodology has gained popularity for designing traditional computer-based information systems. This methodology has several advantages:

- It is easier to design a system.
- It is easier to modify a system.
- It is easier to maintain a system.

Top-down design may not be suitable for DSS design. The major reason for its unsuitability to DSS environment is its long development process. It takes months or even years until a user sees the final product. By that time, the requirements may already have been changed. Also, top-down methodology assumes prespecification, which is not always true in DSS environment.

Bottom-up methodology starts in a piecemeal fashion and may suffer from lack of direction. The solution offered to a subproblem may not be entirely suitable for a particular situation. This methodology may not keep in touch with the organizational needs of a particular setting.

Middle-out methodology begins close to the level of the problem at hand [22], and it develops a process of generalizing (bottom-up) and specifying (top-down) at each stage of the problem-solving process. Middle-out methodology begins with a much less global view of the problem than top-down methodology. This approach is justified because of the lack of understanding of all the dimensions (lack of structure in the problem) of the problem under investigation. Middle-out methodology advocates the utilization of a prototype, which provides quick feedback on the suitability of the solution to a particular problem. The feedback to the prototype may either support the final construction of the system or its complete abandonment. In middle-out methodology, the prototype usually addresses a part of a problem under investigation. Later, several prototypes may be linked together in order to solve the entire problem. Although the prototype is a small-scale version of the system, it can be used to illustrate the value of a DSS and guide its final construction.

Iterative Design

Iterative design concentrates on a small but significant part of a problem and, by going through repetitive steps, tries to improve the system until the user's requirements are satisfied. This is different from prototyping, which may not lead to the final system [39, p. 16]. The initial system is real and usable, and the user/designer have already agreed on the subproblem under investigation.

Adoptive Design

Adoptive design advocates an evolving process in building DSS [1,25]. As a short-term solution, a DSS may respond to the immediate needs of the user. Over the medium range, a DSS may have to be modified, and new features may need to be augmented into its architecture in order to respond to the needs of the user. However, over the long range the DSS may have to utilize a totally new technology in order to respond to the changing information needs of the user. The entire computer field is a good example of the adoptive design process. Computers have evolved from first to second, third, and fourth generations. Each generation uses a new technology that is more advanced than the earlier one. Fifth-generation computers are going to be different from the fourth generation in many radical directions. DSS generators have been improving continuously. A specific DSS that is designed by using a DSS generator has the potential to grow in parallel with the DSS generator. In other words, this process may provide an adaptive environment for the specific DSS.

7-7 Unique Features in DSS Systems Analysis and Design

As discussed in Chapter 3, DSSs are somehow different from the traditional EDP/MIS. These differences in operations and objectives require a different approach when it comes to the analysis and design phases of these systems. We summarize these unique features under three major categories.

Decision Objectives of DSS

- Structured, semistructured, and unstructured problems (focus on semistructured and unstructured problems)
- Present decisions and future decisions
- Simple and complex decisions
- Control and planning decisions
- Flexibility in decision making and decision implementation

Design Issues

- User-oriented
- Special tools: prototypes, iterative designs, and DSS generators
- Internal and external data
- Flexible output, and tailor-made to the users' needs
- Modeling and data anlysis
- Ad hoc decisions
- Interactive system
- Ongoing implementation

Evaluation Criteria

- Effectiveness and efficiency of the system (mostly effectiveness)
- Decision making and decision-implementation improvement
- User satisfaction
- Iterative and continuous design process
- Responsiveness of the system to changing needs

In systems analysis and design phases, the analyst or team of analysts must consider the preceding issues, and, by integration of the classic life-cycle approach and product life-cycle approach, follow a new methodology, which we call a *revised approach*. In the next section this approach is explained.

7-8 Systems Analysis and Design for DSS: A Revised Approach

Since DSSs are designed to be used by key decision-makers, their involvement plays a major role in determining the success of these systems. The classic life-cycle approach changes direction in the DSS environment, as outlined by the following steps:

Problem Definition

In the problem-definition step, the objective of the system must be defined. The user must be informed and in agreement with the following four W's:

Why issue. Why is the system going to be designed? What decision(s) will be effected? How will the organization use this system?

Who issue. Who is going to use the system? Is it going to be used by one decision maker or a group of decision makers?

When issue. When will the system be operational? From now until the final implementation, how will decisions affected by DSS be made?

What issue. What kind of capabilities will be provided by the DSS? Is it a modeling type, a DBMS type, or a combination? How will these different capabilities be used and how will the system provide these capabilities?

Formation of the Task Force

For the continued success of the DSS, different users of the DSS must have input in the construction and maintenance of the system. Their views must be highly regarded. This issue is of considerable significance, particularly if the system is going to be used by more than one user.

The task force should include representatives from different user departments, top management, and technical staff. Preferably the task force should include individuals presented in Figure 7-6. [32] There should be a continuous discussion among the task force members until the user needs are precisely defined.

Construction of an On-Line Prototype

To show the user how the system will work, a simple prototype greatly improves the chances of success [40]. An on-line prototype will give the user a

Figure 7-6 DSS Task Force

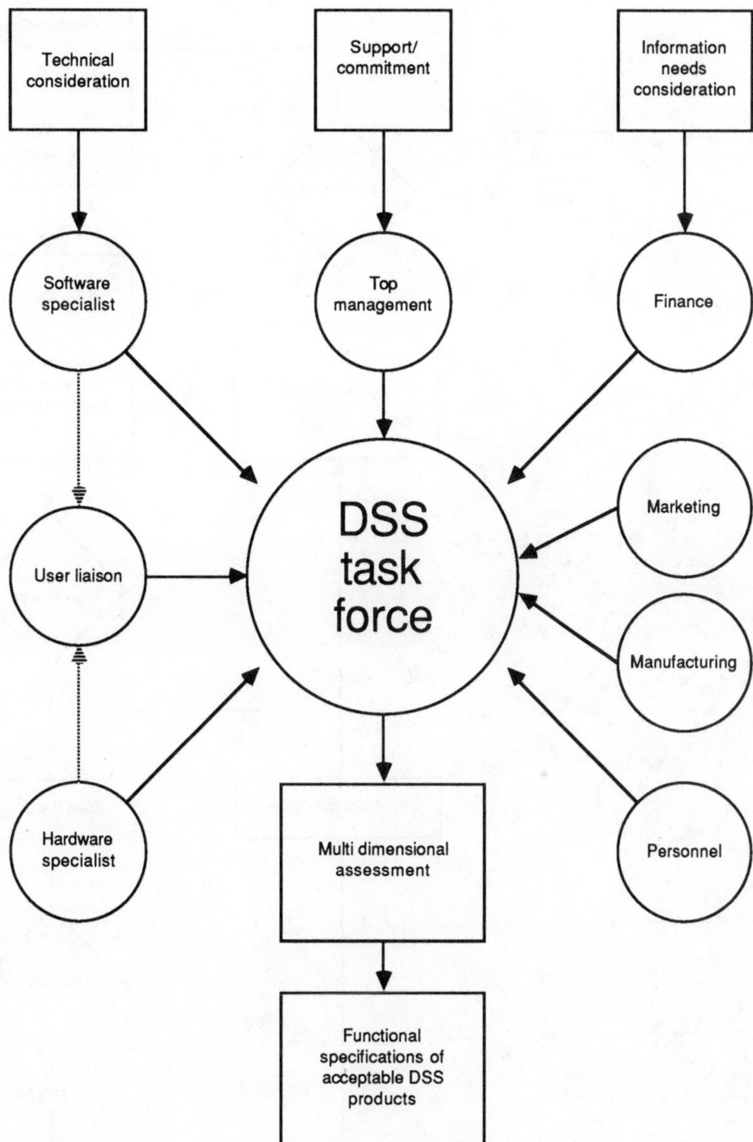

chance to see the system in action. Also, the designer will find out the possible problems associated with the system. As we discussed earlier, there are two types of prototypes. A prototype may even be developed into the final system.

The process of prototype design and modification should continue until the user is satisfied with the system. Then the construction of the final system can be started.

Figure 7-7 The Iterative Process of DSS Design

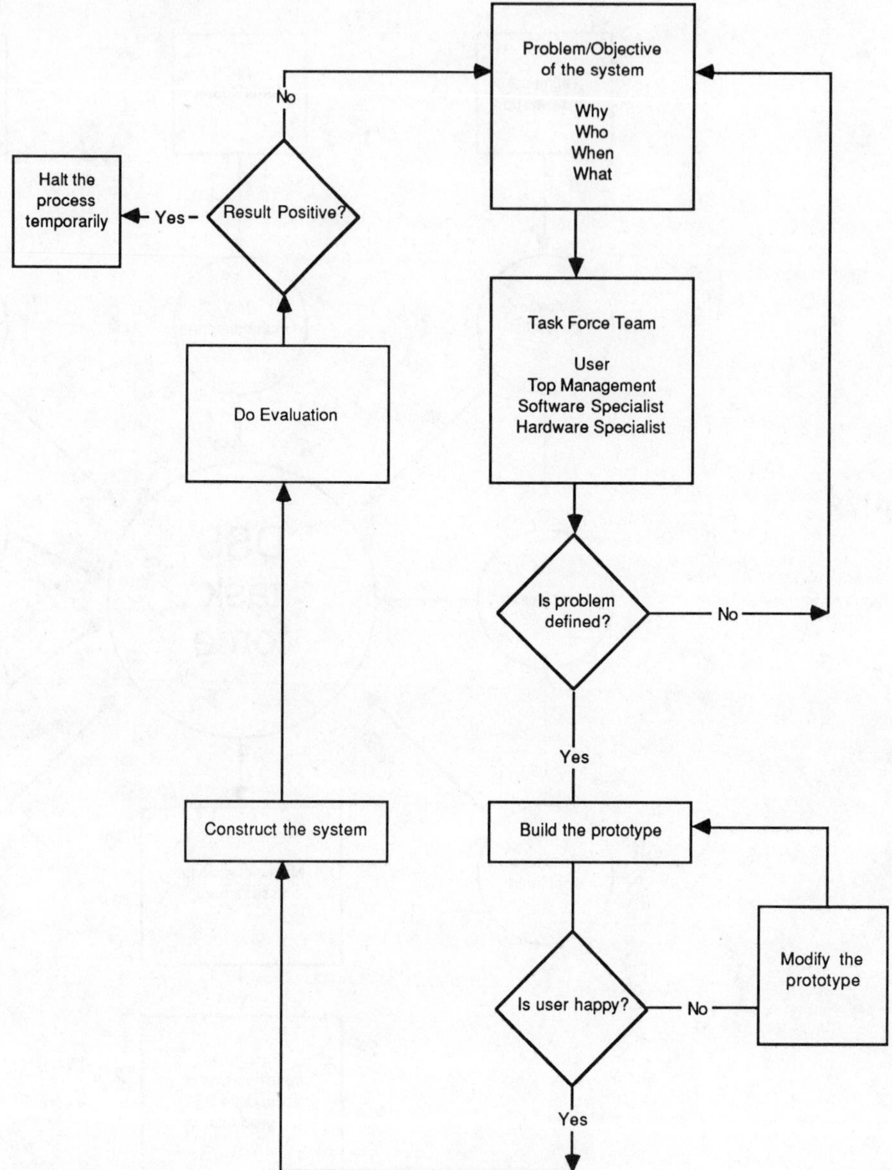

Evaluation

As discussed in Chapter 3, the evaluation of a DSS is not usually based on the monetary benefits generated by the system. Such factors as the impact of the system on decision making, decision implementation, the learning impact of the system, and the overall effectiveness of the system are the more important concerns here.

Based on the result of the evaluation, the process of modification may continue or be halted temporarily until the user tries to use new features of the system or add new features to the system. Figure 7-7 illustrates this process. As this figure shows, all phases of the classic life-cycle approach are combined into one phase, and this phase continues in an iterative manner until the system is constructed. After construction of the system, the monitoring mechanism assures the quality of life for the system and suggests any corrective action that must be taken to guarantee the user's satisfaction.

7-9 Summary

This chapter discussed systems analysis and design in the DSS environment. The classic life-cycle approach and the product life-cycle approach were integrated into a revised approach that is more suitable for DSS design. This discussion should provide a good background for the next chapter, which discusses the process of building an effective DSS.

Review Questions

1. What is the classic life-cycle approach?

2. What phases are included in this life cycle?

3. What is the outcome of the system analysis phase?

4. What is a feasibility study?

5. What are the five major issues concerning feasibility?

6. Why is social feasibility important?

7. What are some of the tools used by systems analysts in the systems-analysis phase of the life cycle?

8. What is a data-flow diagram?

9. What are some of the tasks performed in the system-implementation phase?

10. What are the major types of conversion techniques?

11. Why may direct conversion be dangerous?

12. Why is a postimplementation audit important?

13. What are the four phases of a DSS in the product life-cycle approach?

14. What are the characteristics of each phase?

15. What should a systems analyst do in each phase?

16. What is a half-life? Does a DSS experience a half-life? If yes, how?

17. What are the four major considerations in the product life cycle as it may apply to DSS design? (*Hint:* User is one of them.)

18. What are some of the monitoring mechanisms in the product life-cycle approach?

19. What is prototyping? Why is prototyping so important?

20. What is iterative design? What is the difference between prototyping and iterative design?

21. What is adoptive design? Why must DSS be adoptive?

22. What is middle-out approach? How is it different from top-down or bottom-up methodologies?

23. What are the unique features of DSS as they apply to system analysis and design?

24. What is the revised approach? What are the phases in the revised approach?

Projects

1. Southern CRAFT, a manufacturer of wood products, is implementing a cost-control DSS. What are the phases of systems design in this project as it applies to the classic life cycle? What is the outcome of each phase? Conduct a feasibility study for the system. Which type of feasibility is the most important one in this particular case?

2. How do you apply the product life cycle to the Southern CRAFT problem? How do you establish a monitoring mechanism? How do you establish a planned abandonment?

3. Why and how is design of DSS different than that of MIS/EDP? Choose an organization of your choice and investigate the differences.

4. Mention five monitoring mechanisms for Southern CRAFT as they utilize the cost-control DSS.

5. The president of a state university needs advice for construction of a student-monitoring DSS. This system should help the president to monitor all the students enrolled in different disciplines and display different graphs showing the number, age, nationality, and sex of the different students in each discipline. The system should also generate exception reports regarding these four important variables. Apply systems analysis and design in DSS environment to this specific DSS. Who should participate in the task force? What should the prototype do? How do you build the monitoring mechanism?

Key Terms

Classic life-cycle approach
Problem definition
Feasibility study
Economic feasibility
Tangible cost/benefit
Intangible cost/benefit
Technical feasibility
Operational feasibility
Social feasibility
Time feasibility

Systems analysis
Interview
Questionnaire
Observation
Work measurement
Form investigation and control
Flow chart
Data-flow diagram (DFD)
Systems design
Coding
Testing
Parallel conversion
Phased-in, phased-out conversion
Pilot conversion
Direct (crash) conversion
Implementation
Postimplementation audit
Product life cycle
System introduction
System growth
System maturity
System decline
Top management
Monitoring mechanisms
Task force for DSS
Prototyping
Iterative design
Adoptive design
Middle-out approach
On-line prototype

References

[1] Alavi, Maryann, and H. Albert Napier. 1984. An Experiment in Applying the Adoptive Design Approach to DSS Development. *Information & Management 7*, no. 1 (July): 21–28.

[2] Alexander, David J. 1986. Planning and Building a DSS. *Datamation* (March 15): 115–21.

[3] Alter, Steven L. 1978. Development Patterns for Decision Support Systems. *MIS Quarterly* 2, no. 3 (September): 33–42.

[4] Alter, Steven L. 1980. *Decision Support Systems Current Practice and Continuing Challenges.* Reading, Mass.: Addison-Wesley Publishing Company, pp. 111–16.

[5] Anderson, Evan E. 1985. Managerial Consideration in Participative Design of MIS/DSS. *Information & Management* (September): 201–07.

[6] Bahl, Harish C., and Raymond G. Hunt. 1985. Problem Solving Strategies for DSS Design. *Information & Management:* 81–88.

[7] Bidgoli, Hossein, and Howard Rudd. 1985. Information Systems Life Cycle as a Tool for Design and Implementation of Computer-Based Management Information Systems. *Proceedings S.E. AIDS* (New Orleans) (February-March): 316–18.

[8] Bidgoli, Hossein. 1983. *A Descriptive/Predictive Model for the Employment of Computer-Based Management Information Systems for the Government of a Developing Country.* Ph.D. diss., Portland State University, pp. 64–74.

[9] Benbasat, Lzak, and Yair Wand. 1982. A Dialogue Generator and Its Use in DSS Design. *Information Management* (May): 231–41.

[10] Blake, Robert R., and Jane S. Mouton. 1981. *The Versatile Manager.* Homewood, Ill.: Richard D. Irwin, Inc., pp. 126–27.

[11] Burch, John G., Jr., Felix R. Strater, and Gary Grudnitski. 1979. *Information Systems: Theory and Practice.* New York: John Wiley and Sons, pp. 435–36.

[12] Carlson, Eric D. 1978. An Approach for Designing Decision Support Systems. In *Building Decision Support Systems,* by John L. Bennett. Reading, Mass.: Addison-Wesley Publishing Company, 1983, pp. 15–39.

[13] Davis, Gordon B. 1974. *Management Information Systems Conceptual Foundations, Structure, and Development.* New York: McGraw-Hill Book Company.

[14] Diprimio, Anthony. 1984. Develop a Five-Step Plan to Launch Decision Support Systems. *Bank Systems Equipment* (September): 56–58.

[15] Eliason, Alan L. 1987. *Systems Development Analysis, Design and Implementation.* Boston: Little, Brown and Company.

[16] Fitzgerald, Jerry, and Ardra Fitzgerald. 1987. *Fundamentals of Systems Analysis Using Structured Analysis and Design Techniques.* 3d ed. New York: John Wiley and Sons.

[17] Gaydesch, Jr., Alexander. 1982. *Principles of EDP Management.* Reston, Va.: Reston Publishing Company, Inc., pp. 79–90.

[18] Gore, Marvin, and John W. Stubbe. 1988. *Elements of Systems Analysis.* 4th ed. Dubuque, Ia.: William C. Brown Company.

[19] Henderson, John C., and David A. Schilling. 1985. Design and Implementation of Decision Support Systems in the Public Sector. *MIS Quarterly* (June): 157–69.

[20] Howard, Ted. 1980. *Entropy: A New World View.* New York: The Viking Press.

[21] Huber, George P. 1983. Cognitive Style as a Basis For MIS and DSS Designs: Much Ado About Nothing. *Management Science* 29, no. 5 (May): 567–82.

[22] Hurst, E. G., Jr., D. N. Ness, T. J. Gambino, and T. H. Johnson. 1983. Growing DSS: A Flexible Evolutionary Approach. In *Building Decision Support Systems* by John L. Bennett. Reading, Mass.: Addison-Wesley Publishing Company. pp. 111–32.

[23] Jackson, John F., and Susan W. Adams. 1979. The Life Cycle of Rules. *Academy of Management Review* (October): 269–73.

[24] Janson, Marius A., and L. Douglas Smith. 1985. Prototyping for Systems Development: A Critical Appraisal. *MIS Quarterly* (December): 305–16.

[25] Keen, Peter G. W. 1980. Adaptive Design for Decision Support Systems. *Data Base* 12, nos. 1 and 2 (Fall): 15–25.

[26] Kendall, Penny A. 1987. *Systems Analysis and Design: A Structure Approach.* Newton, Mass.: Allyn and Bacon, Inc.

[27] Kendall, Kenneth E., and Julie E. Kendall. 1988. *Systems Analysis and Design.* Englewood Cliffs, N.J.: Prentice-Hall, Inc.

[28] Kiran, Ali S., and Alex Loewenthal. 1985. An Integrated Decision System for Inventory Management. *Computers & Industrial Engineering* 9, no. 4: 379–86.

[29] Lawrence, Paul R. 1980. How to Deal with Resistance to Change. In *Organization and People.* Ed. J. B. Ritchie and Paul Thompson. St. Paul, Minn.: West Publishing Company, pp. 361–374.

[30] Lantz, Kenneth. 1986. The Prototyping Methodology: Designing Right the First Time. *ComputerWorld* (April 7): 69–72.

[31] Mahmood, Mo A., and Jeanette N. Medewitz. 1985. Impact of Design Methods on Decision Support Systems Success: An Empirical Assessment. *Information & Management:* 137–51.

[32] Meador, C. Lawrence, and Richard A. Mezger. 1984. Selecting an End User Programming Language for DSS Development. *MIS Quarterly* (December): 267–80.

[33] Multinovich, Jugoslav, and Vladimiv Vlahorich. 1984. A Strategy for a Successful MIS/DSS Implementation. *Journal of Systems Management* (August): 8–16.

[34] Plant Shutdowns: States Take a New Tack. 1983. *Business Week* (October 24): 73, 76.

[35] Semprevivo, Philip C. 1982. *Systems Analysis Definitions, Process, and Design.* Chicago: Science Research Associates, Inc.

[36] Senn, Arun. 1983. Decision Support System: An Activity-Oriented Design. *Journal of Information Science* (July): 23–30.

[37] Smith, E. Paul. 1978. Measuring Professional Obsolescence: A Half-Life Model for the Physician. *Academy of Management Review* (October): 914–17.

[38] Sprague, Ralph H. Jr. 1980. A Framework for the Development of Decision Support Systems. *MIS Quarterly* (December): 1–26.

[39] Sprague, Ralph, Jr., and Eric D. Carlson. 1982. *Building Effective Decision Support Systems*. Englewood Cliffs, N.J.: Prentice-Hall, Inc.

[40] Sroka, John M., and Martha H. Rader. 1986. Prototyping Increases Chance of Systems Acceptance. *Data Management* (March): 12–19.

[41] Thierauf, Robert J. 1986. *Systems Analysis and Design a Case Study Approach*. 2d ed. Columbus, Oh.: Merrill Publishing Company.

[42] Wetherbe, James C. 1988. *Systems Analysis and Design*. 3d ed. St. Paul, Minn.: West Publishing Company.

[43] Whitten, Jeffery L., Lonnie D. Bently, and Thomas I. M. Ho. 1986. *Systems Analysis & Design Methods*. St. Louis: Times Mirror/Mosby College Publishing.

[44] Willoughy, Theodore C., and James A. Senn. 1975. *Business Systems*. Cleveland, Oh.: Association for Systems Management.

8 Building Effective DSS

8-1 Introduction

This chapter reviews the process of building a DSS, stressing managerial design. The methodology developed in the last chapter, which focused on user involvement and utilization of prototypes, is emphasized. Five major areas of a business organization, manufacturing, marketing, personnel, and financial and strategic planning, are chosen and the data base and model-base components of a DSS are analyzed. The behavioral issues in DSS design are explained, and system characteristics are identified for different levels of the organization. This chapter concludes with a series of guidelines for building a DSS, and the next chapter provides guidelines for selection of a DSS product. The material presented in this chapter is supported throughout the literature (consult Appendix C).

8-2 Building a DSS

To build an effective DSS, we use the methodology that was introduced in the last chapter under the revised approach:

- Problem definition
- Formation of the task force
- Construction of an on-line prototype
- Evaluation

In the problem-definition phase, the team of designers must define the problem to be addressed by the DSS. Although most problems in a DSS environment cannot be fully defined and do not possess a well-defined structure, the need for the DSS must be articulated during the problem-definition phase. This phase should leave users with a distinct impression that there is a need for constructing a DSS. A feasibility study (as explained in the last chapter) also should be conducted during this phase. The feasibility study may include economic, technical, social, time, and operational issues. Ideally, in this phase the design team will identify the organization's critical-success factors and explain how the DSS can achieve information about these factors to assist the organization in achieving its goals. This phase should not leave any ambiguity about why the system has to be built, and the design team must make sure that all the participants support the DSS.

In the second phase, the task force is formed. In order to achieve a balanced and effective DSS, all the affected departments and user groups must be represented in the task force. As has been emphasized, managerial and technical issues are equally important, and the task force must make sure that both dimensions are fully defined.

In the third phase, the design team builds a small-scale prototype of the system. The prototype must be significant enough to demonstrate the value of the DSS. If the user is not satisfied with the prototype and the operation of the system as represented by the prototype, the prototype must be returned to the design team for change. However, if the user reaction is positive, it is possible that the prototype can evolve to the final DSS or be used temporarily until the final DSS is constructed.

In the fourth, or evaluation, phase an iterative approach is used to add or delete features until the user is fully satisfied with the system, a process that may never be finished. Also in the evaluation phase, the design team should consider the principles of adoptive design and must remember that the effectiveness of the DSS has to be evaluated in a certain time frame. For the short term the DSS may respond by utilizing its existing features. In the medium range (3 months to a year), new features may have to be added or existing ones modified to improve the effectiveness of the DSS. However, over the long term (more than two years), the DSS may need to utilize a completely new technology, including new tools or generators.

8-3 Building Effective DSS in Functional Areas

As mentioned earlier, a DSS includes three components: data base, model base, and dialog management. The dialog component can be designed by using the facility provided by DSS generators. Also, a high-level language such as FORTRAN or Pascal can be used to develop the user/system interface. These facilities were discussed in Chapter 6. In this chapter, we emphasize the data base and model base components of a DSS from a managerial designer's viewpoint. We identify the types of data, sources of data, types of analyses, and particular models needed to perform these analysis. Figure 8-1 illustrates two views of DSS design. To establish a functional DSS, we assume the organization already has a comprehensive accounting information system (AIS) in place, since this system serves as one of the major input components to DSSs in all functional areas.

Figure 8-1 Two Views of DSS Design

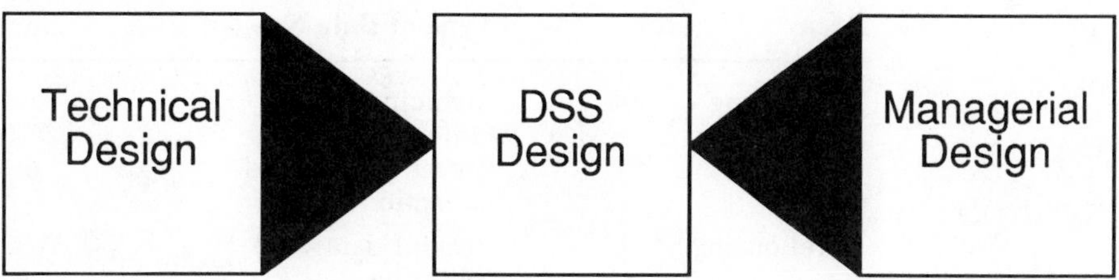

8-4 Manufacturing DSS (MFDSS)

By using internal and external data, mathematical models with what-if capabilities, and a user-friendly dialog, a manufacturing DSS (MFDSS) can provide valuable information in all aspects of manufacturing operations [3, 4]. An MFDSS, like any other DSS, includes three important components: dialog management, data base, and model base. The goal of an MFDSS is to provide timely, accurate, and integrated information regarding production planning and control. To achieve this goal, the data base of an MFDSS must collect and store different types of data both internally and externally. The model base must include a number of mathematical and statistical models for diverse analyses. Table 8-1 illustrates types of data and Table 8-2 illustrates types of models for a MFDSS.

MFDSS and Inventory Control

An MFDSS is primarily useful for managers responsible for inventory control. Their objective is to reduce the total inventory costs to the lowest possible level consistent with desired service. The total inventory costs consist of carrying or holding costs, which vary directly by inventory level; and purchasing or ordering costs, which vary inversely with the number of units ordered. The two key decisions in inventory management are when to order and how much to order.

If the demand for finished goods' inventory is constant and known in advance, the economic order quantity (EOQ) model balances these two inventory costs and identifies the optimum order quantity.

These two decisions can be made with little management intervention using the MFDSS. Management uses the accounting and purchasing/inventory files in the data base to determine the total holding and ordering costs. The EOQ model will determine the optimum quantity to order. The specific vendor is then selected from information provided by the procurement/purchasing file.

Another area where MFDSS can be helpful in inventory control decisions is material requirement planning (MRP). MRP schedules what is wanted in each time period and plans the acquisition of the items. To derive maximum benefit from an MRP system, a large, integrated data base is needed.

Table 8-1 ▪ Types of Data Needed by MFDSS in its Data Base

Area	Type of Data Needed	Source of Data
Accounting	Invoicing Order scheduling Credit control and collection	Accounting information systems
Warehousing	Receipt data Shipping Storage Replenishment Packing	Accounting information systems
Transportation	Loading Trip log Overall costs/units/miles Commodity-movement information Carrier-movement patterns	Accounting information systems Trade publications
Marketing	Current and potential customers Customer service demands Current and potential competitors Competitors' strategies Market potential Market share Demographic profiles Regional changes and shifts	Marketing research Sales force reports Trade publications Syndicated services Census guide data Survey of buying power Marketing information guide
Purchasing/Inventory	Vendor file (lead time, price, financial strength, and so on) Procurement Bidding Overall purchasing Inventory records Lot sizing Overall inventory management	Accounting information systems Trade publications Securities and Exchange Commission reports
Production	Aggregate scheduling Priority planning Capacity planning Facility planning Production control Material planning Work force planning Shop floor data collection Research and development planning Output design Layout of facilities Overall production management	Industrial engineering information systems Personnel information systems

Area	Type of Data Needed	Source of Data
Economy	General level of economic activity Economic activity within industry	Economic indicators *Survey of Current Business* *U.S. Industrial Outlook* *Standard and Poor's Industry Survey* *Across the Board* Trade publications
Legal environment	Changes impacting all businesses Changes impacting industry	General business publications such as *Business Week* and *Wall Street Journal*
Technology	Available technology and expected trends	Trade publications Trade shows

Reprinted by permission from BUSINESS Magazine. Mohsen Attaran and Hossein Bidgoli, "Developing an Effective Manufacturing Decision Support System" (October-December 1986).

Table 8-2 ▪ Examples of Types of Analyses and Models Needed for MFDSS

Types of Analyses	Description	Examples of Models
Inventory	When to order and how much Cost calculation Safety stock Priorities for inventory management	EOQ (economic order quantity) ELS (economic lot size) MRP (material requirements planning) TPOP (time-phased order point)
Warehousing	Storage structures Space utilization analysis Control of equipment	AS/RS (automatic storage and retrieval systems) Simulation modeling
Procurement/Purchasing	The supplier rating/ selection decision Vendor rating/selection decision Price change/discount analysis Bid evaluation	Vendor rating/selection models
Logistics and Location	Distribution improvements Routing/scheduling Selection of modes of transportation Transportation budgeting Shipment planning Regional/international selection Community selection Site selection	Transportation model Center of gravity/ incremental analysis Weighted score model Break-even model

continued

Table 8-2 ▪ Continued

Types of Analyses	Description	Examples of Models
Transformation/Process design	Selection of the process Design of the transformation process Layout design Balancing a line Tools/equipment/facilities selection	Computerized line balancing CPM/PERT CRAFT (computerized relative allocation of facilities) ALDEP (automated layout design program) CORELAP (computerized relationship program)
Capacity planning and scheduling	Short-term capacity planning Long-term capacity planning Capacity versus investment Aggregate scheduling Priority planning Sequencing Detailed scheduling What-if production/ inventory trade-offs	CPM/PERT GERT (graphical evaluation review technique) Learning curve Linear programming Decision tree Linear decision rule MRP II (manufacturing resource planning)
Quality control	Design quality Quality/cost analysis Where to inspect/how to inspect Handling of defects Setting optimal control limits Process control Acceptance sampling	Fraction production charts (P charts) Number of defects (C charts)

Reprinted by permission from BUSINESS Magazine. Mohsen Attaran and Hossein Bidgoli, "Developing an Effective Manufacturing Decision Support System" (October-December 1986).

The MRP requires input regarding what should be produced, when it is needed, a record of the actual inventory level, a record of the lead times needed to replenish inventory levels, product structure, raw materials, and components and subassemblies. These data can be obtained from various files in the MFDSS data base. For example, data regarding lead times and on-hand balance is obtained from inventory files. The number of finished goods needed during each time period and the part numbers of components required to make each individual part are gained from production files, and so forth.

Management then uses the MRP model (computer software) to determine the quantity to order and to generate some optional management reports. The output usually includes (1) what should be ordered, (2) what order should be canceled, (3) exception reports (items that need management attention), and (4) how well the system is operating. Properly designed and integrated, the MFDSS is a powerful support tool that enhances the effectiveness and capabilities of decision-makers in a manufacturing environment. By using an

MFDSS, it becomes easier to collect more data, make forecasts, schedule operations, remove bottlenecks, perform sensitivity and what-if analysis, and optimize, monitor, and control the system. These features offer today's production manager—pressed more than ever to maximize efficiency, quality, and flexibility—unprecedented benefits in the management of resources

8-5 Marketing DSS (MKDSS)

The importance and versatility of computer applications in general, and DSS in particular, are well documented in the literature [7]. Appendix C provides the result of a survey of such applications. A marketing DSS (MKDSS), like any other DSS, includes three important components: dialog management, data base, and model base. An effective MKDSS should provide timely, accurate, and integrated information regarding the marketing mix (price, promotion, place, and product). To achieve this goal, the MKDSS data base must collect and store certain data. The model base component of this system should also be able to perform certain analyses. Table 8-3 illustrates the data base component and Table 8-4 illustrates the model base components of an MKDSS.

Table 8-3 ▪ Types of Data Needed by MKDSS to be Stored in its Data Base

Area	Type of Data Needed	Source of Data
Economy	General level of economic activity Economic activity within industry	Economic indicators Survey of current business *U.S. Industrial Outlook* *Standard and Poor's Industry Survey* *Conference Board Record* Trade publications
Legal environment	Changes impacting all businesses Changes impacting industry	General business publications such as *Business Week* and *Wall Street Journal* Trade publications
Technology	Available technology and expected trends	Trade publications Trade shows
Consumers	Current and potential customers Tastes and preferences Characteristics	Marketing research Sales force reports Census data *County and City Data Book* *A Guide to Consumer Markets* *The Average American Book* *Survey of Buying Power* *Commercial Atlas and Marketing Guide*

continued

Table 8-3 ▪ Continued

Area	Type of Data Needed	Source of Data
Competition	Current and potential competitors Strengths and weaknesses Strategies Customers Sales	Marketing research Sales force reports Syndicated services Trade publications *F & S Index of Corporations and Industries* *Standard and Poor's Register of Corporations* *Thomas Register of Manufacturers*
Sales	Market potential Market share Sales by product, customer, and so on	Sales force reports Market research Accounting information Syndicated services
Markets	Size of various segments Demographic changes and shifts Regional changes and shifts Segment identification Market share Market position	Marketing research *Measuring Markets: A Guide to Federal and State Statistics* *Marketing Information Guide* *Marketing Information Professional Reference Guide*
Cost	Expense ratios Financial ratios	Accounting information systems

Reprinted by permission from *Business Insights*. Hossein Bidgoli and Robert Harmon, "Marketing Decision Support Systems," 3, no. 1 (Spring 1987).

Table 8-4 ▪ Examples of Types of Analyses and Models Needed for MKDSS

Type of Analysis	Description	Examples of Models
Market analysis	Study of the nature and composition of the market including market size, market segments, and market potentials	Market demand function, demographic analysis
Market share analysis	Study of a firm's sales relative to competition	Market share determination, market response models
Sales analysis	Study of the composition of a firm's sales by product, brand size, territory, customer type, and so on	Sales response function, territory analysis

Type of Analysis	Description	Examples of Models
Cost analysis	Study of a firm's expenses and financial position for the overall company and by products	Financial ratio analysis
Sales forecasting	Prediction and estimation of a firm's sales	Regression analysis, time series analysis, Box-Jenkins
Simulation	Performance of "what-if" analysis by simulating various decision-making situations	Competitive analysis, sales response, profit response
Comparative analysis	Simulation of various strategies and alternatives to compare outcomes of various decisions	Competitive analysis
Sales force analysis	Study of the effectiveness and efficiency of sales staff	Scheduling and routing, sales force size, territory assignment, optimal number of customer calls
Media selection analysis	Comparison of alternative media choices	Linear programming, stepwise regression, simulation models, advertising allocation model
Price analysis	Determination of the elasticity of price changes on demand	Competitive bidding model, price change models, product line pricing models

Reprinted by permission from *Business Insights*. Hossein Bidgoli and Robert Harmon, "Marketing Decision Support Systems," 3, no. 1 (Spring 1987).

8-6 Personnel DSS (PDSS)

A personnel DSS (PDSS) is designed to provide information to assist decision-makers in the personnel department in carrying out their tasks in a more effective way. PDSS deals with the human element, the most valuable resource in the organization. Due to the complexity and diversity of skills utilized by a typical large organization, retention and promotion of a skilled labor force is a challenging task. Affirmative action decisions, minority employees, and work force planning all have made management of human resources more complex. An effective PDSS, when designed properly can serve as a valuable tool for human-resource directors. The data base component of a PDSS should include data presented in Table 8-5. The model base component should perform analyses highlighted in Table 8-6.

Table 8-5 ▪ Types of Data Needed by PDSS in its Data Base

Type of Data Needed	Source of Data
Employee personal data	Personnel files
Positions held in the organization	Personnel files
Skills	Personnel files
Employee work hours	Personnel files
Employee education	Personnel files
Employee work experience	Personnel files
Employee ethnic background	Personnel files
Training requirement	Personnel files
Labor union requirements	Labor union information
Job market data	Colleges, universities, trade schools
Government requirements	Published government data
Affirmative action data	Published government data
Equal opportunity employment data	Published government data

Table 8-6 ▪ Examples of Types of Analyses and Models Needed for PDSS

Type of Analysis	Description	Examples of Models
Recruitment analysis	To choose the best candidate	Sort routine Simple statistical models Correlation analysis
Skills evaluation	To maintain and update the most recent skills of employees	Data base management system
Scheduling assignment	To schedule and assign employees to the most suitable assignments	Assignment models, simulation models
Job-appraisal analysis	To promote the most competent employees	Correlation analysis Performance analysis
Job-pattern analysis	To trace the pattern of employee growth internally and externally	Markov analysis models
Achieving worker objectives	To achieve worker objectives within the internal and external constraints	Goal programming
Work force planning	To determine work-force requirements of the organization	Forecasting models
Training and skill development	To assess and implement the training needs of the organization	Forecasting and statistical models

Type of Analysis	Description	Examples of Models
Affirmative action requirements	To provide affirmative action reports	Statistical models
Resource allocation	To allocate human and financial resources	Budgeting models Linear programming models Simulation models

8-7 Financial DSS (FDSS)

The goal of a financial DSS (FDSS) is to provide diverse financial information to finance executives in a timely manner. An FDSS uses internal and external data, mathematical and statistical models, and a user-friendly interface to achieve this goal. By using what-if, goal-seeking, and sensitivity analyses, an FDSS should be able to highlight and analyze different financial scenarios. To achieve the financial goals of an organization, the data base of an FDSS should include data presented in Table 8-7. For performing different analyses, an FDSS should include models presented in Table 8-8.

8-8 Strategic Planning DDS (SPDSS)

The goal of strategic planning DSS (SPDSS) is to help chief executives make long-range strategic decisions [6], even though the majority of these decisions are either semistructured or unstructured. An SPDSS can generate timely information regarding long-range planning, corporate planning, simulation, and decisions regarding new products and new plants. An SPDSS utilizes data presented in Table 8-9 from various functional areas; the models and analyses are presented in Table 8-10. In the near future, the integration of DSS and AI technologies may improve the effectiveness of an SPDSS.

8-9 The Behavioral Issues in Information Technology

Design and implementation of any computer-based information system will affect employees in an organization in different ways. Resistance to change may play an important role in the success or failure of any new system.

Resistance to change is directly related to the position of an employee in an organization (e.g., operational management, tactical management, and strategic management) [9]. It is also related to the age and experience of the employees. Older employees tend to be less receptive to new technology than younger employees, and employees on the whole react differently to the introduction of new technology. Hostile reactions may appear as aggression, projection, and/or avoidance [9].

Table 8-7 ▪ Types of Data Needed by FDSS in its Data Base

Area	Type of Data Needed	Source of Data
Accounting	Raw materials Labor Overhead	Accounting information systems
Budgeting	Sources and uses of funds including sales, production and operating expenses	Accounting information systems
Auditing	Related internal and external audit data	Accounting information systems External sources for the same industry
Internal financial data	Financial management and control	Accounting information systems
External financial data	Interest rate, financial regulation	Financial community, published government material, Federal Reserve Banking Index

Table 8-8 ▪ Examples of Types of Analyses and Models for FDSS

Type of Analysis	Description	Examples of Models
What-if analysis	To allocate budget	Spreadsheet models
Financial forecast	To predict financial needs	Forecasting models, regression, exponential smoothing, and so on
Risk assessment	To minimize capital investment risks	Risk analysis models Expected value analysis models
Why and when analysis	To justify financial allocation	Expert systems/DDS
Cost analysis	To monitor cost trends	Forecasting models Correlation analysis
Financial management	To manage cash flows	Cash flow models
Financial control	To control financial resources	Financial ratio analysis (current ratio, acid test, and so on)
Investment analysis	To determine portfolio structure	Portfolio models
Borrowing analysis	To determine timing of borrowing decision	Present value, future value, rate of return

Table 8-9 ▪ Types of Data Needed by SPDSS in its Data Base

Area	Type of Data Needed	Source of Data
Marketing	Customers	Accounting information systems
	Competition	Marketing information systems
Corporate planning	Competition	Marketing information systems
Forecasting	Sales	Accounting information systems Marketing information systems
Finance	Funds management	Accounting information systems
Plant location	Production	Accounting information systems and manufacturing information systems
Product planning	Production	Marketing information systems and manufacturing information systems
Merger and acquisition	Finance Marketing	Financial information systems Marketing information systems
Personnel planning	Personnel	Personnel information systems

Table 8-10 ▪ Examples of Types of Analyses and Models Needed for SPDSS

Type of Analysis	Description	Examples of Models
Finance	To analyze financial policy	Portfolio models Capital budgeting models Forecasting models
Marketing	To analyze marketing policy	Market analysis models Segmentation analysis models, simulation models
Manufacturing	To analyze production policy	Plant location models Product planning models Optimization models
Personnel	To analyze personnel policy	Statistical models Forecasting models

An employee harboring aggression may go so far as to harm the system physically. He or she will take advantage of any opportunity to stop the operation of the system. In the case of an avoidance reaction, the employee simply will continue to use the old system until the new system fails. In the case of projection, the employee attributes real or imagined difficulty to the system. For more discussion on these three reactions, aggression, avoidance, and projection, see Dickson and Simmons [9].

Employees may resist the changes for many reasons. The employee may think he or she is unable to use the system, or the system may create time pressures, role ambiguity, feelings of insecurity, added complexity, and so forth. The employee may falsely conclude that his or her job is threatened.

Resistance issues may be more severe in EDP/MIS than in DSS. Since DSSs are usually designed to support a decision-maker and since they are not intended to replace the human element, they may be more easily accepted than the EDP/MIS type. However, by active user and management involvement, by clear definition of the objectives of the system, and by use of a prototype, the DSS designers may eliminate or at least minimize these troublesome issues.

Table 8-11 [2, 16] highlights some of the common problems associated with information technology and some suggested solutions. A successful DSS designer will consider these factors, and incorporate them into DSS design methodologies.

8-10 Information Technology and Organization Levels

A DSS designer must distinguish the characteristics of information systems to be designed and utilized by each level of the organization. This is essential, since each level has different needs and different personal and organizational styles. This distinction—made possible through identification of sources of data, types of data, output format, and so on—will expedite the introduction and utilization of these systems.

Table 8-12 [12, p. 59] summarizes the major attributes of a DSS at various organizational levels.

The format of the information provided by the DSS may need to be different for each organizational level. For example, graphs are more useful in strategic planning than in operational control, since it is easier to show trends and forecasts through graphs rather than through other types of data format.

8-11 Guidelines for Building a DSS

To summarize the presentation in this chapter, we would like to provide you with a series of guidelines for building a DSS. These guidelines, summarized in Table 8-13, may serve as a checklist [10, 20, 23].

Table 8-11 ▪ Behavioral Problems and Suggested Solutions

Problem	Suggested Solutions
Styles and status	Modify output format to suit the user's preference (Chapter 6)
Organizational roles or status	Modify input device to fit organizational roles or status (Chapter 6)
Habit, experience with the old system	Make use of the new system mandatory
Unfamiliarity with the new system	Sell the system by providing continuing education (Chapter 7)
Too technical for a typical user	Design a flexible and easy to use system (Chapters 6 and 7)
Problems with formal system	Use informal as well as formal channels of information
Ambiguity in the goals and objectives of the system	Define the goals of the system clearly (Chapter 7)
Information provided is too voluminous	Use exception-reporting system (Chapter 6)
The user does not know how his or her job would be improved by the system	Clarify and explain the mission of the system (Chapter 7)
Lack of flexibility in user/system interface	Provide several options for user/system interface (Chapter 6)
Threat to security and familiarity	Keep the impacted employee informed
Resistance to change	Spread the credit, get user/management involved (Chapter 7)
System is more advanced than the user	Provide training and education (Chapter 7)
Turnover and organizational change	Provide comprehensive documentation, provide modularity (Chapter 7)
Organizational readiness	Start readiness (provide training first); then implement the system (Chapter 7)
Gap between user and data processing personnel	Use intermediary and task force design (Chapter 7)
Image problem	Use flexible user/system interface (Chapter 6)
Conflicts between different organizational units	User task force design (Chapter 7)

Table 8-12 ▪ Information Characteristics and Organizational Levels

	Organizational Levels		
DSS Attributes	Operational Management	Tactical Management	Strategic Planning
Currency of data	Highly current	Moderately current	Very old
Frequency of DSS use	Very frequent	Semifrequent	Infrequent
Level of data aggregation	No aggregation	Some aggregation	Very aggregated
Data accuracy	Very high	Moderately high	Low
Scope of collected data	Very narrow	Moderately narrow	Very wide
Sources of data	Mostly internal	Mixed (internal and external)	Mostly external
Time horizon emphasized by the system	Past	(Mostly past, some future)	Future
Output format	Detail reports	(Detail and summary)	Exception reports
Uses of graphs	Very small	Moderate	Large
General user/ system interface	Mostly scheduled reports	Scheduled reports and some exception reports	Exception summary reports

Table 8-13 ▪ Guidelines for Building a Successful DSS

Consider the behavioral issues in DSS design
Identify the DSS attributes and the organizational level at which a DSS is going to be utilized (Table 8-12)
Get top management involved
Get key users involved
Use a task-force design
Conduct analyses of critical-success factors in conjunction with users' needs assessment
Try to use existing hardware/software technologies (if possible)
Develop the system in stages
Use prototypes
Use DSS generators (if possible)
Define goals and objectives of the DSS clearly
Ascertain that there is a need felt for the system
Provide training and education

Consider user requirements in the context of:
feasibility
simplicity
reliability
accuracy
economy
compatibility
Consider user attitudes, psychological reactions, and organizational factors [20, p. 11]
Establish effective communication both for motivation of the effected employees and information transfer
Keep the user/system interface simple
Let decision-makers determine information usefulness

8-12 Summary

This chapter provided a series of guidelines for building DSSs in different functional areas. To build a DSS two important views must be carefully analyzed: managerial and technical. This chapter emphasized the managerial view. If the components of a DSS are designed from the managerial designer perspective, then the technical designer can take over and construct the system. The chapter discussed the behavioral issues in DSS design and provided DSS characteristics and their relationships to different organizational levels. It concluded with a series of guidelines for building a successful DSS. The next chapter provides guidelines for successful DSS product selection.

Review Questions

1. What is the objective of the problem-definition phase for building a DSS?

2. Why must a task force be found prior to the construction of a DSS?

3. Who usually are the participants of the task force?

4. Why should top management have a representative in the task force?

5. Why must a prototype be designed first before the final construction of a DSS?

6. Will this prototype be converted into the final DSS or will it be abandoned?

7. How do you use the adoptive design methodology in building a DSS?

8. Where does an iterative design come into the design of a DSS?

9. Why is the managerial designer's viewpoint so important?

10. Discuss the input/output of a manufacturing DSS.

11. Discuss the input/output of a marketing DSS.

12. What are some of the internal data sources for a manufacturing DSS? For a marketing DSS?

13. What are some of the external data sources for a personnel DSS? For a financial DSS?

14. What is the role of a manufacturing DSS in inventory-control operations?

15. What are some of the decisions that may be supported by a personnel DSS? By a financial DSS?

16. How may strategic planning benefit from DSS?

17. Why are DSS generators preferred to DSS tools in building an operational DSS?

18. What is the importance of critical-success factors in building a DSS?

19. How do you relate the critical-success factors and the user needs?

20. How do you conduct cost/benefit analysis in building a DSS?

21. What are the behavioral issues in DSS design? Why must the designer of a DSS identify these issues?

22. What are DSS characteristics and their relationships with organizational levels? Why is such identification so crucial?

Projects

1. Research an operational DSS in the marketing area. How was this DSS built? Which tools were used? What decisions are supported by this DSS? (*Hint:* See Appendix C).

2. Neighbor Community Bank is trying to establish a DSS for its credit department. It needs your advice. What are five important points which you may give to the bank prior to the construction of its DSS?

3. Research MRP as a DSS for the manufacturing area. What are the input/process/output of this system? What is really needed to establish an MRP system? What are the strengths and weaknesses of a system of this type?

4. Research an organization of your choice. Conduct an interview with the chief financial officer. How is this individual making his or her financial decision? Is any DSS involved? If yes, what type of information is provided by this system?

5. Using any DSS tool or generator with which you are familiar, design a small-scale DSS in finance, marketing, manufacturing, and personnel. What are the advantages of a system like this? Can these small-scale systems be developed into a final DSS?

Key Terms

Problem definition
Formation of the task force
Construction of an on-line prototype
Evaluation

Small-scale system
Prototype
User reaction
Iterative approach
Design team
Adoptive design
Short-range needs
Medium-range needs
Long-range needs
DSS tools
DSS generators
Managerial design
Technical design
Manufacturing DSS (MFDSS)
What-if analysis
Inventory control
Internal data
External data
Material requirement planning (MRP)
Economic order quantity (EOQ)
Marketing mix
Personnel DSS(PDSS)
Human element
Financial DSS (FDSS)
Strategic planning DSS (SPDSS)
Top-management involvement
User involvement
Critical success factor
Stage development
Feasibility
Simplicity
Reliability
Accuracy
Economy
Compatibility
Psychology reaction
Behavioral issues
Material resource planning (MRP II)

References

[1] Alexander, David J. 1986. Planning and Building a DSS. *Datamation* (March 15): 115–21

[2] Alter, Steven, and Michael Ginzburg. 1978. Managing Uncertainty in MIS Implementation. *Sloan Management Review* (Fall): 23–31.

[3] Attaran, Mohsen, and Hossein Bidgoli. 1986. Developing an Effective Manufacturing Decision Support System. *Business* (October-December): 9–16.

[4] Attaran, Mohsen, and Hossein Bidgoli. 1988. CBMFIS: Core of the Factory of the Future. *Industrial Management & Data Systems* (May): 6–12.

[5] Bariff, M. L., and E. J. Lusk. 1977. Cognitive and Personality Tests for the Design of Management Information Systems. *Management Science* 23, no. 8 (April): 820–28.

[6] Bidgoli, Hossein, and Mohsen Attaran. 1988. Improving the Effectiveness of Strategic Decision Making Using an Integrated Decision Support System. *Information and Software Technology* 30, no. 5 (June): 278–284.

[7] Bidgoli, Hossein, and Robert R. Harmon. 1987. Marketing Decision Support Systems. *Business Insights* 3, no. 1 (Spring): 20–26.

[8] Carper, William B. 1977. Human Factors in MIS. *Journal of Systems Management* (November): 48–50.

[9] Dickson, G. W., and John K. Simmons. 1970. The Behavioral Side of MIS. In *Marketing Information Systems: Selected Readings* by Charles D. Schewe. American Marketing Association, 1976, pp. 65–77.

[10] Diprimio, Anthony. 1984. Develop a Five-Step Plan to Launch Decision Support Systems. *Bank Systems and Equipment* (September): 56–58.

[11] Ginzberg, M. J. 1978. Redesign of Managerial Tasks: A Requisite for Successful DSS. *MIS Quarterly* 2, no. 1 (March): 39–52.

[12] Gorry, G. A., and Michael Scott-Morton. 1971. A Framework for MIS. *Sloan Management Review* 13, no. 1 (Fall): 55–70.

[13] Howard, Geoffry S., and G. Jay Weinroth. 1987. Users' Complaints: Information System Problems From the User's Perspective. *Journal of Systems Management* (May): 8–15.

[14] Huff, Sid L. 1986. DSS Development: Promise and Practice. *Journal of Information Systems Management* (Fall): 8–15.

[15] Hurst, E. G., Jr., D. N. Ness, T. J. Gambino, and T. H. Johnson. 1983. Growing DSS: A Flexible, Evolutionary Approach. In *Building Decision Support Systems* by John L. Bennet. Reading, Mass.: Addison-Wesley Publishing Company, pp. 111–32.

[16] Keen, P. G. W. 1981. Value Analysis: Justifying Decision Support Systems. *MIS Quarterly* 5, no. 1 (March): 1–16.

[17] Keen, P. G. W., and T. J. Gambino. 1983. Building a Decision Support System: The Mythical Man-Month Revisited. In *Building Decision Support Systems* by John L. Bennet. Reading, Mass.: Addison-Wesley Publishing Company, pp. 133–72.

[18] Keen, P. G. W., and G. R. Wagner. 1974. DSS: An Executive Mind-Support System. *Datamation* 25 (November): 117–22.

[19] Moore, J. H., and M. G. Chang. 1983. Meta-Design Considerations in Building DSS. In *Building Decision Support Systems* by John L. Bennet. Reading, Mass.: Addison-Wesley Publishing Company, pp. 173–204.

[20] Multinovich, Jugoslav S., and Vladimir Vlahovich. 1984. A Strategy for Successful MIS/DSS Implementation. *Journal of Systems Management* (August): 8–16.

[21] Niven, Celestine A. 1980. The Seven 'R' Paradigms: What Managers Should Know About Decision Support Systems. *Industrial Management* (January-February): 19–20.

[22] Partow-Navid, Parviz. 1987. Misuse and Disuse of DSS Models. *Journal of Systems Management* (April): 38–40.

[23] Reck, Robert H., and James R. Hall. 1986. Executive Information Systems: An Overview of Development. *Journal of Information Systems Management* (Fall): 25–30.

[24] Stabell, Charles B. 1983. A Decision-Oriented Approach to Building DSS. In *Building Decision Support Systems* by John L. Bennet. Reading, Mass.: Addison-Wesley Publishing Company, pp. 221–60.

[25] Wright, D. J., G. Capon, R. Page, J. Quiroga, A. A. Tassen, and F. Tomasini. 1986. Evaluation of Forecasting Methods for Decision Support. *International Journal of Forecasting*: 139–52.

9 An Integrated Model for DSS Products Evaluation

9-1 Introduction

This chapter provides a series of guidelines for selection and implementation of DSS products. Since there are so many of these products on the market, the selection process has become a complicated task. Each DSS user has different needs and desires. The guidelines provided in this chapter should provide a comprehensive model for DSS users and designers. This model should assist in a successful selection of a DSS product—one that will meet the organizational and personal needs of DSS users.

This chapter first provides a series of methodologies for assessing information needs of DSS users. Then three stages related to DSS product selection—software, hardware, and vendor—are analyzed. After this analysis, three important components of a DSS, data base, model base, and dialog, are analyzed. For sophisticated users, extended features are also explored. Finally, a quantitative model for final selection of each DSS product is provided.

9-2 Why DSS Products?*

DSS products, DSS generators, end-user programming languages, and fourth-generation languages (4 GLs) present a viable option for design and implementation of a DSS in a variety of organizational settings. If these products are used for developing a functional DSS, they contain some unique features [1, 16, 18] in comparison with traditional high-level programming languages such as FORTRAN, and COBOL:

*A version of this chapter has been published by the author in *Journal of Systems Management* (November 1988). These materials are reprinted by special permission of JSM.

- They are easier to use.
- They require shorter installation time.
- They present unique prototyping features.
- They facilitate adoptive design.
- It is easier to train end users on these products.
- They are less expensive.
- They increase a programmer's productivity.
- They are more powerful than their counterparts.

Since there are so many of these products available for both mainframes and microcomputers, selecting such products requires diligent research and multidimensional analysis. In the following pages we provide some guidelines for selecting and implementing these products in a comprehensive manner.

9-3 Information Needs Assessment: A Wish List Approach

Decision-makers have different information needs, styles, and preferences. At the same time, DSS products present different types of analysis with many kinds of formats such as modeling products and products that are data-management oriented. In any case, analysis of information needs should provide a sound background for further analyses of these products.

Assessment of needs must include the present information needs and general information needs of different decision-makers for the next 3 to 5 years. A needs assessment must determine and analyze the organizational styles and preferences of decision-makers.

Defining the information needs of a decision-maker is crucial prior to choosing a DSS product. Each DSS product has distinct capabilities. Types of analyses provided by these products, their output formats, the way in which they interface with the users, and so on, are different. Considering a decision-maker's personal and organizational styles, therefore, plays an important role in selecting a DSS product.

There are several ways to define the information needs of a decision-maker. Traditionally, either data analysis or decision analysis has been used for information needs assessment.

The data analysis approach *first* determines what information a decision-maker is currently receiving and *second* determines the decision-maker's information needs that are not met. The data analysis approach uses techniques, such as questionnaires, interviews, and observations, to determine the decision-maker's information needs. This bottom-up approach has some shortcomings. The decision-maker may not know his or her information needs. Also, this information may not be directly linked to decisions made by a decision-maker.

The decision analysis approach first identifies all the decisions made by a decision-maker. Then a system is designed that uses different data and models in order to provide the information required by a decision-maker. The decision analysis (top-down) approach presents more structure. In addition, the information provided by this approach is closely related to the needs of a decision-maker. However, this may be difficult.

Another approach, the critical success factor (CSF), introduced by John Rockart [14], focuses on an individual decision-maker and his or her current information needs. Time is essential in this approach because the information needs of a decision-maker change continuously. In this approach, decision-makers identify the goals and objectives and a series of key factors necessary for the success of their business. (For example, in the automobile industry, customer taste, styling, and dealership locations may be considered as CSFs.) Then information related to these factors is supplied. This approach also recognizes that some of these indicators may be temporary; therefore, it emphasizes the continuously changing information needs of the decision-maker.

The information needs of key users of a DSS can be defined using these tools and techniques. A clear, concise analysis of information requirements will provide a sound background for DSS product-selection.

Ideally, the result of this analysis identifies the needs of a particular user or users. It may identify specific modeling or data management needs, types of forecasting and simulation needs, types of interfaces, and general capabilities of a DSS product. If a careful analysis is done, the final result will be a series of guidelines that can identify which DSS products may be most suitable. Further analysis of the products will be necessary to determine the best of the options.

9-4 Formation of a Task Force for DSS Selection

A DSS may be designed for a functional area of an organization such as finance, marketing, or production; it may be designed for the entire organization; it may be designed for a special purpose, project, or assignment; it may be designed for research; or perhaps other reasons. In any case the key representative of present and/or prospective user groups must participate in the selection of DSS products.

Involving key DSS users from the very beginning should increase the chances of a successful design and implementation of a DSS. As mentioned earlier, since different users have a broad spectrum of information needs and unique decision-making styles, their participation in the selection process plays an important role for functional analysis of a DSS product.

The second group of participants must come from top management. Participation of senior management representatives provides both financial support and commitment for the present and future success of a DSS.

The third group of participants are software and hardware specialists. These individuals can be from inside or outside of the organization. Specialists from the organization are preferred, since they are closer to the users and understand the environment of the DSS better than the outsiders. The main responsibility of the software and hardware specialists is to help define the

Figure 9-1 Participants of DSS Selection Task Force

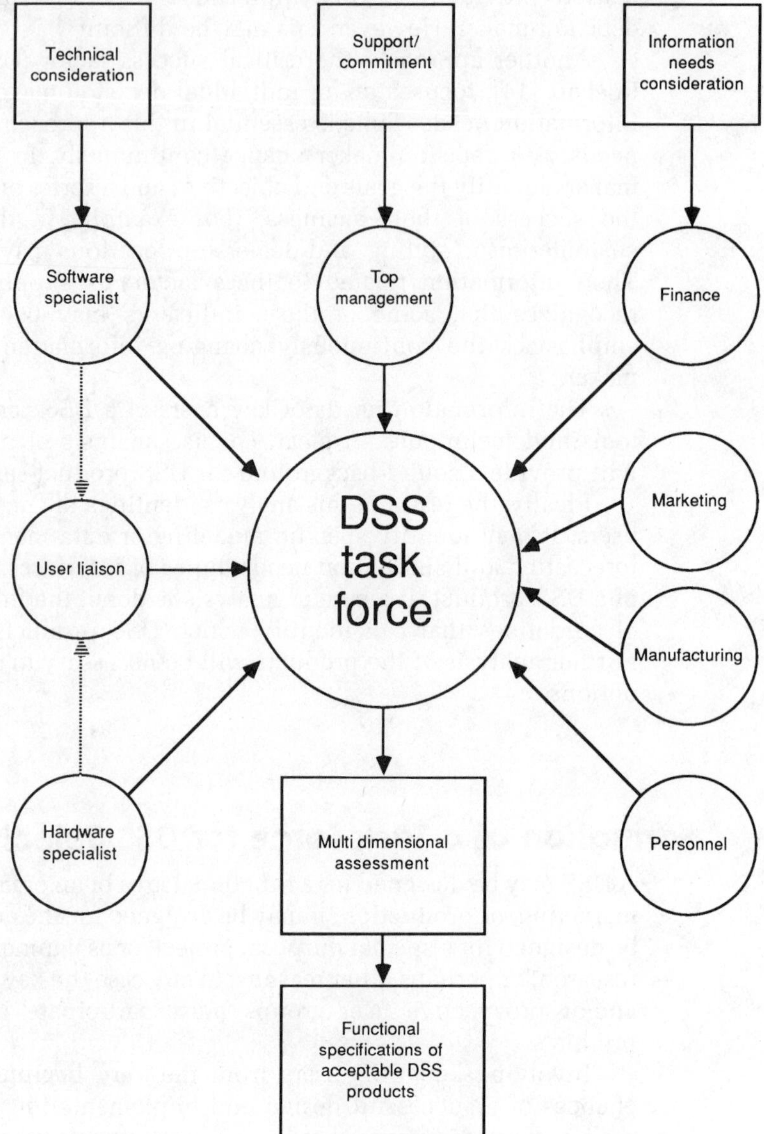

DSS requirements. These may include technical constraints, performance requirements, compatibility issues, and so forth. In other words, these specialists put the user requirements into perspective. Figure 9-1 [12] illustrates the participants of a DSS task force.

This multidimensional participation and analysis should provide a comprehensive understanding of the DSS, and it should also provide realistic guidelines for the DSS product selection.

9-5 The Triangle of Success

Selecting a DSS product involves three stages of analysis. In the first stage the general dimensions of an acceptable product are carefully analyzed. In the second and third stages, the technical capabilities of a DSS product are carefully analyzed. These analyses are performed by the task force team. Figure 9-2 illustrates the first stage of analysis. As this figure shows, this stage involves a careful examination of software, hardware, and vendors of a DSS. In the second and third stages these components are further analyzed.

Software Analysis

One of the most important components of a DSS product is the software. Since the software is usually run on the existing hardware, in many cases the software is the entire system, especially from the user's viewpoint. Several important factors must be carefully considered before selecting software.

Ease of use, or *user-friendliness*, is the key factor in software analysis. As discussed in Chapter 6, the user/system interface is one of the most important features of a DSS. Systems that are menu-driven and work in an interactive fashion are more acceptable to DSS users than the other types of systems, which work either on batch mode or command language. Also, the amount of training needed to get a user started on a DSS is important. The shorter the training time, the more acceptable the system will be.

Figure 9-2 First Stage of DSS Product Analysis

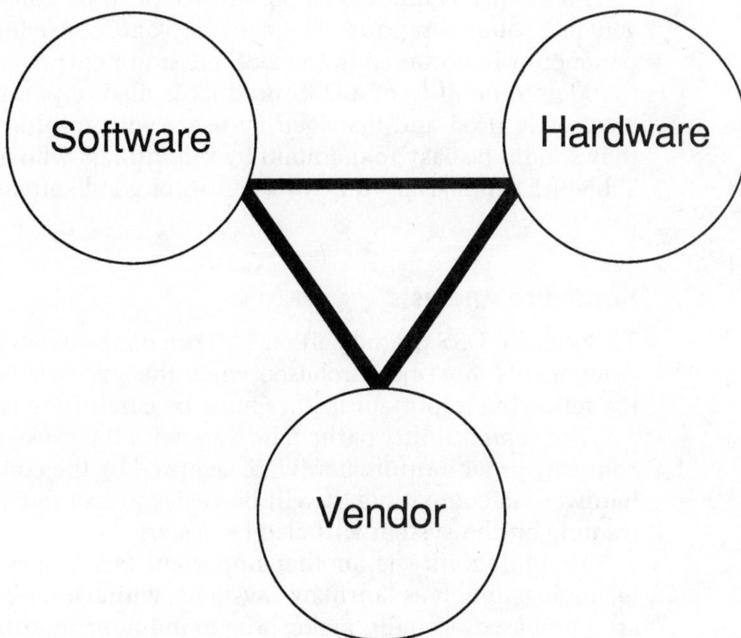

Table 9-1 ▪ Critical Features of Good Software

Easy to learn and use
Good documentation
Availability of error traps and error correction
Update availability
Volume handling
Reliability
Maintainability

Another important factor is documentation, which includes all the supporting documents that accompany a product. Comprehensive documentation has been one of the weakest areas in computer industry. Good documentation must be easy to read and understand, it should include error traps and error correction, and it should also help a user to enter and exit the system at any point. The documentation should include a help screen and a variety of internal documentation to help the user learn to use the software quickly.

Update availability is another important feature. Software products are continuously upgraded and corrected by adding new features and improving technical capabilities, for example. The major concern to DSS users is whether such updates are going to be available; if they are, the cost of gaining access to these updates is also a concern.

Volume handling is another issue that must be considered. This includes the number of fields, records, and files handled by a DSS product. It may also include the number of users who can access the system, processing time, and so on.

Reliability is another important factor to be considered, since DSSs must generate reliable reports. The accuracy and consistency of the reports are of paramount importance in the DSS environment.

Maintainability of a DSS product is also important. Since these products are mostly used and managed by users with minimum technical knowledge, they should be easy to maintain by individuals who are not computer experts. Table 9-1 summarizes the key features of good software.

Hardware Analysis

The selected DSS product either will run on the existing hardware, or hardware components must be purchased when the software is selected. In either case, the following important factors must be carefully analyzed.

The *compatibility* of the hardware with the present hardware system of the company or with future hardware acquired by the company is important. If the hardware is compatible, it will be easier to use the system; maintenance and training on the system will also be easier.

Maintainability is another important factor. The new trend in hardware technology involves "turnkey" systems, which are ready to use as soon as they are purchased. Usually major programming or modification is not needed for immediate operation. These types of systems are easier to maintain, even by individuals with minimum computer training.

Availability, or the degree of access to the system by other users employing access devices from different geographical locations in the organization, of the system is another important feature. Accessibility can also refer to the number of users who use the same program or model at the same time. This feature emphasizes the network capabilities, multiprogramming, and multitasking capabilities of a system.

Reliability usually refers to the downtime of a system and is another factor to be considered. How the system performs during peak times or the performance of the system under "stress" are indicators of system reliability.

Expandability is another important feature. To keep abreast of the future growth of the company, the system, including memory size, speed, throughput, input/output channels, networking capabilities, and so forth, must be expandable. Table 9-2 summarizes the key features of a good hardware system.

Vendor Analysis

There are many vendors offering DSS products. Not all these vendors provide the same service. Careful analysis of key features that must be supported by a good vendor can increase the chances of success in DSS selection and utilization.

Training provided by the vendor on hardware and particularly on software is very important. Some vendors provide on-site training, others provide training at vendor facilities, and some provide both. Some of these training sessions are free to the user, while others are very costly. Also, some vendors provide on-going training in parallel with the system updates. Vendors can also provide significant support and instructions on initial installation and provide on-going support for both training and maintenance of the system. Several vendors offer timely upgrades and assure the user of product reliability.

Hot line availability is another important feature to consider. Many of the questions asked by DSS users can be answered through a hot line service, which often operates on a 24-hour basis. However, few of these hotlines are very helpful, often causing users more confusion and frustration than support.

Availability of *knowledgeable staff* by the vendor is another important feature. Several vendors send their technical staff for on-site visits. These individuals sometimes provide consultation and introduce some of the new capabilities of the DSS product.

Table 9-2 ▪ Critical Features of a Good Hardware System

Compatibility to existing and future hardware
Maintainability
Availability (accessibility)
Reliability
Expandability

Table 9-3 ▪ Critical Features for a Good Vendor

Support training
Hotline availability
Knowledgeable staff
Newsletter/user group (both for business and academic)
Crisis reaction
Number of previous installations
Contract terms for hardware/software maintenance
Bundled and unbundled cost (initial and ongoing)
Local support
Financial stability
Active research and development

Newsletters and *user groups* are also very helpful. Some vendors continuously inform the users about the extended capabilities of the DSS product. They also support user groups by establishing a bulletin board and other on-line facilities.

Crisis reaction is also important. The user must investigate how a particular vendor may react to a crisis. This information can be either asked of other users of the system or of the vendors themselves. A few vendors provide a "loaner" at the time of the crisis and quickly resolve the crisis situation.

The number of *previous installations* is very important. Naturally, if a vendor has installed systems for various organizations, this verifies the quality of a system and vendor. Talking to people using these installations is the best safeguard for a new user when purchasing a new DSS.

Contract terms for both diagnostic and preventive maintenance, terms for maintenance contract renewal, and terms for relocation or reassignment of a DSS product are also important factors to be considered.

Local support of the vendor is also important. Such support may expedite the maintenance procedure in resolving an unexpected crisis situation.

Cost is naturally a very important factor. The DSS user must consider the bundled and unbundled costs, which include both cost of the system as a whole and costs of different components of the system. Table 9-3 summarizes the key features for a good vendor.

9-6 DSS Component Analysis

The triangle of success presents general features of a DSS product. In stages two and three of DSS-selection analysis, the emphasis is more on the technical features of a DSS product. As discussed in Chapters 4 through 6, in order for a DSS to be able to support all phases of decision making (intelligence, design, and choice) it must include three important components. We briefly explain these three components.

Data Base Analysis

As discussed in Chapter 4, a data base is one of the major components of a DSS. Some products are mainly data base–oriented products, and some are more modeling-oriented products. In any event, data base and data base management system components of a DSS must support some minimum capabilities. As mentioned in Chapter 4, the trend for data base is toward the relational data model; it seems this type of data modeling is gaining a lot of support in the user community. It is believed this type of data model is easier for computer novices to use and maintain. Table 9-4 summarizes basic requirements of DBMS components of a DSS.

Model Base Analysis

The model base component of a DSS was discussed in detail in Chapter 5. This DSS component performs some basic analyses. Table 9-5 summarizes the capabilities of a modeling DSS product.

Table 9-4 ▪ Key Features of DBMS Components of a DSS

File creation
File access
File modification
File update
Data dictionary
Automatic audit trails
Simple and multicriteria search
Sort using one key field and multiple key fields
Multifile access
File merge facility
File join facility
Access to both internal and external data bases
Security and privacy protection

Table 9-5 ▪ Key Features of Model Base Component of a DSS

Functions (general and user defined)
What-if analysis
Goal-seeking analysis
Sensitivity analysis
Statistical analysis (bivariate and multivariate)
Forecasting models (time series, regression, curve fitting)
Optimization models
Simulation models
Financial models
Scheduling models
Internal and external model access

Table 9-6 ▪ Key Features of Dialog Management Component of a DSS

Basic user/system interface
- Menu driven
- Question/answer
- Command language

Graphic display with different scaling, labeling, and sizing
Multiple graphs per page
Query capability (procedural and nonprocedural)
Exception type reporting
Multidimensional display
Different report generation and format
Help screens

Depending on a specific need of a decision-maker, one or more of these capabilities may carry a heavier weight. But, again, these capabilities are needed to support the design and the choice phases of decision making.

Dialog Management Analysis

From a user viewpoint, the dialog component of a DSS is the entire system. DSS users are not concerned about how different analyses are done or how a DBMS manages the DSS data base. Their primary concern is how easy and effective the system is to use. The dialog component of DSS was discussed in Chapter 6. For now, it should be emphasized that user-friendliness is perhaps the most important feature of a successful user/system interface. Table 9-6 summarizes the key features of this component of a DSS.

9-7 Extended Feature Analysis

During the third stage of DSS analysis, advanced technical features of a DSS product are examined. These special features are not of the same importance to all DSS users. However, features emphasize what is efficient and effective for the entire system. Table 9-7 summarizes important technical features of a DSS product.

9-8 Evaluation Tools

To make the selection process more rigorous, a series of evaluation tools must be utilized. These tools, if used effectively, can assist the analysis team in the selection of a suitable product. Let us briefly explain these different tools [7].

Benchmarks

A number of DSS products can be compared by evaluating how each performs the same task. A specific task is performed by these different systems; then the run time is measured. Naturally, a shorter run time is preferred.

Simulation

The technique of using a simulation program tries to measure the general capability of a DSS with regard to several important characteristics of a system. This may include system run time, CPU speed, input/output handling and instruction-execution speeds. Different systems can be rated based upon the performance of the simulation test.

Hardware and Software Monitoring

Monitoring is usually used if a DSS product must be installed over the existing hardware/software facility of an organization. This test tries to measure how the existing system must be upgraded in order to handle the new additional task (the new DSS). This may include CPU upgrade, input/output upgrade, number of channels upgrade, and so on.

Performance Power

The performance power technique is used to compare two DSS products by measuring execution times of individual instructions and then using mixed instructions. In other words, first one task is used and then a combination of tasks is examined collectively. The run time and performance of the two or more candidates are compared.

Table 9-7 ▪ Important Technical Features of a DSS Product

Multiuser access (multiprograming and multitasking)
Multidimensional analysis (e.g., product line, geographical location, time, other business variables, and so forth)
Response time
Computational cost
Memory requirement
Source code for the software (some source codes are faster than the others)
CPU cycle
Procedural and nonprocedural languages
Type of operating system
Accuracy and speed of calculations
Linkage capabilities to other hardware/software

Table 9-8 ▪ DSS Product Evaluation Tools

Benchmarks
Simulation
Hardware and software monitoring
Performance power
Programmer productivity
Structured walkthroughs

Programmer Productivity

The programmer productivity technique measures the effectiveness and efficiency of a DSS product in regard to a programmer or application developer. Two DSS products can be used by an application developer to develop a particular application, and then the amount of time spent on each product can be compared. The product that requires less time to develop the same application is more desirable.

Structured Walkthroughs

Structured walkthroughs expose a prospective DSS product to careful scrutiny by the DSS-selection task force. Careful examination of a candidate may highlight its strengths and weaknesses.

Among all these tools, benchmarks are probably the most accurate and commonly used. Even benchmarks have shortcomings, as production conditions may have an impact on the performance of different systems. These techniques should be used with caution. Analysis performed earlier on different components of DSS and hardware, software, and vendor considerations add more validity to these tools. Table 9-8 lists different evaluation tools.

9-9 A Quantitative Model

Quantification in such a multifaceted process is a very difficult task; however, with careful consideration, this quantification may be very helpful in finalizing the selection process. We suggest the following steps:

Step 1. Identify all the features offered by a DSS product.

Step 2. Ask the selection team (task force) to rate each feature of the proposed system from 1 to 7, where 7 means the feature is outstanding and 1 means the feature is either not available or it is extremely poor, 4 is average, under 4 is below average, and above 4 means better than average.

Step 3. Ask individual users to weigh each feature of the proposed system in regard to their specific needs from 1 to 7, where 7 means this feature of the system is extremely important, 4 means average importance, and 1 means unimportant or slightly important.

Step 4. Using different evaluation tools, assign a score between 1 and 3 to each candidate, where 3 means test results are excellent, 2 means average, and 1 means poor. For example, you may conduct a benchmark test of system X and assign a rating of 3 if the result of the test is excellent. If the result of the test is poor, you assign a rating of l.

Step 5. Multiply the scores of Step 2 by the result of Step 3. Add all these scores together. We call this score the gross total score of acceptability. Now multiply this score by the result of Step 4. This new score is the weighted acceptability score.

Step 6. Perform these five steps for all the candidates. Then choose the candidate with the highest total weighted acceptability score.

To illustrate the quantification process, examine the following example. A DSS product called Decision Companion is one of the candidates for selection by Alpha-Tek, a multinational department store chain. You have been asked to calculate the weighted acceptability score for this product.

First identify all the features offered by this system (Table 9-9). Then have each feature rated from 1 to 7 by the task force. After this rating, have each individual user rate each feature from 1 to 7, based on the importance of this feature to his or her needs. The products of Columns 2 and 3 are recorded in Column 4. The scores are summed and then multiplied by the evaluation score (or average evaluation score *if* more than one evaluation technique has been utilized). The final score is the weighted acceptability score.

To conduct a more thorough analysis of a DSS product, a detailed selection matrix can be generated. In this matrix, list all the features first, and then apply the rating system to this particular system. This calculation can be easily performed by any spreadsheet, such as Lotus 1–2–3 or SAS MATRIX.

Table 9-9 ▪ Summary Matrix for Decision Companion Selection Process

1	2	3	4
DSS Product Features	Task Force Rating	User Rating	2 by 3
Software support	6	7	42
Hardware support	7	7	49
Vendor support	7	7	49
Data base facility	3	1	3
Model base facility	7	7	49
Dialog facility	4	7	28
Extended features	3	1	3
Gross total scores of acceptability			223
Average evaluation score			2
Weighted acceptability score			446

To calculate the score for evaluation tools, we can list all the tools and assign a score only to the tool(s) that apply to a particular product or feature. If more than one tool is used, then the evaluation scores must be averaged. If any of the tools are not applicable to a particular DSS product, then in the appropriate column, N/A (not applicable) is recorded. Naturally, this score does not enter into the scoring procedure. For example, if only three tools were used and the other three received N/A, the three scores must be added then divided by 3 in order to calculate the average evaluation score. Evaluation can be performed either by the user or the task force. The quantitative model can be summarized in the following formula:

Weighted acceptability score $= W$
Average evaluation score $= A$
Gross total score of acceptability $= G$
Task force rating $= T$
User rating $= U$

$$W = A \times G, \text{ where } G = \sum_{i=1}^{7} T_i \times U_i$$

This process must be performed for all the candidates and the candidate with the highest value of W must be chosen. Table 9-10 illustrates a detailed selection matrix for Decision Companion.

Table 9-10 ▪ Detailed Matrix for Decision Companion Selection Process

1	2	3	4
DSS Product Features	Task Force Rating	User Rating	2 by 3
Software			
Easy to learn and use			
Good documentation			
Availability of error traps and error correction			
Updates availability			
Volume handling			
Reliability			
Maintainability			
Hardware			
Compatibility to the existing and future hardware			
Maintainability			
Availability			
Reliability			
Expandability			
Vendor			
Support training			
Hotline availability			

1	2	3	4
DSS Product Features	Task Force Rating	User Rating	2 by 3
Knowledgeable staff			
Newsletter/user group			
Crisis reaction			
Number of previous installations			
Contract terms for hardware/ software maintenance			
Bundled and unbundled costs			
Local support			
DBMS			
File creation			
File access			
File modification			
File update			
Simple and multi- criteria search			
Sort with one key and multiple keys			
Multifile access			
File merge facility			
File join facility			
Access to both internal and external data bases			
Security and privacy protection			
Model Base			
What-if analysis			
Goal-seeking analysis			
Sensitivity analysis			
Statistical analysis			
Forecasting models			
Optimization models			
Simulation models			
Financial models			
Scheduling models			
Internal and external model access			
Dialog			
Menu-driven			
Question/answer			
Command language			
Graphic display with different scaling, labeling, and sizing			
Query capability (procedural and nonprocedural)			
Exception type reporting			
Multidimensional display			
Different report generation and format			

continued

Table 9-10 ▪ Continued

1	2	3	4
DSS Product Features	Task Force Rating	User Rating	2 by 3
Extended Features			
Multiuser access (multiprogramming and multitasking)			
Multidimensional analysis (e.g., product line, geographical location, time, other business variables)			
Response time			
Computational cost			
Memory requirement			
Source code for the software			
CPU cycle			
Procedural and nonprocedural languages			
Type of operating system			
Accuracy and speed of calculations			
Evaluation Tools			
Benchmarks			
Simulation			
Hardware/software monitoring			
Performance power			
Programmer productivity			
Structured walkthroughs			

9-10 Summary

In this chapter a series of guidelines for DSS product selection were presented. Different components of a typical DSS, data base, model base, and dialog management were carefully analyzed. Discussion in this chapter attempted to link each feature of a DSS product to the needs of DSS users. The result of this analysis should lead to a DSS product that is closely tied to the needs of DSS users. This presentation should also help DSS users and designers to screen out the most appropriate DSS products from a large number of products available on the market.

Review Questions

1. Why and how is application development using 4GL easier than using high-level programming languages?

2. Mention the advantages of these languages for application development compared with their high-level programming languages counterparts.

3. How do you define the information needs of a decision-maker?

4. What is the difference between data analysis and decision analysis for information need assessment?

5. What is CSF? Why is this approach more effective for assessing information needs than the other approaches?

6. Who are the participants of DSS product-selection task force?

7. What are the important criteria of good software?

8. What are the important criteria of good hardware?

9. What are the important criteria of a good vendor?

10. What are the minimum capabilities of a DBMS in DSS environment?

11. What are some of the important features of the modeling component of a DSS?

12. What are some good features for the dialog management component of a DSS?

13. Among the evaluation tools, which tool is the most versatile one?

14. What is the unique application of hardware and software monitoring?

15. How can programmer productivity serve as an evaluation tool?

16. Describe the quantitative model as the evaluation tool in your own terms. What are some of the shortcomings of this model? What are the strengths?

Projects

1. Using CSF, try to define the information needs of a CEO of a private bank and the president of a state university. Apply data analysis and then decision analysis to the same problem. How do you compare these three techniques? Which technique is superior? Why? Discuss.

2. Compare Lotus Development Corporation and Ashton-Tate as two vendors of DSS products. Which vendor provides a better service? Why?

3. Choose two DSS modeling products for micros from Appendix A; then, using the model presented in this chapter, calculate the total scores of acceptability. We are assuming these two products are evaluated for the head of the forecasting department of a multinational textile company.

4. Research an organization of your choice that has recently installed a DSS. Has it used any evaluation tool discussed in this chapter? If yes, what is its opinion regarding such tools? If not, what is the alternative?

5. SAS as a modeling tool has gained popularity for both microcomputers and mainframe computers. Based on the criteria given in this chapter, investigate this claim.

6. Using the quantitative model given in this chapter, compare and contrast SAS and SPSS for a mainframe computer. Which one gains a higher score? Why?

Key Terms

Information-need-assessment
Data base
Model base
Dialog management
Extended-features
Quantitative-model
DSS products
DSS generators
End-user programming languages
Fourth-generation languages
FORTRAN
COBOL
Data analysis
Decision analysis
Questionnaire
Interview
Observation
Critical success factor
Task force
Top management
Software specialist
Hardware specialist
Technical constraints
Performance requirements
Compatibility issues
Ease of use (user-friendliness)
Documentation
Update availability
Volume handling
Reliability
Maintainability
Availability
Multiprogramming
Multitasking
Expandability
Vendor analysis
Training
Hot line
Knowledgeable staff
Newsletter
User groups
Bulletin board
Crisis reaction
Loaner
Previous installations
Contract terms
Local support
Relational data model
Data dictionary
Bivariate and multivariate analysis
Response time
Benchmarks
Simulation
Hardware/software monitoring
Performance power
Programmer productivity
Structured walkthroughs
Quantitative model
Gross total score of acceptability
Weighted acceptability score

References

[1] Athapilly, Kuria Kose, and Ron S. Galbreath. 1985. Practical Methodology Simplified DSS Software Evaluation Process. *Data Management* (February): 10–28.

[2] Cathe, P. J. 1969. Decide Answer You Need . . . and Leave the System to Us. *Iron Age* (May 15): 66–69.

[3] Cowart, Bob. 1985. Decision Support Software is Starting to Gain Acceptance. *PC Week* 2, no. 48 (December 3): 129–32.

[4] Davis, Michael, and Joseph L. Sardinas. 1985. Creating the Right Decision Support System Pitfalls. *Management Accounting* (June): 12–13.

[5] Digate, Charles. 1985. Integrated Packages Don't Fit Every Need, But They Suit Most. *Information Weekly* (September 30): 49.

[6] Garfinkel, David. 1985. The New Generation of Software That Helps Managers Make Decisions. *International Management* (August): 49–51.

[7] Gaydasch, Alexander. 1982. *Principles of EDP Management.* Reston, Va: Reston Publishing Company, Inc.: 220–22.

[8] Goyette, Richard.1980. Fourth Generation System Soothes End User Unrest. *Data Management* (January): 30–32.

[9] Knittle, Diana L, Stephen Ruth, and Ella Paton Gardner. 1987. Establishing User-Centered Criteria for Information Systems: A Software Ergonomics Perspective. *Information & Management* (November): 163–72.

[10] Kolodzieg, Stan. 1987. 4 GLs Find a Home. *Computerworld* (May 6): 47–54.

[11] Kull, David. 1986. Decision Support With 20/20 Foresight. *Computer Decisions* (May 6): 38–43.

[12] Meador, C. Lawrence, and Richard A. Mezger. 1984. Selecting an End User Programming Language for DSS Development. *MIS Quarterly* (December): 267–80.

[13] Munro, Malcolm C. 1978. Determining the Manager's Information Needs. *Journal of Systems Management* (June): 34–39.

[14] Rockart, John. 1979. Chief Executives Define Their Own Data Needs. *Harvard Business Review* (March–April): 81–93.

[15] Sayena, K. B. C., and Mohan Kaul. 1986. A Conceptual Architecture for DSS Generator. *Information & Management* (October): 149–57.

[16] Seilheimer, Steven D. 1986. Future Solutions to DP Problems Will Integrate Today's Technology. *Data Management* (November): 23–24.

[17] Stahl, Bob. 1986. The Trouble with Application Generators. *Datamation* (April 1): 93–94.

[18] Tinnirello, Paul. 1985. Making a Sensible 4GL Selection. *Computer Decisions* 17, no. 15 (July): 40–45.

part four

New Trends in DSS Environment

10 Microbased DSS and Executive Support Systems

10-1 Introduction

This chapter provides a quick overview of microcomputers and discusses their general capabilities as DSS tools or generators. Some of the most popular PC-DSS products are introduced. General tasks performed by microcomputers used in a DSS environment are discussed, and advantages and disadvantages of micros compared with mainframes in a DSS environment are elaborated. A series of guidelines regarding selection of a PC-based DSS are given, and some popular expert system products for PC's are introduced. Executive support systems as a new "buzzword" introduced in the field of information technology are briefly explored. The chapter concludes with a scenario for the future of microcomputers, which shows an exciting future for this very powerful tool.

10-2 Microcomputers: An Overview

If we mark the beginning of the microcomputer era at 1975, then during a relatively short period this technology has undergone significant changes, improving in every dimension. These computers started as 8-bit machines; they moved to 16-bit, and now 32-bit microcomputers are available. Micros started as single-user and single-tasking machines and are becoming multiuser and multitasking machines. These features enable microcomputers to process more than one task at a time and allow more than one user to process data at the same time.

When using microcomputers in a DSS environment, memory and speed have been two major barriers. It seems in the near future these issues will no longer be a problem. The speed of microcomputers has been steadily increasing because of more advanced chip technology and enhanced operating systems. Since microcomputers are inexpensive and are relatively easy to use, they are more attractive to computer novices.

10-3 Microcomputers as DSS Tools

As we discussed in Chapter 3, a DSS can be built by using either DSS tools or a DSS generator. Microcomputers, with their diverse capabilities, can be used either as tools or generators. These capabilities may be made available through the use of several software packages or through the use of a single integrated package. Let us briefly explain the general capabilities of microcomputers.

Spreadsheet Software

Spreadsheet programs can be broadly classified into two types. Type 1 is a dedicated spreadsheet. This means the program only performs spreadsheet analysis. VisiCalc (by Visicorp) is a good example of this type. The other type of spreadsheet package, such as Lotus, is an integrated software, which means it can perform more than one type of analysis. Lotus is capable of performing spreadsheet analysis as well as data base and graphics. Other popular integrated packages include Symphony, by Lotus Development Corporation; Framework, by Ashton-Tate; Enable, by Alphy Software Corporation; Smart Software System, by Innovative Software, Inc.; UniCalc, by Lattice, Inc.; Multiplan, by Microsoft Corp.; and Electronic Desk, by the Software Group, Inc. In either case, the number of jobs performed by a spreadsheet program is unlimited. Generally speaking, any application suitable for a row and column setting is a candidate for a typical spreadsheet.

Data Base Software

Data base software is designed for performing data base operations, including file creation, deletion, modification, search, sort, merge, and join. The data base portion of Lotus, for example, is capable of performing basic data-management operations. Other popular database programs include dBASE III and III Plus, by Ashton-Tate; Business Filevision, by Telos Software Products; R-Base 5000 by Microrim Corporation; and PC-File III, by Buttonware, Inc.

Graphics Software

Graphics software has been designed to convert business data into graphics. Data can be converted into a line graph to show a trend, to a pie chart to highlight the ingredients of a data item, and to other types of graphs for different analyses.

Graphics are done either by integrated packages such as Lotus or Symphony or by dedicated graphic packages. Two of the popular graphic packages are Freelance, by Graphic Communications; and Energraphics, by Enertronics Research, Inc.

Communications Software

Using a modem and communications software, your microcomputer can easily connect you to a wealth of information available in public and private data bases. Some packages, such as Symphony by Lotus Development Corporation, include a communication program within the package itself. However, there are many other communications software products on the market, among them being On-Line, by Micro-Systems Software, Inc.; Pfs:Access, by Software Publishing Corp.; Smartcom II, by Hayes Microcomputer Products, Inc.; and Crosstalk, by Microstuf, Inc.

Word Processing Software

A microcomputer used as a word processor is very similar to a typewriter with a memory. With such a facility, you can generate documents and do deletion, insertion, cut and paste, and so on. There are numerous word-processing programs on the market. Some of the popular ones include Volkswriter, by Lifetree Software, Inc.; Officewriter, by Office Solutions; and Wordperfect, by Wordperfect Corp.

Financial Planning Software

Financial planning software programs work with large amounts of data and perform diverse financial analysis. These analyses include present value, future value, rate of return, cash flow, regression, depreciation, and budgeting analyses. There are several packages for financial planning on the market. Among them are Micro-DSS/Finance, from Addison-Wesley Publishing Co.; Finar, from Finar Research Systems, Ltd.; Micro Plan, from Chase Laboratories, Inc.; Excel, by Microsoft Corp.; JAVELIN, by Javelin Software Corp.; and DTFPS, by Desk Top Financial Solutions, Inc.

Mathematical Modeling Software

Mathematical modeling software performs diverse operations and research-oriented analysis such as linear programming, queuing, and multiple linear regression. Among the popular products are DSM, by DSS, Inc.; SAS/PC, by SAS Institute, Inc.; SPSS/PC+, by SPSS, Inc.; Lindo (for linear programming), Gino (for nonlinear programming), by Scientific Press; Minitab (for statistical analysis), by Minitab Data Analysis Software; GPSS/PC, by Minuteman Software; and SYSTAT (for statistical analysis), by Systat, Inc.

Micro-Mainframe Linkage Software

Micro-mainframe linkage software packages allow a microcomputer to link to other micros or mainframes for downloading (bringing information to the executive site) and uploading (sending information outside of the organization) purposes. Through this feature a microcomputer can connect an organization to a wealth of external data bases. There are problems that must be overcome before true connectivity can take place, but there have been some successful operations. MFE-Control from Cupertino, California, allows IBM PCs to communicate with different mainframe computers. With MFE-control, the minicomputer functions in a PC controller mode, connecting up to 16 PCs [5]. Symphony Link from Lotus Development Corporation is a vendor-oriented link that connects Lotus and Symphony with IBM mainframes.

Table 10-1 highlights popular PC-based DSS tools and generators. This table also highlights the user/system interface and the memory requirements for these packages. These packages can be used for diverse applications for both modeling and DBMS types of DSS. Depending upon the particular needs of an organization, these packages can serve as DSS tools and/or DSS generators. Since a majority of microcomputers are able to export and import ASCII (American Standard Code for Information Interchange) files, a DSS can be built by a combination of several of these packages. For example, one package may perform the spreadsheet and DBMS operations, and the second package may offer a stronger graphics capability which is not available in the first package. For more diverse coverage of micro-DSS products, consult Appendix A.

10-4 DSS Tasks Performed by Microcomputers

At the present time, a PC-based DSS performs all the operations performed by a mainframe-based DSS but on a smaller scale. For example, microcomputers are capable of performing operation research analyses on a smaller scale than mainframes. The limitations may affect the number of variables and constraints involved or the techniques used. As an example, a microcomputer is capable of performing simulation analysis; however, it cannot perform sophisticated simulation models, which include thousands of variables and expanded time periods. Today's microcomputers are capable of doing the following tasks in a DSS environment, capabilities are improving continually:

Query operation. This may include simple query in a nonprocedural fashion issued by a user through his or her terminal.

Data management. This includes simple data management operations such as file creation, update, addition, deletion, merge, search, and sort.

Report writing capability. Microcomputers are able to generate different reports with varying formats. This can be done either by word-processing programs or by report generator software.

Statistical analysis. Basic statistical analysis, such as bivariate and multivariate analyses, simple and multiple regressions, exponential smoothing, and so on, can be done by microcomputers.

Table 10-1 ▪ Popular DSS products for microcomputers

Product Name	Interface Mode	Vendor	Minimum Required Memory
20/20	Command	Access Technology	256K
Personal W	Menu	ComShare	320K
Expert Choice	Menu	Decision Support Software	256K
IFPS Personal	Menu	Execucom Systems Corp.	512K
Decision Aide II	Menu	Kepner Tregoe Inc.	256K
DSS Workbench	Menu	Lloyd Bush Software Products	512K
MDS Outline	Menu	MDS, Inc.	256K
Smartforecast II	Menu	Smart Software, Inc.	256K
EXEC**U**STAT	Menu	Exec**U**Stat, Inc.	320K
EXPRESS/PC	Menu	Information Resources	640K
Focus/PC	Menu	Information Builders, Inc.	640K
Forecast Plus	Menu	Walonick Associates	192K
NOMAD 2	Menu	Must Software International	640K
PARADOX	Query by example	Ansa Software	512K
Q&A	Menu	Symantic Corporation	512K
RAMIS/PC	Menu	On-Line	512K
RATS	Command	RATS VAR Econometrics, Inc.	256K
SAS/PC	Menu	SAS Institute, Inc.	512K
Superbase Personal	Menu	Progressive Peripherals	256K
SPSS/PC+	Menu	SPSS, Inc.	512K

What-if, goal-seeking, and sensitivity analyses. These standard DSS tasks either are directly built into the package such as IFPS/Personal or users can write simple codes to perform these tasks.

Micro/mainframe link. Microcomputers have been successfully used as intelligent terminals in order to connect the DSS user to the wealth of information outside of the organization as well as to corporate data bases within the firm. Also, PC/DSS generators such as IFPS Personal and EXPRESS enable the user to access the mainframe versions of these products for enhanced computing power.

Template operation. Microcomputers provide the DSS user with templates (prewritten models or formulas) for easy access. These templates can cover diverse areas.

Plotter link. Microcomputers can link the DSS user to sophisticated plotters or graphic printers for high-resolution and advanced graphics.

10-5 Advantages/Disadvantages of PC-Based DSS

A PC-based DSS offers several advantages compared to a mainframe-based DSS [33]:

- They are easier to use.
- They are less threatening to noncomputer experts.
- They provide faster testing and refining.
- The user has more control.
- They are relatively inexpensive.
- They provide screen display with graphics.
- They provide laser printer output.

The major disadvantages of PC-based DSS include speed and memory constraints. To design a large-scale DSS, a large main memory is needed. Also, to run sophisticated statistical, optimization, or simulation models, high-speed processing is required, which is not available on the majority of microcomputers. Most microcomputers are single-user and single-tasking machines. This limitation may present problems in the design of a high-powered DSS, but it seems the majority of these problems will be resolved in the new generation of microcomputers. We talk about this in detail later in this chapter.

10-6 How to Choose a Microbased DSS

Table 10-1 introduces only a few of the microbased products. There are numerous other products being marketed under PC-DSS, which makes the selection task difficult. Since these products offer different capabilities and offer different levels of performance, the user must first identify his or her needs then find a product that matches those specific needs. The following are some of the important questions that must be asked before choosing a microbased DSS [13]:

1. The complexity of the task for which a PC-DSS is being purchased. This may include a variety of factors:
   - Size of the spreadsheet (2000 rows, 8000 rows, 500 columns, and so on)
   - Types of graphs (line, bar, pie, and so on)
   - Sophistication of the graphs (size, labeling, color graphics, number of data points, three-dimensional analysis, and so forth)
   - Types and complexity of the built-in functions (financial, statistical, logical, and so on)
   - DBMS operations (search, sort, query operations, join, merge, and so forth)
   - Capability of the linkage of different worksheets
   - Security provision by the package

2. Is there a mainframe support? Due to memory and speed limitations of micro-DSS, mainframe support may be needed. If this is the case, the user will be better off if he or she chooses a package supported directly by a mainframe. For example, IFPS Personal and EXPRESS/Personal can directly utilize the power of their mainframe counterparts. This factor provides more power to the user of these packages for enhanced capabilities.
3. Is an expert system (ES) DSS needed? If the user requires expert system capabilities, he or she may have to examine only the packages that support these types of capabilities. Expert systems products provide reasoning capability to the DSS user. This capability may assist the user better to understand the problem under investigation. We talk about ESs in Chapter 13. For now, remember that these systems try to mimic the human expert thought behavior in a particular discipline. For example, GURU by Micro Data Base is one of these packages that support spreadsheet operations as well as ES capabilities. An expert system enables the user to ask not only what-is questions but also why questions. Table 10-2 introduces some of the ES tools and shells available [4] for microcomputers. These products have diverse applications, and many specific expert systems can be developed using these products. Also, the guidelines provided in Chapter 9 would be of significant help to a DSS user for choosing a specific package.

Table 10-2 ▪ Expert systems for microcomputers

Product Name	Vendor	Memory	Operating System
ADS	Aion Corp.	512K	PC-DOS; VM/CMS; MVS/TSO, CICS
Arity/Expert	Arity Corp.	512K	PC/MS-DOS
Xi Plus	Expertech, Inc.	512K	PC/MS-DOS
EXSTS	Exsys, Inc.	256K	PC-DOS
MKS	Humanic Systems	640K	MS-DOS
Rule Master	Radian Corp.	640K	PC/MS-DOS
Auto Intelligence	IntelligenceWare	512K	PC/MS-DOS
Auto-Compiler	IntelligenceWare	512K	PC/MS-DOS
KDS	KDS Corp.	512K	PC/MS-DOS
EXSYS	EXSYS	512K	PC/MS-DOS
IEW/WS	KnowledgeWare	640K	PC-DOS
COCOMOL	Level Five Research	512K	PC/MS-DOS
VP-Expert	Paperback Software	256K	MS/PC-DOS
GURU	Micro Data Base	640K	PC-DOS; VAX/VMS; Utrix
M.1	Technowledge, Inc.	512K	PC/MS-DOS

10-7 Executive Support Systems (ESS)

In recent years, some new buzzwords have been introduced to the field of information technology: executive information systems (EIS), executive support systems (ESS), and executive management systems (EMS). While their definitions and place among EDP, MIS, and DSS are still evolving, we consider these systems to be a branch of DSS. At the center of the systems, there is always a microcomputer that serves as an intelligent terminal. The microcomputer can serve as a stand-alone system or be used as a workstation in order to connect the executive decision-maker to a wealth of information from both internal and external data bases.

Executive information systems attempt to deliver only information critical to a decision-maker and are user- or business-problem-driven [28]. There is a heavy emphasis on a format in which executives can use the provided information. One of the primary objectives of these systems is to eliminate amounts of information bombarding executives [18]. An EIS combines the decision-maker's imagination and judgment with the computer's ability to store, retrieve, manipulate, and compute internal and external data.

Executive information systems utilize integrated office technologies for planning, forecasting, and controlling managerial tasks. It may use [22]:

- Touch screens versus traditional keyboards
- Menu-driven system
- Key commands that are close to user verbs
- Local area network (LAN)
- Electronic mail
- Facsimile equipment
- Voice mail
- Teleconferencing, both audio and video
- Graphics
- Spreadsheets
- Lap-top computer
- Scanners
- Image-transmission systems through facsimile

Comparing EIS with DSS, some specific advantages can be highlighted [18]:

- More timely delivery of information
- More informed decisions
- More understandable format for the provided information
- Increased executive productivity
- Better information
- A better understanding of the information and its interrelationships
- Improved information tracking

We will discuss distributed data processing and teleconferencing in the next chapter. For now, remember that through communication systems an organization can share the same data among many decision-makers in an effective way.

10-8 Designing an Executive Information System

Design and implementation of an executive information system is basically the same as designing a DSS. However, in an EIS environment more emphasis is placed on the critical success factors (CSF).

As mentioned earlier, the core of an EIS is a microcomputer that has access to all the productivity tools. Productivity tools for micros may include:

- Spreadsheet
- DBMS
- Graphics
- Electronic mail
- Office automation software

The microcomputer must have access to both key internal and external data. An EIS must be able to generate information regarding [28]:

- What-is
- What does it mean
- What-if
- What to do

The what-is operations include the basic query operation performed by any computer-based information system. The following questions are examples of the what-is operation:

- What are the total sales for Product X?
- What is the advertising budget for Division Y?
- What is the research and development budget for 1990?

The what-is scenario tells the executive about the important events in the organization. The "what does it mean" scenario explains all the what-is operations. For example, if the total sales of product X is $5,000,000 it may mean the total sales for this product have increased by 32% compared to the last year. If the budget for research and development is $800,000, it may mean that this particular company is spending 10% below average. The "what does it mean" analysis is usually performed by intermediaries. As mentioned in Chapter 6, an intermediary may explain the output provided by an information system to the user. An executive information system may provide a feature that automatically answers these types of questions. For example, a comparison of the sales for product X with the last year's data and the data available for the same product from other competitors may tell the executive where his or her particular organization stands.

The familiar what-if analysis monitors the effect of change of one variable on the entire system. For example, if the advertising expenses are increased by 10%, the total sales may be increased by $200,000. Special versions of what-if may include goal-seeking and sensitivity analysis.

The last feature addressed by an EIS is the "what to do" scenario. This feature should tell the executive what to do with the provided information, what action may have to be taken, and so on.

By integrating the artificial intelligence products into EIS, the reasoning features of these systems may be significantly improved. The process of building an EIS may be summarized by the following key guidelines [29]:

- Get the top management involved.
- Get the user involved.
- Identify critical success factors.
- Provide the easiest user/system interface possible.
- Observe simplicity.
- Develop a system with a reasonable response time.
- Develop an on-line prototype.
- Do evaluation.
- Build the final system.
- Repeat the iterative process.

10-9 Future of Microcomputers and DSS

The future of microcomputers is not separated from the future of computers in general. Chapter15 explores the future of computers in general. In this section, we make some specific references to microcomputers. This outlook supports the idea of mainframe micros and the existence of PC-based DSS as a reality.

During the last 15 years, microcomputers have undergone some significant changes. They have improved in all aspects and already possess more power than the earlier minicomputers. Already, the total number of millions of instructions per second (MIPS) available in all microcomputers is larger than the total number of MIPS available in all of the mainframe computers [16]. Further improvement in microcomputer technology may make a mainframe micro a reality. This new development will make a micro-based DSS more powerful than ever. Reed McManus [21] provides a very interesting scenario regarding the future PC. If the past 15 years is any indication about the future, we may be well on schedule. McManus' presentation includes microprocessors, storage, display, output devices, communication, and software. The following is a summary of his presentation:

Microprocessors

Intel's 80386 microprocessor will already process 4 million instructions per second (MIPS) and will easily attain speeds of 10 MIPS within the next few years. Considering how much microprocessors have speeded up during the past few years, it is possible that a microprocessor will be doing 30 MIPS by the year 2000. In order to obtain these goals, the PC will have to become a general-purpose microprocessor with additional functions in the areas of artificial intelligence, communications, and graphics. Multitasking will become the rule rather than the exception. When combined with parallel architecture, RISC (reduced instruction set computer—the processors are encoded with fewer and simpler instructions) technology, and the use of gallium arsenide rather than silicon for chips, the PC of the future may be very "human." These computers will be able to understand English and recognize and synthesize speech.

Storage

A 10MB hard disk was once considered a large amount of storage for a PC; no more will this be true. But as hard disk access time is reduced, more users will look for larger amounts of storage space. Where that storage will be found depends on technology in two areas: software development and research in the area of read/write optical disk drives. While the experts do not foresee the end of the hard or floppy disk drive in the near future, storage capacities of up to 100MB for both hard and floppy disks may become the standard.

Displays

CRTs are not on the way out, even though the technology to make a truly portable computer with excellent resolution is not possible at this time. Research in the area of LCD (liquid crystal display) displays and active-matrix addressing continues, as does research in EL (electroluminescent) backlighting. Experts are not yet confident that the technology will be available; if it is available, they are not completely certain that manufacturing will be able to keep pace. However, if the future PC is a slim computer-to-go, place your bets now that the active-matrix LCD will be the display of choice.

Output Devices

According to Timothy Onosko, the PC printer of the year 2000 is already available—it is the laser printer. Because of the higher print resolution, it already offers users great clarity. In the future, it may become more colorful and may provide output in more than two dimensions. Beyond that, however, the laser printer will still be around or will be replaced by a printer that we cannot imagine today.

Communications

Analog telephone lines and modems are on the way out; ISDN (integrated services digital network) and fiber optics are on the way in. Additionally, as the year 2000 approaches, more people will use LANs (local area networks) to be truly connected to the outside world by their computers. Communication technologies will be discussed more fully in Chapter 11.

Software

The software of the future will, according to Charles Seiter and Daniel Ben-Horin, have the computer ". . . do(ing) everything but chang(ing) the baby."

The typical PC will evolve from "a dumb terminal emulator into a smart, fully powered workstation." The only real problem will be to create software that will allow users everywhere to access the software they are familiar with while being involved with other, unfamiliar software. Software is the area the experts seem the most skeptical about; the marketplace and most users are somewhat conservative and do not rapidly accept change. Development of unique and innovative software may indeed be the slowest developing area in the year 2000.

Disk Operating System

DOS, from version 1.0 to version 3.3, has improved continuously. The newer versions have added new capabilities, and they have also fixed some of the previous bugs. Most recently, a new version of DOS (under several names such as Future DOS, New DOS, Advanced DOS 1.0, DOS 5, and ADOS) has attracted much attention in the microcomputer community.

The new version of DOS has gained popularity through the support of Intel 80286 and 80386 microprocessors and has claimed several specific goals:

- Expanded memory—beyond the traditional 640K
- Multitasking
- Multiprocessing
- Upward compatibility
- Ease of use, or user-friendliness

Memory expansion is essential in order to access more sophisticated software on the market. Also, to improve the user-friendliness, the system may have to use DOS shells, spelling checkers, electronic mail, note pads, pull-down windows, and so forth. All these require enhanced and expanded memory.

Multitasking and multiprocessing will add a new dimension to the microcomputer environment. This feature allows a user to run more than one task or more than one program at the same time. This feature should assist a PC user in performing more sophisticated operations.

The multiprocessing (networking) feature enables more than one user to access the same application program. This feature makes a PC more cost effective. However, a multiprocessing system may run more slowly than single-tasking systems and may cause compatibility problems.

Upward compatibility allows PC users to upgrade to better and more powerful operating systems without losing what they already have.

User-friendliness is of significant importance to PC users. A typical PC user usually is not a computer-trained person. The easier the system to use, the more attractive is the system to the user. User-friendliness can be improved by DOS shells and through graphic interface, e.g., Apple's Macintosh. IBM has developed Top View, and Microsoft has a graphic interface called Windows. To include these features in DOS, the PC must have expanded memory.

The new IBM PC, called Personal System 2 (PS/2), has already entered the market. One version of the new DOS was announced in early 1988. Other versions of this new operating system have been scheduled for the near future.

PS/2 performs multitasking, utilizes the 16-megabyte address space for the 80286 microprocessor, and works with a DOS-compatible environment. At the same time, PS/2 addresses 1 gigabyte of virtual memory. The new operating system also includes many new features for programmers and application developers.

The new microprocessors—286, 386, and possibly, 486—can benefit immensely from the new DOS. However, DOS users should remember that AT&T's Unix Operating System would be a major competitor to the MS-DOS. At the present time, it is too complex for novice computer users.

So what does all this mean to PC-based DSS and EIS? These indications all support the versatility and affordability of PC-based DSS. Having such powerful microcomputers as the core of a PC-based DSS or EIS, these systems will be able to process masses of data in a timely fashion, they will be able to run large operation research models, they will be able to communicate with other computers, and, most important of all, they will be portable. In the near future PC-based DSSs will be an integral part of an executive workstation. As a final note, we should remember that the proliferation of PC use may also create problems—i.e., amateur use of models. Nonexperts may be relying on modeling capabilities such as regression, simulation, or linear programming without the aid of an operations researcher. PCs may enhance this problem by bringing these OR techniques to the fingertips of non-OR people. The role of the operations researcher as intermediary will become evident. In situations like this, the user of a DSS must consult with the intermediary, and the result of such analysis must be used with caution. In the near future, as we discuss in Chapter 14, the interaction of expert systems and DSS may resolve some of these problems.

10-10 Summary

This chapter explored the microcomputer-based DSS and executive support systems. The impressive past and the predictions of a brilliant future for microcomputer technology will certainly have a positive impact on DSS. Using microcomputers in DSS environment should make these systems more attractive than ever. Microcomputer-based DSSs are easier to design, use, and maintain. The positive features of these computers should make them the core of the decision-making process in the near future. In the next chapter, distributed processing is discussed as another frontier in information technology in general and in DSS/EIS in particular.

Review Questions

1. What is a microcomputer?
2. How did the microcomputer industry start?
3. What are some of the general capabilities of a microcomputer?

4. How can a microcomputer be used as a DSS tool?

5. How can a microcomputer be used as a DSS generator?

6. What are some of the popular DSS products for microcomputers?

7. What is the difference between a mainframe DSS product and its PC version? (*Hint:* IFPS and IFPS Personal).

8. What are some of the tasks in DSS environment that can be easily performed by microcomputers?

9. What are some of the advantages of micros compared with mainframes in a DSS environment? What are the disadvantages?

10. How do you choose a PC-DSS? What are some of the critical questions to be asked?

11. What is a PC expert system? What are their general capabilities?

12. What is an executive support system? How is it different from a DSS?

13. What are some of the technologies used in an EIS environment?

14. What are the general capabilities of an EIS?

15. How is an EIS designed?

16. What are some of the indications for future microcomputers?

17. How will future microprocessors be different from today's?

18. What technology will be used for microprocessor design?

19. How will the output devices look in the future?

20. Is the future scenario presented in this chapter realistic to you? Discuss.

Projects

1. Research two of the micro-based products introduced in Table 10-1. What are their major strengths in a DSS environment? What are their major weaknesses?

2. Can a micro-based product be used as a DSS generator? If yes, how? If no, why not? Discuss the specific features in order to justify this claim.

3. Research and compare one of the products in Table 10-1 and one of the products in Table 10-2. What is the major difference between a PC-DSS and a PC-ES? Which product is more powerful in a DSS environment? Why?

4. By referring to the references produced at the end of this chapter, compare and contrast DSS and EIS or ESS. Is EIS something really new? Boeing, Lockheed, and Gillette are among the first users of EIS. Consult one of these companies for specific uses of these systems.

5. If microcomputers are becoming so powerful, why do we need mainframes? What are some of the tasks that cannot be performed by a microcomputer regardless of its sophistication? Discuss.

6. A lot of organizations are using microcomputers at executive workstations. What exactly are these workstations doing? Research this through an organization with which you are familiar.

Key Terms

Microcomputer
8-bit processor
16-bit processor
32-bit processor
Single-tasking
Multitasking
Chip technology
Spreadsheet software
Data base software
Graphics software
Communications software
Word processing software
Financial planning software
Mathematical modeling software
Micro-mainframe linkage software
Query operation
Data management
Report writing capability
Statistical analysis
Template operation
Expert systems
Executive support systems
Executive information systems
Touch screen
Local area network (LAN)
Electronic mail
Facsimile equipment
Voice mail
Teleconferencing
Lap-top computer
Scanners
Image-transmission system
What is
What does it mean
What-if
What to do
Microprocessor
Million instructions per second (MIPS)
Read/write optical disk
Liquid crystal display (LCD)
Active-matrix addressing
Integrated services digital networks (ISDN)

References

[1] Boltz, Walter. 1987. Executive Information Systems Design. *Infosystems* (May): 70.

[2] Davis, Steve, Dennis Schall, Karen Irish, and Kathy O'Neil. 1986. Managing With Micros. *Computers in Health Care* (August): 26–31.

[3] DeSanctis, Gerardine, and Brent Gallupe. 1985. Group Decision Support Systems: A New Frontier. *DataBase* (Winter): 3–9.

[4] Desmond, John. 1987. Bule Propellers Bringing AI to MIS. *Software News* (July): 32–41.

[5] Eblen, P. L., M. Gasaway, L. W. Harm, and S. G. Rae. 1986. A First Class Collection of Software. *Business Software Review* (January): 29–59.

[6] Economides, Spyros, and Mark Colen. 1985. Microcomputer-Based Decision Support Systems Aid Managers in Evaluating Alternatives. *Industrial Engineering* (September): 44–51.

[7] Friend, David. 1986. Executive Information Systems: Successes and Failures, Insights, and Misconceptions. *Journal of Information Systems Management* (Fall): 31–36.

[8] Forman, Ernest H. 1985. Decision Support for Executive Decision Makers. *Information Strategy: The Executive's Journal* (Summer): 4–14.

[9] Gardner, Everette S., Jr. 1987. Analyzing Subjective Decisions With a Spreadsheet. *Lotus* (January): 68–71.

[10] Golden, Bruce L., A. Hevner, and D. Power. 1986. Decision Insight Systems for Microcomputers: A Critical Evaluation. *Computers & Operational Research* 13, nos. 2/3 (April): 287–300.

[11] Guimares, Tor, and Vasudevan Ramanujam. 1986. Personal Computing Trends and Problems: An Empirical Study. *MIS Quarterly* (June): 179–85.

[12] Jennergren, L. Peter. 1985. OR and Micros. *European Journal of Operational Research*, 20, no. 1 (April): 1–9.

[13] Karon, Paul. 1980. Decision Support Systems. *PC Week* (May 6): 101–105.

[14] Keen, P. G. W., and L. A. Woodman. 1984. What to Do With All Those Micros. *Harvard Business Review* 62, no. 5 (September-October): 142–50.

[15] Kersten, Gregory E. 1985. NEGO-Group Decision Support System. *Information & Management* 8, no. 5 (May): 237–46.

[16] Kleninrock, Leonard. 1985. Distributed Systems. *Communications of the ACM* 28, no. 11 (November): 1201–13.

[17] Kull, David. 1985. Executives Tap Into Support Systems. *Computer Decisions* (December 17): 38–83.

[18] Lindholm, Elizabeth. 1988. The View From the Top. *Datamation* (February): 18–22.

[19] Madlin, Nancy. 1986. Executive Information Systems. *Management Review* (August): 21–22.

[20] McLeod, Raymond, Jr., and Jack W. Joes. 1986. Making Executive Information Systems More Effective. *Business Horizon* (September-October): 29–37.

[21] McManus, Reed. 1987. In Pursuit of Tomorrow's PC. *PC World* (May): 260–73.

[22] Menkus, Belden. 1987. Latest Productivity Buzzword—It's Executive Management System (EIS). *Business Month* (March): 64–75.

[23] Milter, Richard G., and John Rohrbaugh. 1985. Microcomputers and Strategic Decision Making. *Public Productivity Review* (Summer/Fall): 175–89.

[24] Morgan, Howard. 1986. The Microcomputer and Decision Support. *Computerworld* (August 19): 39–45.

[25] Parkinson, Chris. 1985. DSS Must Have Long-Term Application. *Software Report* (October): 6–12.

[26] Perlman, Allan. 1986. Building a Successful Executive Information System. *Infosystems* (June): 34–36.

[27] Reck, Robert H., and James R. Hall. 1986. Executive Information Systems: An Overview of Development. *Journal of Information Systems Management* (Fall): 25–30.

[28] Rinaldi, Damian, and Ted Jastvzembski. 1986. Executive Information Systems Put Strategic Data at Your CEO's Fingertips. *Computerworld* (October 27): 37–53.

[29] Rockart, John. 1979. Chief Executives Define Their Own Data Needs. *Harvard Business Review* (March-April): 81–93.

[30] Rockart, John F., and David W. DeLong. 1988. *Executive Support Systems*. Homewood, Ill.: Dow Jones-Irwin.

[31] Rosenthal, Morton. 1985. Integrated Software Past, Present, and Future. *Computerworld Focus* (March 20): 31–35.

[32] Shore, Barry, and T. J. Wharton. 1986. Analysis of Microcomputer DSS Projects. *Journal of Systems Management* (June): 25–31.

[33] Stamps, David. 1987. Modeling With Micros. *Datamation* (April 1): 85–87.

[34] Wood, Richard A. 1985. The Information Center: An Approach to Effective Fourth Generation Computing. *Information Management Review* (Fall): 21–29.

11 Distributed Processing and DSS

11-1 Introduction

This chapter discusses the three different types of data processing organizations: centralized, decentralized, and distributed data processing (DDP), and explains the components of a DDP. Local area network (LAN), a popular type of network system, is also discussed. Then the topologies of LAN are explained and security issues in a network environment are highlighted. A table presents a series of security measures available to a system analyst as they relate to any computer-based information system in a distributed environment. This is followed by a brief discussion of office automation and teleconferencing, and the chapter concludes with a discussion on group DSS (GDSS). Also, a series of software packages used in GDSS is introduced.

11-2 Data-Processing Organizations

During the past 40 years, with advancements in the computer field, three types of data-processing organizations have emerged: centralized, decentralized and distributed data processing.

Centralized

A *centralized* system utilizes one central location for performing the entire data-processing task. In the early days of computer technology this type of processing was well justified because:

- Data-processing personnel were in short supply
- Economies of scale both in hardware and software could be realized
- Only large organizations could afford computers

However, a centralized processing system has a major shortcoming—it is not responsive to the users' needs. Also, the economy-of-scale issue is no longer valid due to the decreasing cost and increasing sophistication of microcomputers.

Decentralized

Decentralized data processing, as the name implies, advocates a decentralized arrangement, meaning that each office, department, or division has its own computer. The entire data-processing task should be implemented within each separate organizational unit.

A decentralized data-processing organization is certainly much more responsive to the user than centralized processing. However, lack of coordination between organizational units, excessive costs of having many systems, and duplication of efforts are some of the common problems associated with it.

Distributed Data Processing (DDP)

Distributed data processing solves two of the major problems associated with the first two types of data-processing organizations: Lack of responsiveness in centralized processing, and lack of coordination in decentralized processing. Distributed data processing (DDP) has overcome these problems by maintaining centralized control and at the same time maintaining decentralized operations.

Generally speaking, in DDP the processing power is distributed among several locations. Data bases, processing units, or input/output devices may be distributed. Since the mid 1970s, with advancement in networking and mini- and microcomputers, this type of data-processing organization has gained a lot of popularity.

Some of the unique advantages of a DDP system include [14]:

1. Modularity in design: Computer power can be added or deleted based on the needs.
2. System reliability: Failure of a system may be limited only to one site.
3. User orientation: The system is more responsive to user needs.

11-3 Components of a DDP System

A typical DDP system, depending on the particular application, may include the following components:

- Source and sink devices

- Modems
- Communication lines
- Communication software
- Communication control units

The *source* (sender) or *sink* (receiver) device may include one of the following devices:

1. Input/output device, or a dumb terminal, which is used only for sending or receiving information with no processing power.
2. Smart terminal, which is also an input/output device having a limited degree of processing capability.
3. Intelligent terminal, or a microcomputer, serving as an input/output device and also as a stand-alone system.
4. Other types of computers (mini, mainframe, and so on).

A modem is used to convert digital signals into analog signals that can be transferred over a regular telephone line. Once the analog signal arrives at its destination, the modem converts it back to a digital signal

Communication lines are used to connect the source and sink. Communication lines can be any one or a combination of the following:

- Regular telephone line
- Coaxial cable
- Microwave
- Satellite
- Fiber optics

Each communication line has advantages and disadvantages. In choosing a communication line, the following criteria are usually considered:

- Quality of transmission
- Security of the line
- Throughput of the line (how much information can be transferred—bits per second, or BPS)
- Range of the line (how far a message can be transmitted)

Telephone lines have been the major method of communication to this date because the system is already well established. However, speed and security issues make these lines less attractive than other options. Also, the lines are not suitable for continent-to-continent transmission.

Satellite systems cover a broad range, but these devices are not completely secure either.

Microwave systems have a shorter range but suffer from the same problems as the satellite.

Fiber optics appear to be the major communication means of the future. This method is capable of a high-quality transmission, high throughput, and very high security.

In a complex DDP system all these communication methods may be utilized at the same time. The system designer(s) must implement a series of measures in order to ensure a comprehensive security system that protects the entire input/process/output cycle. Different security measures are discussed later in this chapter.

Communication software is a dedicated program that enables a user to send messages from one site to another one. The communication control unit (CCU) is usually a minicomputer or a microcomputer that serves as a front-end processor in a network. It is used to perform some processing tasks, such as data condensation, error checking, and simple processing, for the host computer. This unit in the network improves the effectiveness of the host computer by allowing the host to concentrate on the important networking tasks.

11-4 Local Area Network (LAN)

The local area network, or LAN, has received a great deal of attention in recent years. There is no common definition for LAN. Usually this system limits its operation to a certain geographical area, such as a building. However, there are systems that cover a broad geographical range and are still referred to as LANs. The opposite type of network, wide area network (WAN), does not have any specific geographic limit.

LAN is usually a prerequisite for an automated office and many distributed DSSs. To establish a LAN system, careful planning and a thorough assessment of the computer needs of a particular organization are required.

11-5 Network Topologies

There are several different architectures for a network system, each with its own advantages and disadvantages. Depending on the organizational structure, functions, and needs, one or several of these architectures may be implemented. The commonly used topologies are star network, ring network, loop network, bus network, tree network, and web network [2].

Star Network

The *star* network usually consists of a central computer (host computer) and a series of nodes (terminals). The main processing power is performed by the host computer. The breakdown of any of the nodes will not affect the operation of the entire network; however, if the host computer goes down, the entire network is no longer operable.

Ring Network

The *ring* network does not have a central host computer. There may be a variety of computers and input/output devices utilized in this architecture. If any one of the nodes or computers goes down, the effect over the entire network would be minimal.

Loop Network

The *loop* network architecture is used to connect a series of similar-sized nodes, such as word-processing devices. Each node must be capable of communicating to the next node. If any of the nodes fails, the entire network becomes inoperable.

Bus Network

The *bus* network, which is commonly used in a LAN system, connects a series of different nodes. The failure of any of the nodes does not have any impact on any other node. This type of network is usually used for resource sharing in an organization. For example, a bus network allows 20 PCs to use one high-speed laser printer.

Tree (Hierarchical) Network

The *tree* network combines computers with different powers in different levels. It may use microcomputers at the bottom, minicomputers at the middle, and a mainframe computer at the top. This type of architecture may be suitable for organizations that are structured in a compatible fashion as long as that structure does not change. Failure of nodes at the bottom may not have a significant impact on the performance of the entire network; however, the middle nodes and, especially, the top node—which has control over the entire operation of the network—are extremely important for the operation of the network. This is due to the processing power exercised by upper nodes to the lower ones. The lower-level nodes may perform minor processing tasks. The major processing tasks are performed by the node at the top.

Web (Fully-Connected or Cartwheel) Network

In the *web* network every node (which may be of different size and configuration than the others) is connected to every other node. This type of architecture is the most reliable. Failure of one or a few of the nodes may not cause a major problem to the entire network operation. However, this type of architecture is costly and difficult to maintain.

Figure 11-1 [2] illustrates the architecture of each type of network.

11-6 Security Issues and Measures in Network Environment

There are several factors of which any organization must be aware regarding general security issues. Some of the factors are controllable, some are partially controllable, and some are completely uncontrollable. The security issues are as follows [1]:

Figure 11-1 Network Topologies

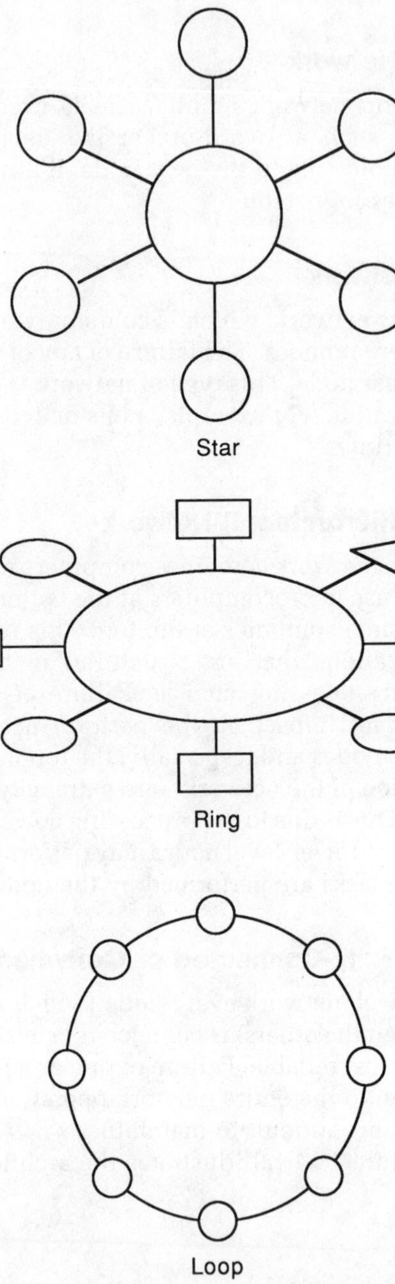

Figure 11-1 Continued

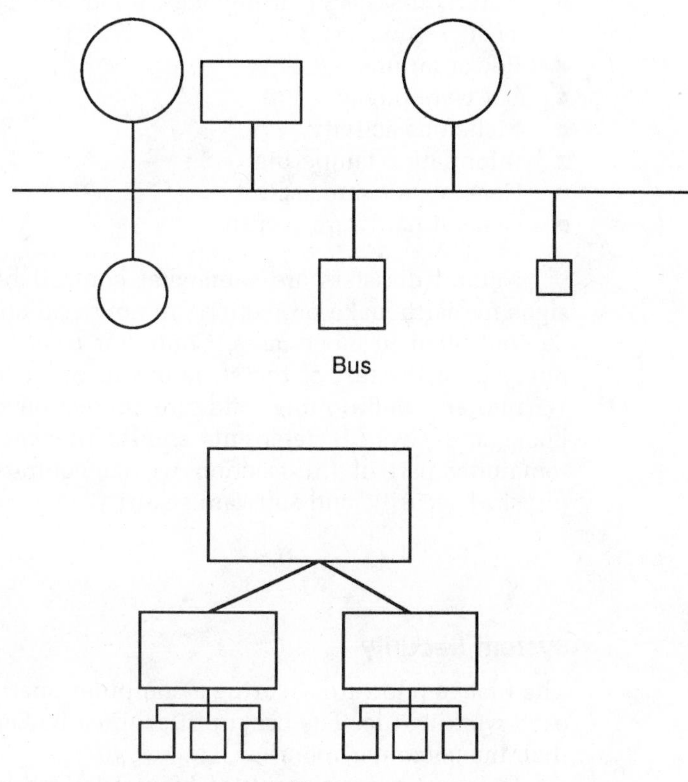

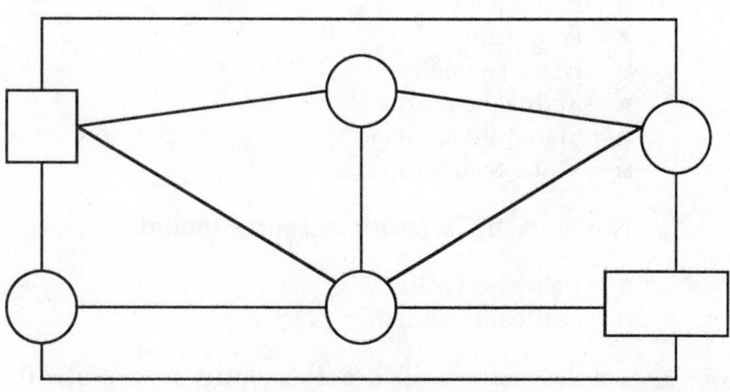

- Fire
- Natural disasters (earthquakes, flood, and so on)
- Theft
- Power failure
- Software piracy
- Malicious activity
- Information tampering
- General software security
- General hardware security

Natural disasters are somewhat controllable. Buildings with special designs for earthquake protection are now available. Potential flood damage can be controlled in most cases. Computer rooms frequently are designed separately from the rest of the structure in order to minimize potential hazards. Wiring, air conditioning, and fire protection should be of special concern. Locks and physical deterrents should prevent most computer thefts. In the remaining part of this section we concentrate on general system security, physical security, and software security.

System Security

The first step toward securing a computer operation is to generate a backup of each working file. The backup files must be kept in a different location other than the computer room.

In recent years a series of biometrics (security measures that involve an element from a human body) have been used to enhance security measures. These include [1]:

- Fingerprint
- Palmprint
- Hand geometry
- Retinal scanning
- Signature analysis
- Voice recognition

Nonbiometric security measures include:

- Data encryption
- Call-back modem

Let us briefly explain each security measure with each group [1].

Fingerprint Whenever a user tries to access the system, his or her fingerprint is checked by scanning and verified against the print stored in a file.

Palmprint The individual characteristics of the palm are used to identify the user.

Hand geometry Hand geometry uses the length of the five fingers on each hand as well as the translucence of the fingertips and the webbing.

Retinal scanning Retinal scanning is one of the most successful methods for security protection. It employs a scanning device contained within a binocular eye camera. Identification is verified by the data about the user stored in a computer file.

Signature analysis Signature analysis uses the signature of the user as well as the user's pattern, pressure deviation, acceleration, and the length of the time needed for the user to sign his or her name.

Voice recognition Voice recognition translates words into digital patterns for transmission to the host computer. This technique is relatively new and research is still ongoing.

These different techniques have been very effective. They may not currently be financially justified for all organizations. However, with rapid cost reduction and improvement in the quality, they present a viable alternative to traditional security systems for the near future.

Data encryption Data encryption is an effective security measure that can be installed in a computer system. Encryption requires the encoding of plain text into unreadable, scrambled text by a source encryptor, which is located between the computer and the modem. Encrypted data are transmitted over a variety of transmission media such as phone lines, satellites, microwaves, coaxial cables, and fiber-optic cables. When the transmission is completed, the receiver can put data into its original form through a cryptor which contains the same prestored key. The cryptor is a key. The delivered key from the source can be any type of secret code based on an organizational scheme. Encryption is becoming a common practice in the networking environment.

Call-back modem A call-back modem is another network security measure. In this process the system tries to verify the validity of a particular access by logging the user off and calling the user back.

Physical Security

Physical security primarily addresses the concerns of access control to computers and the available devices that secure computers from acts of theft.

Physical security is achieved through identification badges, proximity release door openers, corner bolts, steel encasements, or electronic trackers. We briefly explain these measures.

Identification badges Identification badges are checked against a list of authorized personnel. Checks must be done on a regular basis so that any change in personnel is noted.

Proximity release door opener The proximity release door opener is an effective way to control access to the computer room. Access to the computer area is gained through the use of a small radio transmitter located in the authorized employees' identification badges. When the authorized personnel come within a predetermined distance of the entry door, a radio signal sends a key number to a receiver, which opens the door for admittance.

Corner bolts Corner bolts and steel bolts are inexpensive methods of securing a microcomputer to a desktop or counter. These devices are a combination of locks and cables that secure a computer to a table or a counter. Steel bolts are used to secure micros to a heavy-duty locking plate, which is then bonded to an anchor pad that has adhesive on both sides. The pad is then adhered to a desk or counter.

Steel encasement Steel encasements are designed to fit over the entire computer. The encasement is made of heavy-gauge welded steel. The encasement is kept locked and the security administrator or another designated person has control over the key.

Electronic trackers Electronic trackers are secured to the computer at the AC power insert point. If the power cord is disconnected, a coded transmitter sends a message to an alarm, which sounds, and/or a camera, which is activated to record the disturbance [7].

Token A token is a radio transmission device worn around the user's neck. The device activates the computer only when a user wearing a token is seated in front of the screen.

Cable shielding Cable shielding is accomplished by braiding layers of the conductors to form a braided shield. This scheme protects the data from electromagnetic emanations. This is done by either solid shielding or using a conduit. Shielding is more difficult with hardware devices than with cables.

Room shielding Room shielding is done by spraying a conductive material in the computer room. This material reduces the number of signals being transmitted, or completely confines the signals to the computer room.

Software Security

Software security is designed to protect the system from data integrity loss and unauthorized access and to provide data security. Software security is accomplished by passwords, access codes, and terminal resource security.

Passwords Passwords are sets of numbers, characters, words, or combinations that must be entered into the system for access and are the most basic of access controls. The length and the composition of the passwords determines their vulnerability to discovery by unauthorized users. The human element, which plays a major role in the success of the password control, is one of the most notable weaknesses of the password security system.

Access codes The simplest form of access control, the most basic security method, is the missing-character code. Files and/or programs are listed in the directory incompletely. In order for the user to access the data, he or she must fill in the missing character(s).

Terminal resource security Terminal resource security is a software capability that erases the screen automatically and signs the user off after a predetermined length of inactivity. There are also programs that allow users to access data only during certain time slots. Any attempts to access the system other than during the predetermined times results in denial of access [9].

There are several devices available on the market that may help to protect and enhance the security of a distributed environment. Multisentry security devices developed by Tact Technology Corporation install in front of the modem and are available for the standard 16-line version and for the 128-line version. Security Access Multiport (SAM) is another protection device for dial-up port protection. SAM is available from LeeMAH Corporation [22]. The total spent on computer security devices for 1985 was estimated at around $23 billion [3, p. 373].

Table 11-1 [1] illustrates the security measures that must be taken in a distributed environment. This table may serve as a guideline for security protection for designers and users of DSS in a distributed environment. Figure 11-2 illustrates the types of security measures.

In addition to these concerns, there is now a new computer threat, "computer virus." Computer virus replicates itself after entering a computer system and electronically destroys computers. It is not a living organism; it is just a self-propagating computer program. When the program is entered onto a floppy disk or into the operating system, it remains dormant as it infects computer after computer. It moves extremely fast, and a computer user does not even know if the virus exists in his or her computer. When it is entered into the operating system of a particular computer, it forces the operating system to copy the virus onto other programs. This virus has caused severe damage to a number of personal and mainframe computers. At the time of this writing, there is no indication of mainframe computers having been severely infected. Various agencies are hoping to track down the individual(s) who initiated the computer virus in the first place. Again, this new threat adds more significance to computer security in a DDP environment.

11-7 Office Automation

Increasing sophistication and decreasing costs have made microcomputers affordable for even medium and small organizations. This new development has changed the traditional office environment.

Table 11-1 ▪ Security Measures in a Distributed Environment

Measures	Data Entry	Data Base	Data Transmission	Data Output
Reliable operator	X			
Tamper-proof equipment	X	X	X	X
Accurate entry	X			
Double checking	X			X
User code	X			X
Access scope (what to be accessed)	X	X		X
Time access	X	X	X	X
Number of access (how many times to be accessed)	X	X	X	X
Encryption	X	X	X	X
Token	X	X	X	X
Room shielding	X			X
Cable shielding	X			X
Biometric measures	X	X	X	X
Limited use of file	X	X		
Call-back modem	X			X
Automatic shutoff	X	X	X	X

Office automation or office automated systems [8] consist of a series of related technologies such as electronic mail, message distribution, text processing, voice mail, micrographics, facsimile, and reprographics.

The goal of the automated office is to use all the ingredients of an automated office system to make office operation more effective. In the office of the future, we will see voice, data, and images transmitted on a single line. This capability will improve the quality of the information being provided. The office of the future should improve the effectiveness of decision-makers by providing timely access to the information needed for decision-making purposes. The technology is already here, in the form of integrated services digital networks (ISDN). ISDN is still evolving, and its future development should enhance the operation of a typical office. When costs are reduced and telecommunication systems are improved, we should see more applications of office automation.

11-8 Teleconferencing and DSS

Teleconferencing, as Johansen and Bullen [12] call it, is a "managerial support system." There are many different definitions of a teleconferencing system. One such definition is [12, 17, 18]:

Interactive electronic communication among two or more people in two or more locations.

A teleconferencing system can include different types of technologies. In its simplest form it may include a meeting room and a basic telecommunication system. A teleconferencing system may enable face-to-face interaction, interaction between local groups, or interaction with remote groups. It may be a one-time process, or it may be a continuous process.

Significant cost savings have been reported by organizations using teleconferencing systems. The most notable case is Honeywell, which has saved $150,000 a month in travel expenses alone [17].

Advantages of Teleconferencing

A teleconferencing system may include some unique advantages [12, 16, 17, 18]:

1. Cost savings occur because decision-makers do not have to travel from place to place and pay for planes, hotels, and meals.
2. More contacts are possible. Since the decision-makers are not traveling long distances, they have more time to talk with each other and to resolve organization problems.

Figure 11-2 Security Measures in Distributed Environment

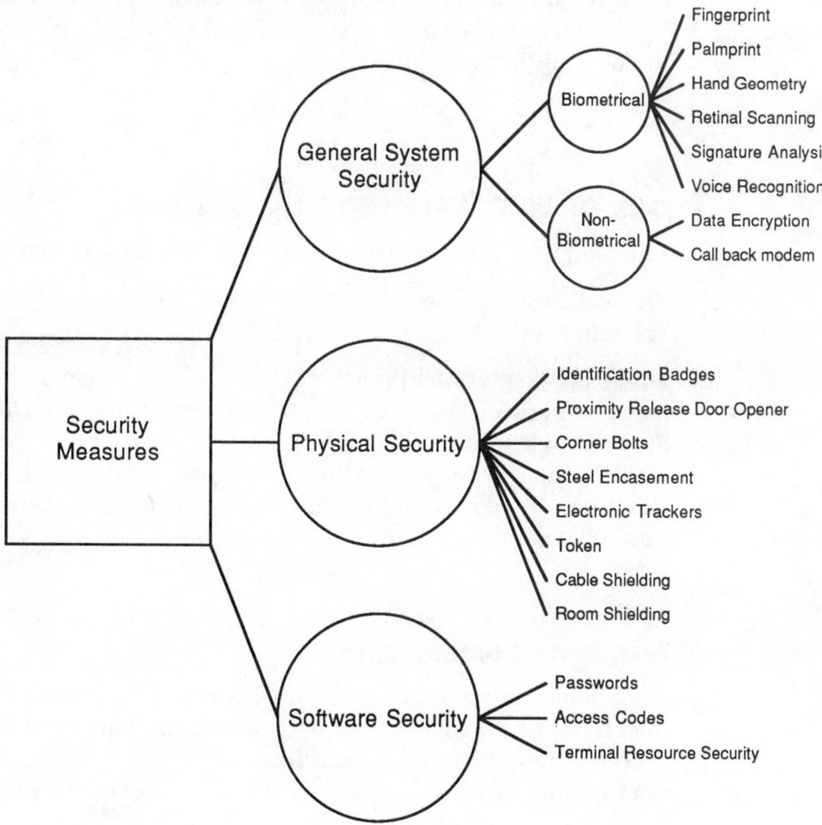

3. Shyness may not be as severe in a teleconference as it is in a face-to-face meeting. This is particularly helpful to those decision-makers who are shy in face-to-face settings.
4. Less stress exists because fewer hours are spent traveling. The decision-makers, by using a teleconferencing system, may be able to spend more time with family and friends, which may improve the morale of these individuals.

Disadvantages of Teleconferencing

Teleconferencing systems, also have some disadvantages [12, 16, 17, 18]:

1. Lack of human touch. In a teleconferencing system gestures, face-to-face impressions, handshakes, and eye contacts are lost. This in turn may hinder the effectiveness of regular meetings. At this point only two of the five senses, sound and vision, are present in a teleconferencing system.
2. Unnecessary meetings. Since teleconference meetings are so easy to arrange, some unnecessary meetings may be held, and time and energy may be wasted.
3. Security problem. Teleconferencing has the same security problem as any other telecommunication system. There is always the risk that valuable and private organizational information may get into the hands of unauthorized individuals.

11-9 Types of Teleconferencing Systems

Teleconferencing systems can be classified within two general groups [13]:

1. Telepresentations
2. Telemeetings

Telepresentation systems offer a one-way video and a two-way audio. The participants can hear and see the presenter; however, the presenter can only hear the participants.

Telemeeting systems allow a two-way video and audio. This is a more effective way of communication. Teleconferencing systems have been grouped into four classes.

Telephone Conferencing

Telephone conferencing, which is the oldest type, has a simple structure. Using telephone lines, several people can call in. This type of conferencing can be used by one person from each location or, by using a special device such as a microphone, several people can call in and exchange ideas.

Limited Image Conferencing

Limited image conferencing adds limited images, such as pictures, graphics, and data charts, to the audio conferencing. These images are transmitted over ordinary telephone lines. One form of this system is slow-scan television, in which it takes several seconds or minutes to transmit images. Limited image conferencing can be more effective than telephone conferencing when it is necessary to display important graphs, figures, and charts.

Video Teleconferencing

Video teleconferencing approximates face-to-face meetings. Television sets and cameras are used to transmit live pictures and sounds. This is markedly more effective than the telephone and limited image conferencing; however, it is more costly.

Computer Teleconferencing

Computer teleconferencing uses both computer hardware and software to establish a communication line between two or more sites. Participants may use electronic mailboxes to leave messages for each other. At the same time that they are viewing a particular document on their CRTs, they have access to telephones and can express their thoughts, make corrections, examine data, and, lastly, can finalize the documents. This type of teleconferencing is particularly useful in a Group DSS environment, as is discussed in the next section.

11-10 Group Decision Support Systems

A DSS is usually designed to be used by a particular decision-maker. That is, a decision is made basically from the input provided by one particular person. Group DSS are designed to be used by more than one decision-maker. These systems are useful for committees, review panels, board meetings, task forces, and decision-making sessions that require the input of several decision-makers [5].

DeSanctis and Gallupe [5] define a GDSS as an interactive, computer-based system that facilitates solution of unstructured and semistructured problems by a set of decision-makers working as a group.

This definition is very similar to the definition of DSS given in Chapter 1. The only difference is the existence of the group versus individual decision-makers. By this definition, the components of a GDSS, hardware, software, people, and procedures, are basically the same as the components of DSS in general. To be more specific, consider the hardware/software components of a GDSS. The software components include:

Figure 11-3 A Model of a GDSS *Source:* DeSanctis and Gallupe [5, p. 4]. Reprinted with permission.

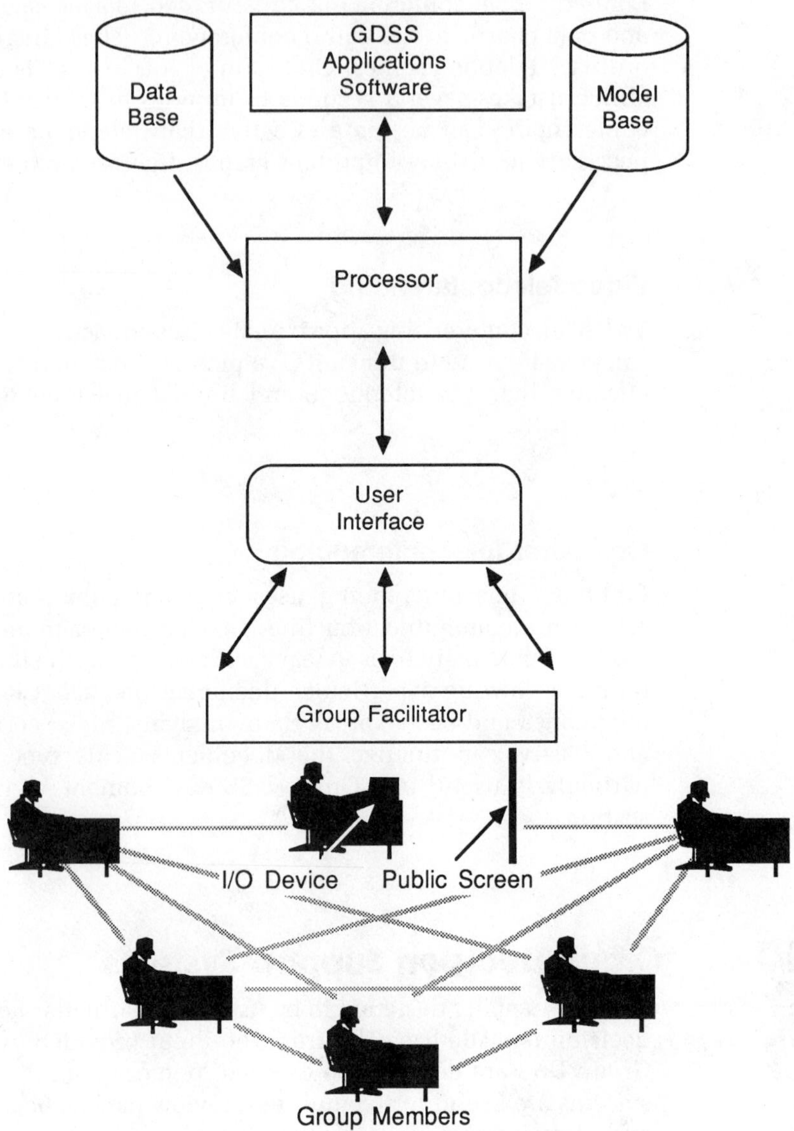

- Data base capabilities (data base)
- Modeling capabilities (model base)
- Dialog management with multiple-user access (dialog management)
- Specialized application program to facilitate group access

The hardware components of GDSS include:

- General purpose I/O devices (terminal, CRT, voice I/O)
- Central processor

- Common viewing screen (for the group) or individual monitor (for each participant)
- A network system linking the different sites/participants to each other

A general model of a GDSS is provided in Figure 11-3.

A GDSS may include all the advantages of teleconferencing systems discussed earlier. As will be seen in the next section, teleconferencing is indeed one special version of a GDSS.

Applications of a GDSS may include any areas that require the input of several decision-makers, such as corporate planning, crisis management, engineering projects, conflict resolution, and evolutionary development.

11-11 Different Types of GDSS

DeSanctis and Gallupe [5] have presented four different architectures for a GDSS.

Decision Room

In the *decision room* GDSS, decision-makers sit around a horseshoe-shaped desk facing a large screen. Each participant has access to a terminal for individual participant input, but at the same time can see the large screen. The large screen is used to summarize the input from the individual participants.

Local Decision Network (LDN)

In *LDN*, the participants are dispersed in a limited geographical area. They can participate from their own offices and express their views. This architecture includes a central processor with dedicated software for storing the results.

Teleconferencing

Teleconferencing, as discussed earlier, enables decision-makers in scattered geographic regions to see and hear each other as they participate in group decision-making.

Remote Decision Making

Remote decision making advocates "uninterrupted communication" [5] on a regular basis among a fixed number of decision-makers in a geographically dispersed organization. In this type of architecture there is no need to schedule meetings in advance as in teleconferencing. A participant may send his or her

Figure 11-4 Framework in Group Decision Support *Source:* DeSanctis and Gallupe [5, p. 6]. Reprinted with permission.

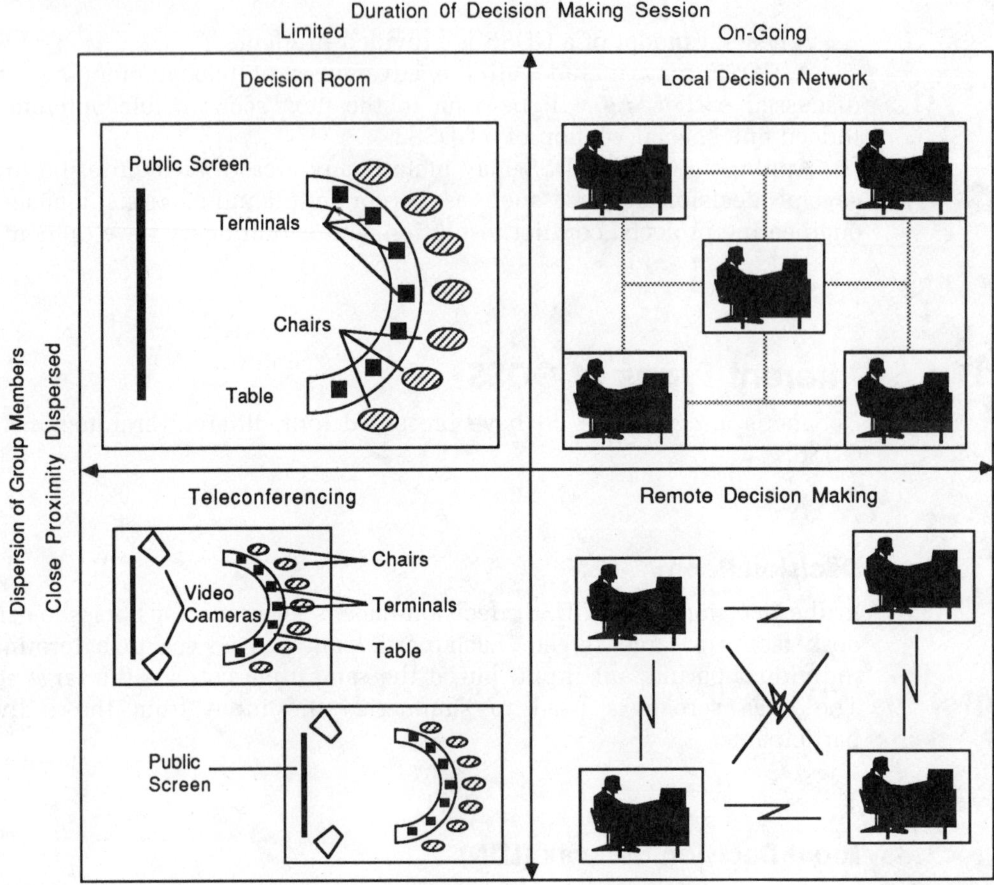

input to the central data base (electronic mailbox); then the other participants respond to this input. Eventually a decision is made by consensus.

Figure 11-4 illustrates these four types of architecture. Rathwell and Burns [18] discuss some interesting applications of GDSS in the areas of engineering, development projects, scientific committees, company planning, and crisis management.

11-12 Software Support for GDSS

There are a number of software programs used in GDSS to facilitate group decision making. Table 11-2 highlights these programs.

Table 11-2 ▪ GDSS Software

Name	Application
1. EMISARI (Emergency Management Information and References Index) [9]	For domestic crisis management. Up to 100 participants can participate in decision-making process.
2. MONSTR [4, 6]	Computer-based message system used for development projects.
3. CONSENSOR [20]	An electronic decision tool that facilitates discussion and decision making in meetings.
4. NEGO [18]	Used for decision making and finding a compromise.

11-13 Summary

In this chapter, types of data-processing organizations, and the components of a DDP system were explained. LAN was explained as it relates to DSS, and possible security measures that could be used in a distributed environment were discussed. Teleconferencing and Group DSS were briefly described. This discussion should highlight some of the issues that may come into play in DSS design and utilization in the near future.

Review Questions

1. What are the three categories of data-processing organizations?

2. What are the advantages and disadvantages of each?

3. What are the major components of a DDP system?

4. Is a modem always needed in a DDP system?

5. What is the best communication line as far as security is concerned? What is the least attractive line in this regard?

6. How do you choose a communication line? What criteria must be considered?

7. What are the network topologies discussed in this chapter?

8. What are the major uses of each?

9. What are security issues? Can they all be controlled?

10. What are the biometrics measures?

11. What is data encryption?

12. What is a call-back modem?
13. What is physical security?
14. What is software security?
15. What are the components of an automated office?
16. What is teleconferencing?
17. What are the advantages and disadvantages of a teleconferencing system?
18. What are the four major types of a teleconferencing system?
19. What is a GDSS?
19. What are the advantages of a GDSS?
20. What are the components of a GDSS?
21. What are the four types of GDSS architecture?
22. What are some software packages used specifically for a GDSS?

Projects

1. Investigate an organization of your choice that has established a LAN system. What are some of the problems they have run into? How could they have avoided these problems?

2. What are some of the LAN products on the market? What are the major differences between PC and mainframe LAN products? What are some of the actual uses of LAN?

3. By investigating the sources in Table 11-2, identify the strengths and weaknesses of the software products given in the table.

4. Select an organization of your choice that is using a teleconferencing system. Identify the advantage of such systems. If the organization is not using a teleconferencing system, what is the alternative?

5. Research data-processing/MIS journals and highlight some of the security problems faced by data processing managers. How may these problems be resolved?

6. Select an organization of your choice that is using GDSS. What are some of the unique advantages of this system? Why is GDSS becoming popular? The quality of a GDSS may improve in the near future. Why is this claim true?

Key Terms

Centralized processing
Decentralized processing
Distributed data processing (DDP)
Modem
Communication control unit
Coaxial cable

Microwave
Satellite
Fiber optic
Local Area Network (LAN)
Star network
Ring network
Loop network
Bus network
Tree (hierarchical network)
Web (fully connected, cartwheel) network
Information tampering
Fingerprint
Palmprint
Hand geometry
Retinal scanning
Voice recognition
Data encryption
Call-back modem
Token
Cable shielding
Room shielding
Identification badges
Proximity release door opener
Corner bolts
Steel encasement
Electronic trackers
Passwords
Access codes
Terminal resource security
Office automation
Teleconferencing
Telepresentations
Telemeetings
Telephone conferencing
Limited image conferencing
Video teleconferencing
Computer teleconferencing
Group (GDSS)
Decision room
Local decision network (LDN)
Remote decision making

References

[1] Azarmsa, Reza, and Hossein Bidgoli. 1988. Savvy Security Measures Keep Computer Intruders at Bay. *The Executive Educator* (June): 13–15.

[2] Burch, John G. 1985. Network Topologies: The Ties That Bind Information Systems. *Data Management* (December): 34–37, 51.

[3[Carpon, H. L., and Brian K. Williams. 1984. *Computer and Data Processing*. 2d ed. Menlo Park, Calif.: Benjamin/Cummings Publishing Company, Inc.

[4] Cashman, P. M., and A. W. Holt. 1980. A Communication-Oriented Approach to Structuring the Software Maintenance Environment. *ACM Software Engineering Notes* 5, no. 1: 4–17.

[5] DeSanctis, Gerardine, and Brent Gallupe. 1985. Group Decision Support Systems: A New Frontier. *Data Base* (Winter): 3–9.

[6] Dzida, W. 1981. Computer Mediated Messages for Interactive Purposes. In *Computer Message Systems*. Ed. R. P. Uhlig. Amsterdam, Holland: North-Holland, pp. 79–87.

[7] Evans, Sandy. 1986. What's New in Security Accessories. *Security Management* (January): 37–39.

[8] Gibson, Harry L., and Robert Rademacher. 1987. *Automated Office Systems*. New York: Holt, Rinehart and Winston.

[9] Hilz, R. S., and M. Turoff. 1978. *The Network Notion*. Reading, Mass.: Addison-Wesley.

[10] Huber, George P. 1984. Issues in the Design of Group Decision Support Systems. *MIS Quarterly* (September): 195–204.

[11] Jachau, Donald A. 1984. Systems in Action. *Office Administration and Automation* (March): 82–90.

[12] Johansen, Robert, and Christine Bullen. 1983. Thinking Ahead What to Expect From Teleconferencing. *Harvard Business Review* (March-April): 164–73.

[13] Kressler, Suzanne Pierce. 1986. Teleconferencing—Meeting on the Air. *Management Accounting* (May): 14–15.

[14] Leigh, William E., and Clifford Burgess. 1987. *Distributed Intelligence*. Cincinnati, Oh.: South-Western Publishing Co.

[15] Lientz, Bennet P., and Kathryn P. Rea. 1987. *Data Communications for Business*. St. Louis: Times Mirror/Mosby College Publishing.

[16] Panko, Raymond. 1986. Teleconferencing Outlasts Skepticism. *Computerworld* (November 10): 67–72.

[17] Portway, Patrick S. 1984. What Teleconferencing Adds, Not Eliminates. *The Office:* 101, 114.

[18] Rathwell, Margaret A., and Alan Burns. 1980. Information Systems Support for Group Planning and Decision Making Activities. *MIS Quarterly* (September): 255–71.

[19] Rushine, Avi, and Sara Ruchinek. 1986. Distributed Processing: Implications and Applications for Business. *Journal of Systems Management* (July): 21–27.

[20] Simmons, W. W. 1981. Planners Look at Planning Again. *Managerial Planning* (January-February): 11–12.

[21] Synders, Jan. 1984. How Safe is Safe? *Infosystems* (June): 64–65.

[22] Walden, Jerry. 1984. Cracking Down on Micro Crime. *Business Computer Systems* (October): 54.

12 Artificial Intelligence: What Is Really Involved?

12-1 Introduction

This chapter provides an overview of artificial intelligence and its related technologies. AI as a concept is discussed and general problems, including a lack of training and understanding for AI users, associated with the AI field are explained. Also among these problems are maintenance issues that may be overcome in the near future. Natural language processing (NLP), one of the most important areas in the AI field and one that has a direct impact on the design and utilization of a DSS, is discussed in detail. Problems associated with NLP are explained. This chapter will explain why it is so difficult to develop a full-featured NLP at this time, and the reasons that it is unlikely to be developed even in the near future. Simple architecture of an NLP is introduced. Computer interpretation of visual and speech input is explained, and problems that must be overcome in this area before "computers" can receive a voice command and respond to the user are also presented. This chapter also provides a brief review of robotics as one of the successful areas in the AI field including a brief mention of Japanese computers and the so-called "fifth-generation" project. This chapter concludes with a discussion of LISP and PROLOG as two of the AI languages that have been used for developing expert systems. Expert systems are discussed in the next chapter.

12-2 What Is Artificial Intelligence?

There is no commonly accepted definition for artificial intelligence (AI). Generally speaking, AI refers to a series of related technologies that try to simulate and reproduce human thought behavior, including thinking, speaking, feeling, and reasoning.

AI technology applies computers to areas that require knowledge, perception, reasoning, understanding, and cognitive abilities. To achieve this, computers must:

- Understand common sense
- Understand facts and manipulate qualitative data
- Deal with exceptions and discontinuity
- Understand relationships among the facts
- Interface with humans in a free-format fashion
- Be able to deal with new situations based on previous learning

Marvin L. Minsky, one of the pioneers in the AI field, has provided a simple definition for AI:

> Artificial intelligence is the science of making machines do things that would require intelligence if done by man [20].

As an example of how AI works, consider the following: You are searching your file cabinet for a document. Suddenly you find an old notebook that you used during junior high school. This notebook brings many different memories to your mind immediately—memories of your classmates, your close friends, possibly the teacher who taught you biology, the course in which you used this notebook for recording class notes. This can go on and on. Can computers perform in such a way? By seeing an old notebook, all the memories associated with that notebook come to your mind. At this time computers are not capable of doing these tasks, and will probably not be capable of them in the foreseeable future.

Whereas traditional computer-based information systems (CBIS) are concerned with storage, retrieval, manipulation, and display of data, AI-systems are concerned with the reproduction and display of knowledge and facts.

In traditional CBISs programmers and systems analysts design and implement systems that help decision-makers by providing timely, relevant, accurate and integrated information. In the AI field, "knowledge engineers" are trying to discover "rules of thumb" that will enable computers to perform tasks usually performed by humans. Rules employed in AI technology may come from a diverse group of experts in such areas as mathematics, psychology, economics, anthropology, medicine, engineering, and physics.

Some AI experts believe that AI is more of a concept than a solid field. AI encompasses a group of related technologies. Among these technologies are:

- Expert systems (ES)
- Natural language processing (NLP)
- Speech recognition
- Vision recognition
- Robotics

In the next chapter we discuss an ES in detail. ES, among all the AI-related technologies, has achieved a relatively high degree of success. The following is a brief definition of an ES:

> An expert system is a series of computer programs that attempt to mimic human thought behavior in a specific area.

For successful ES design and implementation, the system must be applied to an activity that has already been successfully performed by human experts, such as endeavors in the fields of medicine, geology, or electronics. We talk about this in detail in the next chapter.

In the remaining parts of this chapter we discuss other AI-related technologies and their successes, failures, strengths, and weaknesses.

12-3 General Problems Associated with AI Technologies

Conceptually, AI has been around since the 1950s. Although we have experienced some successes in several areas of AI, such as ES, NLP, and, to some degree, robotics, there are still some significant issues that must be resolved before we can implement AI technologies on a broader scale. A summary of these general problems follows [1, 3]:

1. *Misunderstanding of AI domain.* Various AI users and designers have different views of AI. This lack of a common understanding may generate false expectations regarding the real strengths and weaknesses of AI technologies.
2. *Fear of replacement by AI.* Many workers feel AI technologies are being designed to replace them in their jobs. This fear may cause an obstacle in the further development of AI technologies. Robotics have already replaced many workers on assembly lines in the United States and particularly in Japan.
3. *Cost-effectiveness.* The development and design of AI-related technologies (except robotics) may not be cost-effective at this time. Many resources may be spent on something that does not have a positive economic value. Management is reluctant to invest valuable resources in projects that do not promise a positive economic value.
4. *Lack of training for the user.* Many workers are still not familiar with even traditional computer technology, to say nothing of AI fields. Lack of training may be another obstacle to AI use in the workplace.
5. *Maintenance.* Because AI technologies are still new and evolving, it is difficult for designers and particularly for users to effectively maintain them. More has to be learned about AI technologies before they can be efficiently maintained.
6. *Transportability.* At this time, the AI technology, developed in one discipline may not be able to be used in another discipline. This again may consume valuable resources. It may be necessary to first explore the real potential of AI and then start the development of these systems on a broader scale.

At this time one can conclude that computers that work with AI technologies are smarter than other computer-based information systems; however, they do not approach the human intellect. Figure 12-1 shows this conclusion graphically.

Figure 12-1 Comparison of the AI Technologies with Traditional Information Systems Technologies

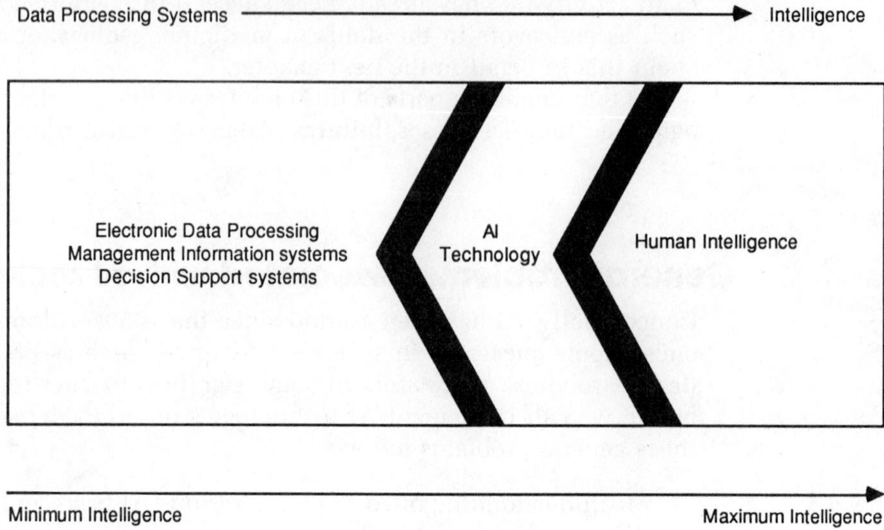

12-4 Natural Language Processing

Computer-based information systems have been designed to be used by users who are somewhat computer literate. No matter how flexible and user-friendly systems are, a specific method must be followed in order to operate these systems or perform queries.

As discussed in Chapter 1, four classes of computer languages have evolved. The first class, a machine language, is a binary system consisting of 1s and 0s. It is the closest to the computer and the farthest from human language. The second class, an assembly language, consists of a series of short codes (mnemonics) to present instructions to the computer. The third class is a high-level language that is more application- and user-oriented and more like English. The fourth class, fourth-generation languages (4 GLs), which are more forgiving than high-level languages and, most importantly, nonprocedural. The nonprocedural quality means that the user does not need to follow a very rigid structure in order to communicate with a computer. The fifth class, natural language, is the ideal language from a user's point of view. This language is supposed to enable a computer user to communicate with the computer in his or her native language.

The goal of NLP is to provide a method for interface that is very similar to our native language. An NLP provides a free-format question-and-answer situation for a typical user.

There are a number of NLPs available on the market. Table 12-1 [1, 11] provides a listing of some of the more successful NLPs. At the time of this writing, none of these products are capable of providing a dialog comparable to a dialog between humans. In the next section we discuss problems and obstacles associated with the development of a full-featured NLP.

12-5 Problems with Natural Language Processing

Many workers are not using computers simply because they do not know how to operate them. Many do not even know how to type. According to senior executives it would be a wonderful idea to be able to talk to the computer and have the computer talk back to you. A natural-language interface can immensely increase the effectiveness of a computer-based information system. However, there are several serious obstacles that have to be overcome before a natural-language interface could be developed:

1. *Ambiguity in our native language.* Human communications contain many ambiguities. Nowhere is this more evident than in language. A word can have many different meanings depending on the context in which it is used. The context that a word is used in can vary widely due to differences between people. We all have different training and backgrounds. Everyone knows people of different backgrounds and status.

   The same word may have different meanings to different people. For example, if I tell you, "The project will be completed soon," soon may mean 10 minutes, 2 days, or 2 months. This depends somewhat on the term *project.* A project can be finishing up a term paper, a textbook, a dissertation, or a house. Another example is this: If you ask an architect, a psychologist, and a construction engineer to study a house, the sentence may have several different meanings to these three individuals. The architect may study the house from a general design or esthetic viewpoint. The psychologist may study the house in terms of relationships among the people living in the house. The construction

Table 12-1 ▪ Natural Language Systems on the Market

NLP Name	Area of Use
BROKER	Standard and Poor's data
CLOUT	Data base management system
EXPLORER	Map generation and display
INTELLECT	Data base management system
LADDER	Ship identification & location
MARKETEER	Market analysis
NATURALLINK	Dow Jones data retrieval and display
POLITICS	Ideological belief system simulation
Q & A	Interface with data base, word processing, and report generator
SAM	Generic story understanding
SHRDLU	Location and manipulation of three-dimensional pictures
STRAIGHT TALK	Interface with word processing/microcomputer worksheet
TDUS	Electromechanical repair
TEAMS	Data base management system

engineer may study the house from the construction point of view, materials used, and so forth. To make a natural language understandable, the particular audience and a particular context must first be defined.

Frequently, we understand a word or a sentence based upon our common sense. How do we tell the computer to understand a given context? How do we tell the computer the same word with a different tone? How does a computer learn common sense? To make this discussion more clear, consider the sentence, "Johnny caught a plane." Everyone knows what this sentence means because of the common use of the word catch: Johnny took a plane to go somewhere. But, this sentence can have several different meanings, depending on the meaning of *catch*.

- Johnny might have seized the plane.
- Johnny might have trapped the plane.
- Johnny might have deceived the plane.
- Johnny might have discovered the plane.
- Johnny might have hit the plane.
- Johnny might have intercepted the plane.
- Johnny might have charmed the plane.

Other examples are the word *get*, with at least 21 meanings, *line* with at least 32 meanings, and *order* with at least 20 meanings.

Computers can make remarkable mistakes if they do not make common-sense connections. A program called FRUMP [7, p. 24], developed at Yale, was supposed to summarize a news story. When in 1978 the shooting of San Francisco's mayor "shook" the city, FRUMP concluded that California had undergone an earthquake. The program, knowing that California is susceptible to tremors, was unable to distinguish the metaphorical meaning of the word *shook* in the mayor's story. Another instance pertains to language translation. In those instances, when computers have been utilized to translate from one language to another, the results have been nothing but amusing. Literal translations of words and phrases may take on totally different meanings in other languages.

2. *Problems with ellipses*. Incomplete sentences, or ellipses, can also present difficulties to computers. These may occur when a word or words are left out, creating grammatical incompleteness. As examples consider:

   If late, don't come (meaning if you are late, do not come).

   If possible, pay the bill (meaning if it is possible, you pay the bill).

   They have fun in Hawaii—me too (meaning you had fun also).

   No pain, no gain (meaning if you don't experience any pain, you may not be rewarded).

   There are many ellipses like these in human language. How can a computer be programmed to understand this?

3. *Problems with metaphors*. Metaphors may also create problems for NLP. Metaphor problems occur when you say something and you mean

something else. Consider the sentence; "He is on top of the world." This sentence usually means the man is happy; it does not mean the man is on the highest point of the world. Consider the following sentences:

He is a straight arrow (meaning he is conventional).

After the race started, I died (meaning I became exhausted).

How are we going to teach these metaphor issues? How does a computer know when we say something, we really mean something else?

4. *Confusion between questions and action.* When a statement requests an action, not just a yes or no answer, still more problems are encountered by an NLP system. Consider the following questions:

   Can you give me a ride?

   Can you hold my briefcase?

   Can you open the door for me?

   Can you answer the phone for me?

   In these cases, the yes or no answer is not the goal; you are asking for an action. Hold my briefcase or answer the phone for me, please.

5. *Idioms in our language.* Idioms and slang also present serious problems to the NLP system. Consider the word "run" as a verb and as a noun. The word run as a verb has at least 16 meanings, and when you use it as slang, the number of meanings becomes very large: Some examples are:

   run up

   run down

   run out

   run on

   Another interesting example is all the slang made with the word go: go around, go far, go at, go down, go into, go off, go over, go to, go under, go with, and so on. The English language is full of slang like this.

6. *Similar sounding words and phrases.* Humans have problems distinguishing similar sounding words and phrases. The same is true about computers. Consider:

Bear	Bare
Chip	Cheap
Fortunes	Four tunes
Flour	Flower
Grade	Great
Night	Knight
Read	Red
Sent	Scent

12-6 How a Natural Language System Works

In a typical natural language system, a user either types a sentence or chooses a sentence from a menu. At this point we are not using voice input. Natural language with voice input is discussed in the next section. When the request is typed or selected through an input device, the NLP goes through the following steps:

1. The parser figures out how a sentence is structured. As an example, consider a user who has typed:

   "John drew a picture"

   The parser may dissect this sentence as follows:

   "John" as noun phrase.

   "drew a picture" as verb phrase.

   In the next round the verb phrase is parsed further to:

   drew

   a picture

   This process continues until the entire sentence is parsed. The result of this process is a parse tree.
2. The NLP starts semantic analysis. The verb is translated first because the verb states the action, then the modifiers of the action are translated, and finally the nouns are translated. In this process the NLP compares the itemized tree with its dictionary in order to figure out the meaning of a statement.
3. If there is any ambiguity, an expert system is used to clear it up. As discussed in the last section, this process is not as easy as it sounds. Figure 12-2 [11] illustrates the process.

At this time NLP systems have been successful only when they are used within a defined context—for example, for DBMS retrieval. CLOUT is one good example of a successful NLP. Table 12-1 illustrates some relatively successful NLPs on the market.

12-7 Perception: Visual and Speech Recognition

As soon as you see an object, your brain instantly gives it a meaning. This is also true of hearing. When somebody talks to you, your brain instantly identifies the person as male, female, an old friend, and so on. Hearing and sight share certain features that are difficult for computers to simulate. Both hearing and sight are responses of the nervous system to the environment. When we see and hear, the stimulation of our nervous system is usually continuous. Our eyes see an entire scene, and our brain effectively separates the scene into individual, understandable objects. Our ears do the same thing with sound stimulation. A continuous stream of sound is received, but the brain can determine where one word starts and ends and where a sentence is finished

Figure 12-2 The Function of a Natural Language Processing System

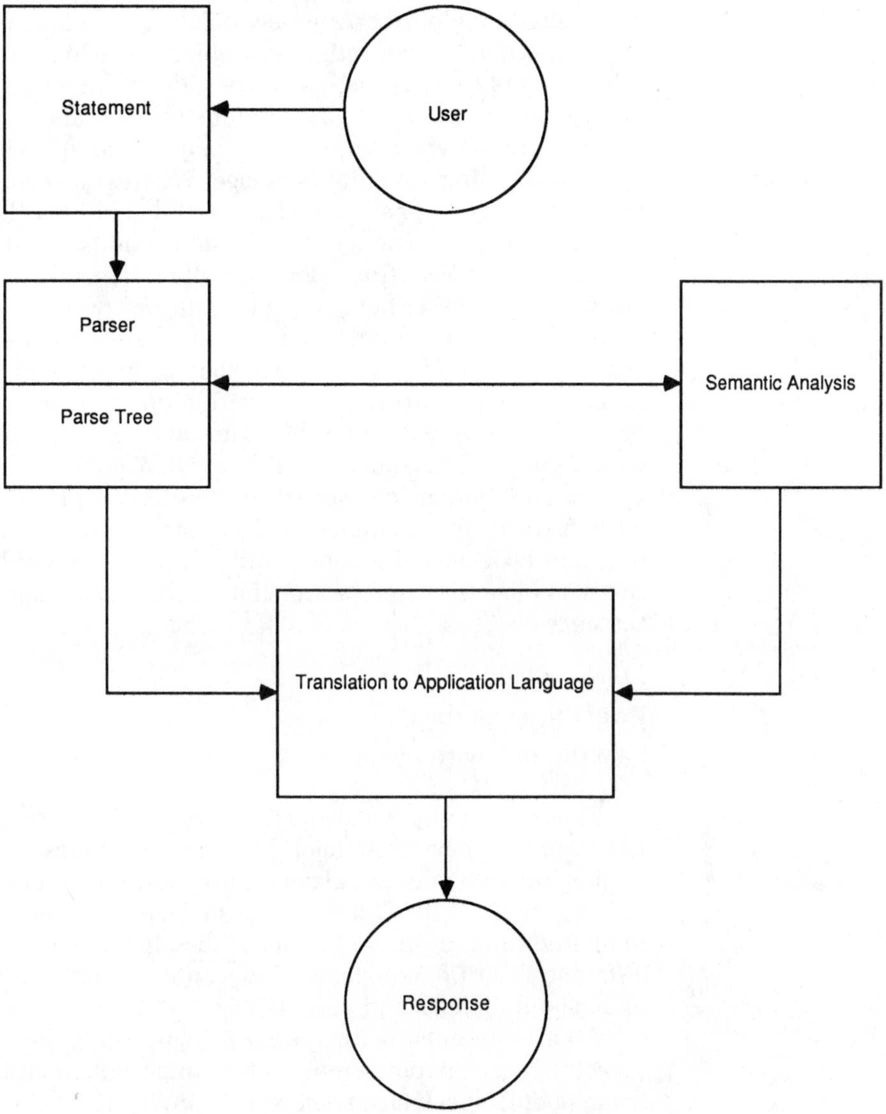

and a new one starts. This is a challenging task for a computer. How does the brain accomplish these tasks so easily? Research to understand how human perception operates has been going on for years. A question more relevant to the study of computer systems, is, "how do computers handle visual and speech recognition?" A discussion of some of the issues involved in perception follows.

1. *Image comprehension.* Image recognition has been achieved by robots. However, a robot, of its own accord, cannot understand and recognize

even a simple shape if it does not have enough information available to build up a sensible interpretation of the scene prior to attempting to comprehend the object. Any new object is a serious challenge. What happens when a robot sees a new object for which it does not have any information [9]? What happens when the robot sticks to a soft surface? What happens when the robot bumps into a wall?

Interpreting visual input is very similar to applying common sense in understanding a natural language. When you see a house, through common sense you have a pretty good idea of how the house should look, even if you have not seen the entire house. Your mind instantly separates this object from a million other objects. Your mind registers the house with all other houses in one category of objects. Computers are still a long way from imitating the visual abilities of humans. Robots can pick up an object from a conveyor belt *only* when an object is oriented in a specific, pre-programmed position on the conveyor belt. What if this part is mixed up with ten other parts in a pile [21]? What if the angle in which the part is standing is slightly changed?

2. *Speech comprehension.* Speech recognition is probably harder than written words for computers to understand. For example, the words bore and boar have the same pronunciation; the words too, to and two also have the same pronunciation. Also consider the following sentences:

   I *threw* a ball.

   I went *through* the door.

   I am *through* with the test.

   These three words may sound very much the same to a computer; however, they have completely different meanings.

   Regional accents can also confuse computers. For example, people in different parts of the United States may say the same word or sentence in totally different tones. Letters of the alphabet are also pronounced differently in different states. How can computers be programmed to understand dialects and accents?

   Another problem with speech recognition is the variety of human speech patterns. Women tend to have high voices and men low ones. Some people speak fast, some speak slowly. Even the same person may have different voice patterns during different hours of the day. In the morning or late afternoon people will have different frequencies in their voices. How can all this be taught to a computer?

The limited success achieved to date on voice recognition is in those areas that are very precise. A voice recognition system can be trained to understand one particular voice [19]. Even when trained for a particular individual, the system may get confused when this person catches a cold, when it is early in the morning and the voice has a different quality, or late in the afternoon when the voice is tired.

12-8 Robotics

Robots and robotics form the field of AI that is least closely related to DSS. However, it is one of the most successful applications of AI, and for this reason we give a quick overview of this field.

Today's robots are the ones seen in movies and factories. They are far from intelligent, but progress has been steady. At the present time, they are slow, clumsy, blind, and mostly stupid! Their major applications have been in assembly lines in factories where they are used as a part of computer-integrated manufacturing (CIM). They have no sense of touch or feeling, and their vision is very limited [22].

Industrial robots cost from $100,000 to $250,000. Their mobility is also limited. A serious challenge that exists is teaching robots how to walk. They will have a very difficult time should they attempt to walk on two feet like humans. How does a robot learn to walk on a soft surface? Which foot has to go first? Even with all these problems, robots have been successfully utilized by Japanese and some American factories. At the present time, the majority of the robots in the world are operating in Japanese assembly lines. Using robots, a Japanese automobile manufacturer can manufacture over 30 cars per day. Developments in AI-related fields such as ES, NLP, vision, and hearing will have a definite impact on the future development of the robotics industry.

A typical robot has a fixed arm, which moves an object repeatedly from point *X* to *Y*. Some robots have limited vision, in which case they can locate objects and pick them up as long as the objects are isolated from other objects. The operation of a robot is controlled by a computer and a program. A computer program written for a robot includes such commands as when and how far to reach, which direction to go or turn, when to grasp an object, and how much pressure to apply. There are numerous computer languages for robot programming: T3, RCL, AL, AML, and PAL, to mention a few. Naturally, these languages are associated with a particular manufacture of a robot. Personal robots have attracted a lot of attention in recent years. These robots have limited mobility, limited vision, and some speech capability. At the present time, they are mostly used as toys. Improvement in speech and vision should improve the usefulness of these robots. In general, robots have some unique advantages compared to humans in the workplace:

- They don't get tired.
- They never ask for a raise.
- They don't ask for a room with a window.
- They are not moody.
- They are consistent.
- They do not take any coffee breaks.
- They do not argue with the boss!
- They don't join unions.
- They don't get emotionally hurt.
- They don't get insulted.
- They can be used in environments hazardous to human health, such as spray painting autos or radioactive work.

12-9 Japanese Computers

As discussed in Chapter 1, four major architectural changes have taken place in the course of computer development: (1) first generation, or the vacuum tube era; (2) second generation, or the transistor era; (3) third generation, or the integrated circuit era; and (4) fourth generation, or the very large scale integration (VLSI) or ultra large scale integration (ULSI) era.

The so-called fifth generation computers refer to AI-type computers currently being developed. There is direct competition between Japanese and U.S. manufacturers to achieve this breakthrough. In Japan, both the Japanese government and private enterprise have been working on the fifth-generation project for years. The Institute for New Generation Computer Technology (ICOT) supervises the fifth-generation computers in Japan. ICOT consists of eight companies: Fujitsu, Hitachi, Oki, Sharp, Toshiba, Nippon Electric, Mitsubishi, and Mitsushita.

The fifth-generation project, which started as a 10-year project in October 1981, has a series of specific goals [7]:

- To implement a logic-processor language such as PROLOG (see the next section).
- To improve the speed of *logic inferences per second* (lips) to gigilips (billion lips) by 1991.
- To generate a machine-translation program between English and Japanese that would have a vocabulary of 100,000 words. This translation should take place with 90% accuracy.
- To generate a speech-understanding program with a 50,000-word vocabulary.
- To make a computer that understands maps, charts, and photographs as well as words.

This project sounds very ambitious, but intense research has been going on for several years, so we must wait and see.

The counterpart of ICOT in the United States is Microelectronics & Computer Technology Corp. (MCC). This organization began operation in 1983 at its headquarters in Austin, Texas. MCC partners include Motorola, National Semi-Conductor, NCR, Rockwell, Sperry, Mostek, Advanced Micro Devices, Allied BMC Industries, Digital Equipment Corporation, Control Data, Eastman Kodak, Lockheed, Martin Marietta, Harris, Gould, and Honeywell. The U.S. Government is backing MCC in many ways. A number of universities, including Stanford, Cornell, and the University of California at San Diego, are also involved in this project [3].

At the time of this writing, we do not know the exact status of the fifth-generation project. Both Japan and the United States are heavily involved in this project, so there is much to be learned in the near future regarding the outcome of this immense research.

12-10 Artificial Intelligence Languages

AI languages are somewhat different from traditional computer languages such as FORTRAN, COBOL, or Pascal. AI languages utilize symbolic representations by using list, graph, matrix, and range.

An AI language needs several unique capabilities. It must:

- Deal with both qualitative as well as quantitative data.
- Deal with words as representatives of meaning, not just a series of characters.
- Deal with data as well as facts.
- Be flexible in order to deal with different types of information, e.g., symbols, tables, graphs, maps, charts, and words.
- Be user-friendly and permit free-format interface.

One of the AI languages on the market is LISP (list processor), which has been in use for over 20 years. While traditional computer languages use data structures such as numeric data, nonnumeric data, array, and matrix, LISP uses only lists as its data structure. A list can include ordered numbers, symbols, expressions, functions, and the like. A LISP list is shown as a group of elements enclosed in parentheses. For example, (SKY IS BLUE) is a list in LISP language consisting of three symbols: SKY, IS, and BLUE.

LISP was developed by John McCarthy in the mid-1950s and was first implemented in 1960. This language facilitates and expedites the development of symbolic expressions in terms of lists and functions. LISP can be compiled by the user or it can be left in the original code. There are two subsets of LISP; MACLISP and INTERLISP, which enhance the capability of the original LISP. For detailed information on LISP, see [23].

PROLOG (programming in logic) is another AI language. This language was developed by Philippe Roussel in France about 1970 and still has a larger market in Europe than in the United States. It defines inferential relationships among groups of objects that could lead to an automatic deduction. Quintus Computer Systems, Inc. is one U.S. company marketing a PROLOG compiler.

PROLOG works on logic. To clarify what we mean by logic consider:

A canary is a bird.

All birds fly.

Therefore, a canary flies.

In comparing LISP and PROLOG, Ross Overbeek [7, p. 51] states that PROLOG or other logic-based languages would be more suitable for the development of expert systems. LISP evaluates each statement in sequence, whereas PROLOG scans all the rules and evaluates those that apply to a particular situation. Because rules that do not apply to the situation under investigation are scanned, PROLOG in general is more efficient than LISP. Also, two important features of AI programming used by most expert systems, forward and backward chaining, are built into PROLOG but must be programmed into LISP. In forward chaining, a series of IF-THEN statements are evaluated in order to reach a goal. In backward chaining, the goal, or the THEN part, is considered first; then the system backtracks until it finds all the rules needed to achieve the goal. In the next chapter we discuss these techniques in more detail. For detailed information on PROLOG, see [4].

12-11 Summary

This chapter reviewed artificial intelligence and its related disciplines. Progress in the AI field will have a direct impact on DSS design and utilization. These issues are discussed in detail in Chapter 14. Among the AI-related disciplines, natural language processing is the most important area as far as a DSS is concerned. Problems related to design of an NLP were explained. The chapter also briefly discussed interpretation of speech and vision perception and robotics and two of the AI languages, LISP and PROLOG. Materials presented in this chapter should provide a good background for understanding expert systems and the possible integration of AI and DSS, which is discussed in the next two chapters.

Review Questions

1. What is AI?

2. Is AI a solid discipline or just a concept?

3. What are AI-related technologies?

4. Among AI-related technologies, which one has a direct impact on DSS? Why?

5. What are some of the problems associated with AI field? Can these problems be resolved in the foreseeable future? If yes, how?

6. What is a natural language processing system? In computer language development where does NLP stand?

7. Why is an NLP so desirable to a computer user?

8. What does an NLP offer that other languages are not capable of offering?

9. What are some of the problems associated with NLP development? Which problem is the most serious? Why?

10. How can computers be taught "common sense"?

11. How does an NLP work?

12. What are some of the problems with visual perception? With speech recognition?

13. What is a robot? What are the advantages of a robot compared to a human? What are some of the disadvantages of a robot?

14. What is the status of computer technology in Japan?

15. What is a Japanese computer? Are they different from American computers? Who are the participants of the fifth-generation project in Japan? Who are their counterparts in the United States?

16. What is an AI language?

17. In what way is an AI language different from a traditional computer language?

18. What is the most popular AI language in the U.S.? In Europe?

19. What is the difference between LISP and PROLOG?

20. PROLOG works based on logic. Give an example of this.

21. LISP is a symbolic language. What does this mean?

22. Which language, LISP or PROLOG, includes built-in forward and backward chaining?

Projects

1. Research the strengths and weaknesses of AI computers. Are they really intelligent? What does "intelligent" mean?

2. Research the function of the brain and the function of computers. How are they similar? How are they dissimilar?

3. Research two of the NLP products presented in this chapter. What are their strengths? Their weaknesses?

4. Research an existing robot in a factory setting. Why are robots unable to see like humans? Are they ever going to see?

5. Research a LISP-based and a PROLOG-based expert system. Do they work differently in principle? Which is more suitable for what situation?

6. Some authors refer to LOGO as an AI-related language. Research this and back up this claim.

Key Terms

Artificial Intelligence
Rules of thumb
Expert systems
Natural language processing
Speech recognition
Vision recognition
Robotics
Transportability
Ambiguity
Ellipses
Metaphors
Idioms
Parser
Semantic analysis
Parse tree
Perception
Image comprehension
Speech comprehension
Computer integrated manufacturing
Japanese computer
Logic processor language
Logic inferences per second (lips)
Gigi lips
Fifth-generation project
Institute for New Generation Computer Technology (ICOT)
Microelectronic and Computer Technology Corp. (MCC)
LISP
PROLOG

References

[1] Andriole, Stephen J. 1985. The Promise of Artificial Intelligence. *Journal of Systems Management* (July): 8–17.

[2] Chang, Alec, Michael Leonard, and Jay Goldman. 1986. Artificial Intelligence: An Overview of Research and Applications. *Industrial Management* (November-December): 14–19.

[3] Chester, Jeffrey A. 1985. Is MIS Ready for the Explosion? *Infosystems* (Fall): 74–78.

[4] Clocksin, W. F., and C. S. Mellish. 1984. *Programming in Prolog.* 2d ed. New York: Springer-Verlag.

[5] Coats, Pamela K. 1986. Artificial Intelligence—Replacing Managerial Judgment with Computers. *The Journal of Business Forecasting* (Spring): 12–14.

[6] Cuadrado, Clara Y., and John L. Cuadrado. 1986. Handling Conflicts in Data. *Byte* (November): 194–202.

[7] Dorothy, Hinshaw, and Patent. 1986. *The Quest for Artificial Intelligence.* New York: Harcourt Brace Jovanovich, Inc.

[8] Firdman, Henry Eric. 1986. MIS and the Corporate View of AI. *Computerworld* (August 25): 61–67.

[9] Forsyth, Richard, and Chris Naylor. 1985. *The Hitch-Hiker's Guide to Artificial Intelligence.* New York: Chapman and Hall/Methuen.

[10] Freedman, David. 1987. AI Meets the Corporate Mainframe. *Infosystems* (February): 32–87.

[11] Fresko-Weiss, Henry. 1985. Natural Language: The Dialog Has Begun. *Personal Computing* (November): 93–96.

[12] Fresko-Weiss, Henry. 1985. Expert Systems Decision-Making Power. *Personal Computing* (November): 97–105.

[13] Grant, Dan, and George McKevitt. 1987. The Fourth Generation Meets the Fifth. *Information Center* (July): 77–79.

[14] Holsapple, Clyde W., and Andrew B. Whinston. 1985. Management Support Though Artificial Intelligence. *Human Systems Management,* pp. 163–71.

[15] Hubert Dreyfus and Stuart Dreyfus. 1986. Why Computers May Never Think Like People. *Technology Review* (January): 44–61.

[16] Johnson, Tim. 1986. NLP Takes Off. *Datamation* (January 15): 91–93.

[17] Kumara, Soundar, Allen L. Soyster, and R. L. Kashyap. 1986. An Introduction to Artificial Intelligence. *Industrial Engineering* (December): 9–20.

[18] Miller, Richard K. 1987. *Fifth Generation Computers.* Lilburn, Ga.: The Fairmont Press.

[19] Minicucci, Rick. 1986. Artificial Intelligence: Fact vs. Fantasy. *Today's Office* (September): 35–46.

[20] Minsky, Marvin. 1982. Artificial Intelligence Applications Called Dead End. *The Institute: News Supplement to IEEE Spectrum* 6, (November-October).

[21] Rohm-Godman, Wendy. 1986. A Remote Promise. *Infosystems* (September): 52–56.

[22] Stevensens, Lawrence. 1985. *Artificial Intelligence: The Search for the Perfect Machine.* Hasbrouck Heights, N.J.: Hayden Book Comapany.

[23] Steele, Jr., Guy, et. al. 1984. *Common LISP: The Language.* Bedford, Mass: Digital Press.

13 Expert Systems: The Products of AI

13-1 Introduction

This chapter covers one of the most successful categories of AI-related technologies, the expert system (ES). ES is defined and the major components of a typical ES are enumerated. Different technologies of ES are discussed, highlighting the similarities between ES and DSS. This chapter explains different types of ES architectures, application and nonapplication situations in the ES environment, and the process involved in developing an ES.

To put the discussion into perspective, several successful ESs on the market are explained in some detail. Products regarding diverse applications of ES present a promising future for these and other ESs. The chapter concludes with legal issues associated with ES use. In the next chapter, the integration of ES/AI and DSS technologies is explored.

13-2 What is an Expert System?

There is no common definition of an expert system. Generally speaking, these systems mimic the human expertise in a particular discipline in order to solve a specific problem in a well-defined area.

Feigenbaum and McCorduck [7, p. 16] have defined an ES as:

> A computer program that has built into it the knowledge and capability that will allow the program to operate at the level of a human expert.

While traditional computer-based information systems generate information by using data and models and a well-defined algorithm, expert systems work with heuristic data. The *American Heritage Dictionary* defines heuristic as:

> Relating to or using a problem-solving technique in which the most appropriate solution of several found by alternative methods is selected at successive stages of a program for use in the next step of the program.

In other words, heuristic does not imply formal knowledge but rather finding a solution to a problem without following a rigorous algorithm. Heuristics sometimes refer to "rules of thumb" or general knowledge available in a discipline.

Expert systems have been around since the 1960s, and have been continually improved during the past 20 years. There are a variety of them on the market. Table 13-1 [2, 16] illustrates a number of successful expert systems.

News about expert systems is kept somewhat secret. Developers of these systems do not reveal the detailed information regarding technical capabilities of these systems until their final release. Practitioners and companies who are using these systems are also reluctant to reveal all the successes achieved by these systems due to the competitive advantages that may be gained by other users of these systems. Even with all the secrecy, significant savings and success are reported in the literature.

R1/XCON, developed by Digital Equipment Corporation in a joint effort with Carnegie-Mellon University, has been used by Digital Equipment Corporation for configuring VAX computers. This system uses more than 3000 rules and more than 5000 product descriptions to configure the specific components of VAX systems based on a particular customer order. When the specifications are defined, the system generates a series of diagrams highlighting the electrical connections and the layout for the 50 to 150 components in a typical order [4]. The system has been continuously improved by modifying the quality and quantity of the rules employed by the system. Until 1983 one out of a thousand orders configured by XCON were misconfigured due to missing or incorrect rules. Overall, only 10% of all the orders had to be corrected for any reason at all. All these correction incidences involved cases where a seldom-used component was part of the system [3, p. 9].

Dipmeter Advisor, developed by Schlumberger Corporation, is another successful expert system in operation. This system utilizes oil well log data with respect to geological characteristics of a well and provides recommendations concerning the possible location of oil in that region.

In the microcomputer environment, Expert Ease, developed by Human Edge Software Corporation for IBM PC and PC compatibles, has demonstrated significant success. Westinghouse, by using this system, has achieved increased productivity in one important factory to the extent of increasing business volume by more than $10 million per year [3].

SRI International, working with the U.S. Geological Survey, has designed the Prospector system. This system provides advice and consultation to field teams during mineral exploration. This system predicted a deposit of molybdenum in the Cascade Mountains in northern California. This mineral deposit is expected to yield over $100 million [19, p. 140].

As this table indicates, expert systems have already been applied to diverse areas of science and technology. The remaining parts of this chapter reinforce this claim and explore the ever-increasing potential of these systems in diverse areas.

Table 13-1 ▪ Popular Expert Systems on the Market

Name	Specific Area
AALPS	Advice to U.S. Army's 82nd Airborne for loading cargo
ADDITOR	Analysis of a company's allowance for bad debts
BUGGY	Medical diagnoses
CADUCEUS	Internal medicine
CALISTO	Project management
CART	Computer faults
CASNET/GLAUCOMA	Diagnosis of glaucoma
CRITTER	Digital, circuitry
CRYSALIS	Protein crystallography
CSA	Nuclear power plant configuration
DELTA	Locomotive troubleshooting
DENDRAL	Chemistry
DIPMETER ADVISOR	Gives oil field log interpretion
ELAS	Analyzes oil well logs
EMPRESS	Planning and scheduling tool for NASA
GUIDON	Medical diagnoses
IMS	Automated factory management
INTERNIST/CADUCEUS	Medical diagnosis
KNOBS	Tactical mission planning
LES	Data monitoring during the liquid oxygen tanking process for NASA
MECHO	Mechanical problems
MEDAS	Critical care medicine
MOLGEN	Molecular genetics
MYCIN	Medical diagnosis
NOAH	Robotics
ONCONCIN	Therapy recommendations for cancer patients
OP-PLANNER	Grand planning
PHOENIX	Oil well log modeling
PICON	Alarms monitoring in an oil refinery
PROSPECTOR	Geology
PUFF	Lung disorder
RAYDEX	Radiology
REACTOR	Nuclear reactor accidents
SPERIL	Earthquake damage assessment
STREAMER	Recruit instruction
SYN	Circuitry synthesis
SYNCHEM	Chemical synthesis
TAX ADVISOR	Estate planning

continued

Table 13-1 ▪ Continued

Name	Specific Area
TAXMAN	Tax consequence evaluation of proposed projects for organizations
TECH	Naval task force threats
TICOM	Internal control system evaluation
XCON/R1	Computer system configuration
XSEL	Computer sales
VISIONS	Vision analysis

13-3 Components of an Expert System

A typical expert system includes the following components:

- Knowledge acquisition facility
- Knowledge base (rule base and data base)
- Knowledge base management system (KBMS)
- Inference engine
- User interface

A *knowledge-acquisition facility* is needed to assure the growth of a system. This subsystem should provide ways to acquire new rules and facts. The availability of new facts creates the opportunity for the KBMS to modify the existing rules and incorporate the new facts into the knowledge base. The knowledge-acquisition facility and KBMS work in conjunction with each other to keep the knowledge base as updated as possible.

A *knowledge base* is very similar to the data base of a DSS. However, a knowledge base not only stores facts and figures, it also keeps track of a series of rules and explanations associated with the facts. For example, the knowledge base of a financial expert system may keep track of all the figures that constitute the current asset. This may include cash, deposits, accounts receivable, and so on. It also keeps track of the fact that the current asset is the type of asset that can be converted to cash within 1 year.

An expert system in an academic environment may include all the facts regarding a classified graduate student, such as number of deficiencies, GMAT score, and GPA. At the same time, it may include a rule that indicates a student may be classified only if he or she has no deficiencies, has a GMAT of 600 or better, has a GPA of 3.40 or better, and so forth.

The knowledge base of an expert system must include three types of knowledge to be considered a true expert system. These include [16, p. 8]:

- Factual knowledge
- Heuristic knowledge
- Metaknowledge

Factual knowledge consists of facts related to a specific discipline—for example, all the facts related to kidney problems, such as size, blood components, pain duration, and location. Heuristic knowledge consists of the rules related to a particular problem or discipline—for example, all the general rules that indicate a patient has a kidney problem.

Incorporation of metaknowledge into an expert system may be the ideal goal of ES designers. This knowledge enables an ES to use and examine the facts, extract those facts, and direct the path used to obtain a solution. In simple terms, metaknowledge suggests the ability for an expert system to learn from experience. This is an area that has not been fully developed and is yet to be seen in the future expert systems.

A KBMS is similar to DBMS in a DSS environment. Its major task is to keep the knowledge base updated with all the facts, figures, and rules. If new facts become available or new rules are added to the existing system, it is the job of KBMS to update the knowledge base of an expert system.

An *inference engine* is similar to the model base of a DSS. Through different techniques, such as forward and backward chaining, an inference engine manipulates a series of rules. In forward chaining, a series of IF-THEN pairs are performed. The condition, IF, is evaluated first, then the appropriate THEN is performed. For example, if the temperature is less than 80° and the grass is 3 inches long, then cut the grass. In a medical diagnostic ES, the system may ask:

- What is the body temperature of the patient?
- Does the patient have a headache?

The system then may conclude it is very likely (95%) the patient has the flu.

In backward chaining, the expert system first starts with the goal, THEN, and backtracks in order to find the right conditions (i.e., to achieve this goal, what conditions must be met?)

As an example, consider a financial expert system that provides advice for financial investment for different investors [20]. In forward chaining, the system may ask 50 questions in order to determine which of the following five categories of investments is more suitable for a prospective investor:

- Oil-gas
- Bonds
- Common stocks
- Public utilities
- Transportation

Let us further assume a particular investor is in a given tax bracket and each investment scenario provides him or her with a different tax shelter.

In forward chaining the system evaluates the IF-THEN conditions and then makes the final recommendation. In backward chaining, the system starts with the goal, THEN. In this example, let us say investment in public utilities is under investigation by an investor. The expert system starts with this goal and then backtracks through all the IF conditions needed to achieve this goal to see if a particular investor qualifies for this type of investment. The backward chaining inference engine may be faster in a particular situation because the

Figure 13-1 A conceptual model for an expert system

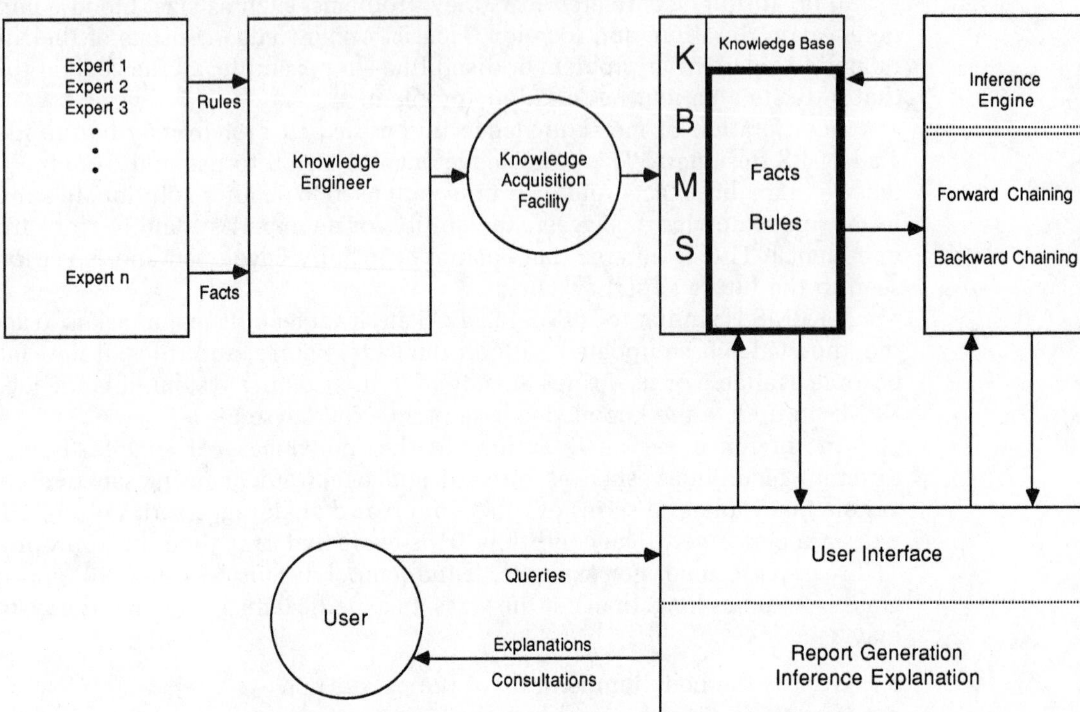

rules irrelevant to a given situation are not considered. However, the solution recommended by the system may not be the optimum one.

Some inference engines work from a matrix of factors. The matrix may include several rows of conditions and rules, which is similar to a decision table. In this case, a number of rules are evaluated at a time and then advice is provided. Also, some inference engines learn from doing [11, p. 30].

User interface is very similar to dialog management of a DSS. It provides a user-friendly access for the user. The goal of AI technology is to provide a natural language for user interface. As we discussed in Chapter 12, natural language processing (NLP) is the ideal goal for user/system interface for any computer-based information system. There are many problems associated with NLP that must be overcome before a full-featured NLP can be introduced.

Figure 13-1 illustrates a conceptual model for a typical expert system.

13-4 Three Technologies of an Expert System

The development process of an expert system closely parallels the development of a DSS. An expert system can be developed in-house or can be a commercial package. As in DSS, in an ES environment there are three technologies:

- ES tools (EST)
- Specific ES (SES)
- ES shell (ESS)

Expert systems tools include AI languages such as LISP, PROLOG, ROSIE, and OPS [16]. These languages can be used directly to develop either a specific expert system or an ES shell. However, other languages, such as C, Pascal, or even COBOL, can be used in the development process. Due to special requirements of ES, symbolic languages such as LISP or PROLOG are more suitable than the usual high-level languages. If symbolic languages are to be used, the developmental period may be long and costly, but at the same time, the final product may be closer to the ES users' needs.

The second group of technologies in the ES environment includes SESs. These systems, developed from either ES tools or shells, are designed to perform specific tasks within a particular discipline. For example, a medical expert system that only does blood analysis falls into the category of an SES. XCON, XSEL, and XSITE, developed by Digital Equipment Corporation and Carnegie-Mellon University to configure VAX computers, are also examples of SESs. Dipmeter Advisor by Schlumberger, Inc., which interprets data from oil logs to determine the amount of oil resources or the possibility of an oil resource, and Prospector, developed by SRI International to provide consultation in mineral exploration, are other SESs.

The third technology, ES shells, is the most versatile. ES shells are readily available for a variety of applications. Three microproducts from Human Edge Software Corporation in Palo Alto, California, are examples of ES shells: Negotiation Edge, Communication Edge, and Management Edge for the IBM PC and Apple. Based on facts fed into the system, these products provide consultation to the user regarding the type of responses to be expected from a prospective customer.

Some ES shells are integrated, so they may run on a company's other computer system and utilize the corporate data base. A good example of this type is the Knowledge Workbench [19] by Silogic, Inc., in Los Angeles. This system incorporates a knowledge base, inference engine, natural language, and universal data base interface. The system runs on 32-bit microprocessors such as IBM PC AT and NCR Tower.

The tool chosen depends on the particular application and the availability of the user and knowledge engineers in an organization. Generally speaking, shells offer a more attractive alternative because of their versatility and relatively low cost. Since a majority of the tools needed to develop a specific ES are already available within the shell, the developmental period is shorter than that needed to develop a specific ES from ES tools.

13-5 Types of Expert System Architectures

Generally speaking, there are two types of ES architectures.

- Rule-based expert system
- Example-based expert system

The rule-based ES, as its name implies, operates based on a series of rules. In a specific situation a series of rules is evaluated; then a conclusion is drawn. A typical rule-based system includes a variety of rules related to a particular discipline. The inference engine compares a given situation by using a series of IF-THEN statements and provides consultation to the user. The number and complexity of rules depends on a particular system and can be anywhere from fewer than 100 to more than several thousand.

In an example-based ES, a conclusion is drawn by comparing a specific situation to an existing example stored in the knowledge base. These examples have been collected from an expert or a number of experts throughout the years of practice within a discipline. Such an example might be:

> A kidney of normal size and normal density with an irregular contour denotes a kidney stone.

These two types of systems can be further classified as one of the following [3, p. 4]:

1. *Assistant system.* This type of system helps a user in making a decision by providing routine analysis and pointing out those areas for which the human experience is needed. Dipmeter Advisor falls into this classification. This system performs a series of tedious tasks and summarizes its findings; then the human expert takes over.
2. *Colleague system.* This type of system works jointly with the human expert to reach a conclusion. For this type of system the why and how features of the ES may be very helpful to the human expert. The system may provide a recommendation regarding a particular situation. The human expert may then ask why this recommendation was given. The ES will explain why it made the recommendation, and it may also say how the recommendation was generated. From this information, the human expert may gain insight about the problem under investigation.
3. *Ideal expert system.* In this type of system, the user accepts the advise of the ES and, based on this advice, a decision is implemented.

At this time the majority of ESs fall in the first two groups.

A successful or ideal ES should:

- Possess common sense for exceptions.
- Learn structuring knowledge and rules.
- Learn to revise and reproduce rules.

As you see, the preceding three factors are characteristic of people. It is yet to be seen if computers can ever possess such human traits.

13-6 Application and Nonapplication Situations of Expert Systems

An expert system should be used if one or a series of the following conditions exist [3, 5]:

1. A great degree of human expertise is needed. This is the case when one expert is not able to investigate all the dimensions of a problem. ES, by integrating the experience and expertise of several experts, may be a more viable option than consulting one human expert.
2. Situations that are not oriented toward mathematical models. As was mentioned earlier in this chapter, ESs usually work based on heuristics. A heuristic is a suitable option in the absence of a well-defined algorithm. Therefore, whenever knowledge can be represented as rules or heuristics, ESs are viable candidates.
3. Situations that have been successfully solved by human experts. Since an expert system is trying to mimic the human expertise, that expertise must be made available to an ES. At this point, problems that have not been previously solved by human experts are not candidates for ES application.
4. Situations that require consistency and standardization. Since computers are more accurate in following a series of standard tasks, in these situations ES may be superior to humans, who tend to vary solutions or tasks based on irrelevant elements in the problem-solving setting.
5. Limited subject domain. Expert systems are successful if the problem under investigation is narrow.
6. Under uncertainty. If a situation involves a degree of uncertainty, e.g., 90% probability or 75% probability and/or some degree of fuzziness, an ES may present a viable option.
7. Many rules. Whenever there are several hundred to several thousand rules or the logic of the problem is complex, an ES may present a more viable option.
8. Why and how situations. For those situations that require some explanation (e.g., Why did you choose this answer? or How was this conclusion drawn?) an ES presents an attractive alternative.
9. Scarcity of experts. For those situations where there are not enough experts to go around, an ES can replace and closely duplicate the scarce knowledge resource.
10. Key experts retiring. An ES may replicate the expertise of these rare individuals.
11. Hazardous situations. To avoid the loss of human life, an ES may present an attractive alternative.

If these situations are not present, the expert system may not provide any advantages when compared with the human expert.

To be more specific, at the present time the following problem areas are unsuitable for expert systems [11, 16, 17]:

1. Problems that include very few rules (e.g., fewer than ten). It is more cost-effective to solve these types of problems using human experts.
2. Problems that include too many rules (e.g., more than 10,000). It may take a long time to develop a system to solve a problem of this magnitude. At the same time, the processing time may be slow.
3. Well-structured numerical problems. These types of problems may be solved by nonexpert systems in a faster and cheaper manner.

4. Problems in areas that are "too wide and shallow." This means the problem area covers a broad range and at the same time does not involve many rules, as opposed to problems that are "deep and narrow" [16].
5. Problem areas in which there are disagreements among the experts.
6. Problems that are solved better by human experts than by ES. This may include areas that involve the five senses (i.e., taste, smell, touch, sight, and hearing).

Generally speaking, an ES generally has the following advantages over a human for performing a task [12]:

- An ES never becomes distracted.
- An ES never forgets.
- An ES never becomes tired.
- An ES never loses its train of thought.
- An ES can be used for tedious, monotonous tasks with no objection.
- An ES can be used for hazardous tasks with no risk of losing life.
- An ES duplicates the expertise of scarce experts.
- An ES can utilize the expertise of more than one expert.

13-7 Process of Building an Expert System: Life-Cycle Approach

The development of an ES is very similar to the development of a DSS. To build an expert system, a series of steps are followed:

1. *Problem definition.* In this stage, the domain of a problem to be solved by an ES is defined. The scope and nature of the problem must be carefully analyzed in order to ascertain its suitability and feasibility for ES application. This stage is comparable to the feasibility study performed in a DSS environment.
2. *Organization readiness.* The user(s) of the prospective expert system should be selected and exposed to the benefits of using an ES. The advantages of using an ES should be clearly identified.
3. *Tool selection.* In this stage, either a language (ES tool) or a shell (ES generator) is chosen. As discussed earlier, the majority of the expert system problems can be solved by using a shell. An ES shell is similar to a DSS generator. In some situations, a particular problem may not be suitable for an ES shell. If this is the case, a language such as LISP or PROLOG may be chosen.
4. *Expert(s) selection.* When the scope of a problem is defined, then one or a series of experts must be selected. These individuals must have a proven record in the field. A problem similar to the problem under investigation must have been solved by these or other experts in the past. This will assure the suitability of ES implementation.
5. *Design team selection.* A design team for an ES usually includes one or more knowledge engineers and experts and one or more prospective

users. Knowledge engineers know how to design the system, how to store knowledge and rules in the knowledge base, and how to design the user interface. Human experts try to explain all the rules involved in the process under investigation. The prospective users may suggest methods for interface and type of queries.

6. *Prototype design.* Before a large-scale system is developed, a prototype, which is a small-scale system, must be designed and demonstrated to the user(s). This will certainly improve the chances of success.
7. *Prototype revision.* Any possible suggestions or problems pointed out by the user and/or design team must be incorporated or removed from the system.
8. *Final construction.* This stage includes the full-scale construction of the system.
9. *Post implementation audit.* This stage tries to evaluate the system for any possible improvements, which includes any modification in any of the components of the expert system.

13-8 Selected Examples of ES Shells

We have chosen three popular micro-based expert system shells that have been very successful. A brief overview of these systems may help you to understand an ES better.

GURU

GURU is from Micro Data Base Systems and includes [30]:

- Spreadsheet (more powerful than 1-2-3)
- Data base (relational, random access)
- Natural language interface
- Communications facility
- Graphics
- Text processor
- Numerous built-in functions
- Report-generation facility

The inference engine of GURU allows for both forward and backward chaining. It deals with operations involving uncertainty and limited fuzzy sets (those data sets that are not clearly defined, such as tall, short, or sweet). It includes a query language similar to structured query language (SQL). This package is written in C and assembly language.

GURU supports full-featured programing language structures such as branching, IF-THEN, PERFORM-RETURN, and other conditional loops. It allows the user to establish priorities for the rules. This may include a weighting procedure (e.g., more important rules are given a higher weight and less important rules are given a lower weight.) Finally, GURU provides an explanation facility. The user can question why a particular conclusion was reached and why a particular question is asked.

Some of the limitations of GURU may include memory (640K) and knowledge-representation facility. Overall, GURU is an exciting expert system shell. It is available for IBM PC, XT, or AT with hard disk and at least 512K of RAM memory. It is also available for VAX-11/780. For more information contact:

Micro Data Base Systems, Inc.
P.O. Box 248
Lafeyette, Indiana 47902
(317)463-2581

Rule Master

Rule Master by Radian is an expert system shell. Rule Master can diagnose a problem given a series of symptoms. It can predict an outcome from a series of given conditions or identify a problem from a series of clues given by the user.

The inference engine of Rule Master performs both forward and backward chaining [33]. Using a CGEN utility, the user can automatically translate a Rule Master program into a compiled C program. This feature makes the program faster to run and more compact.

Rule Master answers and explains why a particular decision was made. Situations involving uncertainty and fuzzy set operations can also be handled by Rule Master.

Rule Master is very easy to use. One of its limitations is memory size (only 640K); thus, the user may not be able to write complex programs. It also has inadequate explanations ability. As Van Horn mentions [33], "Its explanations are limited to statements tied to each rule by the system designer." Rule Master is available for IBM PC, XT, AT, UNIX Systems, AT&T PC 6300, and VAX. It is available for single-user or multiuser workstations. For more information, contact:

Radian Corporation
8501 Mo-Pac Boulevard
P.O. Box 9948
Austin, Texas 78766-0948
(512) 454-4797

Acquaint

Acquaint Version 2.4F by LithP Systems BV is an expert system shell for the IBM PC. Acquaint uses object-oriented representations in its knowledge base. It is written in MULISP (a version of LISP). Acquaint includes three programs [31]: QUAINT.EXE (for user interface), QEDIT.EXE (a text editor), and KAIN-T.EXE (a development tool).

Acquaint offers both forward and backward chaining. It also provides a direct interface to MULISP, which allows the user to use the language's many standard functions and call them from within the rules.

One of the limitations of ACQUAINT is its handling of interactive loops and multiple-choice questions. However, these problems are being resolved in the newer version of Acquaint.

As Tello [31] mentions, two of the most impressive features of Acquaint are:

- Its high speed
- Its capability for building relatively large knowledge bases

Acquaint is available for IBM PC, XT, or AT, and it is 100% compatible with minimum RAM memory of 256K, MS-DOS 2.0 or higher with one or two floppies. For more information on Acquaint, contact:

LithP Systems BV
P.O. Box 65
1120 AB Landsmeer
The Netherlands 011-31-2908-4623

13-9 Legal Issues of Expert Systems

In the near future, the utilization of expert systems may raise serious legal issues in the workplace. If an ES is used for medical purposes and the advice of the system is taken, what happens if the patient dies? Who is responsible? The company that developed the system? The expert(s) who provided the knowledge to the system? The knowledge engineers? The same thing can be said if a company loses a great deal of money by using the advice of an ES. These issues are real, and careful planning must be done before these systems become more common in the workplace [10].

13-10 Summary

This chapter discussed expert systems as one of the most successful products of artificial intelligence technologies. A review of literature shows a promising sign for the further success of these systems. To back up this presentation, the chapter provided a listing of several successful ES products on the market. Components, different technologies, and the architecture of an ES were described. It also discussed applications of an ES as well as areas to which an ES is not applicable and explained the process of building an ES. Three selected ESs on the market were depicted in some detail. This chapter concluded with legal issues in ES design and utilization. This should provide a good background for the next chapter, which explains the process and issues related to the integration of AI/ES and DSS.

Review Questions

1. What is an ES?
2. Discuss several successful applications of ES.
3. In what areas have ESs been the most successful and why?
4. What are the major components of an ES?
5. What type of knowledge should be included in a successful ES?
6. What are heuristic operations?
7. What is backward chaining?
8. What is forward chaining?
9. Generally speaking, to achieve a certain conclusion, which type of inference engine is faster, backward or forward chaining? Why?
10. What is the difference between dialog management in DSS and user interface in ES?
11. What are the three technologies of an ES?
12. Which technology in an ES environment resembles a DSS generator? Which technology resembles a DSS tool?
13. What is the difference between a rule-based and an example-based ES?
14. What is the difference between assistant-type and colleague-type ES?
15. Can any of these types of ES (e.g., assistant or colleague) completely replace the human expert?
16. What are some examples or situations in which an ES can be superior to a human expert?
17. What are some examples or situations in which a human expert can be superior to an ES?
18. Is the process of building an ES different from the process of building a DSS? If yes, how? If no, how is it dissimilar?
19. What is the difference between GURU and a typical spreadsheet such as Lotus 1-2-3?

Projects

1. Select an organization of your choice that has installed an expert system. Discuss some of the successes of this system. Where does the system fail?
2. Conduct a survey through the computer literature and find out ES applications and/or products for law firms or district attorneys' offices.
3. Conduct a survey on XCON, developed by DEC and Carnegie-Mellon University. What are some of the limitations of this system?
4. GURU has been reported to be one of the successful ES shells on the market. Is this claim supported in the literature? Support your conclusion.

5. What are some of the applications of an ES in an academic setting? Is there any product available for this environment? Research this.

Key Terms

Expert systems
Heuristics
Knowledge acquisition facility
Knowledge base
Knowledge base management system (KBMS)
Inference engine
User interface
Factual knowledge
Heuristic knowledge
Metaknowledge
Forward chaining
Backward chaining
ES tools
Specific ES
ES shells
Rule-based ES
Example-based ES
Assistant ES
Colleague ES
Ideal ES
GURU
Rule Master
Acquaint
Legal issues of ES use

References

[1] Akers, Michael D., Grover L. Porter, Edward J. Bocher, and William G. Mister. 1986. Expert Systems for Management Accountants. *Management Accounting* (March): 30–34.

[2] Andriole, Stephen J. 1985. The Promise of Artificial Intelligence. *Journal of Systems Management* (July): 8–17.

[3] Anonymous. 1985. What's Happening with Expert Systems? *EDP Analyzer* 23, no. 12 (December): 1-11.

[4] Bachant, J., and McDemott, J. 1984. R1 Revisited: Four Years in the Trenches. *AI Magazine* (Fall): 21–32.

[5] Blanning, Robert W. 1985. Expert Systems for Management: Research and Applications. *Journal of Information Science* (September): 153–162.

[6] Blanning, Robert W. 1984. Management Applications of Expert Systems. *Information & Management* (July): 311–16.

[7] Chang, Alec, Michael Leonard, and Jay Goldman. 1986. Artificial Intelligence: An Overview of Research and Application. *Industrial Management* (November-December): 14–19.

[8] Curtis, Gary A. 1987. Should You Try to Build Your Own? *Information Center* (March): 43–46.

[9] Degroff, Leslie. 1987. Conventional Languages & Expert Systems. *AI Expert* 2, no. 4 (April): 32–36.

[10] Hinshaw, Dorothy and Patent. 1986. *The Quest for Artificial Intelligence*. New York: Harcourt Brace Jovanovich, Inc., p. 90.

[11] Efroymson, Sharon, and David B. Phillips. 1987. What is an Expert System, Anyway? *Information Center* (March): 29–31.

[12] Fisher, Edward L. 1985. Expert Systems Can Lay Groundwork for Intelligence CIM Decision Making. *Industrial Engineering* (March): 78–83.
[13] Gold, Jordon. 1986. Do-It-Yourself Expert Systems. *Computer Decisions* (January 14): 76–81.
[14] Guterl, Fred. 1986. Computers Think for Business. *Dun's Business Month* (October): 30–37.
[15] Holsapple, Clyde W., and Andrew B. Whinston. 1987. *Business Expert Systems.* Homewood, Ill.: Richard D. Irwin, Inc.
[16] Keim, Robert T., and Sheila Jacobs. 1986. Expert Systems: The DSS of the Future? *Journal of Systems Management* (December): 6–14.
[17] Kolcum, Edward H. 1986. NASA Demonstrates Use of AI with Expert Monitoring System. *Aviation Week and Technology* (March 17): 79–88.
[18] Kull, David. 1986. Decision Support With 20/20 Foresight. *Computer Decisions* (May 6): 38–48.
[19] Lampert, Anne. 1985. Expert Systems Get Down to Business. *Computer Decisions* (January 15): 138–44.
[20] Luconi, Fred L., Thomas W. Malone, and Michael S. Scott-Morton. 1986. Expert Systems: The Next Challenge for Managers. *Sloan Management Review:* 3–13.
[21] Mulsant, Benoit, and David Servan-Schreiber. 1985. Toward a New Paradigm of Health Care: Artificial Intelligence and Medical Management. *Human Systems Management* 5, no. 2: 137–47.
[22] Newquist, Harvey P., Ill. 1986. Expert Systems: The Promise of a Smart Machine. *Computer World* (January 13): 43–57.
[23] O'Keefe, Robert M. 1985. Expert Systems and Operational Research—Mutual Benefits. *Journal of the Operational Research Society.* 36, no. 2 (February): 125–29.
[24] Oxman, Steven W. 1985. Expert Systems Represent Ultimate Goal of Strategic Decision Making. *Data Management* (April): 36–38.
[25] Rajarama, N. S. 1987. Expert Systems Development: Current Problems, Future Needs. *InTech* (April): 25–26.
[26] Santarelli, Mary-Beth. 1987. Stalking the Knowledge Engineer. *Information Center* (March): 33–40.
[27] Sen, Arun, and Gautam Biswas. 1985. Decision Support Systems: An Expert Systems Approach. *Decision Support Systems* (Winter): 197–204.
[28] Singh, Madan G., and Roderick Cook. 1985. A New Class of Intelligence Knowledge-Based Systems With an Optimization-Based Inference Engine. *Decision Support Systems* (Winter): 299–312.
[29] Stoner, Greg. 1985. Expert Systems: Jargon or Challenge? *Accountancy* (February): 142–45.
[30] Tello, Ernest R. 1986. Guru. *Byte* (August): 281–85.
[31] Tello, Ernest R. 1987. Acquaint. *Byte* (June): 265–72.
[32] Tucker, Michael. 1986. Expert Systems Blaze Trails to AI Success. *Mini-Micro Systems* (March): 69–78.
[33] Van Horn, Mike. 1987. Rule Master. *Byte* (January): 341–42.
[34] Williamson, Mickey. 1986. Expert Systems Shells Design Tools Help MIS Answer Management's Call. *Computer World* (July 14): 51–57.

14 AI, ES, and DSS: An Integrated Technology

14-1 Introduction

This chapter gives an overview of AI, ES, and DSS technologies and then compares an ES and a DSS side by side. The comparison reveals striking similarities and some dissimilarities between DSS and ES. After these similarities and dissimilarities are explored, two scenarios for DSS and ES integration are presented. The first scenario advocates the integration of ES into all the components of a DSS. The second scenario recommends ES as an additional component to a DSS. The integration presents a clear gain in DSS operation. Problems and issues related to the integration of ES and DSS are elaborated upon. To support the possibility of integrating the two technologies, a literature survey of the existing integrated hardware/software technologies is presented. This literature survey highlights a diverse area where integration has already taken place. A brief discussion indicating that the integration is not always needed is also presented; there are numerous situations that can be handled by a typical DSS without ES support. The chapter concludes with an "ideal" model for a future DSS.

14-2 Overview of AI: The Second Look

The field of AI is concerned with intelligent computers, those that possess and display behavior similar to that of human beings. AI is more of a concept than a discipline, and it includes a number of related technologies. Among these are the following:

- *Expert systems* (ES) are computer programs that mimic the human thought pattern. Ideally, these programs should learn from past experience and should be able to deal with uncertainties and exceptions.
- *Natural language processing* (NLP) is a language that enables a computer user to interact with the machine in his or her native language.
- *Voice recognition*, like NLP, enables the computer to understand the voice of a computer user and respond to the user in his or her native language.
- *Robotics* are machines that can be programmed to perform a human task in a repetitive, dangerous, or boring operations free of error and with a high degree of speed and accuracy. A sophisticated robot should understand both vision and sound.
- *Pattern recognition* involves computer programs and robots that differentiate between shapes, figures, and graphs and mimic human visual responses.

Chapter 12 discussed these related fields and also explained the limitations and strengths of each. Two of these related technologies, ES and NLP, should play a significant role in improving the quality and usefulness of DSS. We explain these related fields further in the context of DSS and highlight their possible contributions in the next few pages.

14-3 DSS and ES: A Comparison

We have defined DSS as:

> A computer-based information system consisting of hardware/software and the human elements designed to assist any decision maker at any level of the organization. However, the emphasis is on semistructured and unstructured tasks.

An ES was defined as:

> A computer program that has built into it the knowledge and capability that will allow the program to operate at the level of a human expert [Feignbaum and McCorduck].

A close investigation of ES and DSS components presents a striking similarity between these two fields of computer technology. As we will see, these similarities suggest a possible integration between the two. To demonstrate a possible integration, first let us examine the differences between DSS and ES [6, 10, 18].

Objectives

DSS attempts to provide information that helps a decision-maker make a decision or make a better decision. By mimicking a human expert, an ES attempts to make actual decisions, thereby replacing human experts. As we discussed in Chapter 13, there are three types of ESs on the market:

ES as an assistant

ES as a colleague

The ideal ES

The first two types of ES still need a human expert for the execution of the final decision. However, in the third class of ES technology, the human expert is replaced, and the advice provided by the ES becomes a basis for formulating and implementing decisions by the user. In other words, a DSS tries to support a decision maker; an ES tries to replace a decision maker.

Query Operations

The query operations are basically the same in both DSS and ES. However, in the DSS environment the *user* asks the system a number of questions before reaching a decision. In the ES environment the *system* asks the user a number of questions before reaching a decision.

Major Components

As discussed in Chapters 4 through 6, the major components of a DSS include:

- Data base
- Model base
- Dialog management

As discussed in Chapter 13, the three major components of an ES include:

- Knowledge base
- Inference engine
- User interface

Although there are some similarities among these components, at the same time there are some important dissimilarities. Table 14-1 highlights the differences between these components for a DSS and an ES.

Mode of Operations

DSSs and other traditional information systems operate based on specific algorithms. In these systems a "good enough" solution is reached and the process stops. Problems addressed by DSS are too complex to be solved perfectly. Expert systems operate based on heuristics. The major difference between the two modes is that in heuristics operation the system does not follow a well-defined procedure to reach the solution. Different routes may be

Table 14-1 ▪ Comparison of DSS and ES Components

DSS	ES
Data base, which includes:	Knowledge base, which includes:
Internal data	Facts related to a specific field
External data	Rules related to a specific field
Model base	Inference Engine
Optimization models	Forward chaining
Nonoptimization models	Backward chaining
	Frames or matrices
Dialog Management	User Interface
Menu, question/answer, and so on	Natural language, free-format interface

chosen, uncertainty may be considered, and, to some degree, "fuzziness" can also be handled. A DSS works primarily with quantitative data; an ES works with rules, symbols, and qualitative data. DSS works with ad hoc decisions; ES works with routine and repetitive decisions.

Users

DSS users are usually key decision-makers who are not necessarily experts in one specific discipline. They use DSS to improve their effectiveness in design and implementation of a decision. In the majority of decision-implementations processes in a DSS environment, the user and the system consult each other for final implementation of a decision. Most ES users are highly sophisticated experts in specific disciplines. However, because the ideal ES should completely replace the decision-maker, an ES should be able to be used by anyone regardless of his or her technical background.

Design Team

In DSS, the design team includes programmers, systems analysts, and the users, or decision-makers, who participates in the design process in order to express their specific information needs. In ES, the design team includes knowledge engineers, experts, and possibly the prospective users of the system, who may not themselves be the expert. Ideally, the experts should know all the rules and knowledge related to a specific field. The knowledge engineer, with the help of experts, tries to transfer all the existing knowledge and rules to the knowledge base of the ES.

Technology Levels of DSS and ES

As discussed in Chapter 3, a DSS includes three technology levels:

- DSS tools (DSST)
- Specific DSS (SDSS)
- DSS generator (DSSG)

An ES includes three very similar technologies in a different context:

- ES tools (EST)
- Specific ES (SES)
- ES shells (ESS)

Table 14-2 highlights these differences.

Problems Addressed

A DSS usually addresses general problems covering a broad range of managerial issues, while an ES addresses a well-defined and narrow problem area.

Problem Precedence

In the DSS environment, problems addressed by the system usually do not have any precedence. These problems are one of a kind and nonrecurring. Therefore, such problems have not been solved before. On the other hand, the problems addressed by the ES have been solved by experts before. Therefore, for these problems there is a well-defined procedure for proposing a solution.

Nature of Support

Although both DSS and ES are designed to support individual decision-makers, DSS also offers institutional support [17, 18].

Table 14-2 ▪ Comparison of DSS and ES Technology Levels

DSS	ES
DSS tools	ES Tools
FORTRAN, COBOL, Graphics packages, and so on	LISP, PROLOG, and so on
Specific DSS	Specific ES
Forecasting DSS, Optimization DSS, and so on	Medical ES, diagnostic ES, and so on
DSS generator	ES shells
FOCUS, IFPS, NOMAD, and so on	AQUAINT, GURU, EXPERT, and so on

Table 14-3 ▪ DSS and ES Comparison

Key Feature	DSS	ES
Main objectives	To support a decision-maker	To replace a decision-maker
Who makes decisions	Human	ES
Orientation	To support a decision-maker	To mimic expert
Query operation	The user questions the system	The system questions the user
Major components	Data base Model base Dialog management	Knowledge base Inference engine User interface
Mode of operation	Algorithmic Good enough solution Ad hoc Quantitative	Heuristic Uncertainty Fuzziness Optimum solution Qualitative/quantitative Rules, symbols Routine, repetitive
Users	Key decision-makers	Specific experts (one end) Anybody (the other end)
Design team	Programmer/analyst/user	Knowledge engineer/expert/user
Technology levels	DSS tools Specific DSS DSS generators	ES tools Specific ES ES shells
Problems addressed	General	Specific
Problem precedence	No precedence	Always precedence
Nature of the support	Individual and maybe institutional	Individual
Reasoning and explanation capability	None	Some

Reasoning and Explanation Capability

DSSs usually do not include either reasoning or explanation capability. In other words, the user cannot ask why or how a particular solution was reached. On the other hand, the majority of ESs possess some reasoning and explanation capability, which means the system will tell the user why it made a particular recommendation or how particular advice was generated. Table 14-3 summarizes the key characteristics of a DSS compared with an ES.

14-4 Decision Support and Artificial Intelligence Integration

It was mentioned in the last two chapters that AI is a concept, not a solid discipline. AI-related technologies, expert systems, NLP, and voice and pattern recognition can improve the quality of today's DSS. Whereas a DSS presents a what-if scenario to a decision-maker, AI technologies can add why, how, and when scenarios to a DSS. The advantages of the integration are obvious: The result is a much more powerful DSS than is presently available.

Efraim Turban and Paul R. Watkins [18] present an excellent discussion regarding the ES/DSS integration. The next few pages discuss the process of integration and also present some possible problems, advantages, and disadvantages of this integration.

Turban and Watkins present two alternatives for the integration of DSS and ES.

- Integration of ES to all components of a DSS
- ES as an additional component of a DSS

Let us explain in detail each alternative and discuss the problems and issues involved in integration.

14-5 Integration of ES Into DSS Components: Scenario 1

Let us first explain, step by step, how ES capabilities can be integrated into the major components of a DSS, the data base, model base, and dialog management.

Data Base and ES

In Chapter 4 we discussed the data base component of a DSS. Turban and Watkins suggest that the integration of ES capabilities into the data base and data base management systems components of a DSS can improve construction, operation, and maintenance of the data base and DBMS.

Chapter 4 also discussed the rule model as one of the data models used in a DSS environment. This model utilizes AI principles. Integrating ES capabilities into the data base and DBMS of a DSS adds reasoning capability to the operation of the DBMS. After this integration, the user can learn not only what facts are stored in the data base, but what each fact means. The user can broaden the types of questions he/she can ask to why and how questions.

Model Base and ES

In Chapter 5 we discussed the model base component of a DSS. It is difficult for a typical DSS user to select an effective model from all of the available model categories. For example, a user may puzzle over whether an optimization model or a nonoptimization model should be used. With some modeling knowledge, the user may be able to choose the right category, but then has to make a more intricate selection of a model from within a specific category. For example, a user may know that a problem under investigation is an optimization problem; but not whether it is a linear optimization problem or a nonlinear optimization problem. Table 14-4 summarizes the models generally used in a DSS environment.

Table 14-4 ▪ Summary of Models Used in DSS Environment

General Type	Specific Examples
Linear optimization models	Allocation models Assignment models Transportation models
Network models	Program evaluation review techniques (PERT) Critical path method (CPM)
Inventory optimization models	Economic order quantity Economic manufacturing quantity
Portfolio optimization models	Present value Future value Internal rate of return
Dynamic programming optimization models	Deterministic—replacement problems Probabilistic—forecasting problems
Nonlinear optimization models	Quadratic models

Nonoptimization Models

General Type	Specific Examples
Forecasting models	Exponential smoothing Moving average Mean
Regression models	Simple linear regression Multiple linear regression
Decision tree models	Expected value of different decisions
Simulation models	Monte Carlo simulation

Let us assume the user has limited knowledge about modeling techniques but understands that a forecasting model has to be used for solving a particular problem. Which model should be selected from this list? This can be a complex task, and not many DSS users have adequate training in this area. Table 14-5 [12] summarizes the forecasting models and their specific use.

To select an appropriate forecasting technique, a series of factors must be considered. These factors include:

- Time horizon of the forecast
  - Immediate forecast (less than 1 month)
  - Short-range forecast (1 to 3 months)
  - Medium-range forecast (less than 2 years)
  - Long-range forecast (2 years or more)
- Type of data
  - Horizontal (even distribution over a given period)
  - Trend (growth or decline over a given period)
  - Seasonal (growth or decline over a given season)
  - Cyclical (growth or decline over a longer period of time—usually more than 1 year)

Table 14-5 ▪ Summary of Forecasting Models

Smoothing techniques
- Mean
- Simple moving average
- Simple Exponential smoothing
- Linear moving average
- Linear exponential smoothing

Decomposition Techniques
- Classical decomposition
- Census
- Foran system

Control Techniques
- Adaptive filtering
- Box-Jenkins
- Generalized adaptive filtering

Regression Techniques
- Simple linear regression
- Multiple linear regression
- Nonlinear regression
- Econometric models

General Techniques
- Life-cycle analysis
- Surveys
- Leading index or diffusion indexes
- Input/output analysis

Technological (Qualitative) Forecasting
- Delphi
- S-curves
- Historical analogies
- Morphological research
- Relevance trees
- Mission flow diagram

- Number of data points available from the past
- Cost of the forecast
- Accuracy of the forecast

Based on these factors, a forecasting model must be chosen. For detailed discussion of forecasting techniques, consult [11, 12].

At this point ES can assist the DSS user by helping him or her decide which model must be chosen based on specific requirements. BUMP [7] is a package that integrates statistical models with ES capabilities and also tells the user which model to use and provides a user-friendly interface.

There are other areas in which ES can improve the model base component of a DSS [18]:

- By adding heuristics to the existing analysis capability of the model base
- By simplifying simulation models
- By improving sensitivity analysis
- By incorporating imprecise representation (fuzzy sets) in the model-building process, which should help the user/designer of a DSS to build a model that represents a more realistic view of a real-life situation

Dialog Management and ES

As discussed earlier, four classes of computer languages exist to date:

- Machine language (0 or 1 presentation)
- Assembly language (mnemonic presentation, short codes)
- High-level languages (more user and application oriented—COBOL, BASIC, and so on)
- Fourth-generation (4GL) languages (more English-like—IFPS, FOCUS, and so on)

These languages have been improved and have become more user-friendly throughout the years. Although we have come a long way, some computer knowledge is still needed even to use a 4GL. In recent years, another class of computer languages, NLP, has added a new dimension to the computer/user interface. INTELLECT and CLOUT, two examples of these languages, have been in operation for some time, but there are still some problems and obstacles associated with full-featured NLPs that must be overcome before they can effectively be used.

One area that may improve the quality and user-friendliness of the existing DSS is the integration of ES capability into the dialog component of DSS. Such integration should improve and then incorporate the following features into DSS:

- Explanation capability
- Symbolic presentation
- Terminologies more compatible with the user's native language

The integration of vision recognition, speech recognition, and NLP into the dialog component of a DSS should immensely improve the effectiveness of these systems.

Figure 14-1 ES as a DSS Component

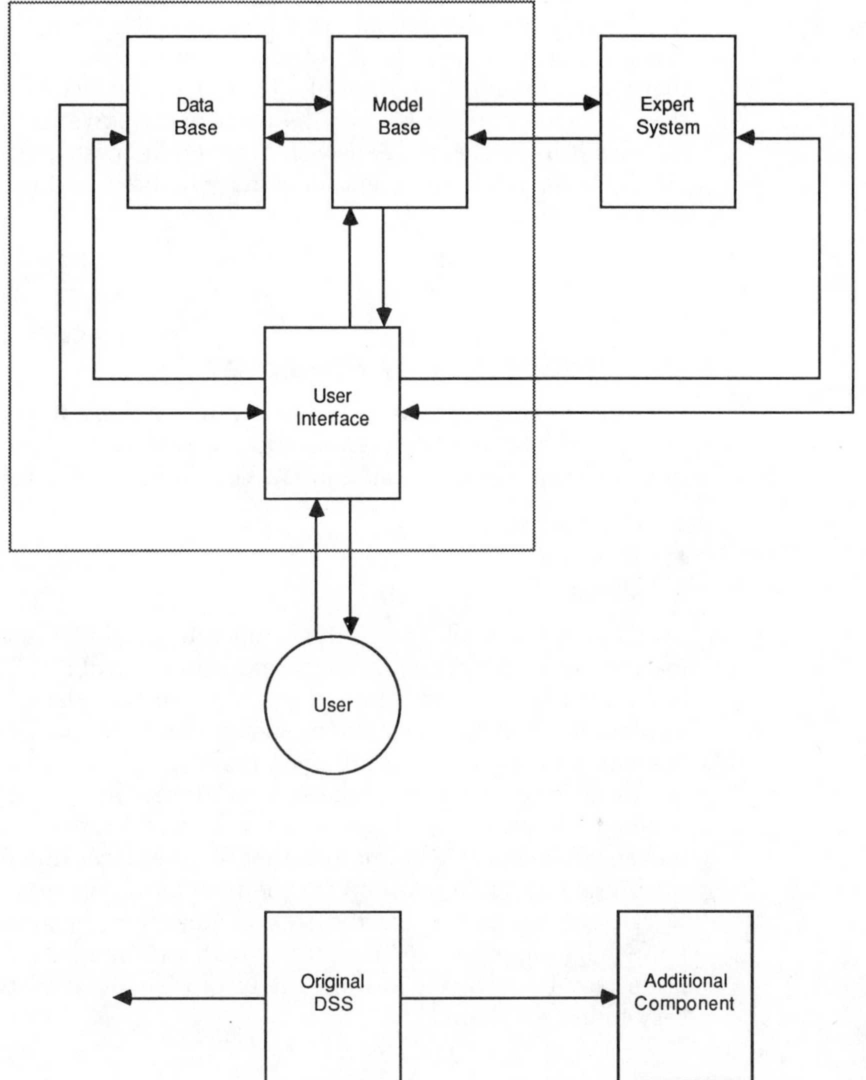

14-6 Integration of ES and DSS: Scenario 2

As Turban and Watkins explained, the second alternative for DSS and ES integration is to add ES as one additional component to the existing DSS components. Figure 14-1 illustrates this possible integration.

If this is the case, the ES output may serve as input to the DSS in order to determine and clarify a problem under investigation. For example, a problem under investigation may be categorized as an optimization problem, but may have several types of applicable optimizations. The ES may help a DSS user to identify the nature and specific category of the problem currently being considered. In another case, the DSS output may serve as input to ES in order to receive recommendations, in which case the ES will function exactly like one or a group of experts. As discussed in Chapter 6, sometimes an intermediary may explain the output of a DSS to a user. Here an ES will do the job of that intermediary. An ES may be even more powerful than an intermediary because it integrates the expertise of several experts [18].

We believe the first scenario is more realistic and more powerful than the second scenario.

14-7 Is Integration Really Possible?

The integration process is more complex than it sounds. A number of managerial and technical issues must be resolved before a successful integration can take place. Turban and Watkins highlight the following issues:

- Compatibility
- Behavior
- Design

The majority of ES products operate on LISP machines, whereas the majority of DSS operate on machines other than LISP. The issue of compatibility must be resolved before integration can take place. This issue may not be as significant in the near future, when computer architectures support both types of processing (i.e., LISP and others).

Behavioral issues may take several forms. One possible issue is resistance to integration because of the notion that an ES replaces the human decision-maker, whereas a DSS supports rather than replaces him or her. Organizational readiness must take place before the integration process starts.

Design issues involve the lack of qualified personnel (e.g., experts and knowledge engineers) to fulfill the human requirements of the integration. This issue may be resolved in the near future by the availability of inexpensive, easy-to-use ES shells.

14-8 Has Integration Already Started?

Integration has already been started in a number of directions. A review of the literature shows promising signs for further integration between DSS and AI technologies. Let us briefly introduce some of the existing examples of DSS/ES integrated systems [18].

1. GURU by Micro Data Base Systems, Inc. (as discussed in Chapter 13) combines ES, DBMS, spreadsheet, graphics, communication and word processing programs. This package can be used for development of numerous DSS/ES-type systems. As Holsapple and Whinston [8] state:

> GURU dramatically extends the conventional AI notions of knowledge representation and processing to embrace well-known business computing methods. Conversely, it can be viewed as an incorporation of traditionally alien AI techniques into a single business problem-solving environment, taking a quantum leap beyond prior business computing methods.

2. M-1 by Teknowledge, Inc., by using AI technology, integrates data base interface by providing easy access.
3. Knowledge Workbench by Silogic Corporation integrates a comprehensive data base and a NLP interface.
4. KEE by Intellicorp, by using AI technology, integrates various modeling and simulation techniques [16].
5. REVEAL by Decision Products, Inc., works based on the "fuzzy sets" theory for financial and corporate planning. This system helps to represent fuzzy words like fairly high, reasonably important, and adequate progress. This presentation should add more flexibility to the model-building process.
6. IFPS Optimum by Execucom helps to identify the nature of a problem under investigation. For example, is a particular problem a linear optimization or a nonlinear optimization?
7. Promoter by Management Decision Systems, Inc., is used with EXPRESS (a 4GL by the same company). This package analyzes the effects of promotional activities on sales in the packaged goods industry.
8. STRUDL (Structural Design Language), developed by Terry Winograd [5], along with its added components helps engineers during the design process by telling them what data to input, what action to take, and so on.
9. Logistics Management System (LMS) by IBM combines DSS/MIS, ES, simulation, computer-aided manufacturing, and DDP. This system is used in IBM's Burlington plant by manufacturing management as a tool for resolving crises and providing accurate planning.
10. DSS/Decision Simulation (DSIM) combines DSS with OR, statistical techniques, data base, query language, and AI. This integration has improved communication, assisted the system users in finding appropriate models, and added heuristic capability to traditional modeling processes.
11. Lambda 2X2 Plus by LISP Machines, Inc., combines and supports both DSS and ES users. This system is equipped with a LISP processor and a UNIX processor and has the capability of adding a PROLOG processor.
12. PLEXSYS, an organizational planning system, is described by Applegate et al. [1] as a:

> Planning System (that) combines advanced microcomputer technology with an understanding of the knowledge requirements for organizational planning to enable the elicitation, representation, storage, and management of planning information. Internal and external organizational planning information, qualitative, and quantitative planning decision aids, and a variety of information structuring and analysis models have been integrated to allow support for the planning process from initial formulation of the planning problem or task to implementation of the plan.

Shane, Fry, and Toro describe a system that uses some DSS/ES/AI integration techniques to provide personal financial investment advice [20]:

> A Personal Financial Investment Decision Support System administered by two expert systems. It . . . combines two expert systems within a decision support system with a database; it uses gaming techniques to measure an investor's risk aversion; it has one expert system working with another by modifying the rules of the second knowledge base; and it uses strong database aspects of a DSS to simulate some aspects of meeting with a consultant.

13. Symbolics' 80386-based coprocessor card allows the user of its LISP machine to run MS-DOS and UNIX systems software. Xerox Corporation's 1185 and 1186 LISP processors support MS-DOS [16].
14. Explorer LX by Texas Instruments provides access to UNIX and LISP files [16].
15. HP Workstations combine C, Pascal, FORTRAN, UNIX, and LISP and PROLOG [16].

14-9 Is Integration Really Needed?

The integration of ES/DSS certainly presents some unique benefits. This does not mean that all the systems must be integrated. There will be a need for all three systems [18]:

- DSS
- ES
- Integrated DSS/ES

However, we foresee that NLP will be used in a majority of DSSs of the future. Since this type of interface makes the user's job easier and provides a greater degree of user-friendliness to the system, there should be more of this type of integration in the near future.

14-10 Architecture of an Ideal DSS

The ideal DSS or expert DSS (EDSS) should borrow some powerful properties from the existing expert systems technology. The components of a EDSS should include the following properties.

1. *Data base.* The data base of EDSS should include both internal and external data. Besides these facts, the data base should include knowledge, or the meanings of facts and associated rules.
2. *DBMS.* DBMS should be able to perform basic data management and data-manipulation operations. It should also perform some reasoning analysis, by which we mean the type of analysis performed by a rule-data model (see Chapter 4).
3. *Model base.* The model base component of an EDSS should include both optimization and nonoptimization models. It also should be able to perform heuristics and deal with uncertainty and fuzzy analysis. The

Figure 14-2 A Model for an EDSS

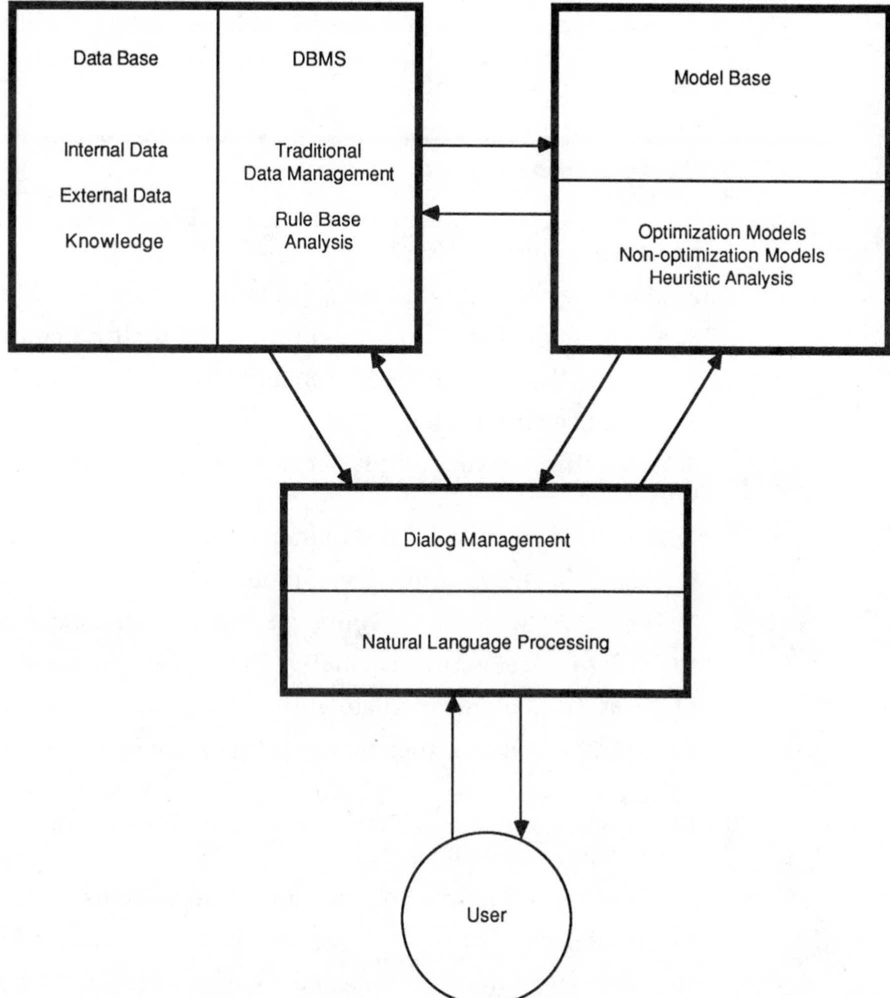

model base component of EDSS should be able to guide the user in selecting an appropriate model. It also should be able to explain the model output to the user.

4. *Dialog management.* The dialog component of EDSS should provide the most flexible type of interface to a typical user. A natural language-type interface would be the ideal. Figure 14-2 presents the structure of EDSS graphically.

14-11 Summary

This chapter, by reviewing the AI/ES and DSS technologies, identified the similarities and dissimilarities between ES and DSS. A detailed comparison between DSS and ES revealed some guidelines for possible integration of ES and DSS given two scenarios. The literature supports the possible integration of the two technologies. However, even though integration is beneficial, it is not a must situation; many managerial problems can be handled by a typical DSS. The chapter concluded with a presentation of a conceptual model for an ideal ES called an expert DSS.

Review Questions

1. Among all the AI-related technologies, which one may improve the quality of a DSS operation? How?

2. What are some similarities and dissimilarities of a DSS and ES?

3. What are the three DSS components and their ES counterparts?

4. What is the difference between an ES design team and a DSS design team?

5. What is a specific ES?

6. Generally speaking, is it faster to develop an ES from ES tools or ES shells? Why?

7. A routine problem is more suitable for a DSS or an ES? Why?

8. What is a "narrow and deep" problem? Give an example.

9. What is a "wide and shallow" problem? Give an example.

10. What is a reasoning capability? What is an explanation capability?

11. Is an ad hoc operation suitable for an ES or a DSS? Why?

12. Is a problem in a specific discipline more suitable for ES or DSS applications?

13. In what way can ES improve the data base component of a DSS? Model base? Dialog management?

14. How can ES help a DSS user in model selection?

15. What criteria must be considered before selecting a forecasting model?

16. What is the most obvious and significant contribution of ES to DSS?

17. If ES is used as an additional component to a DSS, how can it help and improve the operation of a DSS?

18. What are some of the problems involved in the integration of ES and DSS?

19. What are some examples of integrated DSS/ES on the market?

20. Is integration of AI/ES and DSS always needed?

21. Describe, in your own terms, the architecture of an ideal DSS presented in this chapter.

Projects

1. Investigate an organization of your choice that has established an ES/DSS system. What are the strengths and weaknesses of such a system? What are some of the existing problems with such a system?

2. Investigate the potential of GURU as a framework for developing an ES/DSS type system. What are some of the limitations of this system?

3. At the present time, is an "ideal DSS" design possible? If yes, how? If no, why not?

4. Investigate KEE by Intellicorp and describe how some of the problems associated with traditional modeling are resolved by using such a system.

5. Investigate REVEAL by Decision Products, Inc., and describe the operations of fuzzy sets in this system. Is it really possible to handle fuzzy operation? If yes, how?

Key Terms

Expert systems
Natural language processing (NLP)
Voice recognition
Robotics
Pattern recognition
Query operations
Uncertainty
Fuzzy sets
Qualitative
Quantitative
Knowledge engineer
DSS tools (DSST)
Specific DSS (SDSS)
DSS Generator (DSSG)
ES tools
Specific ES
ES shells
Optimization models
Nonoptimization models
Forecasting models
Vision recognition
Speech recognition
Expert DSS

References

[1] Applegate, Lynda M., Tsugn Teng Chan, Benn R. Konsynski, and Jay F. Nunamaker. 1987. Knowledge Management in Organizational Planning. *Journal of Management Information Systems* (Spring): 37.

[2] Bailey, Andrew D., Jr., Rayman Meserly, and Joanne H. Turner. 1986. Decision Support Systems, Expert Systems, and Artificial Intelligence: Realities and Possibilities in Public Accounting. *The Ohio CPA Journal* (Spring): 11–15.

[3] Chester, Jeffrey A. 1985. Artificial Intelligence: Is MIS Ready for the Explosion? *Infosystem* (April): 74–78.

[4] Cuadrado, Clara Y., and John L. Cuadrado. 1986. Handling Conflicts in Data. *Byte* (November): 197–202.

[5] Dorothy, Hinshaw, and Patent. 1986. *The Quest for Artificial Intelligence*. New York: Harcourt, Brace Jovanovich, Inc., pp. 70–72.

[6] Ford, F. Nelson. 1985. Decision Support Systems and Expert Systems: A Comparison. *Information & Management:* 21–26.

[7] Hand, D. J. 1986. Statistical Expert Systems Design. *The Statistician* 33, no. 10 (October): 351–69.

[8] Holsapple, Clyde W., and Andrew B. Whinston. 1987. *Business Expert System.* Homewood, Ill.: Richard D. Irwin, Inc., no. 15, p. 34.

[9] Kehler, Thomas P. 1987. AI, or 'Knowledge Processing,' Will be a Boon to MIS. *Information Week* (January 26): 46–47.

[10] Keim, Robert T., and Sheila Jacobs. 1985. Expert Systems: The DSS of the Future. *Journal of Systems Management* (December): 6–12.

[11] Makridakis, Spyros, and Steven C. Wheelwright. 1978. *Interactive Forecasting.* San Francisco, Calif.: Holden-Day, Inc.

[12] Makridakis, Spyros, and Steven C. Wheelwright. 1978. *Forecasting Methods and Applications.* New York: John Wiley & Sons, Inc.

[13] Martins, G. R. 1984. The Overselling of Expert Systems. *Datamation* 30, no. 18 (November 1): 76–80.

[14] Michaelson, R., and D. Michie. 1983. Expert Systems in Business. *Datamation* (November): 240–46.

[15] Moad, Jeff. 1987. Building a Bridge to Expert Systems. *Datamation* (January 1): 17–19.

[16] Raunch-Hindin, Wendy. 1987. Hardware Dynamos Power AI Deployment. *Mini-Micro Systems* (August): 75–85.

[17] Sen, Arun, and Gautam Biswas. 1985. *Decision Support Systems: An Expert Systems Approach.* New York: Elsevier Science Publishers, pp. 177–204.

[18] Turban, Efraim, and Paul R. Watkins. 1986. Integrating Expert Systems and Decision Support Systems. *MIS Quarterly* (June): 121–36.

[19] Vedder, Richard, and Chadwick H. Nestman. 1985. Understanding Expert Systems. *MIS Quarterly* (March-April): 121–36.

[20] Shane, Barry, Mitchel Fry, and R. Toro. 1987. The Design of an Investment Portfolio DSS Using Two Expert Systems as a Consulting System. *Journal of Management Information Systems* (Spring)): 80.

part five

The Future Outlook

15 DSS: A Future Explored

15-1 Introduction

This chapter concludes the text by providing some projections for the future. It is extremely difficult to provide any decisive predictions in the dynamic field of computer technology; however, careful examination of the past should reveal some insights about the future. The chapter examines hardware and software trends, highlighting the amazing progress of these two areas of technology over the past 40 years. The performance of computers measured in bits of information processed per second is reviewed, and a profile of a typical computer user in general and a DSS user in particular are presented. The artificial intelligence field is briefly reviewed for the second time in order to highlight the important features of this new technology. Promising developments in data base and telecommunications systems are studied. The microcomputer—one of the fastest growing technologies and one that will undoubtedly have an impact on DSS—is reviewed. This chapter elaborates on the present and future use of computers in the home and concludes with organizational changes and cost trends. All these indications strongly suggest that DSS will continue to gain more power and popularity. At the same time, DSS should become more affordable and easier to use and maintain. The major ingredient of any DSS is the computer technology, which has gone through a major revolution during the past 40 years. Based on what has happenned in the past, some general predictions can be highlighted.

15-2 A Look in the Past

To present a relatively clear picture of DSS future, we first must look into the past. How did we get here? In the past 40 years the field of computers has progressed beyond all imagination. Observers in the field claim that computer

Figure 15-1 Different Dimensions of DSS Future

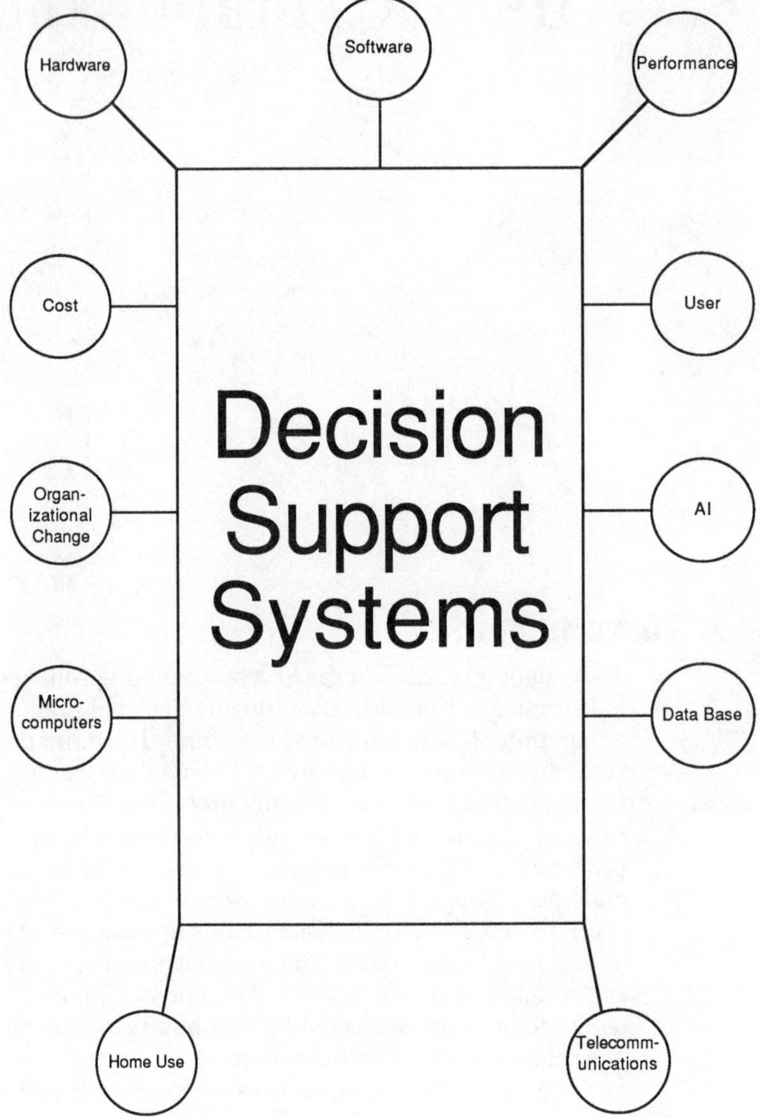

technology has been unique throughout human history with respect to its impressive development. Still, some experts believe this is only the beginning, and there is much to be seen in the near future. To back up this claim and highlight a trend for the future, we investigate several dimensions of computer technology that have direct impact on the growth of DSS. Figure 15-1 illustrates different dimensions of computer technology that are closely related to DSS design, implementation, and utilization. Let us discuss these different dimensions.

15-3 Hardware Trends

If we mark the beginning of today's computers as 1946, over the past four decades hardware has experienced major developments. Computers started with vacuum-tube technology. At that time rudimentary computers were bulky and unreliable. They generated lots of heat, and they were very difficult to program. Then the second generation came into being roughly in 1957. The second generation, which used transistors, was indeed a significant improvement over the first. Computers were improved in every dimension. They became faster, more reliable, and easier to program and maintain. The third generation began in 1964 with computers that operated on integrated circuits (IC). They became smaller, faster, more reliable, and more sophisticated. Remote data entry and telecommunications were introduced during this generation. The fourth generation began about 1982. This generation of computers is associated with several attributes: miniaturization, very large scale integrated (VLSI) circuits, massive utilization of microcomputers, optical disks, and bubble memories, for example.

The early 1990s are anticipated to be the beginning of the so-called fifth generation of computer technology. All the conventional attributes of computer technology, including speed, sophistication, and size, are believed to be subject to further improvements. However, the major attributes of this generation will include parallel processing (multiple CPUs) (present computers are serial processing-Von Neuman architecture), gallium arsenide, and optical technologies. Gallium arsenide and optical technologies are briefly explained.

Since silicon technology is not able to emit light and has speed limitations, computer designers have concentrated on gallium arsenide technology. In gallium arsenide, electrons are almost five times faster than they are in silicon. Devices made with the synthetic compound can emit light, withstand higher temperatures, and survive much higher doses of radiation [24]. The major problems associated with gallium arsenide are the difficulties in mass producing it and working with it. Gallium arsenide is soft and fragile compared to silicon; it breaks more easily during slicing and polishing. At the present time, due to its high cost and difficulty in production, military systems—where high speed and radiation are vital—are the major users of this technology. However, research continues to eliminate some of the shortcomings of this impressive technology.

Optical technologies offer at least three unique features not found in the earlier technologies [14]: much higher speed, parallelism (several thousand independent light beams can pass through an ordinary device), and interconnection (much denser arrays of interconnections are possible because light rays do not affect each other). Optical computing is in its infancy, and much more research is needed in order to produce a full-featured optical computer. At the present time, the storage devices using this technology are revolutionizing the computer field by allowing massive amounts of data to be stored in a very small space.

The fifth generation will include a revolutionary architecture that did not exist in the first four generations of computer technology. Table 15-1 highlights the trend for hardware technology.

Table 15-1 ▪ Hardware Trends

Generation	Date	Major Attribute	Example
First	1946–1956	Vacuum tubes	ENIAC
Second	1957–1963	Transistors	IBM 7094
Third	1964–1981	Integrated circuits	IBM 360, 370
Fourth	1982–1989	VLSI	Cray XMP
Fifth	1990–?	Gallium arsenide	?

15-4 Software Trends

In parallel with hardware technology, software technology has undergone major changes. The *first* generation of computers utilized machine language. This cumbersome language uses a series of 0s and 1s to present data or instructions to the computer. The *second* generation of computer software used assembly language, which uses a series of short codes, or mnemonics, to present data or instructions to a computer. The *third* generation of computer software introduced several computer languages, including FORTRAN and COBOL. These languages are more user- and application-oriented. They are much easier to learn and use than the first two. Although the third-generation languages are easier than those of the first two, rigorous training is still needed in order to become a proficient and productive programmer. The *fourth* group of computer software introduced fourth-generation languages (4GLs). These languages are more forgiving and nonprocedural, and they utilize "macro codes." The nonprocedural aspect allows the user to enter the code in the order with which he or she is most familiar. Because they are macro-oriented, the languages use vocabularies and grammars that are closer to the users thought pattern. These languages are also more powerful than their third-generation counterparts. Interactive Financial Planning System (IFPS), NOMAD, and FOCUS, to name a few, are examples of 4GLs. Appendix A covers more than two dozen such languages. The *fifth*-generation software promises the widespread utilization of NLP. These languages should enable a user to communicate directly, in a free-format fashion, either orally or in writing with a computer. Table 15-2 summarizes the software trends.

15-5 Computer Performance

The computer performance is usually measured in terms of the number of instructions per second (IPS). In the last 40 years the number of instructions processed per second has increased dramatically, as shown in Table 15-3.

15-6 Users

The users of computers are no longer hardcore computer scientists. User-friendliness has become a reality, and computers are being used and operated all the way from grade schools to households for diverse tasks. In the corporate world, the utilization of computers is unavoidable. Either through industry push or demand pull, computers have become an integral part of the corporate scene.

The general computer awareness of typical users has forced private and public organizations to improve their use of computer technology. A typical investment customer may ask for more diverse and sophisticated analysis when it comes to any business investment. A spreadsheet has become as popular as a calculator in any financial institution.

15-7 Artificial Intelligence and the Fifth-Generation Project

Artificial intelligence and Japanese computers (the fifth-generation project) were discussed in Chapter 12 in detail. Here we would like to highlight the significance of this development for the future of DSS. Development in AI

Table 15-2 ▪ Software Trends

Generation	Major Attribute
First	Machine language
Second	Assembly language
Third	High-level language
Fourth	Fourth-generation language (4GL)
Fifth	Natural language processing (NLP)

Table 15-3 ▪ Computer Performance

Generation	Speed*
First	10 KIPS
Second	200 KIPS
Third	5 MIPS
Fourth	30 MIPS–100 MIPS
Fifth	1 GIPS–1 TIPS

*K stands for kilobyte (1024 bytes); M stands for meagabytes (1024^2), G stands for gigabytes (1024^3), and T stands for terabytes (1024^4).

technology, particularly in the areas of ESs and NLP, undoubtedly will have a significant impact on design and utilization of DSS. As we explained, integration of ES with DSS promises a significant improvement in all aspects of DSS operations.

Further improvements in AI technology will have a direct impact on DSS architecture. As discussed in Chapter 14, AI technology may improve the quality of the data base component of a DSS by incorporating rules and facts in the data base. The model base may be improved by including heuristic analysis in the modeling component. A DSS user may be able to ask why and how questions of a DSS.

NLP, by providing a free-format interface for typical DSS users with minimum computer training, should improve and increase the utilization of DSS significantly. NLP should enable a user to communicate in his or her natural spoken or written language. Computers should understand optical images such as pictures and symbols. These computers are sometimes called sequential-inference machines (SIM) [31]. Their "reasoning" process is based on words, paragraphs, and concepts, not just numbers. The fifth-generation project in Japan has specified some goals [21, p. 3]. The new-generation computer will:

- Listen when spoken to; then do what it is told
- Help program itself
- Sort through volumes of facts to find and use only what is pertinent
- Make logical inferences
- Translate foreign languages
- Treat images and graphs the same as words
- Learn from its own experience
- Be designed for both portable and fixed-based systems

Although these goals seem somewhat ambitious, we have already experienced some progress in this area, and may witness attainment of these specific goals [11, 31].

In parallel with NLP, hardware components of a DSS should also be improved. Mouse, touch technology, and joystick–type interfaces make it easier for a typical user to access a DSS. At the same time, the quality of output devices (such as graphic terminals and laser printers) should be improved and should be reasonably priced. This may make these systems more attractive to a typical DSS user.

Development in automatic programming, one branch of AI that advocates automating the software development cycle, sounds like a significant effort. Automatic programming should make it easier to develop, maintain, and debug software.

In parallel with the fifth-generation project, there is another project underway in Japan called the TRON project [30]. This project, which includes four layers of development, covers both hardware and software technologies. These layers are intended to incorporate and enhance all levels of computer operations:

- The instruction-set processor (ISP) layer
- The operating system kernel layer

- The operating system shell layer
- The application and user-machine interface layer

This project has been divided into four subsystems: ITRON (industry), BTRON (business), MTRON (micro), and CTRON (the central project). The outcome of this project should have a significant impact on all aspects of DSS design and utilization.

15-8 Development in Data Base and DBMS

We discussed the data base as one of the crucial components of a DSS. The trend toward establishing a relational data base that is easy to use and maintain has already started. As a part of the fifth-generation and the TRON project, the Japanese are working on the Delta project, which involves the development of large-scale relational data bases [30]. Also, data base machines with dedicated data bases and DBMS have enjoyed steady development. These advancements in AI technology should have a significant impact on data base design and use. Also, distributed data bases should become more common in the DSS environment. This trend will continue with the progress in distributed processing in general.

15-9 Development in Telecommunications

In Chapter 11 we discussed distributed data processing and telecommunications briefly. During these past 40 years telecommunication technology has undergone major improvements. This branch of computer technology started with the telephone and teletype system as the first generation. During the second generation, digital transmission and pulse-code modulation became common. The third generation was propelled by several major technological breakthroughs, including satellite communications, microwaves, fiber optics, and packet switching. Packet switching (also called value-added networks) offers alternative routes between a sender and receiver. This means there will be more than one route from point A to point B, resulting in more effectiveness in the entire communication system. Encryption and communication control were also made commonly available [18]. With the fourth generation of telecommunication technology, the integrated services digital network (ISDN) has become prevalent. ISDN provides standardization and enables the user to combine voice, video, text, and image. This technology requires further development [18, pp. 90–91]. In the fifth generation we should also see further development in networking and enhanced telecommunication systems, and improvements in security and compatibility.

Improving the quality of telecommunication systems may have a direct impact on the data base of a DSS. A DSS may be able to access a variety of internal and external data bases with a fast turnaround time. At the same time, such an access may be provided with a reasonable cost and a high degree of security.

15-10 Microcomputers

In Chapter 10 we discussed general capabilities of microcomputers. Recent advancements and the projected growth of these computers will affect DSS design and utilization. Already, the total number of millions of instructions per second (MIPS) available and performed in all microcomputers is larger than the total MIPS in all mainframes [32]. It seems this trend will continue. In the last few years, microcomputers have undergone major improvement. The 8086 and 8088 chips are seriously challenged by the 80286 and 80386 series. Microcomputer processing speeds have improved from 4.7 megahertz to 25 megahertz, and the processor size has increased from 8 bits to 32 bits [4]. A 80386-based microcomputer can address 4 gigabytes of memory physically and about 64 terabytes by using the virtual-addressing technique [12], in which the memory of a computer gets partitioned. The entire application program does not need to be loaded in the memory for processing, which provides an almost indefinite amount of memory to a user in a given situation.

Microcomputers started as single-user systems. Now they are becoming multiuser systems. They started as single-tasking and are becoming multitasking. Compact disk read-only memory (CD ROM) offers mass-storage capability, as one of these disks is capable of storing almost 550 megabytes of data [8]. The CD ROM, in conjunction with laser beams, scans a disk extremely rapidly.

CP/M as the major operating system for the PC has been almost replaced by MS-DOS and PC-DOS. Some manufacturers, such as AT&T, have moved to the UNIX operating system. IBM and Microsoft Corporation are pushing a new operating system for personal computers called OS2. Soon a $100,000 computer will make the Cray, a $5,000,000 computer, obsolete [17]. The new super minicomputer will perform at 10 MIPS. Specifically, experts in the field have provided an interesting outlook for microcomputers by the turn of the century [20]. These computers will have:

- Parallel processing power
- High storage capacity
- Read-write optical disks
- Extremely high resolution CRTs or flat-panel LCD displays
- Hard-copy output on typeset-quality color laser printers
- Combined communication of data, voice, video on the same line
- A true user-friendly interface
- Massive CD ROM data base access
- Multitasking and multiprocessing
- Processing speed of 30 million or more instructions per second
- Gallium arsenide instead of silicon (gallium arsenide is five times faster)
- Communication speed of over 19,200 bits per second (BPS)
- Relatively few compatibility problems

15-11 Computers at Home

The advancement of computers, improved user-friendliness, and general computer awareness should significantly increase computer utilization by typical average people. Improvement in telecommunication systems may make telecommuting a common reality [5]. A large portion of the work force may work at home and perform their jobs through telecommunications systems. The office of the future could be your kitchen. Via personal computers, workers at a home workplace should be able to send and receive work assignments from a central office. This approach may have advantages and disadvantages. However, it is a reality and is gaining popularity [5].

A massive job shortfall has been projected to occur by the year 2010 [23] because of advanced applications of computers in areas such as engineering, construction, transportation, finance, government, manufacturing, trade, and services. Jobs are changing, which means education and job training need to change as well. It is not clear exactly how these changes will affect DSS, but it is almost certain that DSS will be a part of this transformation.

Computer development may also change the traditional arrangement at home. For example, voice synthesis and voice-recognition systems used in conjunction with robotics may control appliances such as smoke alarms and heating systems. Furniture and kitchens may be radically different in the future, possibly containing furniture that moves by itself and robots that listen and respond. Also, teleshopping may become a reality by incorporating other senses, such as touch, smell, and taste, into the telecommunication system [9].

15-12 Organizational Change

During the last few years, DSSs have gained acceptance both in academia and in the business world. Major universities offer degree programs in decision support systems. Some large organizations have changed their traditional MIS departments to DSS departments, and many business organizations are now hiring DSS specialists [33]. The notion that a DSS can support rather than replace a manager may finally gain acceptance. All these changes indicate the increasing popularity of DSS.

15-13 Cost Trends

The cost of hardware and software continues to decrease, while the quality and quantity of both is expected to increase. Cost decreases, quality improvement, and improved user-friendliness should make DSS more attractive to organizations regardless of their size and type of operation.

15-14 What Does All This Mean to DSS?

By examining some of the important factors surrounding the design, implementation, and utilization of a DSS, it is possible to make some predictions. Although it is very difficult to provide a long-range projection, we can make a projection that should put us into the mid 1990s. By that time, the status of the fifth-generation project will be more clear, and a more decisive trend for the future can be ascertained:

1. The cost of hardware and software will continue to decline. In other words, it will be cheaper to process 1BPS of information in the future than it is today. This should make DSS a more affordable alternative to all organizations regardless of their size and financial status.
2. AI technology and its related fields will continue to grow. This enhancement will have a definite impact on DSS.
   - AI will have a direct impact on the architecture of a DSS by the integration of this technology into all three components of a DSS: dialog, data base, and model base. This should make DSS more powerful for diverse decision-making purposes.
   - Further development in natural language processing should make DSS easier to use for a typical user.
3. User awareness and computer literacy for typical DSS users will improve.
4. Networking technology should improve. Issues of compatibility are becoming more manageable. Quality of communication should improve as voice, data, and images are integrated. This development should further promote distributed DSS and group DSS.
5. Microcomputers will continue to improve in power and quality. A majority of DSS products will run on microcomputers without any significant problems. This trend should make DSS again more affordable, more maintainable, and more appealing to diverse organizations.
6. Improvement in networking and microcomputers should make distributed data processing a viable option. Microcomputers will be used for downloading information from major data bases to diverse sites. Cost reduction, ease of use, and responsiveness should further make DDP and particularly distributed DSS a more attractive option.
7. Fourth-generation languages will be improved and should become more attractive to organizations of all sizes. Enhanced productivity by users employing these languages is already well documented in the literature [32]. This positive trend will continue due to ease of use, less training for computer novices, faster application development, and enhanced power of these languages. These factors will promote DSS use by organizations of all sizes.

15-15 Summary

In this final chapter the past was studied in order to provide a picture of the future. During the past 40 years computer technology has progressed beyond imagination. All indications show this trend will continue. Hardware/software trends indicate that future computers will be more powerful, easier to use, and cheaper. AI technology will make DSS more powerful and easier to design and use. Microcomputer development will continue to grow, and networking and telecommunications should improve steadily. This indicates that distributed DSS (DDSS) and group DSS (GDSS) should become more popular. In the next few years, DSS will become a reality accepted by a majority of profit and nonprofit organizations and should continue to gain popularity. It is hard to imagine an enterprise in the near future *without* a DSS.

Review Questions

1. How many generations of computers have we seen? What is a distinguishing feature of each generation?

2. What is the main difference between the third and the fourth generation in hardware? Software? Telecommunications?

3. What are different generations of software technology? What is a 4GL? How is a 4GL different from a traditional language like COBOL?

4. How has computer performance improved? How do you measure a computer performance?

5. What is an IPS?

6. How would you describe future computer users?

7. It has been said that the user's computer literacy will increase. Why is this claim true?

8. AI should enhance the DSS operation. How is this true?

9. What area of AI will directly impact DSS? How?

10. NLP should make the use of DSS easier for a typical user. Why is this true?

11. What are the specific goals of the fifth-generation project? Are these goals realistic? Discuss.

12. In what direction will data base and DBMS improve? What about data base machines?

13. Telecommunications should also improve, both in quality and quantity. Discuss.

14. What is an integrated services digital network? Is this a major factor in telecommunications of the future? Why? Discuss.

15. In what aspects will microcomputers improve?

16. What is a multitasking computer?

17. What are some of the features of the future microcomputers?

18. What will the status of computers be in private homes in the future? What is teleshopping? Telecommuting?

19. What organizational changes are expected regarding DSS use in the future?

20. Will DSS replace MIS? If yes, how? If no, why not?

Projects

1. Research the fifth-generation computers. What are some of the obstacles that must be overcome?

2. It has been said that a programmer's productivity has significantly improved by using 4GLs versus a language like COBOL or FORTRAN. Discuss this. (Hint: Consult [32].)

3. The TRON project should have a significant impact on DSS. In what direction will the impact be? Research this? (*Hint:* Consult [30].)

4. Automatic programming may revolutionalize the software development process. Research this claim.

5. How may telecommunications of the future be different from today's? Discuss.

6. Research a 80386-based microcomputer. Compare and contrast this computer with a 80286-based microcomputer. What are the specific improvements in the 80386? Compare the cost of 80386- to 8088-based machines at a local vendor.

7. It has been said that in the near future we will see mainframe micros. What does this mean? Discuss.

Key Terms

Hardware trend
Vacuum tube
Transistor
Integrated circuit
Telecommunications
Miniaturization
Very large scale integration (VLSI)
Microcomputer
Optical disk
Bubble memory
Parallel processing
Gallium arsenide
Optical technology
Machine language
Assembly language
High-level language
Fourth-generation language (4 GL)
Natural language processing (NLP)
Instruction per second (ISP)
Kilobytes
Megabytes
Gigabytes
Terabytes
Artificial intelligence
Fifth-generation project
Expert systems
Heuristic analysis
Logical inferences
Mouse
Touch technology
Joy stick
Laser printer
Automatic programming
TRON project
ITRON
BTRON
MTRON
CTRON

Delta project
Teletype
Pulse-code modulation
Satellite
Microwaves
Fiber optics
Packet switching (value-added network)
Encryption
Integrated services digital network (ISDN)
Microcomputers
Megahertz
MIPS (millions of instruction per second)
Virtual addressing
Single-user
Multiuser
Single-tasking
Multitasking
Compact disk (CD)
Read only memory (ROM)
CD ROM
CP/M
MS-DOS/PC-DOS
UNIX operating system
OS2
Read-write optical disk
Telecommuting
Organizational change
Distributed DSS (DDSS)

References

[1] Alter, Steven L. 1980. *Decision Support Systems Current Practice and Continuing Challenges*. Reading, Mass.: Addison-Wesley Publishing Company, pp. 183–93.

[2] Anonymous. 1984. What's Happening with DSS? *EDP Analyzer* 22, no. 7 (July): 1–12.

[3] Bell, Jon. 1987. Atari's New Computers. *ANTIC, The Atari Resource* (May): 22–24.

[4] Bender, Eric, and Ken Greenberg. 1987. The Soul of the 386. *PC World* (March): 242–55.

[5] Best, Fred. 1986. No Place Like Home. *MW* (July-August): 9–12.

[6] Blanning, R. W. 1983. What Is Happening in DSS? *Interfaces* 13, no. 5 (October): 71–80.

[7] Bonczek, R. H., C. W. Holsapple, and A. B. Whinston. 1980. Future Directions for Developing Decision Support Systems. *Decision Sciences* 11, no. 4 (October): 616–31.

[8] Churbak, David. 1986. CD ROM Databases Attracting User Attention. *PC Week* (July 15): 103.

[9] Cornish, Edward. 1986. Did You Hear the One About the Human Who . . . ? *ComputerWorld* (November): 28–29.

[10] Diebold, John. 1984. Six Issues That Will Affect the Future of Information Management. *Data Management* (July): 10–12, 14.

[11] Emmett, Arielle. 1984. Why Japanese Computers Aren't Selling in America. *Personal Computing* (February): 220–39.

[12] Gibson, Michael L., and John C. Windsor. 1986. PC-DOS: The Next 'De Facto' Standard for Micro-Computer Operating Systems. *Journal of Systems Management* (July): 6–10.

[13] Goyette, Richard. 1986. Fourth Generation Systems Sooth End User Unrest. *Data Management* (January): 30–32.

[14] Hecht, Jeff. 1987. Optical Computers. *High Technology* (February): 44–49.

[15] Kopcych, Tony. 1986. Evolution of the MIS Function. *Infosystems* (April): 56–59.

[16] Lemonick, Michael D. 1987. Superconductors! *Science* (May 11): 64–75.

[17] Lewis, Geoff, Anne R. Field, and Katherine M. Hofner. 1986. Zoom! Here Come the New Micros. *Business Week* (December 1): 82–92.

[18] Lientz, Bennet P., and Kathryn P. Ren. 1987. *Data Communications for Business*. St. Louis: Times Mirror/Mosby College Publishing.

[19] Liskin, Miriam. 1986. Speeding Hard Disk Access. *Personal Computing* (September): 39–47.

[20] McManus, Reed. 1987. In Pursuit of Tomorrow's PC. *PC World* (May): 260–73.

[21] Miller, Richard K. 1987. *Fifth Generation Computers*. Lilburn, Ga.: The Fairmount Press, Inc.

[22] Nadel, Robert B. 1986. The Practitioner and the Computer. *The CPA Journal* 56 (July): 93–94.

[23] Porter, Alan. 1986. The New Information Age. *The Futurist* (September-October): 9–14.

[24] Posa, John J. 1987. Using Silicon and Gallium Arsenide. *High Technology* (March): 38–41.

[25] Raike, William M. 1985. The Fifth Generation in Japan. *Byte* (April): 401–406.

[26] Reed, Sandra R. 1987. Bill Gates On: A Platform for the Next 10 Years. *Personal Computing* (May): 74–81.

[27] Rifkin, Glenn. 1986. Parallel Processing: The Next Generation is Already Under Way. *ComputerWorld* 20 (December 22): 35–37, 39–41.

[28] Rothfeder, Jeffrey. 1986. A Few Words About Voice Technology. *PC Magazine* (September 30): 191–202.

[29] Rothfeder, Jeffrey. 1986. Is There Intelligent Life in the PC? *PC Magazine* (January 14): 139–48.

[30] Sakamura, Ken. 1987. The TRON Project. *IEEE Micro* (April): 8–13.

[31] Seaman, Jon. 1984. Fifth Generation on Track. *Computer Decisions* 16 (November): 24–25.

[32] Seilheimer, Steven D. 1986. Future Solutions to DP Problems Will Integrate Today's Technology. *Data Management* (November): 23–24.

[33] Sprague, Ralph H., Jr., and Eric D. Carlson. 1982. *Building Effective Decision Support Systems*. Englewood Cliffs, N.J.: Prentice-Hall, Inc., pp. 314–16.

[34] Steinbrecher, David. 1986. Next Generation PCs: A Panoply of Pluses. *Today's Office* (October): 38–48.

part six

DSS Products and Applications

DSS Products: What Is Available

Introduction

In this appendix, brief summary of some of the most commonly used DSS products (DSS generators) on the market is presented. Part I presents the mainframe-based products and Part II introduces the micro-based products. These products are capable of designing many powerful specific DSS in a variety of disciplines. If you have further questions regarding the suitability of these products for your specific needs, contact the vendor. This listing should give an idea regarding what is available.

This is not an exhaustive listing; there are many other products available. Also, these products are not being endorsed. This is only a fact sheet and is accurate at the time of this writing. Part I includes the following products:

- A-1. Accent R
- A-2. DB2
- A-3. EIS
- A-4. Empire
- A-5. Express
- A-6. FCS-EPS
- A-7. FOCUS
- A-8. IFPS
- A-9. MODEL
- A-10. Nomad
- A-11. RAMIS II
- A-12. SAS
- A-13. Simplan
- A-14. System W

Part II includes the following products:

- A-15. Exec*U*Stat
- A-16. EXPRESS/PC
- A-17. FOCUS/PC
- A-18. Forecast Plus
- A-19. IFPS/Personal
- A-20. NOMAD 2
- A-21. Oracle
- A-22. Paradox
- A-23. Q&A
- A-24. RAMIS/PC
- A-25. RATS
- A-26. SAS/PC
- A-27. Superbase Personal

Part I—Mainframe Based DSS

Table A-1 ▪ Accent R

Vendor:	National Information Systems, Inc. 1190 Saratoga Avenue, Suite 100 San Jose, California 95129
Telephone number:	(408) 985-7100
Systems it runs:	DEC-10, DEC-20, VAX
Operating system:	TOPS-10, TOPS-20, VMS
User support or vendor support:	Local/newsletter, manual, on-site training, hot-line, case materials
English-like:	Yes
Nonprocedural:	Yes, at different levels
Forecasting:	N/A
Statistical analysis:	Through interface with SPSS
Financial analysis:	Through interface with NYPLAN
Optimization:	N/A
Goal seeking:	Yes
What-if:	Yes
Multidimensional analysis:	No
DBMS:	Relational, hierarchical, network
Report generation:	Yes
Graphic display:	Through interface with TELL-A-GRAF
Security:	Separated from data and applications
PC version:	No
Related products:	NYPLAN, WordMARC, SPSS, TELL-A-GRAF
Third-party products with which it works:	COBOL, FORTRAN, C, and MACRO
Number of terminals supported:	Unlimited
Sensitivity analysis:	No
Monte Carlo:	Yes
Risk analysis:	No
Source language:	C
Query operation:	Yes

Table A-2 ▪ DB2

Vendor:	IBM Corporation P.O. Box 50020 Programming Publishing San Jose, California 95150
Systems it runs:	Any processor supported by MVS/System product Version 1 Release 3.6, MVS/System product, Version 2 Release 1.3, IBM 3033 Processor
Software requirements:	For an MVS/XA environment: 1. MVS/SP-JES2 or JES3 Version 2, Release 1.3 2. MVS/XA Data Facility Product Version 2, Release 1 3. TSD Extensions Release 2.1 For an MVS/370 environment: MVS/S system product—JES2 or JES3 Version 1, Release 3.6 For both MVS/XA and MVS/370 environments: DFSORT, Release 8
User or vendor support:	Yes
English-like:	Yes
Nonprocedural:	Yes
Forecasting:	Yes
Statistical analysis:	Yes
Security:	Yes
Query:	Yes
Source language:	PPL2, BASIC, COBOL, PL/I, FORTRAN, assembly language
DBMS:	Relational
Financial analysis:	Yes
Modeling:	Yes
Monte Carlo:	Yes
Report generation:	Yes
Graphic display:	Yes
Optimization:	Yes
Related products:	Host Access, PC Access, Performance Management, Query, and Report Writing

Table A-3 ▪ EIS

Vendor:	Boeing Computer Services P.O. Box 24346 Seattle, Washington 98124
Telephone number:	(206) 644-6708
Systems it runs:	IBM 370, XT, AT, or IBM PC
Operating system:	N/A

continued

Table A-3 ▪ Continued

User support or vendor support:	Manual, on-site training, materials, hotlines, newsletter
English-like:	Yes
Nonprocedural:	Yes
Forecasting:	Nine different regression techniques
Statistical analysis:	Moving average, exponential smoothing, seasonal adjustment, regression
Financial analysis:	IRR, ROI, NPV, loss-carry-forward, amortization
Optimization:	None
Goal seeking:	Yes
What-if:	Yes
Multidimensional analysis:	Yes
DBMS:	Multidimensional array
Report generation:	Display Command, EZ Writer, Standard Writer, DB Extract
Graphic display:	Line, pie, bar, scatter diagrams, histograms, bubble charts
Security:	Extensive security at several levels
PC version:	Yes, EIS Micro Workstation
Related products:	RAMIS, SAS
Third-party products with which it works:	FORTRAN, PASCAL
Number of terminals supported:	N/A

Table A-4 ▪ Empire

Vendor:	Applied Data Research, Inc. 601 Gateway Blvd., Suite 1000 South San Francisco, California 94080
Telephone number:	(415) 875-1600
Any licensing agreement:	Yes
Systems it runs:	IBM and IBM look-alikes and in a network environment
Operating system:	N/A
User support or vendor support:	Hotlines, examples of use available, detailed manual, and case study materials for academic users
English-like:	Yes
Nonprocedural:	Procedural only
Forecasting:	Arina/Box-Jenkins and seasonal decomposition
Statistical analysis:	Averaging, growth (inflation), sum of the columns or rows, plus others

Financial analysis:	Depreciation, loan amortization, present value, return on investment, and yield to maturity
Optimization:	None
Goal seeking:	Yes
What-if:	Yes
Multidimensional analysis:	Only two
DBMS:	No; however, A.D.R. does offer DATACOM DBMS
Report generation:	Yes
Graphic display:	Bubbles charts, pie charts, multiple graphs on one page, color graphs, line graphs, color fills under lines, and alternate shading for pen plotters
Security:	N/A
PC version:	No
Related products:	Yes
Third-party products with which it works:	Yes; specifics N/A
Number of terminals supported:	Depends on the amount of memory
Sensitivity analysis:	N/A
Monte Carlo:	Yes
Risk analysis:	Yes
Source language:	N/A

Table A-5 ▪ Express

Vendor:	Information Resources, Inc. 200 Fifth Avenue Waltham, Massachusetts 02254
Telephone number:	(617) 890-1100
Any licensing agreement:	Yes
Systems it runs:	IBM 43XX series, 30XX series and up under VM/CMS or MVS, Prime 250 and up, DEC VAX family, IBM PC
Operating system:	N/A
User support or vendor support:	Hotline, manuals, on-site and classroom training, applications consulting, case materials, extended support, newsletters
English-like:	Yes
Nonprocedural:	Procedural and nonprocedural
Forecasting:	Regression, trend analysis, Box-Jenkins, Holt-Winters, exponential smoothing, and others
Statistical analysis:	Major functions and interface with SAS. Exploratory data analysis (e.g. mean, median), time series analysis & forecasting
Financial analysis:	DCF and IRR analysis and other financial functions

continued

Table A-5 ▪ Continued

Optimization:	Most OR techniques including linear programming, PERT/CPM, and EOQ
Goal seeking:	Yes
What-if:	Yes
Multidimensional analysis:	Yes
DBMS:	Multidimensional relational
Report generation:	Nonprocedural query language, procedural report generator, many formats
Graphic display:	Time series, scatter plot, logarithmic, and pie plots, histograms, bar charts, color, and filled bars
Security:	Password, encryption, read/write file access, protection down to cell level, data backup
PC version:	Yes
Related products:	EASYCAST*, EASYTRAC*, PROMOTER*, FCRS*
Third-party products with which it works:	SAS, FOCUS, Telegraph, DB2, SQL, Import and Export data through VKS, WK1, DIF, ASCII
Number of terminals supported:	Depends on hardware
Sensitivity analysis:	Yes
Monte Carlo:	Yes
Risk analysis:	Yes
Source language:	N/A
Query:	Yes

*EASYCAST: Known as Sales Forecasting System (SFS); enables marketing and production planners to combine statistical forecasts with management judgement to produce highly accurate forecasts.
*EASYTRAC: Known as Marketing Management System (MMS); distributes information and analysis throughout the marketing and sales organization.
*PROMOTER: Measures response to sales promotion at the manufacturer, retailer, and consumer levels.
*FCRS: Financial Consolidation and Reporting System provides a complete facility for specifying, performing, and reporting on financial consolidations.

Table A-6 ▪ FCS-EPS

Vendor:	THORN EMI Computer Software 285 Mill Road Chelmsford, Massachusetts 01824
Telephone number:	(508) 256-3900
Systems it runs:	IBM, DEC, UNIVAC, Wang, Honeywell, HP, DG, PRIME, Sperry
Operating system:	CMS, TSO, CICS, VMS, (DOS-MICROFCS), MPE, VS, AOS
User support or vendor support:	Manual, on-site training, materials, hotlines

English-like:	Yes
Nonprocedural:	Yes
Forecasting:	Correlated curve fit, Multiple Linear regression, Box-Jenkins, FCS-X11—Shishkin XII seasonal analysis
Statistical analysis:	11 types available: basic statistics, Durbin-Watson coefficient, shape, autocorrelation, correlation, T-test for means, Theil U statistic, Spearman's rank correlation coefficient, runs test, data entry, list data
Financial analysis:	Time series, curve fitting, Monte Carlo, risk analysis
Optimization:	N/A
Goal seeking:	"Target" option
What-if:	Yes
Multidimensional analysis:	Yes
DBMS:	Hierarchical, relational, multidimensional
Report generation:	Yes
Graphic display:	Discrete, plotting, continuous line, pie, bar, scatter, histogram, three-dimensional tower charts, star charts
Security:	Strong Security
PC version:	Yes—Micro-Subset, IBM compatible, WANG
Related products:	Micromulti, FQS, Tempus Link, EIA
Third-party products with which it works:	FORTRAN, COBOL, DB2, SQL/DS, IDMS, FOCUS
Number of terminals supported:	Depending on installation
Sensitivity analysis:	Yes
Risk analysis:	Yes
Source language:	Assembler, C
Query:	Yes (FQS) Friendly Query System

Table A-7 ▪ FOCUS

Vendor:	Information Builders, Inc. 1250 Broadway New York, New York 10001
Telephone number:	(212) 736-4433
Systems it runs:	IBM or compatible mainframes (VM/CMS, DOS/VSE, MVS/TSO), DEC/VAX and Wang/VS mini computers, and personal computers
User or vendor support:	Customer support representative, training, hotline, customer mailbox system
English-like:	Yes
Nonprocedural:	Menu-driven
Forecasting:	Yes
Statistical analysis:	Time series, correlation, regression

continued

Table A-7 ▪ Continued

Financial analysis:	Yes
Optimization:	Yes
Goal seeking:	Yes
Multidimensional analysis:	Yes
DBMS:	Share relational structure, can access and combine data from any files VSAM, QSAM, IMS, SQL/DS, DB2, ADABAS
Report generation:	Customized reports, automatic formatting
Graphics:	Yes
Security:	Yes
Related products:	PC/FOCUS, PC/FOCUS-multi user
Third-party products with which it works:	Lotus 1-2-3, DB2
Number of terminals supported:	Multiple
Source language:	COBOL, FORTRAN, PL/1
Query:	Yes

Table A-8 ▪ IFPS

Vendor:	Execucom P.O. Box 9758 Austin, Texas 78766
Telephone number:	(800) 531-5078
Systems it runs:	9 product lines (specifics N/A)
Operating system:	Over 20 operating systems
User support or vendor support:	
Local offices	Several
International offices	Several
International agents	Several
Case materials	Yes
Manuals	Yes
Student guides	Yes
Hotlines	Yes
On-site training	Yes
Education centers	Several
Newsletter	Yes
Magazine	Yes
User week conventions	Yes
User groups:	
Regional	Yes

National	Yes
International	Yes
English-like:	Yes
Nonprocedural:	Yes
Forecasting:	Regression, trend analysis
Statistical analysis:	Descriptive statistics
Financial analysis:	DCF, PV, NPV, IRR
Optimization:	Linear programming, EOQ
Goal seeking:	Yes
What-if:	Yes
Multidimensional analysis:	Three-dimensional
DBMS:	Relational
Report generation:	Yes
Graphic display:	Yes
Security:	N/A
PC version:	Yes
Related products:	N/A
Third-party products with which it works:	N/A
Number of terminals supported:	Limited by hardware and/or operating system
Sensitivity analysis:	Yes
Monte Carlo:	Yes
Risk analysis:	N/A
Source language:	FORTRAN
Query:	Yes

Table A-9 ▪ MODEL

Vendor:	Lloyd Bush Software 156 William Street New York, New York 10038
Telephone number:	(212) 962-4004
Systems it runs:	Control Data, IBM, HP, DEC, PRIME, Sperry Perkin-Elmer, 16 bit microprocessors
User support or vendor support:	Yes
English-like:	Yes
Nonprocedural:	Yes
Forecasting:	Yes
Statistical analysis:	Yes

continued

Table A-9 ▪ Continued

Financial analysis:	Yes
Optimization:	Yes
Goal seeking:	Yes
What-if:	Yes
Multidimensional analysis:	Yes
DBMS:	No, but interfaces with most data base systems
Report generation:	Yes—variable
Graphic display:	Yes—limited
Security:	Yes
PC version:	Yes
Related products:	Yes
Third-party products with which it works:	Most DBMS products
Number of terminals supported:	Limited by hardware
Sensitivity analysis:	No
Monte Carlo:	N/A

Table A-10 ▪ NOMAD

Vendor:	MUST Software International 1 Merritt 7, 4th Floor Norwalk, CT 06856
Telephone numbers:	(203) 845-5000 FAX 203-845-5252
Vendor or customer support:	Yes
Systems it runs:	IBM 370, 30XX, 43XX/VM/LMS, MVS/TSD compatible
English-like:	Yes
Nonprocedural and procedural language handling facilities:	Yes
Report generation:	Yes
DBMS:	Supports relational, hierarchical and hybrid data base systems
Statistical analysis:	Yes
Graphics:	Yes
Financial analysis:	Yes (budgeting, portfolio, cashflow, rate-case analysis)
Modeling analysis:	Yes
What-if:	Yes

Goal seeking:	Yes
Forecasting:	Yes
Decision support system capabilities:	Yes
Menu-driven or command-driven:	Nomad Assistant, Nomad 2 Data dictionary is menu-driven
Third-party products with which it works:	SQL NOMAD, Reporter NOMAD, RUN-TIME NOMAD, BEAMIT DB2, SQL/DS
Source code:	Assembly source code

Table A-11 ▪ RAMIS II

Vendor:	On-Line Software International, Inc. Fort Lee Executive Park Two Executive Drive Fort Lee, New Jersey 07024-9990
Telephone numbers:	Information 800-642-0177 Customer Support 800-257-9426
Systems it runs:	IBM and plug-compatible machines
Operating system:	N/A
User support or vendor support:	Manuals
On-site training	Yes
Case materials	Teaching done by case method
Hotlines	Provided with package
Newsletter	Quarterly newsletter
English-like:	Yes—with natural language knowledge-based architecture
Nonprocedural:	Yes—with syntax-based language or AI-based natural language
Forecasting:	Only limited*
Statistical analysis:	22 built-in functions
Financial analysis:	Array processing structure available*
Optimization:	No*
Goal seeking:	No*
What-if:	Limited*
Multidimensional analysis:	No*
DBMS:	Tree & relational structures. Can access external DBMS, i.e., DB2, SQL/DS, IMS, IDMS, ADABAS, dBASE III, LOTUS 1-2-3, and so on
Report generation:	Four options provided: AI-based natural language, menu assistance, syntax-based language, checklist

continued

Table A-11 ▪ Continued

Graphic display:	Variety available with options for color, format, captions, and labels
Security:	Down to value of data items
PC version:	Yes. RAMIS/PC Workstation. Any IBM or compatible requires hard disk
Other related products:	DSS packages for modeling
Third-party products with which it works:	Most IBM-compatible software packages
Number of terminals supported:	Limited only by hardware
Sensitivity analysis:	No*
Monte Carlo	No*

*Modeling is handled better by specifically designed packages with RAMIS used to extract the information needed to feed these packages.

Table A-12 ▪ SAS

Vendor:	SAS Institute, Inc. Box 8000, SAS Circle Cary, North Carolina 27511-8000
Telephone number:	(919) 467-8000
Systems it runs:	(a) Runs on batch and interactive under OS, TSO, CMS, DOS/VSE, SSX, and ICCF on IBM 370/30XX/43XX and compatible machine (b) On Digital Equipment Corporation's VAX 8XXX and 11/7XX series under VMS and Micro VAX II under Micro VMS (c) On Data General Corporation's ECLIPSE MV series under AOS/VS (d) On Prime Computer Inc.'s Prime 50 series under PRIMOS (e) On IBM PC AT/370 and XT/370 under VM/PC and IBM PC XT and PC AT under PC DOS The PL/I Optimizing Transient Library is required for IBM Mainframe and VM/PC Systems
Operating systems:	MVS, MVS/XA
User or vendor support:	Yes (on-site training, computer-based training publications)
English-like:	Yes
Nonprocedural:	Menu-driven
Forecasting:	Yes
Statistical analysis:	Yes
Financial analysis:	Yes
Optimization:	Yes
What-if:	Yes
DBMS:	Yes

Multidimensional:	Yes
Report generation:	Yes
Graphic display:	Yes
Security:	Yes
Related products:	SAS/STAT, SAS/IML, SAS/FSP, SAS/OR, SAS/GRAPH
Third-party products with which it works:	DB2
Number of terminals supported:	Multiuser environment
Source language:	N/A

Table A-13 ▪ Simplan

Vendor:	Simplan Systems, Inc. 300 Eastowne Drive, Suite 100 Chapel Hill, North Carolina 27514-0098
Telephone numbers:	800-334-8660, (919) 493-2495
Systems it runs:	IBM and PRIME
Operating system:	IBM: OS/TSO, VM/CMS; PRIME: PRIMOS
User support or vendor support:	Customer support services, quarterly newsletter, toll-free telephone technical and application support (continental U.S.), consulting, annual user group conference
English-like:	Yes
Nonprocedural:	Yes
Forecasting:	Can be linked to SAS
Statistical analysis:	Can be linked to SAS
Financial analysis:	N/A
Optimization:	No
Goal seeking:	Yes
What-if:	Yes
Multidimensional analysis:	Yes
DBMS:	Three-dimensional
Report generation:	Yes
Graphic display:	Yes
Security:	Yes
PC version:	MicroSimplan
Related products:	Yes
Third-party products with which it works:	SAS and other IBM compatible DBMS
Number of terminals supported:	Limited by hardware
Sensitivity analysis:	Yes
Source language:	PL/1, assembly

Table A-14 ▪ System W

Vendor:	Comshare, Ann Arbor, Michigan P.O. Box 1588 Ann Arbor, Michigan 48106
Telephone number:	(213) 387-1177
Any licensing agreement:	Restricted use
Systems it runs:	IBM System/370
Operating system:	VM/CMS; MVS/TSO
User support or vendor support:	
Local offices:	Numerous
Case materials:	Yes
Manuals:	Yes
Hotlines:	Yes
On-site training:	Yes
Education centers:	In numerous locations
Newsletter:	Yes
User week conventions:	Yes
User groups:	Yes
English-like:	Yes
Nonprocedural:	Yes
Forecasting:	Regression, trend analysis
Statistical analysis:	Descriptive statistics
Financial analysis:	DCF, PV, NPV, IRR
Optimization:	Linear programming, EOQ
Goal seeking:	Yes
What-if:	Yes
Multidimensional analysis:	Nine dimensions
DBMS:	Relational
Report generation:	Yes
Graphic display:	Yes
Security:	Yes
PC version:	Yes
Related products:	Commander EIS, W/communications, W/Information Gateway, W/File Power, W/Datman, W/Modelling
Third-party products with which it works:	dBASE, Lotus, Focus
Number of terminals supported:	Limited by hardware and/or operating system
Sensitivity analysis:	Limited
Monte Carlo:	No
Risk analysis:	N/A
Source language:	Pascal
Query:	Limited

Part II: Micro-Based DSS

Table A-15 ▪ Exec*U*Stat

Vendor:	Exec*U*Stat Inc. 5 Independent Way Princeton, New Jersey 08540
Telephone number:	(609) 924-9357
Systems it runs:	IBM PC, AT, XT, and compatibles; Tandy 1000, 2000; Eagle PC; Corona; AT&T 6300
Operating systems:	IBM PC DOS (2.0 or higher)
User and vendor support:	User manuals, on-line tutorial
English-like:	Yes
Nonprocedural:	Menu
Forecasting:	Yes
Statistical:	Yes
Financial:	Yes
Optimization:	Programmable
Goal seeking:	Yes
What-if:	Yes
Multidimensional analysis:	Yes
DBMS:	Limited
Report generator:	Yes
Graphics:	Yes
Third-party products with which it works:	Imports a file: DIF, ASCII, Lotus 1-2-3, Symphony, dBASE II, dBASE III, and Multiplan SYLK Files
Number of terminals supported:	Executive level DSS/single user
Sensitivity analysis:	Yes
Monte Carlo:	Programmable
Risk analysis:	Yes
Source language:	APL, C
Query:	Menu-driven
Requirements:	IBM XT, AT, or compatible 320K RAM min.

Table A-16 ▪ EXPRESS/PC

Vendor:	Information Resources 150 North Clinton Street Chicago, Illinois 60606
Telephone number:	(312) 726-9221

continued

Table A-16 ▪ Continued

Systems it runs:	IBM PC/XT, PC/AT, 3270/PC or 100% compatibles
Operating system:	DOS 2.0 or later version
User or vendor support:	Hot-line, customized training materials
English-like:	Yes
Nonprocedural:	Menu-driven
Forecasting:	Yes
Statistical analyses:	Time series, regression, and so on
Financial analyses:	IRR, NPV
Optimization:	Yes
Multidimensional analysis:	Yes
DBMS:	Yes
Report generation:	Yes
Graphics:	Yes
Related products:	EasyEXPRESS, PowerEXPRESS, BuilderEXPRESS
Third-party products with which it works:	Imports & Exports: Lotus 1-2-3, Symphony, DIF, ASCII files
Query:	Yes
Modeling:	Yes
Memory required:	640K RAM

Table A-17 ▪ FOCUS/PC

Vendor:	Information Builders, Inc. 1250 Broadway New York, New York 10001
Telephone numbers:	(212) 736-4433 (213) 615-0735
Any licensing agreement:	No, but volume discounts available
Systems it runs:	IBM 43XX, 30XX, DEC and VAX/VMS; Wang VS, IBM PC, XT, and AT, 3270-PC, XT/370, AT/370
Operating systems:	IBM Mainframe OS, Unix, Wang VS, IBM PC DOS
User and vendor support:	Hotline, manuals, training, newsletters and so on
English-like:	Nonprocedural English Also, add-on package called "English Query Language" that allows natural language interface
Nonprocedural:	Some functions. Mainly a programmable language like dBASE
Forecasting:	Programmable
Statistical:	Yes—standard statistics
Financial:	Yes
Optimization:	Programmable
Goal seeking:	Programmable
What-if:	Programmable

DBMS:	Relational and hierarchical and network
Report generator:	Yes
Graphics:	Yes
Security:	Yes
Related products:	EQL (English Query Language), dBASE interface, Focus Vision, Foccalc (spreadsheet), Host Language interface, FOCTALK, PC Screen Painter
Third-party products with which it works:	Lotus 1-2-3 files, dBASE III files
Number of terminals supported:	Using Multiuser version for networks, 16 at the same time
Source language:	Assembler, C, FORTRAN, Pascal
Query:	English Query Language add-on package
Requirements:	IBM AT or compatible 80286; 640K RAM minimum; 5-megabyte hard drive; uses LIM expanded memory

Table A-18 ▪ Forecast Plus

Vendor:	Walonick Associates 6500 Nicollet Avenue, S. Minneapolis, Minnesota 55423
Telephone number:	(612) 866-9022
Any licensing agreement:	Yes
Systems it runs:	IBM PC, AT, XT, and compatibles
Operating systems:	IBM PC DOS (Version 2.0 or higher)
User and vendor support:	Users manuals, tutorial manuals
English-like:	Semi—nonprocedural
Nonprocedural:	Menu
Forecasting:	Yes
Statistical:	Yes
Financial:	Yes
Optimization:	Programmable
Goal seeking:	Yes
What-if:	Yes
Multidimensional analysis:	Yes
DBMS:	Yes
Report generator:	Yes
Graphics:	Yes
Security:	Limited
Related products:	STATPAC and STATPAC GOLD, goodness of fit
Third-party products with which it works:	Data Interchange—1-2-3, Symphony, ASCII, DIF
Source language:	Compiled BASIC
Query:	Menu-driven
Requirements:	192K RAM minimum; two disk drives; DOS 2.0 or later

Table A-19 ▪ IFPS/Personal

Vendor:	Execucom System P.O. Box 9758 Austin, Texas 78766
Telephone number:	(800) 531-5078
Systems it runs:	IBM 43XX, 30XX, 9370, Prime, DEC and VAX, HP (older version), IBM PC, XT, AT, PC3270, ITT EXTRA, Sperry PC, TI Pro, TI Business Pro, Zenith 150
Operating systems:	IBM Mainframe VMS IBM PC DOS (2.1 or higher)*
User and vendor support:	Hotline, manuals, training quarterly magazine (*Planner*)
English-like:	Nonprocedural
Nonprocedural:	Menu
Forecasting:	Yes
Statistical:	Yes
Financial:	Yes
Optimization:	Built-in—mainframe only; add-on package—"Optimum"
Goal seeking:	Yes
What-if:	Yes
Multidimensional analysis:	Yes
DBMS:	Not on PC; uses a spreadsheet-like file
Report generator:	Yes
Graphics display:	Add-on package called Impressionist
Security:	Yes
Related products:	Impressionist (graphing), Macintosh version, Optimum (optimization)
Third-party products with which it works:	Lotus 1-2-3 files
Sensitivity analysis:	Yes
Monte Carlo:	Mainframe only
Risk analysis:	Yes
Source language:	PC—Pascal and Assembly; Mainframe—FORTRAN
Query:	English-like natural language
Requirements:	IBM XT, AT, or compatible 512K RAM min.

*(LANs require PC DOS 3.0 or higher; LANs supported on 3 Com, 3Com3+, Novell Network, and IBM Token Ring)

Table A-20 ▪ NOMAD 2

Vendor:	MUST Software International 187 Danbury Road Wilton, Connecticut 06897

Telephone number:	(203) 762-2511
User and vendor support:	Yes
Systems it runs:	IBM XT, AT or 100% compatibles with DOS 3.0 or higher, IBM PC/2 models 30, 50, 60 with DOS 3.3
English-like:	Yes
Nonprocedural:	Both (procedural and nonprocedural)
Graphics:	Yes
Report generation:	Yes
Financial analysis:	Yes
Statistical analysis:	Yes
DBMS:	Yes
Security:	Yes
Query:	Yes
Forecasting:	Yes
What-if:	Yes
Goal seeking:	Yes
Multiple user:	Yes
Related products:	PC Nomad, ReporterNOMAD, Teredata NOMAD, The Nomad Assistant
Third-party products with which it works:	Lotus 1-2-3, dBASE III
Memory requirements:	640K

Table A-21 ▪ Oracle

Name of the vendor:	Oracle Corporation 20 Davis Drive Belmont, California 94002
Telephone number:	(415) 598-8000
User or vendor support:	Yes
Systems with which it works:	IBM PC, XT, AT, RT; IBM S/88, 370, 30XXX, 43XX; DEC DPDP-11, VAX, VAXCLUSTER; UNIX; DG MV Series; Haris 700, 800, 1000; HP 9000 Series 500; Sperry; Honeywell; Prime; NCR; Wang VS compatibles
Operating system:	286/386-based PC running DOS 3.1 or higher with a minimum of 1 MB extended memory and at least 7.5 MB of hard disk space. VM SP, MVSSP, MVSXA, MS-DOS, UNIX, VMS, AOS VS PRIMOS
DBMS:	Relational
Graphic:	Yes
Query:	Yes
Single or multipler user:	Multiple user
Security:	Yes

continued

Table A-21 ▪ Continued

Nonprocedural:	Menu-driven
Report generation:	Yes
Optimization:	Yes
Related products:	SQL *Star, SQL*Forms, Easy*SQL
Third-party products with which it works:	IBM's DB2 and other SQL-based DBMS products
Source code:	C Source Code
Memory:	512 KB required

Table A-22 ▪ Paradox

Vendor:	Ansa Software 1301 Shoreway Road Belmont, California 94002
Telephone number:	(415) 595-4469
Systems it runs:	IBM PC (two floppy drives or one floppy drive and one hard disk drive Monochrome or color monitor)
Operating system:	IBM Mainframe VMS IBM PC DOS (2.0 or higher)
User and vendor support:	Manuals and vendor support
English-like:	Syntax sensitive query by example; script language
Nonprocedural:	Menu
Forecasting:	Programmable
Statistical:	Programmable
Financial:	Programmable
Optimization:	Programmable
Goal seeking:	Programmable
What-if:	Programmable
Multidimensional analysis:	Yes
DBMS:	Fully relational
Report generator:	Custom-designed and tabular
Graphics:	No; can import Lotus 1-2-3 graphics
Security:	Passwords
Third-party products with which it works:	Lotus 1-2-3 files, Symphony, dBASE II, III, pfs:FILE, DIF, VisiCalc, ASCII
Number of terminals supported:	Multi-user environment
Sensitivity analysis:	Programmable
Monte Carlo:	Programmable
Risk analysis:	Programmable
Source language:	PAL (Paradox Application Language)
Query:	Intuitive query by example
Requirements:	IBM PC, XT, AT, or compatible 512K RAM min.)

Table A-23 ▪ Q&A

Vendor:	Symantec Corporation 10201 Torre Avenue Cupertino, California 95014
Telephone number:	(408) 253-9600
Licensing agreement (site license):	Yes; will not sell directly to the end users. Exclusive distributors.
Systems it runs:	IBM PC, AT, XT, COMPAQ compatibles; monochrome or color monitor; supports CGA and EGA cards
Operating systems:	IBM PC DOS, MS DOS (version 2.0 or higher)
User and vendor support:	Hotline, manuals, training
English-like:	Yes—The best to date!
Nonprocedural:	Yes—menu
Third-party products with which it works:	Lotus 1-2-3 files, Symphony, dBASE II, III, MultiMate, pfs: File and Write, IBM Filing and Writing Assis., WordStar, and all programs that create DIF and ASCII format files
Number of terminals supported:	Single-user environment
Query:	English-like natural language
Requirements:	IBM XT, PC, AT, or compatible 512K RAM min., 640K recommended
Report generator:	Excellent; custom-designed.
Graphics:	No; importable through Lotus 1-2-3
Security:	Yes

Table A-24 ▪ RAMIS/PC

Vendor:	On-line P.O. Box 2392 Princeton, New Jersey 08540
Telephone number:	(800) 526-0272
Systems it runs:	IBM 43XX, 30XX, 9370 IBM PC, XT, AT, and compatibles with hard disk; monochrome or color monitor
User and vendor support:	Hotline, manuals, training, newsletters, and so on
English-like:	Menu-like dBASE Assist, also add-on package called "RAMIS English" for English-language Query (a lot like "Intellect")
Forecasting:	Programmable
Statistical:	Programmable
Financial:	Programmable
Optimization:	Programmable
Goal seeking:	Programmable

continued

Table A-24 ▪ Continued

What-if:	Programmable
Multidimensional analysis:	KeepIT allows multifield join
DBMS:	Relational
Report generator:	Yes
Graphics:	No, but works with Lotus
Security:	Encription for files
Related products:	RAMIS for mainframe; PC RAM Learn—tutorial; RAMIS English—query
Memory requirements:	512K, 640K recommended
Third-party products with which it works:	
(Spreadsheet interfaces)	Lotus 1-2-2 (vers. 1A and 2) files, dBASE III files, VP Planner, Farsight, Twin, Supercalc, Multiplan, CalcIT
(Word processing)	MultiMate, Wordstar/Mailmerge, Volkswriter, Easywriter, Peachtext, Office Writer, XYWrite II, Spellbinder, Display Write III, Samna Word III, Microsoft Word, Wordperfect
(Graphics)	Chartmaster, Energraphics, Lotus 1-2-3 Graphics, Microsoft Chart, Twin Graphics, VP Planner Graphics
(Compatible data formats)	DBF (dBASE III), WKS and WK1 (Lotus 1-2-3), Quote/Comma Delimited, Fixed Length, Sequential, RAMIS SAVE
Number of terminals supported:	Single user; LAN version.
Source language:	C
Query:	"RAMIS English," English query language add-on package

Table A-25 ▪ RATS

Vendor:	RATS VAR Econometrics, Inc. 1800 Sherman Ave., Suite 612 Evanston, Illinois 60201
Telephone numbers:	(312) 864-8772 (800) 822-8038 (612) 822-9690
Licensing agreement:	No
Systems it runs:	IBM PC
Operating systems:	PC DOS (2.0 or higher); requires two disk drives, color graphics card
User and vendor support:	Tutorial, manuals, training guide, on-line help
English-like:	Semi—command-driven
Nonprocedural:	Command language
Forecasting:	Yes

Statistical:	Yes
Financial:	Yes
Optimization:	Yes
Goal seeking:	Yes
What-if:	Yes
Multidimensional analysis:	N/A
DBMS:	Not on PC; uses a spreadsheet-like file
Report generator:	Yes
Graphics:	Yes
Security:	Limited
Related products:	E-Z-RATS (menu-driven program)
Third-party products with which it works:	Lotus 1-2-3 files, ASCII files, DIF files
Number of terminals supported:	Single PC user environment
Sensitivity:	Programmable
Monte Carlo:	Yes
Risk analysis:	Yes
Source language:	FORTRAN
Query:	Intuitive query by example
Requirements:	IBM PC, XT, AT, or compatible; 256K RAM minimum; two disk drives; color graphics card

Table A-26 ▪ SAS/PC

Vendor:	SAS Institute, Inc. Box 8000, SAS Circle Cary, North Carolina 27511-8000
Telephone number:	(919) 467-8000
Systems it runs:	IBM PC XT, PC AT, 3270 PC, compatibles, and the IBM Personal System/2
Operating systems:	PC DOS 2.0 or later
User or vendor support:	On-site training, computer-based training publications
English-like:	Yes
Nonprocedural:	Menu-driven
Forecasting:	Extensive
Statistical analysis:	Yes
Financial analysis:	Yes
Optimization:	Yes
What-if:	Yes
DBMS:	Yes

continued

Table A-26 ▪ Continued

Multidimensional:	Yes
Report generation:	Yes
Graphic display:	Yes
Security:	Yes
Related products:	SAS/STAT, SAS/IML, SAS/FSP, SAS/OR, SAS/GRAPH
Third-party products with which it works:	DB2, Lotus 1-2-3
Number of terminals supported:	Multiuser environment
Source language:	N/A
Memory:	640K and hard disk

Table A-27 ▪ Superbase Personal

Vendor:	Progressive Peripherals & Software 464 Kalamath Street Denver, Colorado 80204
Telephone number:	(303) 825-4144
Systems it runs:	IBM PC, XT, AT, or compatible (Atari & Amiga versions available)
Operating systems:	GEM (Graphic Environment Manager)
User and vendor support:	Manuals
English-like:	Pictorial, menu-driven, mouse-driven
Nonprocedural:	Menu-driven (mouse)
Forecasting:	No
Statistical:	Yes, depending upon application
Financial:	Yes
Optimization:	No
Goal seeking:	Programmable
What-if:	Programmable
Multidimensional analysis:	N/A
DBMS:	Digital's (GEM), Graphics Research Manager
Report generator:	Yes
Graphics:	Can store CAD drawings, business graphics
Security:	Passwords
Related products:	Superbase Professional, Subscript, Superbase Starter
Third-party products with which it works:	Can import data from dBASE, dBASE II, dBASE III

B DSS In Action

Introduction

This appendix introduces over a dozen specific decision support systems. As was said in Chapter 3, a specific DSS (SDSS) can be built either by using DSS tools or DSS generators. The majority of the systems in this appendix have been built from DSS tools such as FORTRAN and PL/1. Most of these systems were designed in the early 1970s, and at that time the majority of DSS generators either were not in existence or did not have the necessary power. Conversely, the majority of the applications encountered in the next appendix are designed using DSS generators because most of them were developed in recent years. Generally speaking, the development of a specific DSS from a DSS generator is a step forward. Since the majority of the functions needed by a SDSS are already present in a DSS generator, the development process is shorter and the process itself is easier.

SDSSs are designed to perform a specific task or a series of related tasks that encompass a diverse area. Generally speaking, these tasks include a variety of data analysis, data retrieval, query operation, modeling analysis, ad hoc analysis of information, and what-if, sensitivity, and goal-seeking analysis. This appendix should give you an idea regarding the actual uses of DSS in a practical setting. These systems include:

B–1 An Analytic Information Management System (AAIMS)
B–2 BRANDAID
B–3 Capacity Information System (CIS)
B–4 Computer-Assisted Underwriting System at Equitable (CAUSE)
B–5 Generalized Management Information System (GMIS)
B–6 Generalized Planning System (GPLAN)

B–7 Geographic Data Analysis and Display System (GADS)
B–8 Goal-Directed Decision Structuring System (GODDESS)
B–9 Interactive Market Systems (IMS): A Media Decision Support System
B–10 Plan Analysis and Modeling System (PAMS)
B–11 Portfolio Management System (PMS)
B–12 PROJECTOR
B–13 Relational General Information System (REGIS)

Only the major aspects of these systems are highlighted. To understand the detailed operation of each system, you must consult the references provided for the system.

Table B-1 ▪ An Analytic Information Management System (AAIMS)

General Features	References
Used for data analysis and report generation	[6], [13]
An APL-based DSS (APL—a programming language—is a high-level programming language)	[1, pp. 287–304]
Major interface mode is command language	
Easy to learn and use; interactive	
Suitable for users with different backgrounds	
Can be used for both ad hoc or standard reporting	
Initially developed in 1976 by R. Klass, C. Weiss, and J. D. Kingsley	
Implemented by American Airlines	
Has grown continually both in terms of scope and capabilities	
Is being used by many other organizations besides American Airlines	
Modeling analysis is limited	
Report formatting is relatively limited	

Table B-2 ▪ BRANDAID

General Features	References
Used for marketing mix analysis (price, promotion, place, product)	[7, p. 138–143]
Helps a decision-maker to evaluate the overall situation regarding the market by integrating all the variables and allowing the use of the decision-maker's judgment	[8], [9]
Does forecasting	
Developed by John D. C. Little	

General Features	References
Implemented in 1975	
Demonstrates the coexistance of computer and decision-maker	
Adaptive in terms of parameters and structures	
Very easy to communicate with	
Uses EXPRESS for implementation (EXPRESS, a DSS generator, is discussed in Appendix A)	
Is modular (has been developed in a series of independent segments; this makes it easier to develop the system further)	

Table B-3 ▪ Capacity Information System (CIS)

General Features	Reference
Graphics-based DSS	[7, pp. 131–38]
Used in production planning environments	
Primary emphasis on profit analysis	
Has helped decision-makers to pinpoint bottlenecks in a timely manner	
Allows various what-if analyses	
Implemented in 1975	
Used by Ztrux, a major truck manufacturer	
Supports the plan modification process	
Through an interactive session, generates forecasts, analyzes capacity, modifies the forecast, and so on	
FORTRAN-based and uses more than 40,000 lines of codes	

Table B-4 ▪ Computer-Assisted Underwriting System at Equitable (CAUSE)

General Features	References
Assists insurance underwriters in calculating renewal rates on group insurance policies	[1, pp. 197–224], [4]
Used for training underwriters and production staff	
Provides various underwriting reports and numerous calculations accompanied with statistical analysis	
Includes over 200 FORTRAN subroutines, two assembly-language subroutines, and 24 COBOL modules	
Successfully implemented in several versions	

continued

Table B-4 ▪ Continued

General Features	References
Improved accuracy, is responsible for great cost savings, and has eliminated clerical tasks	
Provides statistical analysis to support underwriter's action	
Improved communication among the underwriters and the organizations who are using CAUSE	

Table B-5 ▪ Generalized Management Information System (GMIS)

General Features	Reference
Includes a modeling language, TROLL, for econometric analysis, TSP (Time Series Processor), DYNAMO (simulation language) (used in the Limits of Growth World Model by the Club of Rome), APL/EPLAN for econometric analysis and forecasting; also includes statistical and DBMS operations	[7, pp. 160–166]
Used by NEEMIS (New England Energy Management Information System) from 1974 to 1976	
Developed in 1970 at MIT	
Developed under the supervision of J. J. Donovan and S. E. Madnick	
Based on the concept of the virtual machine, which provides the opportunity of several incompatible computers and data bases to communicate and be simulated on a real computer	
Allows a user to access a SQL data base, a FORTRAN subroutine, and some data in a relational data base, for example	
Interactive and user-friendly	

Table B-6 ▪ Generalized Planning System (GPLAN)

General Features	Reference
Allows for ad hoc decision making	[3]
Developed at Purdue University	
Does data analysis as well as data retrieval	
Uses a nonprocedural English-like query	
Has been used for inventory management and water-quality planning	
FORTRAN IV-based	
Has been used on a CDC 6500 and IBM 360, 370	
Uses a network-type DBMS	

Table B-7 ▪ Geographic Data Analysis and Display System (GADS)

General Features	References
Includes optimization algorithms	[12, pp. 41–54]
Performs statistical analysis	[7, pp. 147–60]
Developed by IBM Research Division	
Interactive graphics system capable of drawing maps by utilizing data from an existing data base	
Used in 1974 to design a police beat plan for a city in order to minimize response time	
Used in 1976 to help a school superintendent to design a zoning plan for the school district	
Graphics capabilities, its most distinguishing feature	
Very user-friendly	

Table B-8 ▪ Goal-Directed Decision Structuring System (GODDESS)

General Features	Reference
Developed by J. Pearl, A. Leal, and J. Saleh in the cognitive systems laboratory at UCLA; designed in 1980 and revised in 1981	[11]
Based on a unique, goal-directed structure for representing decision problems	
At any point in time, focuses the user's attention on the issues that are most crucial to the problem at hand	
Functions very similarly to human behavior in perceiving a problem	
Helps to discover new alternatives	
Includes an English-like dialog component	
Allows the user to state relations among aspects, conditions, and goals, which is similar to a decision-tree approach	

Table B-9 ▪ Interactive Market Systems (IMS): A Media Decision Support System

General Features	Reference
Initially designed by David Ness and Christopher Sprague	[1, pp. 225–46]
Designed to assist advertisers to reach potential customers	
Designed to assist media representatives to sell space to advertisers	
Offers ten different products; among them are: cross-tabulation analysis, market segmentation analysis, reach and frequency analysis, and optimization	

continued

Table B-9 ▪ Continued

General Features	Reference
FORTRAN-based	
Unique features of the system are: speed and convenience, capability to monitor results and testing alternatives, personnel development, and security	

Table B-10 ▪ Plan Analysis and Modeling System (PAMS)

General Features	Reference
Used to support capital investment decisions	[2]
Allows diverse data analysis	
Uses English-like query	
Provides graphics or tabular output	
Allows external model access to diverse routines	
Developed by Getty Oil Corporation	

Table B-11 ▪ Portfolio Management System (PMS)

General Features	Reference
Used in financial and bank-related industries	[7, p. 101–26]
Provides investment services to manage security portfolios	
Designed to maximize return for a given level of risk or minimize portfolio risk for a given level of return	
Uses three levels of data: portfolio, securities, and price	
Includes diverse operations such as STATUS to display the contents of a portfolio, TABLE to display portfolio values, and SCATTER and HIST to display scatter plots and histograms, respectively	
Designed by T. P. Gerrity	
Implemented in four banks beginning in 1974	

Table B-12 ▪ PROJECTOR

General Features	Reference
Supports financial planning	[7, pp. 126–30]
Offers multiple regression, trend, and seasonal analysis, and exponential smoothing	
Offers optimization algorithms such as goal programming	
Developed by C. L. Meador and D. N. Ness in 1970	
Used in 1974 by a small New England manufacturing company to investigate the acquisition of a new subsidiary	
Includes four categories of models: merger/acquisition, cash flow, forecasting, and project analysis	
Interactive, easy to use and learn	
Major limitation: lack of graphic capabilities	

Table B-13 ▪ Relational General Information System (REGIS)

General Features	Reference
Used for project control, personnel files, warranty analysis, quality-control applications, and engineering test analysis	[5]
Uses relational DBMS	
Performs statistical analysis	
Provides graphics	
Uses English-like query	
Allows external model access written in PL/1, FORTRAN, or assembly language	
Allows external data access	
Has been used by General Motors	

Summary

This appendix overviewed thirteen specific DSSs from among the many that have been successfully implemented. These systems were among the earliest DSSs in operation. This brief coverage, which is by no means exhaustive, should give you an idea regarding the actual applications of DSS. For detailed information regarding actual use, consult the references provided for each system.

References

[1] Alter, Steven L. 1980. *Decision Support Systems Current Practice and Continuing Challenges*. Reading, Mass.: Addison-Wesley Publishing Company.

[2] Cooper, D. O., L. B. Davidson, and W. K. Denison. 1975. A Tool for More Effective Financial Analysis. *Interfaces* (February): 91–109.

[3] Haseman, William D. 1977. GPLAN: An Operational DSS. *Data Base* (Winter): 73–78.

[4] Johnson, James. 1976. The Implementation of Computer Assisted Underwriting. *Interfaces* 6, no. 2 (February): 2–13.

[5] Joyce, John D., and N. N. Oliver. 1977. Impacts of a Relational Information System on Industrial Decisions. *Data Base* (Winter): 15–21.

[6] Klass, Richard L. 1977. A DSS For Airline Management. *Data Base* (Winter): 3–8.

[7] Keen, Peter G. W., and Michael S. Scott-Morton. 1978. *Decision Support Systems: An Organizational Perspective*. Reading, Mass.: Addison-Wesley Publishing Company.

[8] Little, John D. C. 1975. BRANDAID: A Marketing-Mix Model, Part 1: Structure. *Operations Research* 23, no. 4, (July-August): 628–55.

[9] Little, John D. C. 1975. BRANDAID: A Marketing-Mix Model, Part 2: Implementation, Calibration, and Case Study. *Operations Research* 23, no. 4 (July-August): 656–73.

[10] Nash, David R. 1977. Building EIS, A Utility for Decisions. *Data Base* (Winter): 43–45.

[11] Pearl, Judea, Antonio Leal, and Joseph Saleh. 1981. "GODDESS: A Goal-Directed Decision Structuring System," Cognitive Systems Laboratory, School of Engineering and Applied Science, UCLA, California (August).

[12] Sprague, Ralph H., Jr., and Eric D. Carlson. 1982. *Building Effective Decision Support Systems*. Englewood Cliffs, N.J.: Prentice-Hall, Inc.

[13] Taplin, Janet M. 1973. AAIMS: American Airlines Answers the What-Ifs. *Infosystems* (February): 40–41.

C DSS Capabilities in Different Disciplines

Introduction

In this appendix a comprehensive survey of literature regarding applications of DSS in diverse disciplines is provided. This list is by no means exhaustive; there are numerous other applications of DSS that are not mentioned. Those areas that have an immediate use for a typical DSS practitioner have been chosen.

As discussed in Chapter 1, DSSs, by utilizing data, models, and user-friendly interfaces, are capable of performing many tasks in diverse disciplines. These applications are:

- What-if analysis
- Goal-seeking analysis
- Sensitivity analysis
- Exception reporting
- General modeling analyses, including optimization, forecasting, simulation, and time series
- Data base management systems and diverse data analysis
- Micro-mainframe linkage

We start this discussion by first providing the results of a survey regarding applications of DSS in different industries. Then we provide a list of over a dozen disciplines that have benefitted from DSS. If you are interested in a particular discipline, consult the reference list provided in each section. When we were conducting this survey, many software packages were discovered that have directly utilized in the disciplines listed. To save space, we decided not to mention and discuss individual software packages. Once again, if you are interested in knowing more about the application and/or the software package, consult the reference list. Disciplines covered include:

Table C-1 ▪ DSS Applications Used By Selected Companies

Company	DDS Use
American Airlines	Price and route selection
American Petrofina	Corporate planning and forecasting
Central and Southwest Corporation	Corporate planning and forecasting
Champlin Petroleum	Corporate planning and forecasting
First United Bank Corporation	Investment evaluation
Frito-Lay, Inc.	Price, advertising and promotion section
General Dynamics	Price evaluation
Gifford-Hill and Company	Corporate planning and forecasting
Lear Petroleum	Evaluation of potential drilling sites
Mercantile Texas Corporation	Corporate planning and forecasting
National Gypsum	Corporate planning and forecasting
Southern Railway	Train dispatching and routing
Texas–New Mexico Power	Corporate planning and forecasting
Texas Oil and Gas Corporation	Evaluation of potential drilling sites
Texas Utilities Company	Corporate planning and forecasting
The LTV Corporation	Terms of sale of downtown office tower
The Western Company	Corporate planning and forecasting
Zale Corporation	Evaluation of potential store sites

Jack T. Hogue and Hugh J. Watson. "Management's Role in the Approval and Administration of Decision Support Systems." *MIS Quarterly* 7, no. 2 (June 1983): 18.

Table C-2 ▪ Manufacturing

Specific Applications	References
Forecasting	[4], [20]
Master scheduling	[37], [38], [14]
Order processing	[13]
Capacity planning	
Shop-floor planning	
Computer-aided design (CAD)	
Computer-aided manufacturing (CAM)	
Computer-integrated manufacturing (CIM)	
Multilevel planning	
Product design	
Resource management	
Forecasting expected delivery date	
New-product planning	
Material requirements planning	
Inventory management	
Dispatching work to workstation	
Capacity control	
Distribution planning analysis	
Robot selection	
Production/sales/inventory (PSI) planning	
Manufacturing/distribution coordination	
Facility location analysis	

Table C-3 ▪ Marketing

Specific Applications	References
Product evaluation	[66], [30], [25], [62]
Pricing	[61], [49], [10], [23]
Sales territory assignment	[16], [17]
Analysis of dealership location	
Advertising analysis	
Media selection	
Salesperson routing	
Marketing research	
Demographic analysis	
Profitability analysis	
Competitive advantage analysis	

continued

Table C-3 ▪ Continued

Specific Applications	References
Product distribution analysis	
Monitoring sales objective analysis	
Market testing and simulation	
Marketing mix (price, promotion, product, place) analyses	
Different statistical analysis for customer and market analyses	
Sales forecasting for new products	
Sensitivity analysis (regarding different promotional activities, advertising budget, and salespeople compensation)	
Distribution-center analysis	

Table C-4 ▪ Accounting and Budgeting

Specific Applications	References
Integrated spreadsheet for budget preparation and analysis	[15], [68], [45], [67] [19], [39]
What-if analysis with budget	
What-if with budget allocation	
Goal-seeking analysis with budget	
Integrated budgeting and forecasting models	
Creation of integrated budget, which includes: Sales Production Purchase Cost of goods sold Direct labor Overhead Operating expenses Cash budget	
DSS in auditing: For staff scheduling to create more harmonic audit team To provide more cost/effective service to clients	
Risk assessment	
Interpreting analytical review results	
Improving financial accounting by using ES/DSS	
Monitoring cost trend	
Monitoring profit trend	

Table C-5 ▪ Purchasing

Specific Applications	References
Vendor-selection system (VSS)	[8], [56]
Cost analysis	
Contract analysis	
Statistical analysis on different vendors, parts, contacts, and so on	
What-if analysis with vendors	
Integrated mixed integer programming (MIP) to: Adjust cost breaks Fixed costs Linkage among commodities and contracts	
Bid analysis	
Material management	

Table C-6 ▪ Finance and Investment

Specific Applications	References
Financial management	[36], [44], [9], [65],
Financial control	[22], [27], [7], [42],
What-if analysis	[48], [32]
Investment analysis	
Risk analysis	
Capital budgeting analysis	
Funds allocation	
Timing of borrowing decisions	
Cash-flow analysis	
Financial projection	
Setting financial objectives	
Portfolio analysis	
Investment structure analysis	

Table C-7 ▪ Sales

Specific Applications	References
Planning new industrial sales	[16], [69], [18], [11],
Controlling new industrial sales	[36]
Sales forecast	

continued

Table C-7 ▪ Continued

Specific Applications	References
Improving communication between the saleperson and the company	
Territory analysis	
Seasonal analysis	
More effective allocation of sales crew	
Price elasticity analysis	
Measuring financial performance	
Measuring the effectiveness of marketing activities such as promotion and advertising	
Sales force analysis	
Sales through electronic mail (teleshopping)	

Table C-8 ▪ Office Automation

Specific Applications	References
Automated filing system	[63], [6], [52]
Time management	
Electronic mail	
Scheduling appointments	
Improving office operations by using integrated DSS to combine: Word processing Electronic mail Message distribution	
Mainframe-micro linkage for office applications	

Table C-9 ▪ Banking

Specific Applications	References
Merger and acquisition analysis	[28], [17], [29], [35], [71]
Integrated electronic funds transfer	
Financial modeling and simulation	
Customer analysis	
Credit analysis	
Geographical service analysis	
Improved customer service by providing exception reporting system	

Specific Applications	References
Improved customer service in investment area by providing dynamic analysis, showing different investment scenarios, and conducting risk analysis	
Marketing-segment analysis	
Cost analysis	
Internal and external data base access	
Mortgage analysis	
Portfolio analysis	
Sensitivity analysis	
What-if analysis	
Check-clearing model	
Interest-rate analysis	

Table C-10 ▪ Insurance

Specific Applications	References
Brokers analysis	[54], [40], [50], [70],
Geographical analysis	[58]
Competition analysis	
Policy analysis	
Agent-compensation analysis	
Budgeting analysis	
Long-range planning	
Claim analysis	
Agent activity model	
Insurance-modeling analysis	
Internal/external data access	
Long-range planning	
Underwriting reports analysis	

Table C-11 ▪ Facility Planning

Specific Applications	References
Computer-aided facilities planning and design	[37], [33], [2]
Factory planning	
Warehouse planning	

continued

Table C-11 ▪ Continued

Specific Applications	References
Office planning	
Laboratory planning	
Computer-aided design (CAD)	
Dynamic simulation via CAD	
Integrated DSS/CAD/MIS systems	
Multistory assignments analysis	
Block layouts analysis	
Geographical analysis for a site	
Population analysis for a site	

Table C-12 ▪ Strategic Planning

Specific Applications	References
Market research	[64], [66], [59]
Competition analysis	
Identification of relevant environment	
Corporate planning	
Long-range marketing planning	
Long-range manufacturing planning	
Long-range financial planning	
Long-range personnel planning	
Prioritizing corporate objectives	
Plant-location analysis	
New-product planning	
Competition analysis	
Market-segment analysis	
Policy analysis	
Merger and acquisition analysis	
Profitability analysis	

Table C-13 ▪ Personnel/Human Resource Management

Specific Applications	References
Recruitment analysis	[51], [45], [1], [3],
Candidate-selection analysis	[39]

Specific Applications	References
Skills inventories	
Work force analysis	
Employee-scheduling analysis	
Job-appraisal analysis	
Compensation analysis	
Markov analysis to show the flow of personnel from period to period	
Goal programming to determine the best way to achieve a set of manpower objectives under a series of constraints	
Job-person assignment models to assign the best person to the most suitable job	
Labor force planning with what-if	
Salary administration with what-if	
Personnel policy and planning	
Training and skill development analysis	
Staff selection, assessment, and evaluation	
Industrial disputes	
Job evaluation	
Attitude surveys	
Resource allocation in personnel department	

Table C-14 ▪ Health Care Management

Specific Applications	References
Hospital administration	[24], [60]
Healthcare-cost analysis and control	
Market and competition analysis	
Various applications of DSS/expert systems for diagnostic purposes	
Physician performance analysis	
Nurse-performance analysis	
Resource allocation	
Improving scheduling of doctors and medical staff	
Budgeting analysis	
Service analysis	
Patient and family structure analysis	
Improving emergency room operation by fast retrieval system	
Medical-staff skills inventory	

References

[1] Algie, Jimmy, and William Foster. 1985. New Aides for Personnel Decision Making. *Management Decision* 23, no. 4: 14–27.

[2] Anonymous. 1982. Decision Support Helps Dominion Choose Store Sites. *Canadian Data Systems* (Canada) 14, no. 10 (October): 85.

[3] Anonymous. 1986. Managing Human Resources with Computers. *Small Business Report* 11 (December): 71 (1).

[4] Ayers, Allan F. 1985. Decision Support Systems — New Tool for Manufacturing. *Computer-World* 19, no. 24A (June 19): 35–38.

[5] Bailey, James E. 1986. Personnel Scheduling with Flexshift: A Win/No Win Scenario. *Personnel* (September): 62–67.

[6] Barnes, Kate. 1983. Integrating MIS and Office Automation: What's Involved. *The Office* (September): 113–16.

[7] Bell, Peter C. 1985. Emerging Technology to Improve Managerial Productivity—Special Supplement: Generating Profit from New Technology, *Business Quarterly* 50 (Winter): 103–08.

[8] Bender, Paul S., Richard W. Brown, Michael H. Isaac, and Jeremy F. Shapiro. 1985. Improving Purchasing Productivity at IBM with a Normative Decision Support System. *Interfaces* (May-June): 106–15.

[9] Brooke, G. M., and N. M. Duffy. 1986. The Use of Financial Modeling in Strategic Planning. *North-Holland Information & Management* 11, no. 1 (August): 13–24.

[10] Brown, Daniel C. 1985. The Anatomy of a Decision Support System: How Abbott Labs Puts DSS to Work for 2,000 Products. *Business Marketing* 70, no. 6 (June): 80–86.

[11] Buchin, Stanley, and Timothy A. Davidson. 1983. Computer-Aided Sales Forecasting: How the Skeptics Can Learn to Love It. *Business Marketing* 68, no. 8 (August): 74–81.

[12] Burrows, B. C. 1986. Computer-Aided Design and Manufacturing—A Manager's Guide. *Long Range Planning* 19 (October): 76–83.

[13] Cartwright, Geoffrey. 1986. Making the Right Decisions in Financial Management Development. *Management Accounting* (UK) 64, no. 10 (November): 41–42 (2).

[14] Chakravarty, Amiya K., and Avraham Shtub. 1985. New Technology Investments in Multistage Production Systems. *Decision Science* (Summer): 248–64.

[15] Chan, Hung, and Bajiis Dodin. 1986. A Decision Support System for Audit-Staff Scheduling with Precedence Constraints and Due Dates. *The Accounting Review* (October): 726–34.

[16] Choffray, Jean, and Gary Lilien. 1986. A Decision—Support System for Evaluating Sales Prospects and Launch Strategies for New Products. *Industrial Marketing Management* 15, no. 1: 75–85.

[17] Coats, Pamela K. 1984. Electronic Funds Transfer Networks: Modeling Their Impact on Bank Service Goals. *Computers & Operations Research* (UK) 11, no. 4: 415–26.

[18] Cravens, David W., and Raymond W. Laforge. 1983. Salesforce Deployment Analysis, *Industrial Marketing Management* 12, no. 3 (July): 179–92.

[19] De Kluyver, Cornelis A., and Edgar A. Pessemier. 1986. Benefits of a Marketing Budgeting Model: Two Case Studies, *Sloan Management Review* 28, no. 1 (Fall): 27–38.

[20] De, Suranjan, Shimon Y. Nof, and Andrew B. Whinston. 1985. Decision Support in Computer-Integrated Manufacturing. *Decision Support System* 1: 37–56.

[21] Despres, Charles J., and Thomas H. Rowley. 1986. Desktop Computing and HRM: A Professional Challenge. *Personnel Administrator* 31 (May): 65–73.

[22] Donath, Bob. 1986. Computer Age Media Selection. *Business Marketing* (April): 118–26.

[23] Edelman, Franz. 1981. Managers, Computer Systems and Productivity. *MIS Quarterly* 5, no. 3: 1–18.

[24] Edwards, Carl N. 1985. Information Management in the Health Industries. *Information Management Review* (Summer): 65–75.

[25] Evans, Steven R., and John P. Norback 1985. The Impact of a DSS for Vehicle Routing in a Foodservice Supply Situation. *Journal of Operation Research Society* 36, no. 6 (June): 467–72.

[26] Filley, Richard D. 1984. A Survey of Software for Facilities Planning & Decision. *Industrial Engineering* 16, no. 5 (May): 71–79.

[27] Frank, Jonathan, and Jacques Schnabel. 1983. Timing of Borrowing Decisions—A Decision Support System. *Journal of Systems Management* (April): 6–9.

[28] Gillis, Arthur M. 1985. The Micro's Proper Place in Banking. *NABW Journal* 61, no. 2 (January/February): 19–23.

[29] Goldberg, Joan B. 1984. RB3 Boosts Personal Selling, Enhances Bank's 'Pro' Image. *Bank Systems & Equipment* 21, no. 4 (April): 72–73.

[30] Goslar, Martin D., and Stephen W. Brown. 1986. DSS: Advantages in Consumer Market Settings. *Journal of Consumer Marketing* 3, no. 3 (Summer): 43–50.

[31] Gremillion, Lee L., and Philip J. Pyburn. 1985. Justifying Decision Support and Office Automation Systems. *Journal of Management Information Systems* 2, no. 1 (Summer): 5–17.

[32] Guisseppi, Forgionne A. 1986. Effective Resource Allocation Through Decision Support Systems. *Journal of Systems Management* (December): 26–31.

[33] Hales, Lee H. 1984. Computerized Facilities Planning and Design: Sorting Out the Options. *Industrial Engineering* 16, no. 5 (May): 60–70.

[34] Harris, Donald. 1986. Beyond the Basics: New HRIS Developments. *Personnel* (January): 49–56.

[35] Horn, Sheri. 1984. Managers Analyze Data with DSS, Make Future Planning Decisions. *Bank Systems & Equipment* 21, no. 4 (April): 66–69.

[36] Hughes, David G. 1983. Computerized Sales Management. *Harvard Business Review* 61, no. 2 (March-April): 102–12.

[37] Hurrion, Robert D. 1985. Implementation of a Visual Interactive Consensus Decision Support System. *European Journal of Operational Research* 20: 138–44.

[38] Jones, Marilyn S., Charles J. Malmborg, and Marvin H. Agee. 1985. Decision Support System Use for Robot Selection. *Industrial Engineering* (September): 66–73.

[39] Juris, Robbin. 1986. Managing Human Resources Online. *Computer Decisions* 18 (January 14): 44 (5).

[40] Justice, Karen. 1982. Electronic Decisions for Bankers. *Interface: Banking Industry* 7, no. 4 (Winter): 6.

[41] Keith, Dale. 1986. A Decision Support System for New Technologies. *Public Utility Fortnightly* (December): 21–25.

[42] Khan, Feroze, and John Morrison. 1985. Financial Modeling for Decision Makers: Opening a Window on the Future? *CA Magazine* 118 (September): 28–35.

[43] Kleeman, Michael J. 1987. Data Communication—Not Perfect But Better Here Than Elsewhere and Due to Improve. *Administrative Management* 48 (January): 58–60.

[44] Leary, Edward J. 1985. Decision Support Systems Aid in Management of Operations, Resources and Finances. *Industrial Engineering* (September): 26–34.

[45] Lederer, Albert L. 1984. Information Technology: 1. Planning and Developing a Human Resources Information System. *Personnel* (May-June): 14–27.

[46] Livingston, David. 1985. A System to Grow With. *Datamation* 31, no. 19 (October 1): 89 (8).

[47] Main, Liz. 1986. Decision Support Systems: Help for Tough Decisions. *ICP Insurance Software* 11, no. 1 (Spring): 12.

[48] Main, Liz. 1986. Think Big! How Business Planning Systems Can Help You Grow. *Business Software Review* 5, no. 3 (March): 34–36.

[49] Mallinson, Don. 1984. How DEC Sells Computers with Computers. *Business Marketing* 69, no. 10 (October): 162–66.

[50] Mann, Ned. 1984. The Manager Prototype. *Managers Magazine* 59, no. 8 (August): 22–26.

[51] Manos, Susan. 1987. Human Resource Decisions—Better Evaluations, More Computerization. *Data Management* 25 (February): 32–33.

[52] McCallum, John C. 1982. Computers in the Office of the Future. *Optimum* 13-4: 63–81.

[53] Menou, Michel J. 1985. An Information System for Decision Support in National Information Policy-making and Planning. *Information Processing & Management* 21, no. 4: 321–61.

[54] Mercer, Alan. 1985. A Decision Support System for Insurance Marketing. *European Journal of Operational Research*, pp. 10–16.

[55] Minch, Robert P., and G. Lawrence Sanders. 1986. Computerized Information Systems Supporting Multicriteria Decision Making. *Decision Sciences* 17 (Summer): 395–411.

[56] Monezka, Robert M. 1984. User Friendly Software Now Available for Purchasing. *Purchasing World* (October): 70–71.

[57] Mulvihill, Lee P. 1983. Creating the Rosetta Stone. *Best's Review (Life/Health)* 84, no. 1 (May): 47.

[58] Pyatt, Gary R. 1984. Management Information Systems. *Journal of Information Management* 5, no. 2 (Winter): 9–14.

[59] Raimondi, Donna. 1984. Strategic Planning Eases Southwestern Bell Transition. *Computerworld* 18, no. 40 (October 1): 14.

[60] Rash, Robert M. 1986. Decision Support or Support Decision? *Computers in Health Care* (April): 24–26.

[61] Reiling, Lynn G. 1984. System Organizes Marketing Data to Aid Executives' Decision-Making. *Marketing News* 18, no. 24 (November): 2.

[62] Rosenfeld, Judith. 1984. Ready. . .Aim. . .Computer! *Marketing Communications* 9, no. 12 (December): 35–40, 66.

[63] Sachs, Randi T. 1984. A Manager's Guide to OA User Groups. *Office Administration and Automation* 45 (March): 38–39, 48–50.

[64] Schultz, David I. 1986. Strategic Information Systems Planning Sharpens Competitive Edge. *Data Management* (June): 20–29.

[65] Sena, James, and Murphy Smith. 1987. The Controller's Computerized Workstation. *Journal of Accounting and EDP* (Winter): 4–12.

[66] Simith, Douglas, et al. 1985. Decision Support for Marketing Research and Corporate Planning. *North-Holland Information & Management* 8, no. 3 (March): 133–45.

[67] Smith, Russell W. 1985. Resource Programming in Large Organizations. *The Bureaucrat* 14, no. 2 (Summer): 49–58 (5).

[68] Stoner, Greg. 1985. Expert Systems: Jargon or Challenge? *Accountancy* (February): 142–45.

[69] Taylor, Thayer C. 1984. Honeywell's Computer Makes Managers Out of Salespeople. *Sales and Marketing Management* 132, no. 7 (May 14): 59–61.

[70] Viste, Gerald D. 1984. Making Decisions Are a Snap Because of DSS at Warsaw Insurance. *Data Management* 22, no. 6 (June): 22–24.

[71] Weaver, William C., and Joseph D. Albert. 1984. Support for Pricing Decisions—Part II. *Mortgage Banking* 44, no. 7 (April): 73–82.

[72] Wilkinson, Joseph W. 1984. Financial Modeling Within Distributed Systems. *Journal of Systems Management* 35 (March): 33–37.

D Comprehensive Bibliography on DSS

This appendix provides a comprehensive and updated bibliography on Decision Support Systems and their related technology. The bibliography includes articles on DSS foundation, applications, microcomputer-based DSS, executive information systems, artificial intelligence and expert systems. This collection includes both classic and contemporary articles on DSS.

Abdolohammadi, Mohammad J. 1987. Decision Support and Expert Systems in Auditing: A Review and Research Directions. *Accounting & Business Research* (UK) 17, no. 66 (Spring): 173–85.

Akers, Michael D., Grover Porter, Edward J. Blogher, and William G. Mister. 1986. Expert Systems for Management Accountants. *Management Accounting* 67, no. 9 (May): 30–34.

Akoka, J. 1981. A Framework for Decision Support System Evaluation. *Information and Management* 4, (July): 133–41.

Alavi, M., and J. C. Henderson. 1981. Evolutionary Strategy for Implementing a Decision Support System. *Management Science* 27, no. 11 (November): 113–21.

Alexander, David J. 1986. Planning and Building a DSS. *Datamation* 32, no. 6 (March 15): 115–21.

Anderson, Evan E. 1985. Managerial Considerations in Participative Design of MIS/DSS. *Information and Management* (Netherlands) 9, no. 4 (November): 201–07.

Anonymous. 1988. Move to Intelligent Work-Stations. *Banking World* (UK) 6, no. 2 (February): 42.

Anonymous. 1987. Executive Systems: Corner Office Computing Heats Up. *Business Software Review* 6, no. 9 (September): 16–17.

Anonymous. 1987. Executive Information Systems. *EDP Analyzer* 25, no. 4 (April): 1–11.

Anonymous. 1987. Group Decision Support Systems. *EDP Analyzer* 25, no. 1 (January): 1–11.

Athappilly, Kuriakose. 1985. Successful Decision Making Starts with DSS Evaluation. *Data Management* 23, no. 2 (February): 24–28.

Ayati, M. B. 1987. A Unified Perspective on Decision Making and Decision Support Systems. *Information Processing & Management* 23, no. 6: 615–28.

Badiru, Adedeji. 1988. Expert Systems and Industrial Engineers: A Practical Guide to a Successful Partnership. *Computers & Industrial Engineering* 14, no. 1: 1–13.

Bahl, H. C., and R. G. Hunt. 1984. Decision Making Theory and DSS Design. *Data Base* 15, no. 4 (Summer): 12–19.

Bailey, Andrew D., Jr., Rayman Meservy, and Joanne H. Turner. 1986. Decision Support Systems, Expert Systems and Artificial Intelligence: Realities and Possibilities in Public Accounting. *Ohio CPA Journal* 45, no. 2 (Spring): 11–15.

Baird, Patricia J., and Thomas J. Kazamek. 1988. Moving to Micro-Based Cost Accounting. *Computers in Healthcare* 9, no. 3 (March): 29–31.

Barbera, Anthony T. 1987. Artificial Intelligence in Accounting: The Future Has Arrived. *Review of Business* 9, no. 2 (Fall): 17–21.

Barki, Henri, and Sid L. Huff. 1984. Change, Attitude to Change, and Decision Support System Success. *Information and Management* (Netherlands) 9, no. 5 (December): 261–68.

Barrow, Craig. 1988. Executive Information Systems: Automating the CRO Function. *Bank Administration* 64, no. 5 (May): 52, 54.

Basu, Amit. 1986. Computer Based Support of Reasoning in the Presence of Fuzziness. *Decision Support Systems* (Netherlands) 2, no. 3, (September): 235–56.

Benbasat, I., and A. S. Dexter. 1982. Individual Differences in the Use of Decision Support Aids. *Journal of Accounting Research* 20, (Spring): 1–11.

Benbasat, I., and R. N. Taylor. 1978. The Impact of Cognitive Styles on Information Systems Design. *MIS Quarterly* 2, no. 2 (June): 43–54.

Bernstein, Amy. 1985. Decision Support Graphics Draw a Better Bottom Line. *Business Computer Systems* 4, no. 8 (August): 38–48.

Blanning, Robert W. 1987. Sensitivity Analysis in Logic-Based Models. *Decision Support Systems* (Netherlands) 3, no. 4 (December): 343–49.

Blanning, Robert W. 1987. The Application of Metaknowledge to Information Management. *Human Systems Management* (Netherlands) 7, no. 1: 49–57.

Blanning, Robert W. 1984. Management Applications of Expert Systems. *Information and Management* (Netherlands) 7, no. 6 (December): 311–16.

Blanning, Robert W. 1985. A Relational Framework for Joint Implementation in Model Management Systems. *Decision Support Systems* (Netherlands) 1, no. 1 (January): 69–81.

Blanning, R. W. 1984. What is Happening in DSS? *Interfaces* 13, no. 5 (October): 71–80.

Bonczek, R. H., C. W. Holsapple, and A. B. Whinston. 1980. The Evolving Roles of Models in Decision Support Systems. *Decision Sciences* 11, no. 2 (April): 337–56.

Bonczek, R. H., C. W. Holsapple, and A. B. Whinston. 1980. Future Directions for Developing Decision Support Systems. *Decision Sciences* 11, no. 4 (October): 616–31.

Braun, Helmut. 1987. Predicting Stock Market Behavior Through Rule Induction: An Application of the Learning-from-Example Approach. *Decision Sciences* 18, no. 3 (Summer): 415–29.

Briggs, Warren. 1985. Software Tools for Planning: DSS and AI/Expert System. *Planning Review* 13, no. 5 (September): 36–43.

Brightman, H. 1978. Differences in Ill-Structured Problem Solving Along the Organizational Hierarchy. *Decision Sciences* 9, no. 1 (January): 1–18.

Brody, Herb. 1988. Computers Invade the Executive Suite. *High Technology Business* 8, no. 2 (February): 41–45.

Brown, Daniel C. 1985. The Anatomy of a Decision Support System: How Abbott Labs Puts DSS to Work For 2000 Products. *Business Marketing* 70, no. 6 (June): 80–86.

Bullers, William I. 1987. Management Systems: Four Options, One Solution. *Journal of Information Systems Management* 4, no. 2 (Spring): 54–62.

Burd, Stephen D. 1987. Logic-Based Decision Support for Computer Capacity Planning. *Information & Management* (Netherlands) 13, no. 3 (October): 125–33.

Bush, Chandler M., and W. Douglas Cooper. 1988. Inventory Level Decision Support. *Production & Inventory Management* 29, no. 1 (First Quarter): 69–73.

Calantone, Roger J., and Michael H. Morris. 1985, The Utilization of Computer-Based Decision Support Systems in Transportation. *International Journal of Physical Distribution and Materials Management* (UK) 15, no. 7: 5–18.

Camillus, John C. and Albert L. Lederer. 1985. Corporate Strategy and The Design of Computerized Information Systems. *Sloan Management Review* 26, no. 3 (Spring): 35–42.

Canada, John R., and George L. Hodge. 1988. Microcomputer Software Costing Less than $1000 for Economic and Multi-Attribute Decision Analysis. *Engineering Economist* 33, no. 2 (Winter): 130–44.

Canning, R. G. 1976. APL and Decision Support Systems. *EDP Analyzer* 14, no. 5 (May): 1–12.

Canning, R. G. 1984. What's Happening with DSS. *EDP Analyzer* 22, no. 7 (July): 1–12.

Canning, R. G. 1984. Interesting Decision Support Systems. *EDP Analyzer* 20, no. 3 (March): 1–12.

Carlis, J. V., G. W. Dickson, and S. T. March. 1983. Physical Database Design: A DSS Approach. *Information and Management* 6, (August): 211–24.

Carlsson, Christer. 1985. Decision Support Systems - Dawn or Twilight for Management Science? *Human Systems Management* (Netherlands) 5, no. 1 (Spring): 29–38.

Casey, David. 1987. EIS: Turning a Toy into a Tool. *Euromoney* (UK) Information Technology Supplement (August): 47–48.

Chakravarthy, Bala, Worth Loomis, and John Vrabel. 1988. Dexter Corporation's Value-Based Strategic Planning System. *Planning Review* 16, no. 1 (January-February): 34–41.

Chen, Michael C. and Lawrence J. Henschen. (1985). On the Use and Internal Structure of Logic-Based Decision Support Systems. *Decision Support Systems* (Netherlands) 1, no. 3 (September): 205-19.

Choffray, Jean Marie and Gary L. Lilien. 1986. A Decision-Support System for Evaluating Sales Prospects and Launch Strategies for New Products. *Industrial Marketing Management* 15, no. 1 (February): 75–85.

Conlon, Grace. 1988. Computers Can't Be Intelligent Without the Right Data Base. *Marketing News* 22, no. 6 (March 14): 42.

Cooper, Randolph B. 1988. Review of Management Information Systems Research: A Management Support Emphasis. *Information Processing & Management* (UK) 24, no. 1: 73–102.

Coor, Robert M. 1988. Successful EIS Implementations Require Commitment from Top Management. *InfoWorld* 10, no. 6 (February 8): 39.

Courtney, James F., Jr., David B. Paradice, and Nassar H. Ata Mohammed. 1987. A Knowledge-Based DSS for Managerial Problem Diagnosis. *Decision Sciences* 18, no. 3 (Summer): 373–99.

Cowan, William M. 1985. Business Graphics Add New Dimension to Decision Support. *Office Administration and Automation* 46, no. 4 (April): 32–35, 66.

Cullum, R. L. 1985. Iterative Development. *Datamation* 31 (February): 92–98.

Cunningham, Lloyd, Lynn Heinrich, and Joanna Hoit. 1985. Developing a Database Management System for Decision Support. *Computers in Healthcare* 6, no. 8 (August): 34–36.

Dauphinais, G. William. (1987). The Information Drought in the Executive Suite. *Price Waterhouse Review* 31, no. 1: 40–47.

Davis, Michael and Joseph L. Sardinas, Jr. 1985. Management Information Systems: Creating the Right Decision Support System. *Management Accounting* 66, no. 11 (May): 10, 15, 17.

Davis, Michael and Joseph L. Sardinas, Jr. 1985. Creating the Right Decision Support System - Pitfalls. *Management Accounting* 66, no. 12 (June): 12, 69.

De, P., and A. Sen. 1981. Logical Data Base Design in Decision Support Systems. *Journal of Systems Management* 32 (May): 28–33.

Dery, David and Theodore J. Mock. 1985. Information Support Systems for Problem Solving. *Decision Support Systems* (Netherlands) 1, no. 2 (April): 103-9.

DeSanctis, Gerardine, and R. Brent Gallupe. 1987. A Foundation for the Study of Group Decision Support Systems. *Management Science* 33, no. 5 (May): 589–609.

Dick, John R. 1986. Automating Your Chairman . . . The Theory of System Support for Executives/Putting Theory to the Test: Executive Use of Personal Computers at UVB. *Magazine of Bank Administration* 62, no. 7 (July): 36–38.

Dos Santos, Brian L., and Martin L. Bariff. 1988. A Study of User Interface Aids for Model-Oriented Decision Support Systems. *Management Science* 34, no. 4 (April): 461–58.

Eblen, Pamela L. 1986. Tough Decisions Get Easier. *ICP Banking Software* 11, no. 1 (Spring): 11.

Eblen, Pamela L., Marilyn Gasaway, Louis W. Harm, Liz Main, and Sharon Gamble Rae. 1986. *Business Software Review* 5, no. 1 (January): 29–59.

Economides, Spyros and Mark Colen. 1985. Microcomputer-Based Decision Support Systems Aid Managers in Evaluating Alternatives. *Industrial Engineering* 17, no. 9 (September): 44–51.

Eiger, Amir, Johnathan M. Jacobs, Donald B. Chung, and James L. Selsor. 1988. The U.S. Army's Occupational Specialty Manpower Decision Support System. *Interfaces* 18, no. 1 (January/February): 57–73.

Elam, Joyce J., and Benn Konsynski. 1987. Using Artificial Intelligence Techniques to Enhance the Capabilities of Model Management Systems. *Decision Sciences* 18, no. 3 (Summer): 487–02.

Elam, J. J., and J. C. Henderson. 1983. Knowledge Engineering Concepts for Decision Support Design and Implementation. *Information and Management* 6, no. 2 (April): 109–14.

Eliot, Lance B. 1987. Information Management and Expert Systems: A Pedagogical Approach. *Information Management Review* 2, no. 3 (Winter): 63–69.

Elson, John L. 1985. Policy and Procedure Program Is a Support System for Executive Decision Making. *Industrial Engineering* 17, no. 9 (1985): 36–42.

Erickson, D. C. 1984. A Synopsis of Present Day Practices Concerning Decision Support Systems. *Information and Management* 7, (October): 243–52.

Fedorowicz, Jane, and Gerald B. Williams. 1986. Representing Modeling Knowledge in an Intelligent Decision Support System. *Decision Support Systems* (Netherlands) 2, no. 1 (March): 3–14.

Firdman, Henry Eric. 1986. Choice of Technology Guides Thrust of Expert System Effort. *Computerworld* 20, no. 2 (January 13): 50–56.

Ford, F. Nelson. 1985. Decision Support Systems and Expert Systems: A Comparison. *Information Management* (Netherlands) 8, no. 1 (January): 21–26.

Forgionne, Giusseppi A. 1988. Building Effective Decision Support Systems. *Business* 38, no. 1 (January/February/March): 19–30.

Forman, Ernest H. 1985. Decision Support for Executive Decision Makers. *Information Strategy: The Executive Journal* 1, no. 4 (Summer): 4–14.

Franz, L. S., S. M. Lee, and J. C. Van Horn. 1981. An Adaptive Decision Support System for Academic Resource Planning. *Decision Sciences* 12, no. 2 (April): 276–93.

Fredericks, Peter, and N. Venkatraman. 1988. The Rise of Strategy Support Systems. *Sloan Management Review* 29, no. 3 (Spring): 47–54.

Friend, David. 1986. Are Information Systems Your Friend or Foe? *Chief Executive*, no. 36 (Summer): 26–27.

Gantz, John. 1987. Office Automation and DP: A 40-Year Side Trip. *Telecommunication Products & Technology* 5, no. 11 (November): 54–55.

Garelick, Howard. 1987. Executive Information Systems: Marketing Hype or Invaluable Management Aid? *Industrial Management & Data Systems* (UK) (March/April): 20–22.

Garfinkel, David. 1985. The New Generation of Software That Helps Managers Make Decisions. *International Management (UK) 40, no. 8 (Europe Edition) (August): 49–51.*

Garsombke, H. Perrin, and Larry M. Parker. 1987. Decision Support Systems and Expert Systems: Auditing in the Information Age. *Journal of Accounting & EDP* 2, no. 4 (Winter): 20–25.

Gertosio, Christine. 1988. A Decision Support System for Wine-Making Cooperatives. *European Journal of Operational Research* (Netherlands) 33, no. 3 (February): 273–278.

Gilbert, G. Nigel. 1988. The Alvey DHSS Demonstrator Project: Applying Intelligent Knowledge-Based Systems to Social Security. *Information Age* (UK) 11, no. 2 (April): 113–115.

Goldman, Tamara. 1988. PCs Help Marketers Enter Info Loop. *Marketing Communications* 13, no. 2 (February): 30–31.

Gorry, G. A., and M. S. Scott Morton. 1971. A Framework for Management Information Systems. *Sloan Management Review* 13, no. 1 (Fall): 55–70.

Goslar, Martin D. and Stephen W. Brown. 1986. Decision Support Systems: Advantages in Consumer Marketing Settings. *Journal of Consumer Marketing* 3, no. 3 (Summer): 43–50.

Goul, Michael. 1987. On Building Expert Systems for Strategic Planners: A Knowledge Engineer's Experience. *Information & Management* (Netherlands) 12, no. 3 (March): 131–141.

Hara, Jacques E. 1987. Operations Support Systems in the 1990s. *Telecommunications* 21, no. 8 (North American Edition) (August): 64–67.

Harris, Donald. 1986. Beyond the Basics: New HRIS Developments. *Personnel* 63, no. 1 (January): 49–56.

Haskell, Robert E. 1987. Decision Support Systems: The Next Step. *Topics in Health Care Financing* 14, no. 2 (Winter): 42–51.

Heap, John. 1985. Management Information Systems and Their Impact on Productivity. *Management Services* (UK) 29, no. 3 (March): 14–17.

Henderson, John C. 1987. Finding Synergy Between Decision Support Systems and Expert Systems Research. *Decision Sciences* 18, no. 3 (Summer): 333–49.

Henderson, John C. and David A. Schilling. 1985. Design and Implementation of Decision Support Systems in the Public Sector. *MIS Quarterly* 9, no. 2 (June): 157–69.

Hill, John B. and William A. Wallace. 1985. Decision Support in a Guaranteed Student Loan Program: Design and Implementation of a Model-Based System. *Information and Management* (Netherlands) 9, no. 4 (November): 215–25.

Hogue, Jack T. and Hugh J. Watson. 1985. An Examination of Decision Makers' Utilization of Decision Support System Output. *Information Management* (Netherlands) 8, no. 4 (April): 205–12.

Holsapple, Clyde W. and Andrew B. Whinston. 1985. Management Support Through Artificial Intelligence. *Human Systems Management* (Netherlands) 5, no. 2: 163–71.

Hruschka, Harald. 1988. Use of Fuzzy Relations in Rule-Based Decision Support Systems for Business Planning Problems. *European Journal of Operational Research* (Netherlands) 34, no. 3 (March): 326–35.

Hunter, Bob. (1988). A Bigger "What-If." *Systems/3X World* 16, no. 3 (March): 74–78.

Inmon, William. 1986. Building the Best Database. *Computerworld* 20, no. 27A (July 9): 73–75.

Janson, Marius A. and L. Douglas Smith. 1985. Prototyping for Systems Development: A Critical Appraisal. *MIS Quarterly* 9, no. 4 (December): 305–16.

Jelassi, M. Tawfik, Karen Williams, and Christine S. Fidler. 1987. The Emerging Role of DSS: From Passive to Active. *Decision Support Systems* (Netherlands) 3, no. 4 (December): 299–307.

Jelassi, M. Tawfik, and Renee A. Beauclair. 1987. An Integrated Framework for Group Decision Support Systems Design. *Information & Management* 13, no. 3 (October): 143–53.

Jones, Jack Williams and Raymond McLeod, Jr. 1986. The Structure of Executive Information Systems: An Exploratory Analysis. *Decision Sciences* 17, no. 2 (Spring): 220–49.

Jones, Kirk. 1987. "Intelligent" Computers for Business Needs. *Financial Executive* 3, no. 5 (September/October): 13–15.

Jordan, Mary Lou. 1988. Executive Information Systems Make Life Easy for the Lucky Few. *Computerworld* 22, no. 9 (February 29): 51, 55–57.

Karten, Naomi. 1987. Executive Info Systems: But Do They Inform? *Canadian Datasystems* (Canada) 19, no. 6 (June): 74–75.

Keen, Peter G. W. 1987. Decision Support Systems: The Next Decade. *Decision Support Systems* (Netherlands) 3, no. 3 (September): 253–65.

Keen, P. G. W. and G. R. Wagner. 1980. DSS: An Executive Mind-Support System. *Datamation* 25, no. 12 (March): 117–22.

Kersten, Gregory E. 1987. On Two Roles Decision Support Systems Can Play in Negotiations. *Information Processing & Management* (UK) 23, no. 6: 605–14.

Klein, Heinz K. and Rudolf A. Hirschheim. 1985. Fundamental Issues of Decision Support Systems: A Consequentialist Perspective. *Decision Support Systems* (Netherlands) 1, no. 1 (January): 5–23.

Klein, Michel R. and Florence Klein-Estrabaud. 1985. A Decision Support System for Production and Financial Planning in a Tannery. *Engineering Costs & Productions Economics* (Netherlands) 9, no. 1–3 (April): 239–47.

Kosaka, T., and T. Hirouchi. 1982. An Effective Architecture for Decision Support Systems. *Information and Management* 5, (March): 7–17.

Kull, David. 1985. Executives Tap Into Support Systems. *Computer Decisions* 17, no. 25 (December 17): 38–46, 83.

Kull, David. 1986. Decision Support With 20/20 Foresight. *Computer Decisions* 18, no. 10 (May 6): 38–43.

Lamberti, Donna M., and William A. Wallace. 1987. Presenting Uncertainty in Expert Systems: An Issue in Information Portrayal. *Information & Management* (Netherlands) 13, no. 4 159–69.

Langendorf, Richard. 1985. Computers and Decision Making. *Journal of the American Planning Association* 51, no. 4 (Autumn): 422–33.

Larreche, J. and V. Srinivasan. 1981. STRATPORT: A Decision Support System for Strategic Planning. *Journal of Marketing* 45 (Fall): 39–52.

Lauer, Joachim, and David M. Stettler. 1987. New Directions for Information Centers. *Journal of Systems Management* 38, no. 10 (October): 6–11.

Law, Curt. 1988. Financial Modeling: Are Execs Ready for Encore Plus? *Business Software Review* 7, no. 2 (February): 6-7.

Leary, Edward J. 1985. Decision Support Systems: A Look at Hardware, Software, and Planning Procedures. *Industrial Engineering* 17, no. 10 (October): 82–94.

Leary, Edward J. 1985. Decision Support Systems Aid in Management of Operations, Resources, and Finances-Part I. *Industrial Engineering* 17, no. 9 (September): 26–34.

Lehman, John A. 1986. Microcomputer Use of Mainframe Databases. *Journal of Systems Management* 37, no. 1 (January): 18–22.

Lewis, L. Floyd. 1987. A Decision Support System for Face-to-Face Groups. *Journal of Information Science Principles & Practice* (Netherlands) 13, no. 4: 211–19.

Liang, Ting-peng, and Christopher V. Jones. 1988. Meta-Design Considerations in Developing Model Management Systems. *Decision Sciences* 19, no. 1 (Winter): 72–92.

Liang, Ting-peng. 1985. Integrating Model Mangement with Data Management In Decision Support Systems. *Decision Support Systems* (Netherlands) 1, no. 3 (September): 221–32.

Long, Robert H. 1986. Procedural vs. Intelligent Decision Systems. *United States Banker* 97, no. 8 (August): 68.

Lopes, Peter F., and John F. Cingari. 1988. Expert Systems Key to Decision Support. *Manufacturing Systems* 6, no. 4 (April): 58–61.

Luconi, Fred L., Thomas W. Malone, and Scott Morton, Michaels. 1986. Expert Systems: The Next Challenge for Managers. *Sloan Management Review* 27, no. 4 (Summer): 3–14.

Mackay, Alex. 1985. DSS Concept is Often Misunderstood. *Computing Canada* (Canada) 11, no. 13 (June 27): Software Report 6–7.

Madey, G. R., M. H. Wolfe, and J. Potter. 1987. Development of an Expert Investment Strategy System for Aerospace RD&E and Production Contract Bidding. *IEEE Transactions on Engineering Management* EM-34, no. 4 (November): 252–58.

Madlin, Nancy. 1986. Executive Information Systems. *Management Review* 75, no. 8 (August): 21–22.

Magnusson, Cecilia. 1988. Introducing Knowledge-Based Systems in the Swedish Social Insurance Organization. *Information Age* (UK) 11, no. 2 (April): 103–06.

Mahmood, Mo A. and Jeanette N. Medewitz. 1985. Impact of Design Methods on Decision Support Systems Success: An Empirical Assessment. *Information & Management* (Netherlands) 9, no. 3 (October): 137-51.

Major, Michael J. 1987. Microsoftware Trends. *Business Software Review* 6, no. 1 (January): 33–35.

Main, Liz. 1986. Decision Support Systems: Help for Tough Decisions. *ICP Insurance Software* 11, no. 1 (Spring): 12.

McLaughlin, Hugh S., and Timothy G. Sullivan. 1988. Recent Spreadsheet Innovations: Expansion Paths from Lotus 1-2-3. *Journal of Accounting & EDP* 4, no. 1 (Spring): 8–17.

Meador, C. Lawrence, Martin J. Guyote, and William Rosenfeld. 1986. Decision Support Planning and Analysis: The Problems of Getting Large Scale DSS Started. *MIS Quarterly* 10, no. 2 (June): 159–77.

Meador, C. Lawrence, Peter G. W. Keen, and Martin J. Guyote. 1984. Personal Computers and Distributed Decision Support. *Computerworld* 18, no. 19 (May 7): 7–16.

Menkus, Beldon. 1987. Latest Productivity Buzzword: It's Executive Management System (EIS). *Business Month* 129, no. 3 (March): 64–75.

Mercer, Alan. 1985. A Decision Support System for Insurance Marketing. *European Journal of Operational Research* (Netherlands) 20, no. 1 (April): 10–16.

Milter, Richard G. and John Rohrbaugh. 1985. Microcomputers and Stategic Decision Making. *Public Productivity Review* 9, nos. 2 and 3 (Summer/Fall): 175–89.

Moad, Jeff. 1988. The Latest Challenge for IS Is the Executive Suite. *Datamation* 34, no. 10 (May 15): 43–52.

Monk, J. Thomas, and Kenneth M. Landis. 1988. Decision Support Systems Move Treasurers Beyond Flipping a Coin. *Cash Flow* 9, no. 5 (May): 56–57.

Moody, H. Gerald. 1988. Emerging Technologies: Decisions, Decisions. *Information Strategy: The Executive's Journal* 4, no. 2 (Winter): 43–46.

Morris, Richard M., III. 1986. Management Control and Decision Support Systems—An Overview. *Industrial Management* 28, no. 1 (January/February): 8–15.

Moser, Jorge, and Richard Christoph. 1987. Management Expert Systems (M.E.S.): A Framework for Development and Implementation. *Information Processing & Management* (UK) 23, no. 1: 17–23.

Meyers, Edith. 1988. EIS Provides Critical Details—Without Paper. *Administrative Management* 49, no. 2 (March): 23–26.

Myers, Edith. 1986. Expert Systems—Not For Everyone. *Datamation* 32, no. 10 (May 15): 28, 32.

Needle, David. 1985. Deciding About Decision Support. *Personal Computing* 9, no. 6 (June): 85–91.

Nestman, Chadwick H. and John C. Windson. 1985. Decision Support Systems: A Perspective for Industrial Engineers. *IIE Transaction* 17, no. 1 (March): 38–46.

Newquist, Harvey P. III. 1986. Expert Systems: The Promise of a Smart Machine. *Computerworld* 20, no. 2 (January 13): 43–46, 51–57.

Newsome, Michael. 1986. Micros Need Mainframes for DSS. *Computing Canada* 12, no. 5 (March 6): 22–23.

Ntuen, Celestine A, and Arup K. Mallik. 1987. Applying Artificial Intelligence to Project Cost Estimating. *Cost Engineering* 29, no. 5 (May): 8–13.

Ntuen, Celestine A. 1986. The Seven "R" Paradigms: What Managers Should Know About Decision Support Systems. *Industrial Management* 28, no. 1 (January/February): 19–21.

Nute, Donald. 1988. Defeasible Reasoning and Decision Support Systems. *Decision Support Systems* (Netherlands) 4, no. 1 (March): 97–110.

O'Leary, Daniel E. 1987. Validation of Expert Systems—With Applications to Auditing and Accounting Expert Systems. *Decision Sciences* 18, no. 3 (Summer): 468–86.

Ow, Peng Si, and Stephen F. Smith. 1987. Two Design Principles for Knowledge-Based Systems. *Decision Sciences* 18, no. 3 (Summer): 430–47.

Pajor, Wladyslaw. 1986. DSS Integrates Computer Net. *Canadian Datasystems* 18, no. 5 (May): 83–84.

Paller, Alan. 1988. Business Graphics Are Ready for a New Move. *Canadian Datasystems* 20, no. 3 (March): 32–35.

Paller, Alan. 1987. Getting Started with Executive Information Systems. *EDP Analyzer* 25, no. 1 (January): 13–14.

Patterson, William Pat, and John Teresko. 1988. Managing in the '90s: New Tools. *Industry Week* 236, no. 8 (April 18): 61, 67–68.

Pottruck, David S. 1988. Strategic Information Systems Ignite Successful Offensives. *Bank Marketing* 20, no. 5 (May): 32–42.

Puzzanghera, Paul. 1984. Micro Users Looking for Mainframe Power. *Computerworld* 18, no. 18 (April 30): Special Report 56.

Rash, Robert M. 1986. Decision Support or Support Decision? *Computers in Health Care* 7, no. 4 (April): 24–26.

Reid, Ian. 1986. Artificial Intelligence in the Market. *Banker* (UK) 136, no. 724 (June): 73, 76.

Reimann, Bernard C. 1988. Decision Support Software for Value-Based Planning. *Planning Review* 16, no. 2 (March/April): 22–32.

Reimann, Bernard C. 1985. Decision Support Systems: Strategic Management Tools for the Eighties. *Business Horizons* 28, no. 5 (September/October): 71–77.

Reimann, Bernard C. 1985. Decision Support for Planners: How to Pick the Right DSS Generator Software. *Managerial Planning* 33, no. 6 (May/June): 22–26, 60.

Robin, Michael. 1988. The Evolution of Management Accounting Systems at Chase Manhattan Bank. *Journal of Accounting & EDP* 3, no. 4 (Winter): 15–29.

Rockhart, John, and David De Long. 1988. ESS Shakes Up the System. *Computerworld* 22, no. 9 (February 29): 58.

Samples, James E. and Cyrus C. Wilson. 1985. How Senior Management Can Cash in on the Information Revolution. *Retail Control* 53, no. 8 (April/May): 22–31.

Sanders, G. Lawrence and James F. Courtney. 1985. A Field Study of Organizational Factors Influencing DSS Success. *MIS Quarterly* 9, no. 1 (March): 77–93.

Sanders, L. C., J. F. Courtney, and S. L. Loy. 1984. The Impact of DSS on Organizational Communication. *Information and Management* 7 (June): 141–48.

Sankar, C. S. 1986. Integrating Information System In Bank Administration. *Information Management Review* 2, no. 1 (Summer): 37–47.

Sargent, John S. 1988. Downloading for Credit Decision Support. *Business Credit* 90, no. 1 (January): 33–36.

Saxena, K. B. C. and Mohar Kaul. 1986. A Conceptual Architecture for DSS Generators. *Information & Management* (Netherlands) 10, no. 3 (March): 149–157.

Scherer, William T. and Chelsea C. White III. 1986. A Planning and Decision Aiding Procedure for Purchasing and Launching Spacecraft. *Interfaces* 16, no. 3 (May/June): 31–40.

Schmidt, Reinhart. 1985. The Usage of an Interactive Modeling System. *European Journal of Operational Research* (Netherlands) 22, no. 2 (November): 166–177.

Schubert, Donald S. 1988. Risk Reduction the Electronic Way. *Best's Review* (Prop/Casualty) 89, no. 1 (May): 84–88.

Schussel, George. 1988. Applications Development: Tools of the Trade. *Computerworld* 22, no. 5A (February 3): 32–34.

Schussel, George. 1986. DBMS and 4GL Technology: Pressing Questions — And Answers. *Journal of Information Systems Management* 3, no. 4 (Fall): 82–87.

Schwarz, Brita. 1988. Income Redistribution Policies and Decision Support Systems — Problems and Potentials. *European Journal of Operational Research* (Netherlands) 34, no. 2 (March): 139–48.

Seagle, John P. and Belardo Salvatore. 1986. The Feature Chart: A Tool for Communicating the Analysis for a Decision Support System. *Information Management* (Netherlands) 10, no. 1 (January): 11–19.

Seither, Mike. 1988. Oracle Extends DBMS Reach Into On-Line Processing. *Mini-Micro Systems* 21, no. 2 (February): 15–16.

Sharda, Ramesh, Steve H. Barr, and James C. McDonnell. 1988. Decision Support System Effectiveness: A Review and an Empirical Test. *Management Science* 34, no. 2 (February): 139–59.

Shpilberg, David. 1986. One Giant Step for Insurers. *Best's Review* (Prop/Casuality) 87, no. 1 (May): 54–60, 110.

Siegel, Paul. 1987. Expert 87: This Decision Support System Uses Your "Expert" Intuition. *InfoWorld* 9, no. 36 (September 7): 70–72.

Simmons, LeRoy R., and Laurette Poulos. 1988. DSS The Successful Implementation of a Mathematical Programming Model for Strategic Planning. *Computers & Operations Research* (UK) 15, no. 1: 1–5.

Sonnen, Jan. 1988. Aiding You with Decision Support Capabilities. *Computers in Healthcare* 9, no. 5 (May): 24–32.

Smith, L. Douglas, John Blodgett, Marius Janson, and Vince Barle. 1985. Decision Support for Marketing Research and Corporate Planning. *Information & Management* (Netherlands) 8, no. 3 (March): 133–45.

Snitkin, Sidney R. and William R. King. 1986. Determinants of the Effectiveness of Personal Decision Support Systems. *Information & Management* (Netherlands) 10, no. 2 (February): 83–89.

Sorgensen, Karen. 1986. Expert Systems Emerging As Real Tools. *Infoworld* 8, no. 16 (April 21): 32–38.

Stretch, Terrance T. 1988. Overcoming Resistance to Strategic and Executive IS Planning and Implementation. *Journal of Information Systems Management* 5, no. 1 (Winter): 63–65.

Sullivan, Cornelius H., Jr., and Charles E. Yates. 1988. Reasoning by Analogy — A Tool for Business Planning. *Sloan Management Review* 29, no. 3 (Spring): 55–60.

Sussman, Philip N. 1986. The Art of Managing Decision Support Tools. *Computerworld* 20, no. 12 (March 24): 17–18.

Sutcliffe, Roy. 1988. Software: Supporting Decisions. *Systems International* (UK) 16, no. 4 (April): 87–88.

Teresko, John. 1985. Delivering Desktop Decision Support. *Industry Week* 226, no. 3 (August 5): 33–35.

Thiriez, Herve. 1988. OR Software: STORM. *European Journal of Operational Research* (Netherlands) 35, no. 1 (April): 124–25.

Turban, Efraim, and Paul R. Watkins. 1987. The Impacts of Emerging Management Support Systems. *Human Systems Management* (Netherlands) 7, no. 1: 7–10.

Turban, Efraim and Paul R. Watkins. 1985. Integrating Expert Systems and Decision Support Systems. *MIS Quarterly* 10, no. 2 (March/April): 121–36.

VanGundy, Arthur B. 1987. Idea Collection Methods: Blending Old and New Technology. *Journal of Data Collection* 27, no. 1 (Spring): 14–19.

van Hee, K. M., and R. J. Wijbrands. 1988. Decision Support System for Container Terminal Planning. *European Journal of Operational Research* (Netherlands) 34, no. 3 (March): 262–72.

van Hee, K. M., B. Huitink, and D. K. Leegwater. 1988. PORTPLAN, Decision Support System for Port Terminals. *European Journal of Operational Research* (Netherlands) 34, no. 3 (March): 249–61.

Vedder, Richard G., and Richard O. Mason. 1987. An Expert System Application for Decision Support in Law Enforcement. *Decision Sciences* 18, no. 3 (Summer): 400–14.

Violano, Michael. 1988. Friendly Software for the Bank CEO. *Bakers Monthly* 105, no. 5 (May): 44–48.

Weisman, Randy. 1987. Six Steps to AI-Based Functional Prototyping. *Datamation* 33, no. 15 (August 1): 71–72.

Williamson, Mickey. 1986. Expert System Shells: Design Tools Help MIS Answer Management's Call. *Computerworld* 20, no. 28 (July 14): 51–60.

Wright, David J., Gabriela Capon, Robin R. Page, Jose Quiroga, Arshad A. Taseen, and Franco Tomasini. 1986. Evaluation of Forecasting Methods for Decision Support. *International Journal of Forecasting* (Netherlands) 2, no. 2: 139–52.

Young, Lawrence F. 1987. The Metaphor Machine: A Database Method for Creativity Support. *Decision Support Systems* (Netherlands) 3, no. 4 (December): 309–17.

Zeleny, Milan. 1987. Management Support Systems: Towards Integrated Knowledge Management. *Human Systems Management* (Netherlands) 7, no. 1: 59–70.

Index